CHAPTER 71: INDIAN POKER

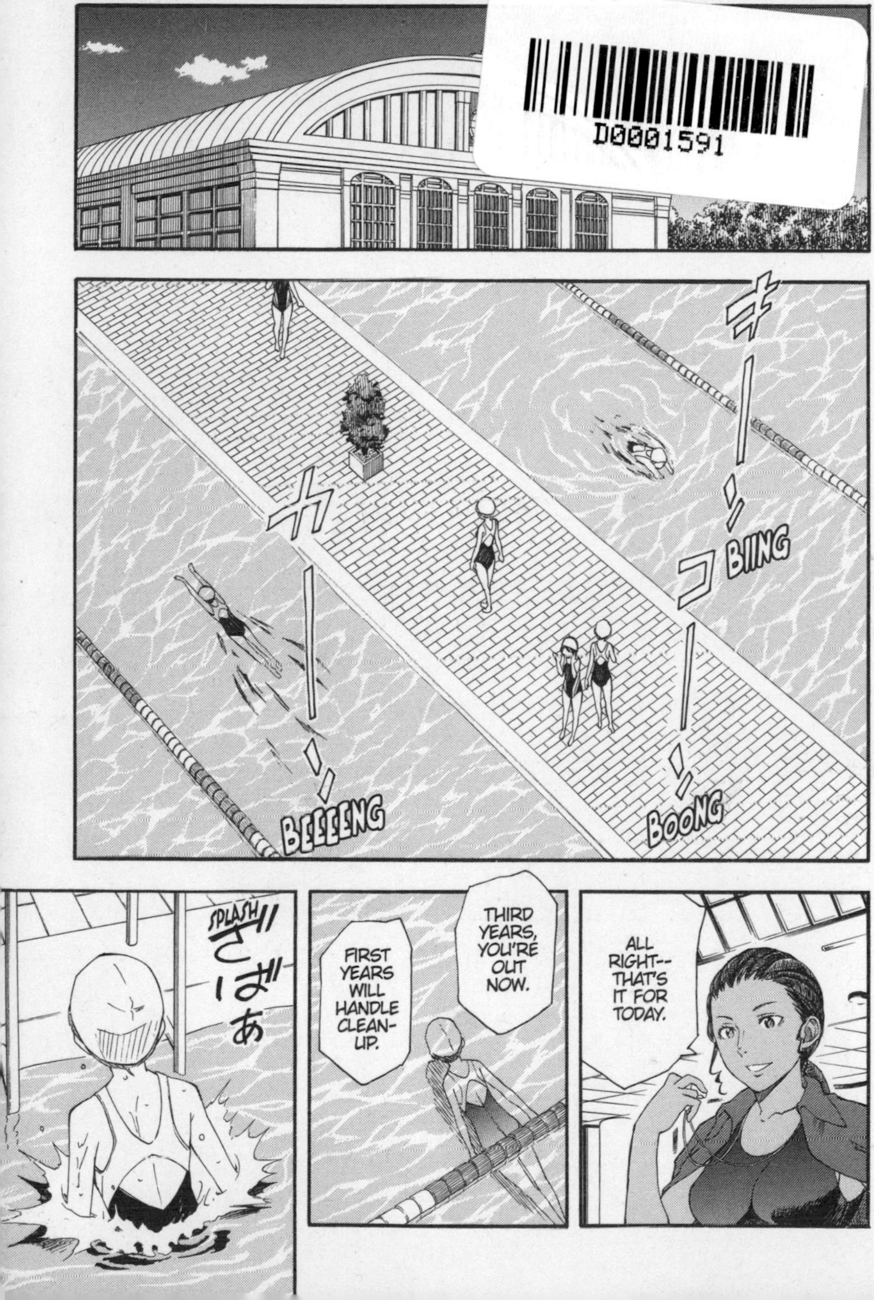
BIING
BOONG
BEEEENG
ALL RIGHT--THAT'S IT FOR TODAY.
THIRD YEARS, YOU'RE OUT NOW.
FIRST YEARS WILL HANDLE CLEAN-UP.
SPLASH
ざばぁ

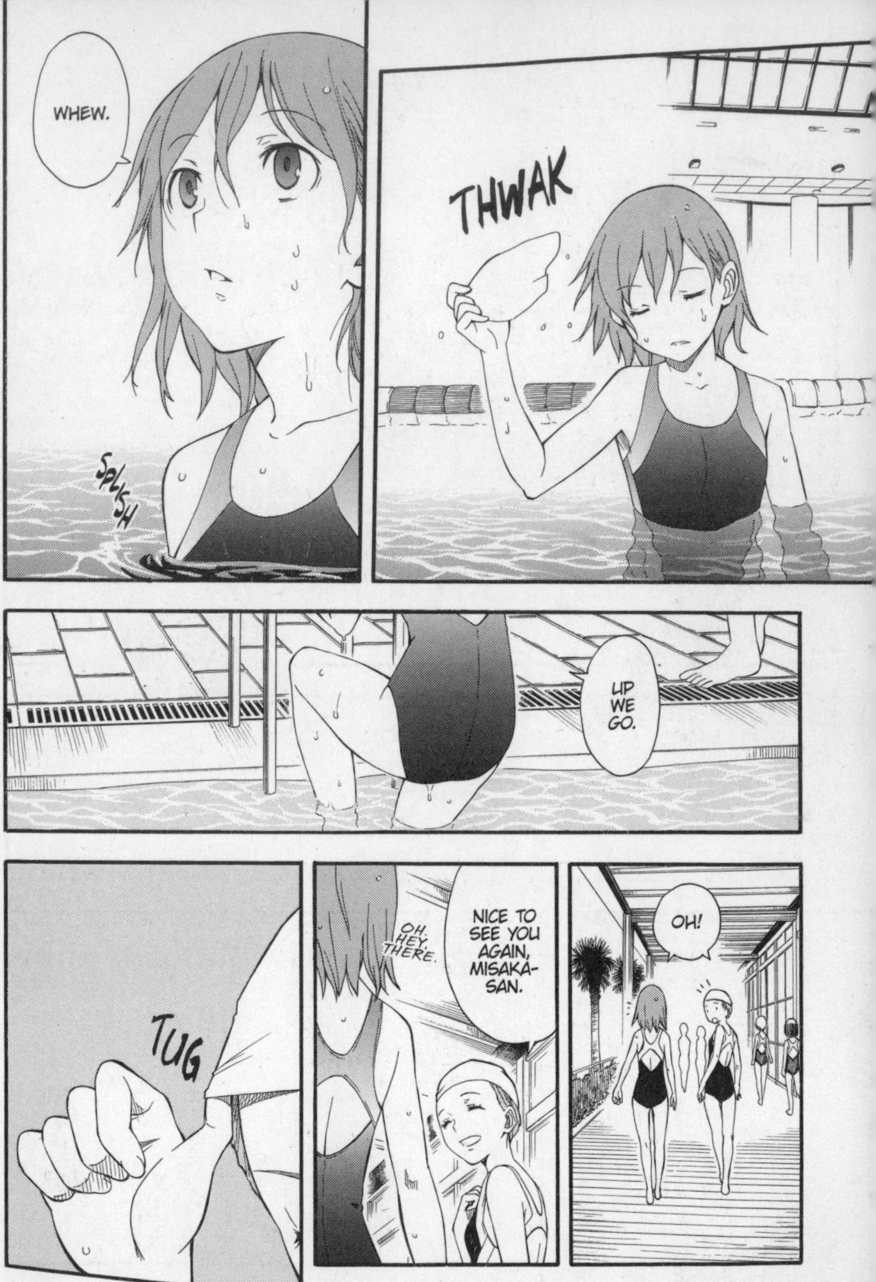
THWAK
WHEW.
SPLISH
UP WE GO.
OH!
NICE TO SEE YOU AGAIN, MISAKA-SAN.
OH. HEY, THERE.
TUG

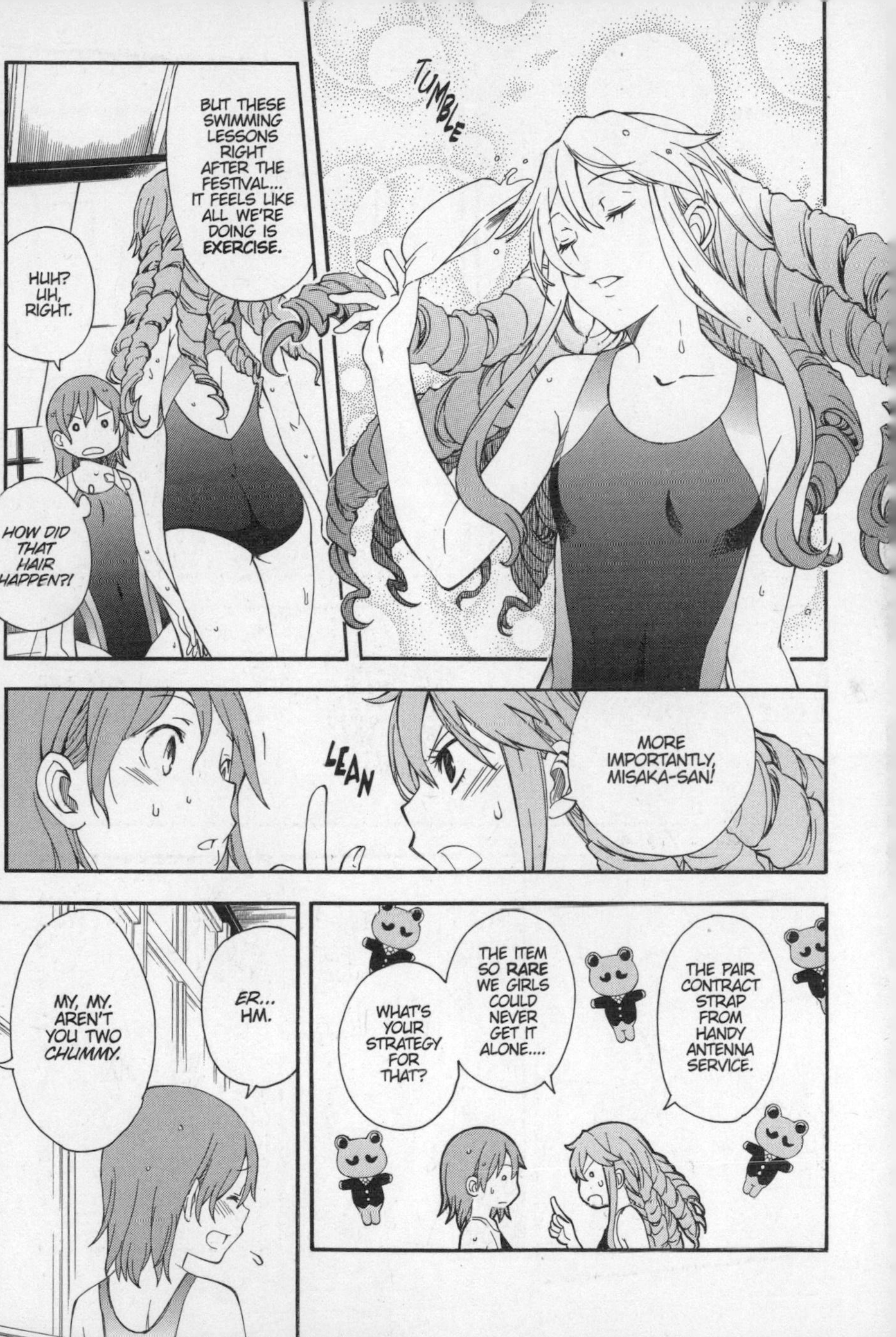
TUMBLE
BUT THESE SWIMMING LESSONS RIGHT AFTER THE FESTIVAL... IT FEELS LIKE ALL WE'RE DOING IS EXERCISE.
HUH? UH, RIGHT.
HOW DID THAT HAIR HAPPEN?!
MORE IMPORTANTLY, MISAKA-SAN!
LEAN
THE PAIR CONTRACT STRAP FROM HANDY ANTENNA SERVICE.
THE ITEM SO RARE WE GIRLS COULD NEVER GET IT ALONE....
WHAT'S YOUR STRATEGY FOR THAT?
ER... HM.
MY, MY. AREN'T YOU TWO CHUMMY.

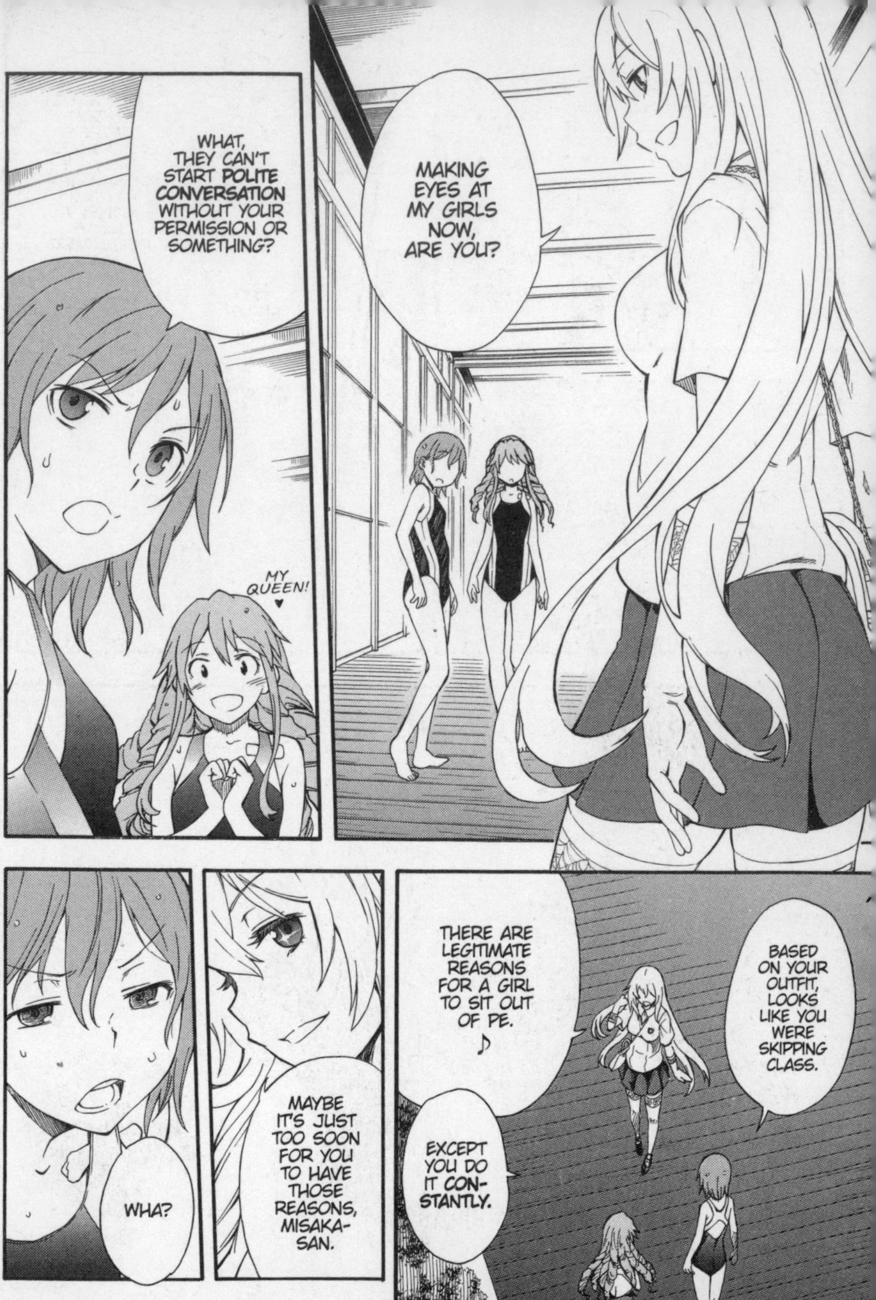
MAKING EYES AT MY GIRLS NOW, ARE YOU?
WHAT, THEY CAN'T START POLITE CONVERSATION WITHOUT YOUR PERMISSION OR SOMETHING?
MY QUEEN! ♥
BASED ON YOUR OUTFIT, LOOKS LIKE YOU WERE SKIPPING CLASS.
THERE ARE LEGITIMATE REASONS FOR A GIRL TO SIT OUT OF PE. ♪
EXCEPT YOU DO IT CONSTANTLY.
MAYBE IT'S JUST TOO SOON FOR YOU TO HAVE THOSE REASONS, MISAKA-SAN.
WHA?

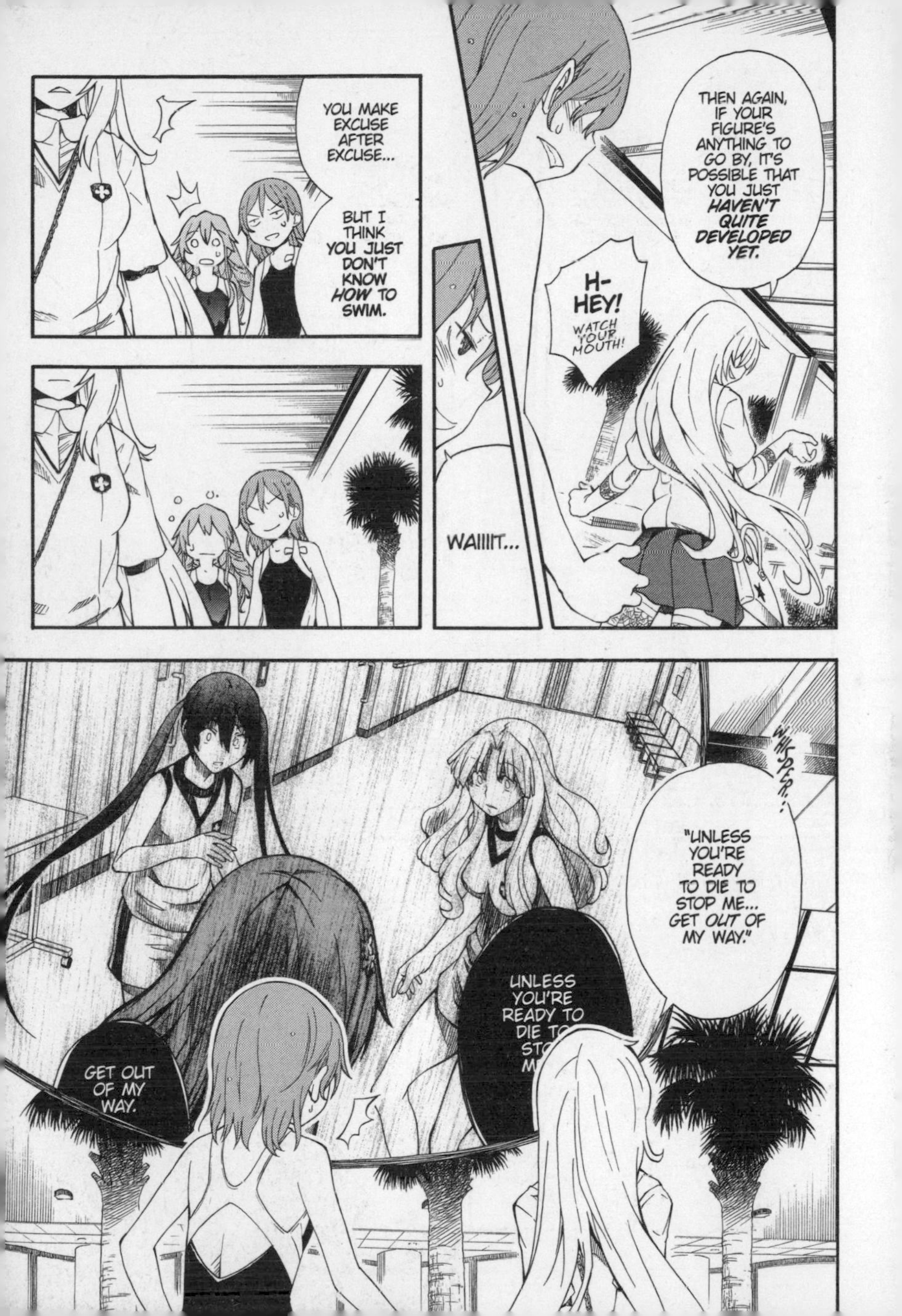
THEN AGAIN, IF YOUR FIGURE'S ANYTHING TO GO BY, IT'S POSSIBLE THAT YOU JUST ***HAVEN'T QUITE DEVELOPED YET.***
H-HEY!
WATCH YOUR MOUTH!
WAIIIT...
YOU MAKE EXCUSE AFTER EXCUSE...
BUT I THINK YOU JUST DON'T KNOW *HOW* TO SWIM.
WHISPER...
"UNLESS YOU'RE READY TO DIE TO STOP ME... GET *OUT* OF MY WAY."
UNLESS YOU'RE READY TO DIE TO STO
GET OUT OF MY WAY.

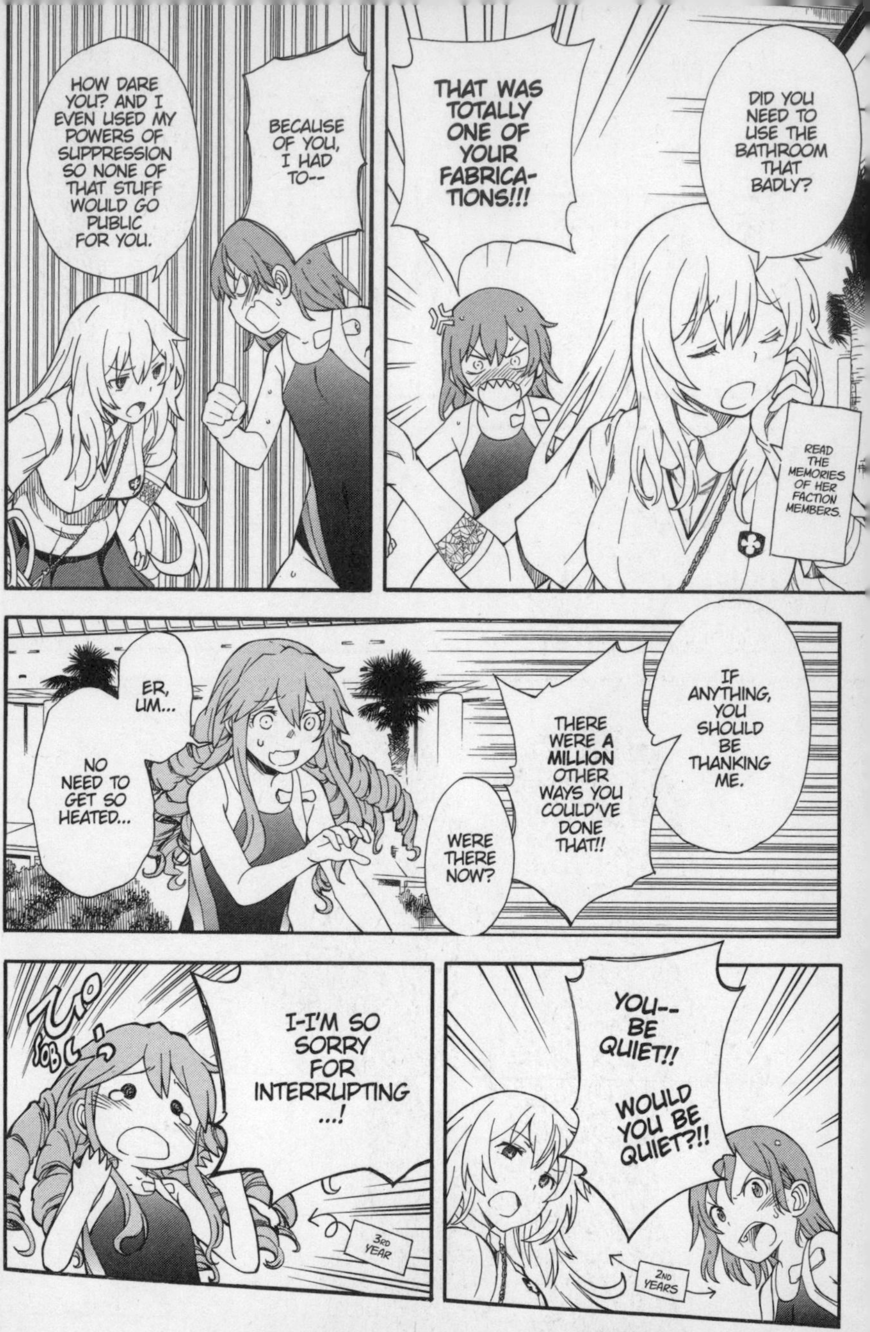
DID YOU NEED TO USE THE BATHROOM THAT BADLY?
READ THE MEMORIES OF HER FACTION MEMBERS.
THAT WAS TOTALLY ONE OF YOUR FABRICATIONS!!!
BECAUSE OF YOU, I HAD TO--
HOW DARE YOU? AND I EVEN USED MY POWERS OF SUPPRESSION SO NONE OF THAT STUFF WOULD GO PUBLIC FOR YOU.
IF ANYTHING, YOU SHOULD BE THANKING ME.
THERE WERE A MILLION OTHER WAYS YOU COULD'VE DONE THAT!!
WERE THERE NOW?
ER, UM...
NO NEED TO GET SO HEATED...
YOU-- BE QUIET!!
WOULD YOU BE QUIET?!!
2ND YEARS
I-I'M SO SORRY FOR INTERRUPTING ...!
SOB
3RD YEAR

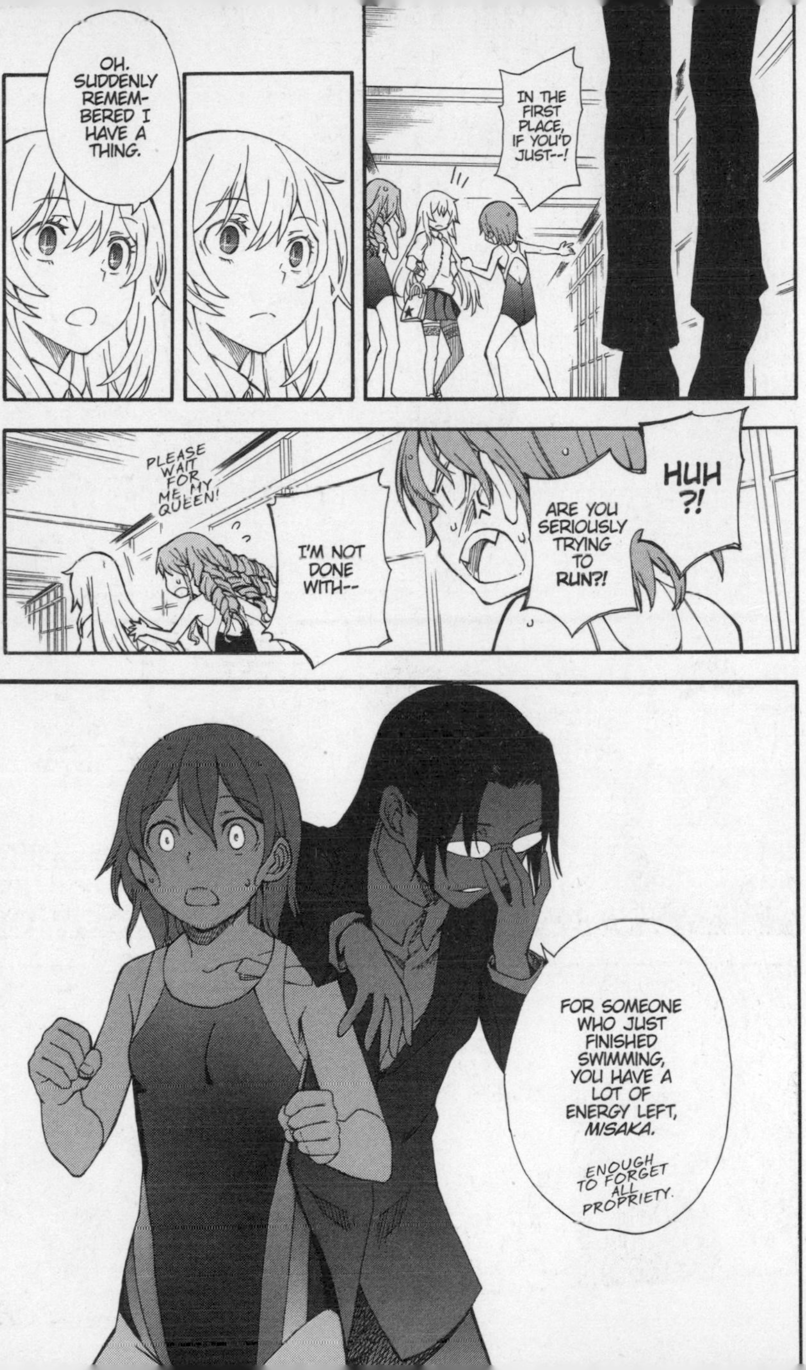
IN THE FIRST PLACE, IF YOU'D JUST--!
OH. SUDDENLY REMEMBERED I HAVE A THING.
HUH?!
ARE YOU SERIOUSLY TRYING TO RUN?!
I'M NOT DONE WITH--
PLEASE WAIT FOR ME, MY QUEEN!
FOR SOMEONE WHO JUST FINISHED SWIMMING, YOU HAVE A LOT OF ENERGY LEFT, *MISAKA.*
ENOUGH TO FORGET ALL PROPRIETY.

SHALL WE HAVE YOU USE THAT ENERGY...

HMM?

...TO *CLEAN THE POOL* DURING YOUR LUNCH BREAK?

UH... N-NO!

I'D LIKE TO EAT LUNCH, PLEASE AND THANK YOU.

IF THERE'S ONE THING THAT GIRL'S GOOD AT, IT'S PICKING FIGHTS.

RRGH!

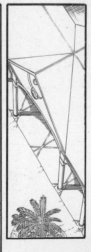

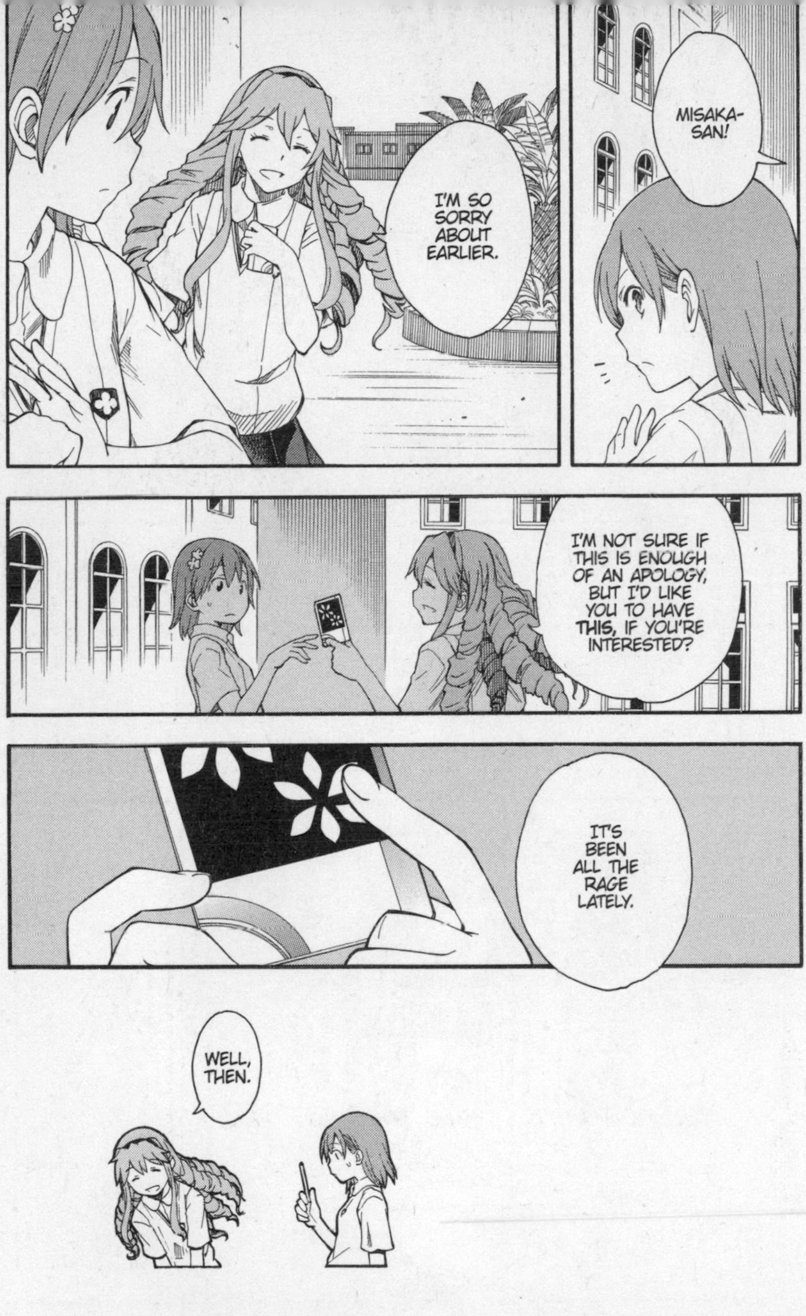
MISAKA-SAN!
I'M SO SORRY ABOUT EARLIER.
I'M NOT SURE IF THIS IS ENOUGH OF AN APOLOGY, BUT I'D LIKE YOU TO HAVE THIS, IF YOU'RE INTERESTED?
IT'S BEEN ALL THE RAGE LATELY.
WELL, THEN.

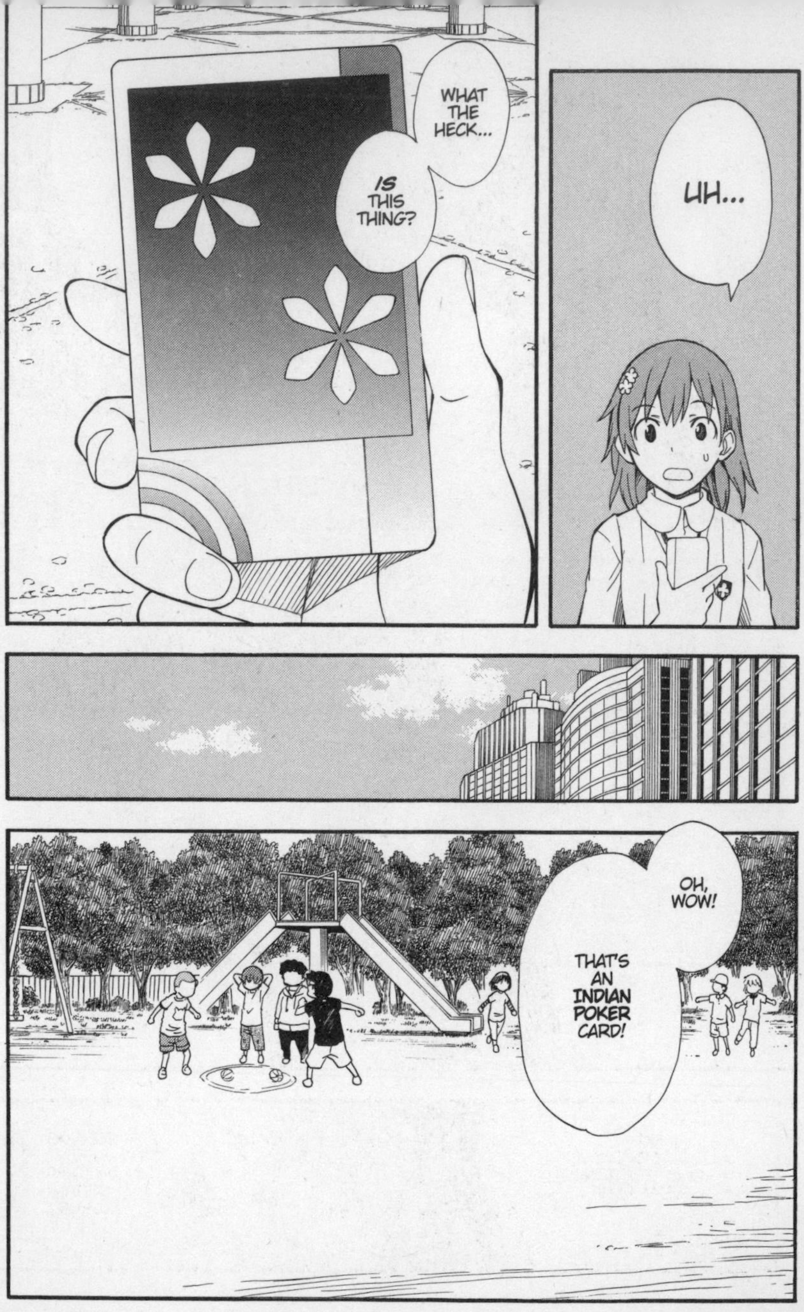
UH...
WHAT THE HECK...
IS THIS THING?
OH, WOW!
THAT'S AN INDIAN POKER CARD!

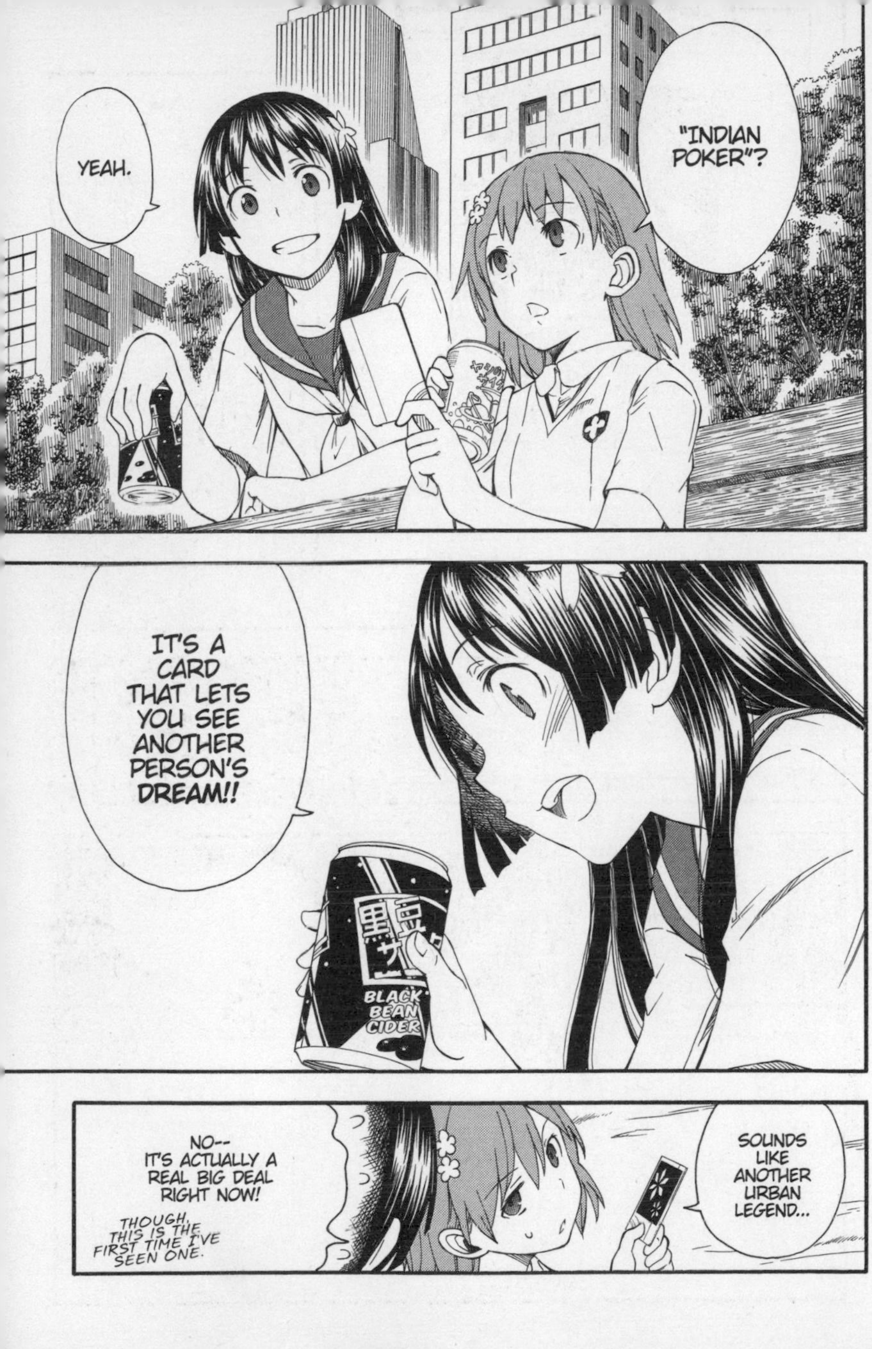
"INDIAN POKER"?
YEAH.
IT'S A CARD THAT LETS YOU SEE ANOTHER PERSON'S DREAM!!
BLACK BEAN CIDER
SOUNDS LIKE ANOTHER URBAN LEGEND...
NO-- IT'S ACTUALLY A REAL BIG DEAL RIGHT NOW!
THOUGH, THIS IS THE FIRST TIME I'VE SEEN ONE.

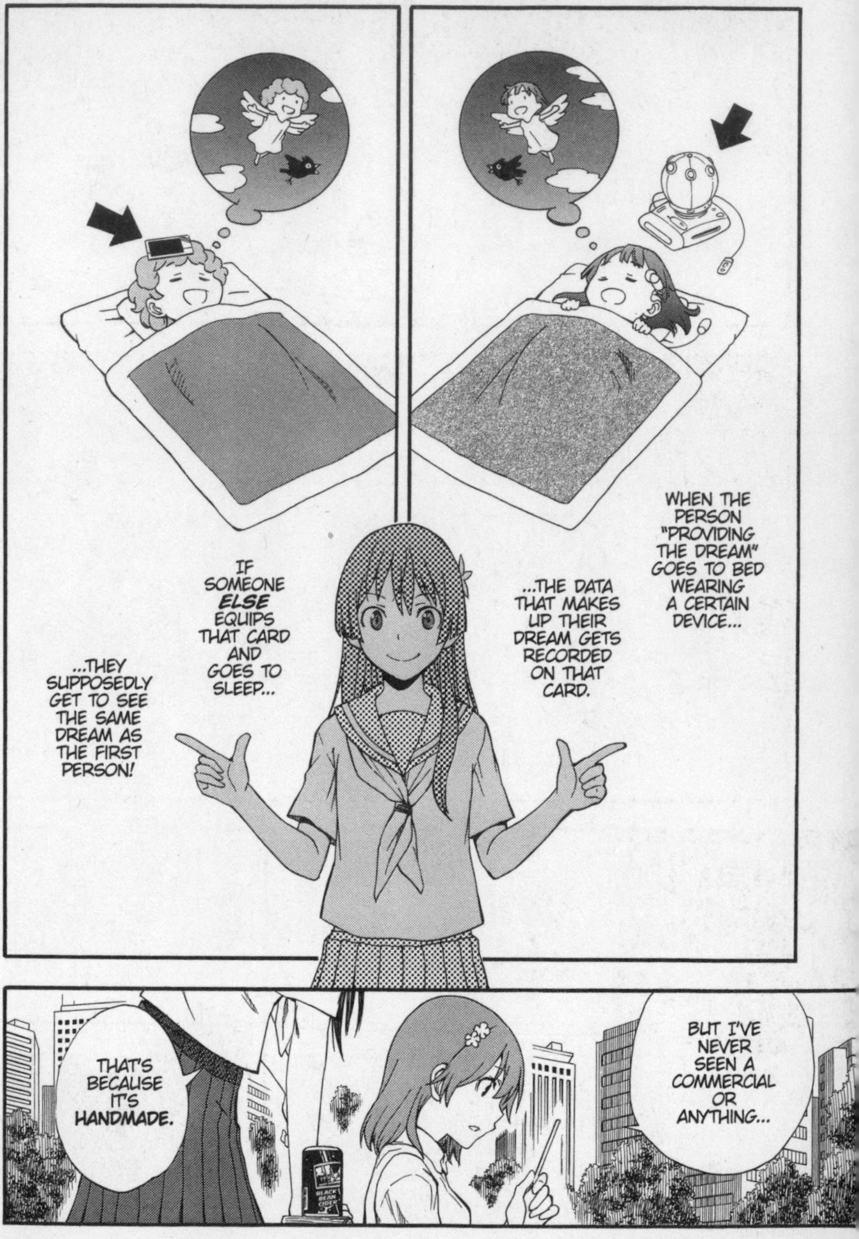
WHEN THE PERSON "PROVIDING THE DREAM" GOES TO BED WEARING A CERTAIN DEVICE...
...THE DATA THAT MAKES UP THEIR DREAM GETS RECORDED ON THAT CARD.
IF SOMEONE *ELSE* EQUIPS THAT CARD AND GOES TO SLEEP...
...THEY SUPPOSEDLY GET TO SEE THE SAME DREAM AS THE FIRST PERSON!
BUT I'VE NEVER SEEN A COMMERCIAL OR ANYTHING...
THAT'S BECAUSE IT'S **HANDMADE.**

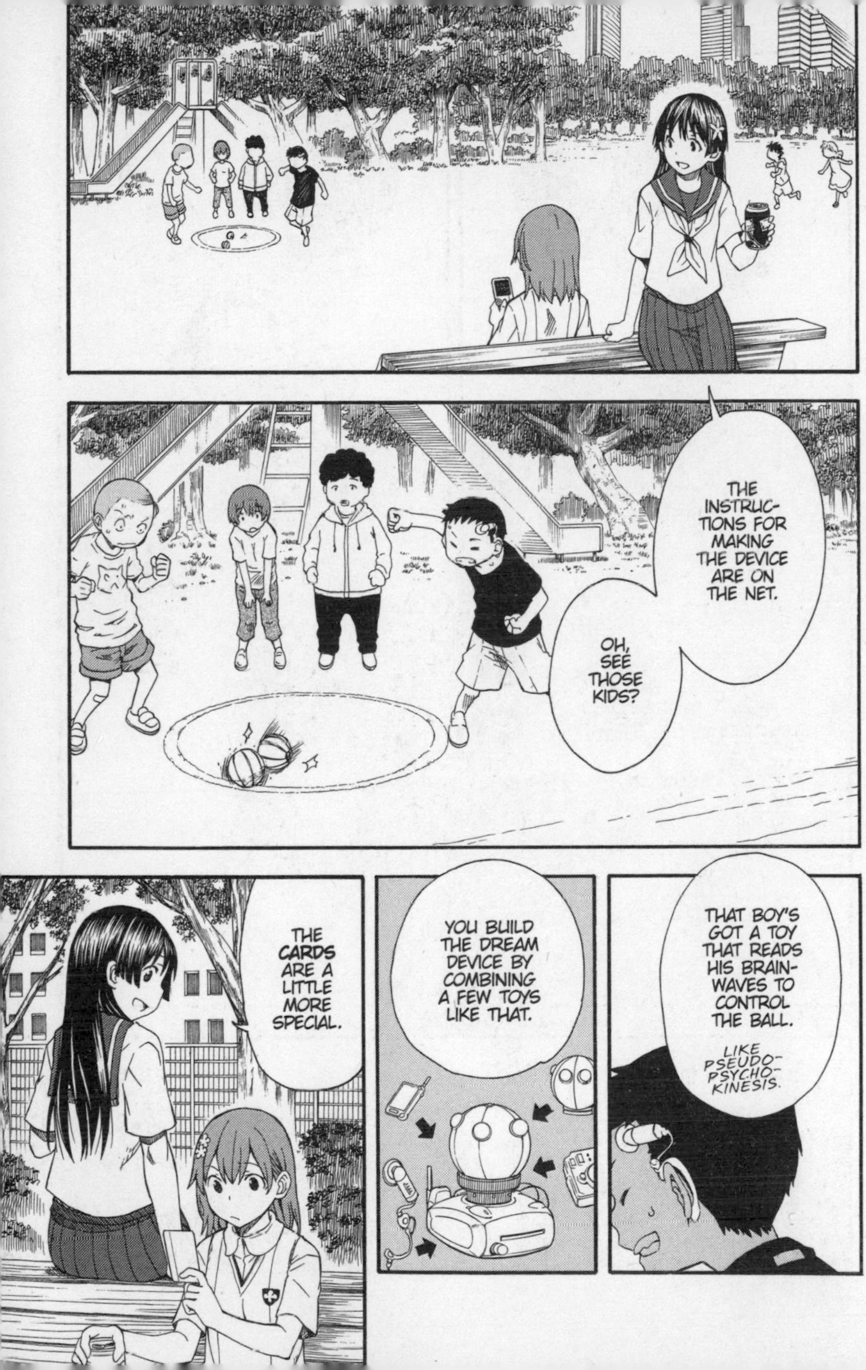
THE INSTRUCTIONS FOR MAKING THE DEVICE ARE ON THE NET.
OH, SEE THOSE KIDS?
THAT BOY'S GOT A TOY THAT READS HIS BRAIN-WAVES TO CONTROL THE BALL.
LIKE PSEUDO-PSYCHOKINESIS.
YOU BUILD THE DREAM DEVICE BY COMBINING A FEW TOYS LIKE THAT.
THE CARDS ARE A LITTLE MORE SPECIAL.

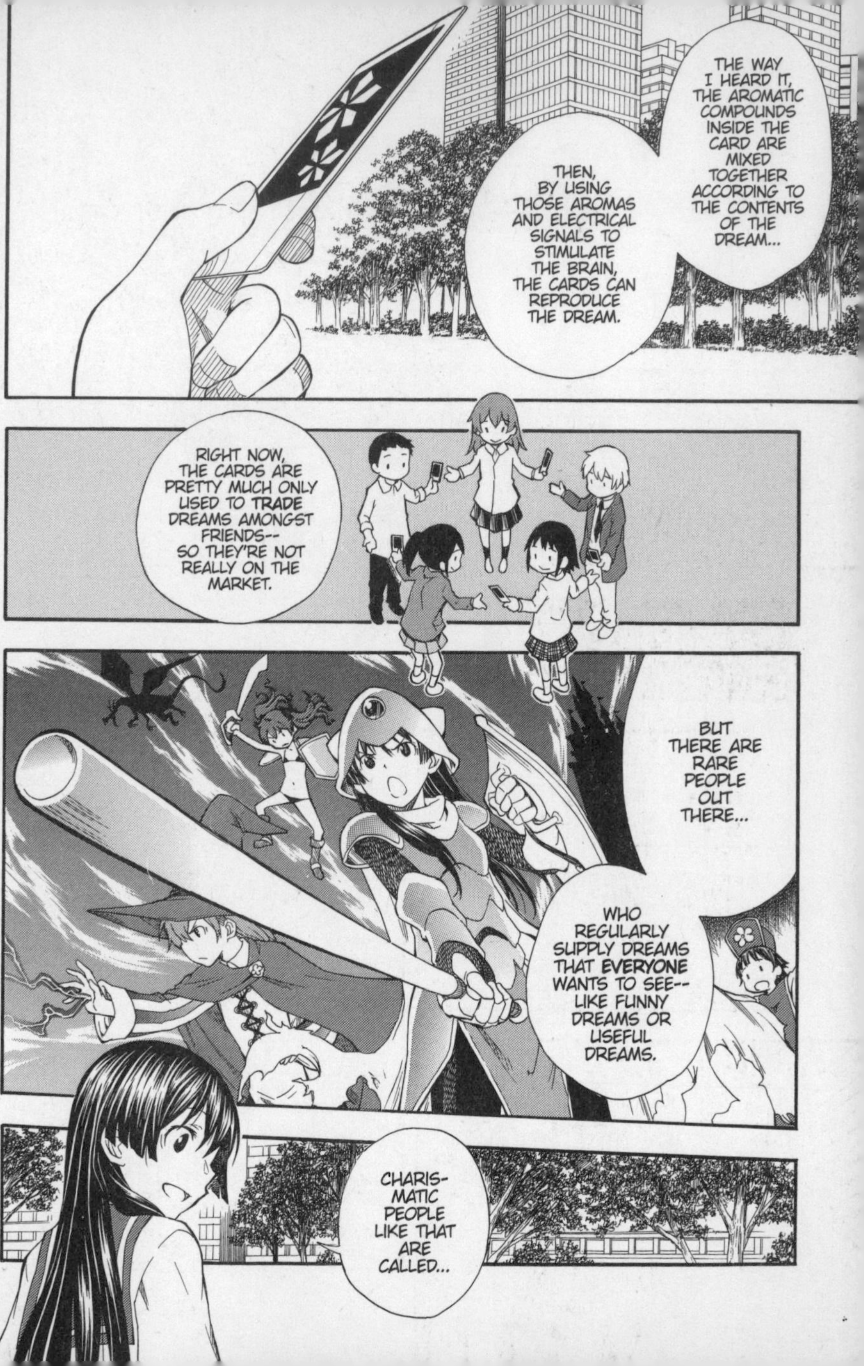
THE WAY I HEARD IT, THE AROMATIC COMPOUNDS INSIDE THE CARD ARE MIXED TOGETHER ACCORDING TO THE CONTENTS OF THE DREAM...
THEN, BY USING THOSE AROMAS AND ELECTRICAL SIGNALS TO STIMULATE THE BRAIN, THE CARDS CAN REPRODUCE THE DREAM.
RIGHT NOW, THE CARDS ARE PRETTY MUCH ONLY USED TO **TRADE** DREAMS AMONGST FRIENDS-- SO THEY'RE NOT REALLY ON THE MARKET.
BUT THERE ARE RARE PEOPLE OUT THERE...
WHO REGULARLY SUPPLY DREAMS THAT **EVERYONE** WANTS TO SEE-- LIKE FUNNY DREAMS OR USEFUL DREAMS.
CHARIS-MATIC PEOPLE LIKE THAT ARE CALLED...

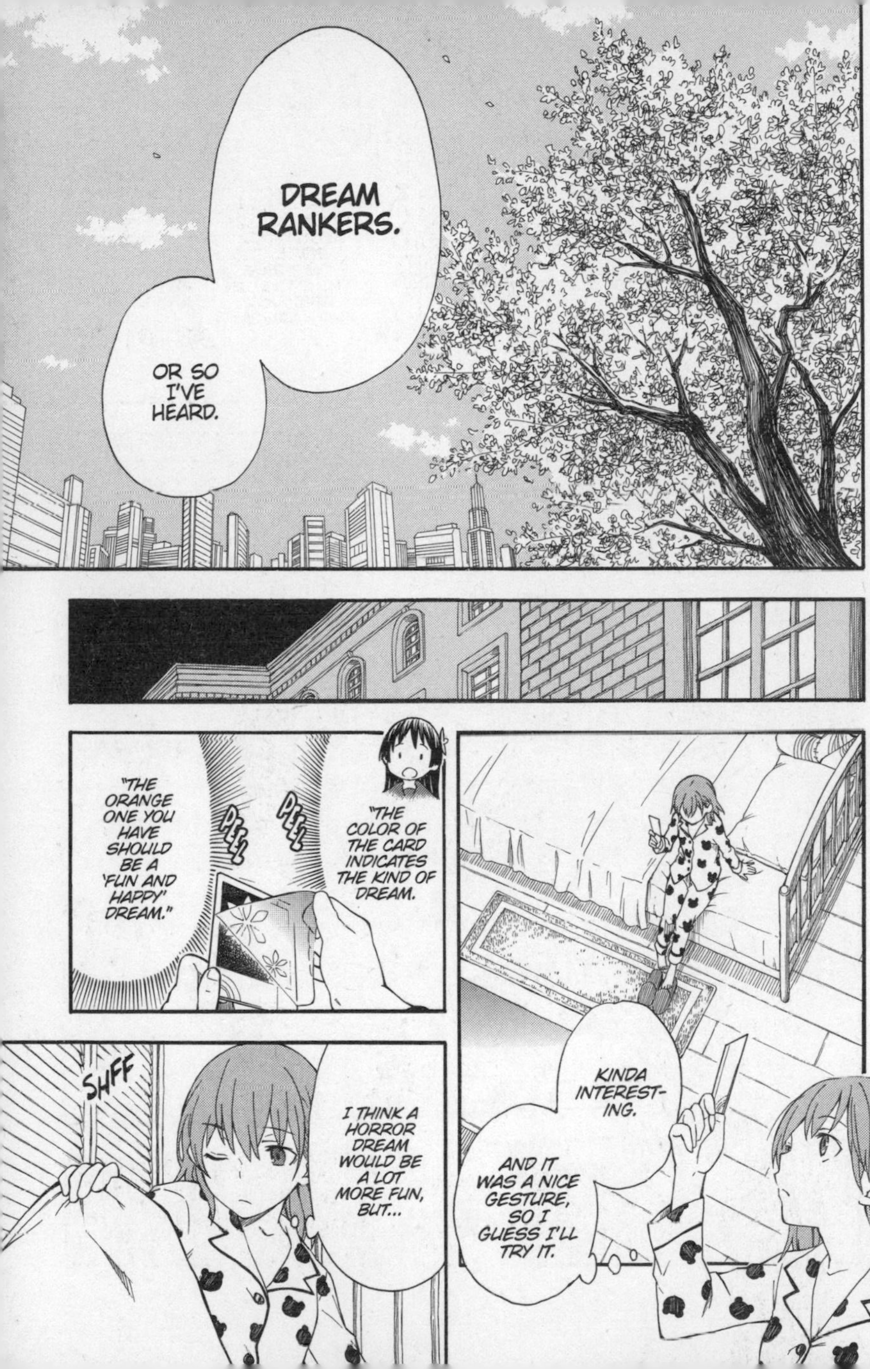
DREAM RANKERS.
OR SO I'VE HEARD.
"THE COLOR OF THE CARD INDICATES THE KIND OF DREAM.
PEEL
PEEL
"THE ORANGE ONE YOU HAVE SHOULD BE A 'FUN AND HAPPY' DREAM."
KINDA INTEREST-ING.
AND IT WAS A NICE GESTURE, SO I GUESS I'LL TRY IT.
SHFF
I THINK A HORROR DREAM WOULD BE A LOT MORE FUN, BUT...

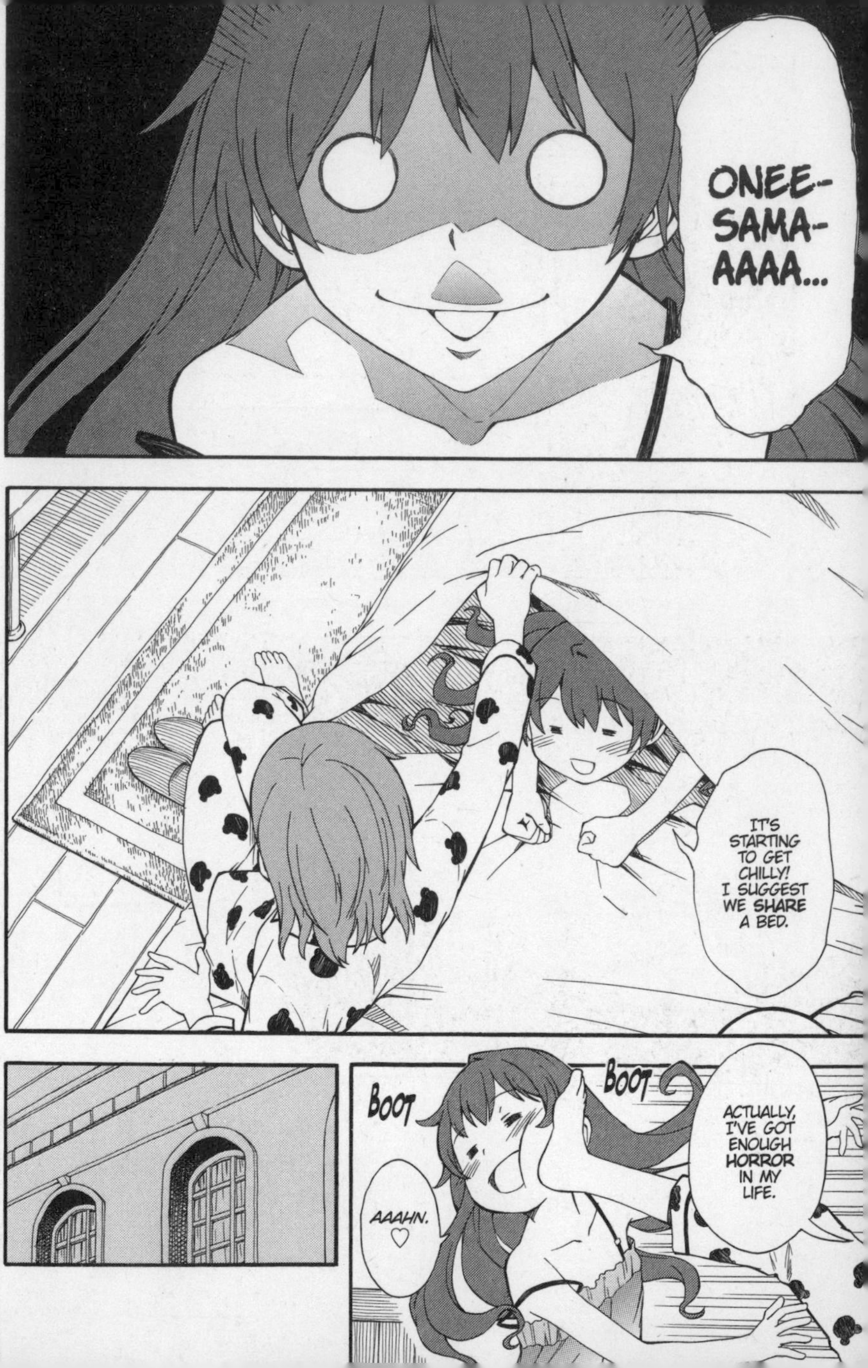
ONEE-SAMA-AAAA...
IT'S STARTING TO GET CHILLY! I SUGGEST WE SHARE A BED.
ACTUALLY, I'VE GOT ENOUGH HORROR IN MY LIFE.
BOOT
BOOT
AAAHN. ♡

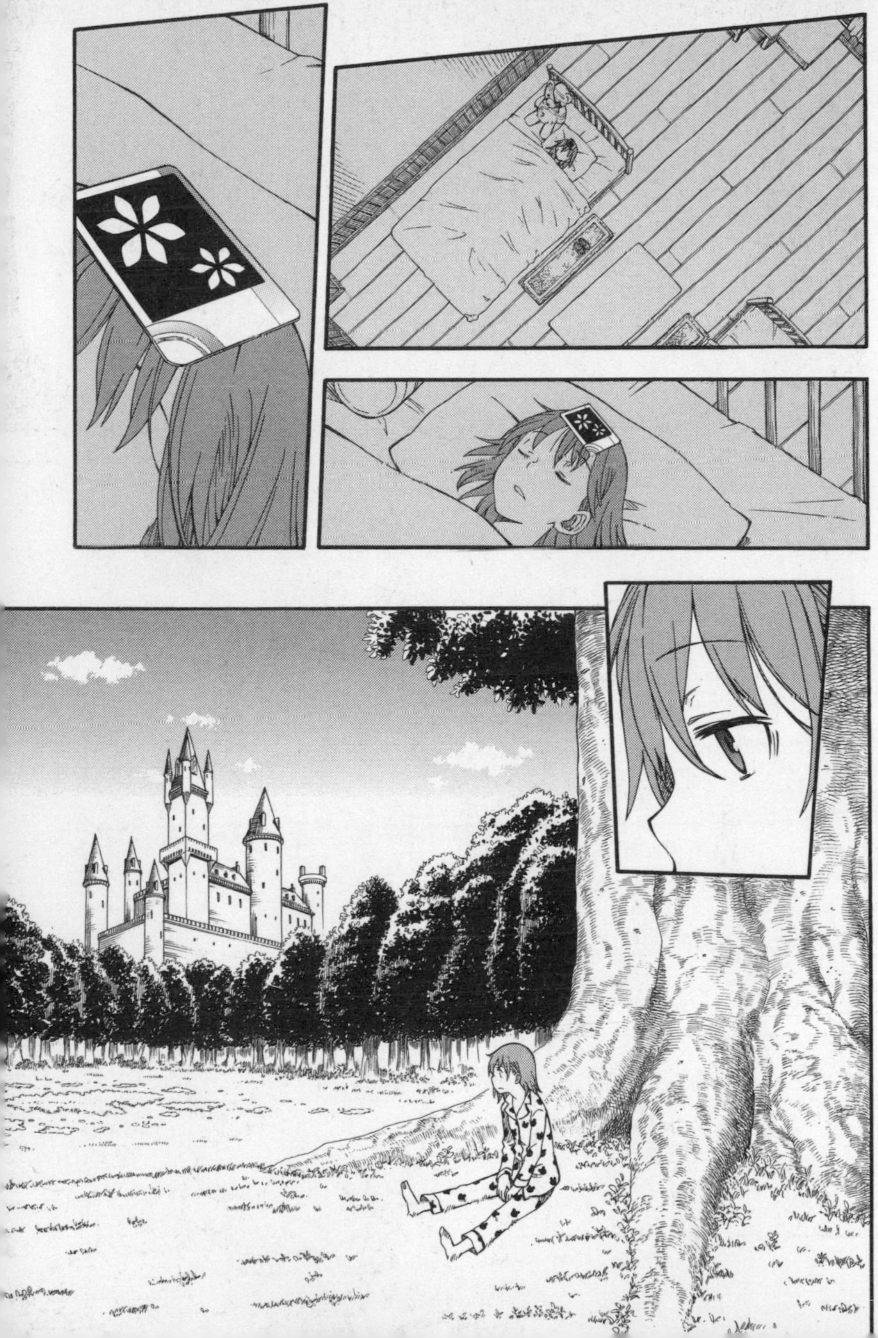

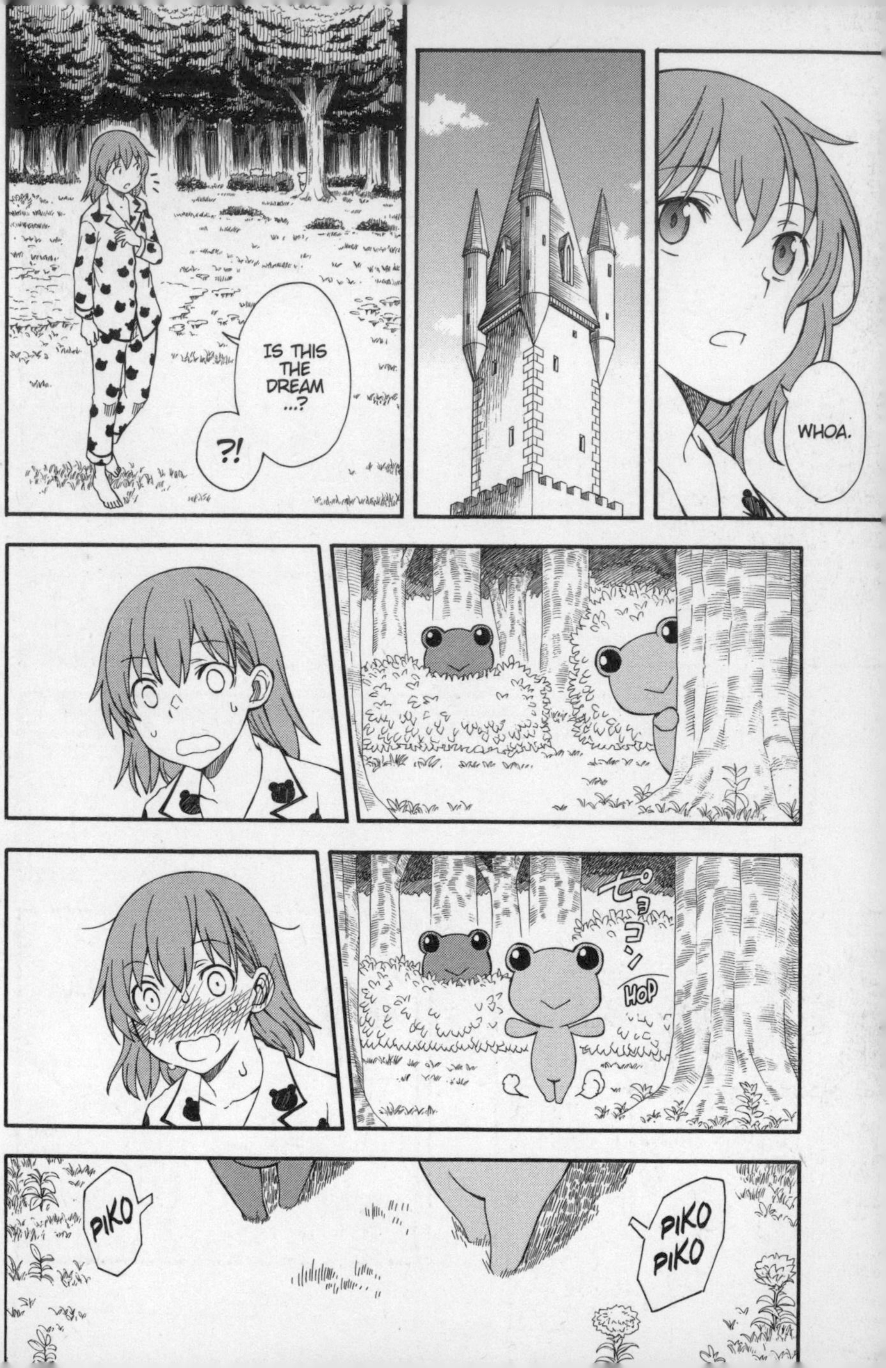
WHOA.
IS THIS THE DREAM ...?
?!
ピョコン
HOP
PIKO PIKO
PIKO

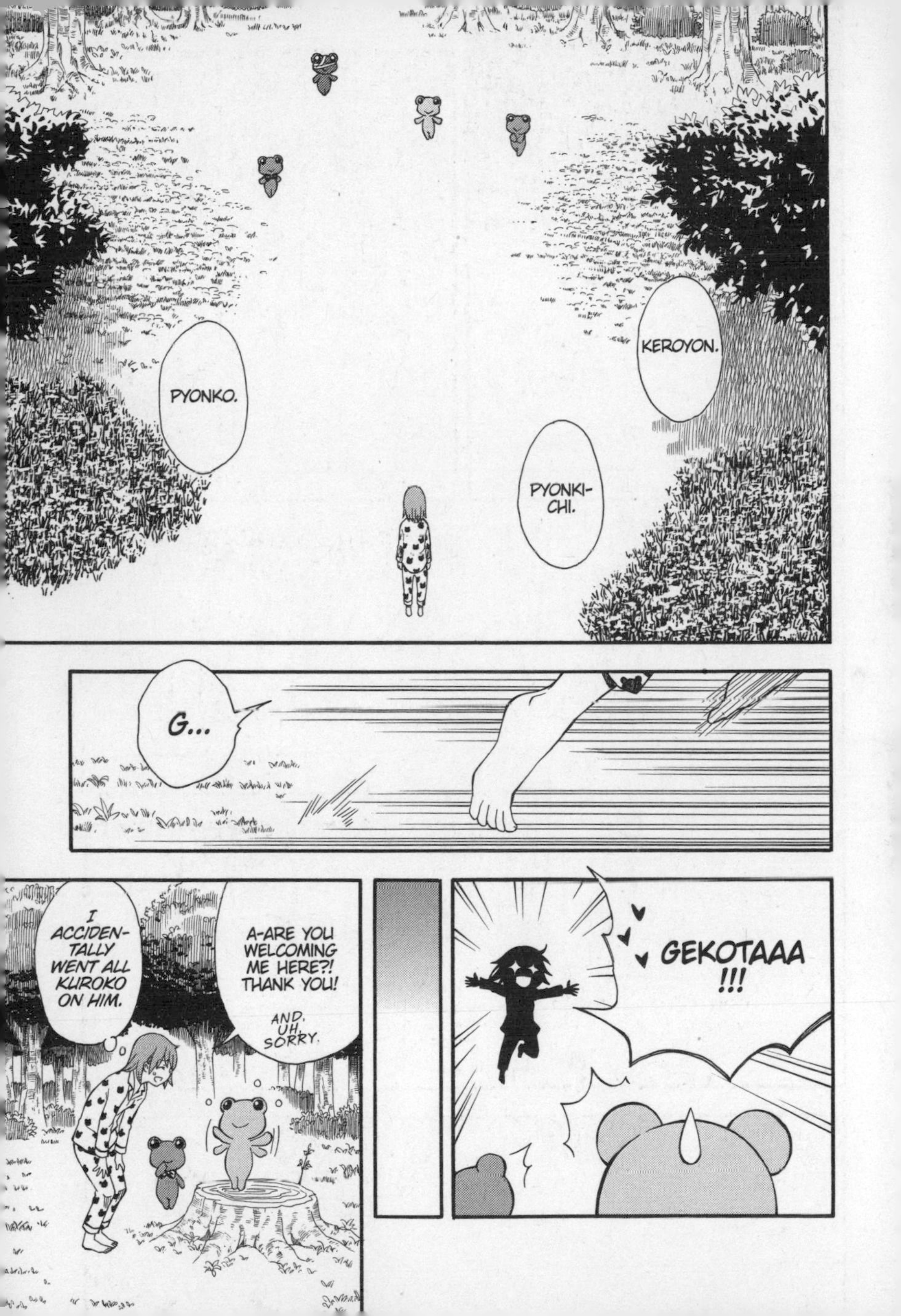
KEROYON.
PYONKI-CHI.
PYONKO.
G...
GEKOTAAA!!!
A-ARE YOU WELCOMING ME HERE?! THANK YOU!
AND, UH, SORRY.
I ACCIDEN-TALLY WENT ALL KUROKO ON HIM.

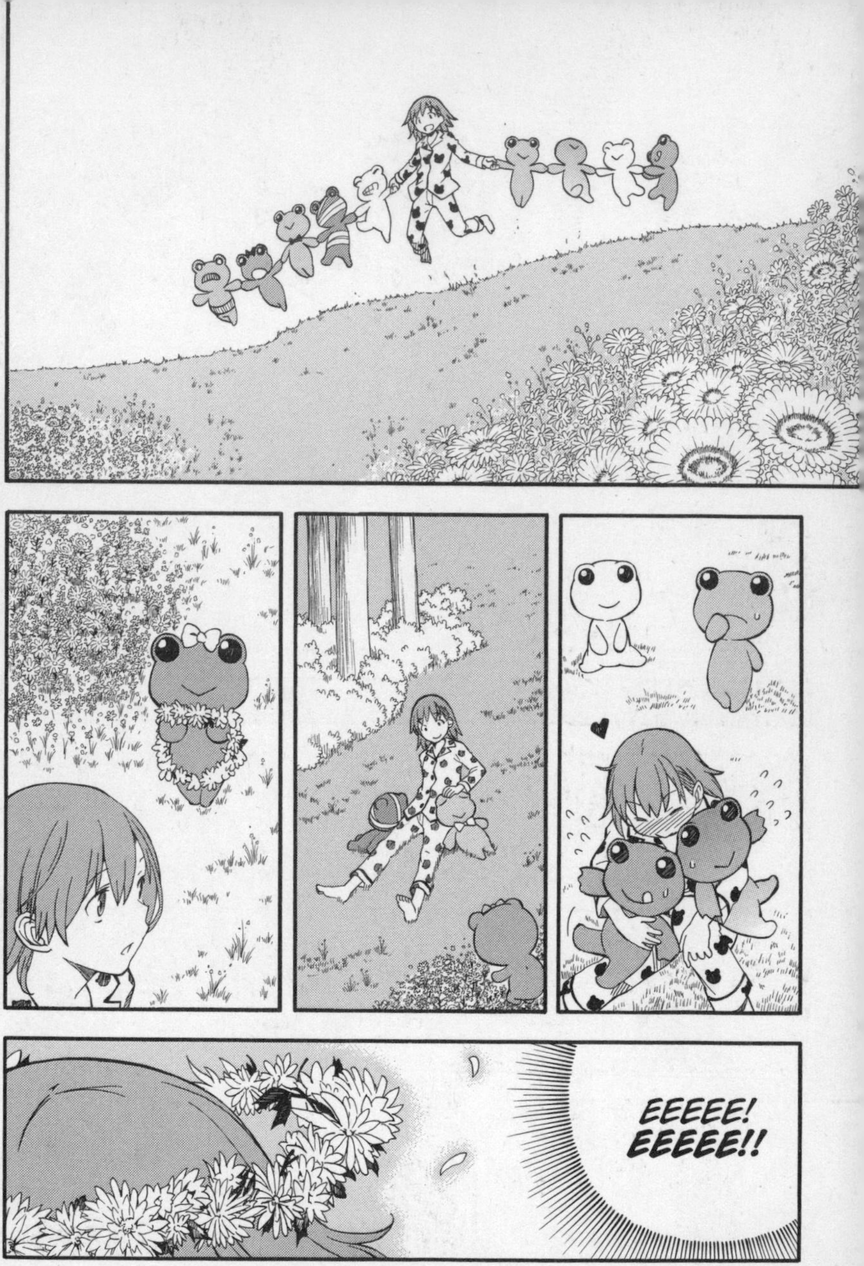
EEEEE!
EEEEE!!

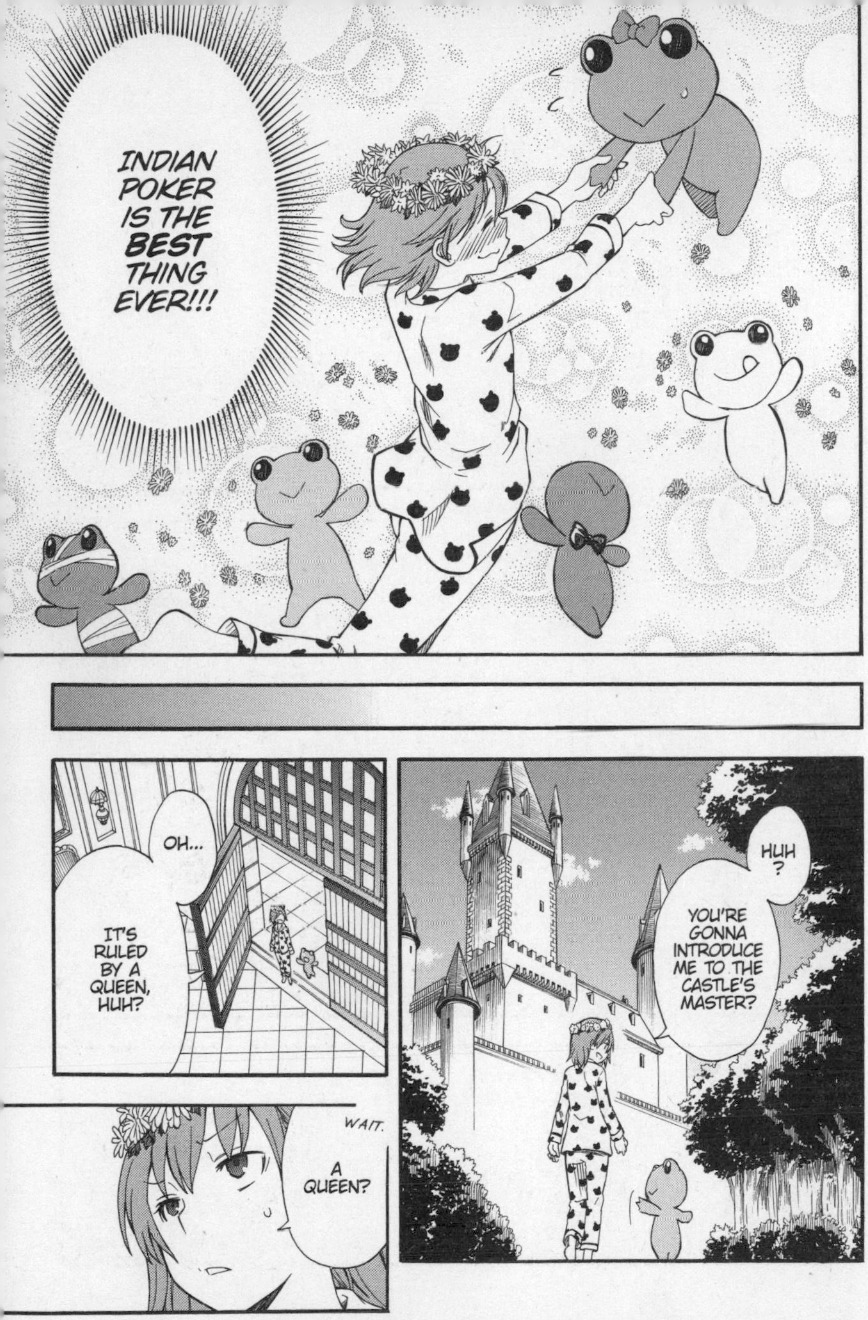
INDIAN POKER IS THE BEST THING EVER!!!
HUH?
YOU'RE GONNA INTRODUCE ME TO THE CASTLE'S MASTER?
OH...
IT'S RULED BY A QUEEN, HUH?
WAIT.
A QUEEN?

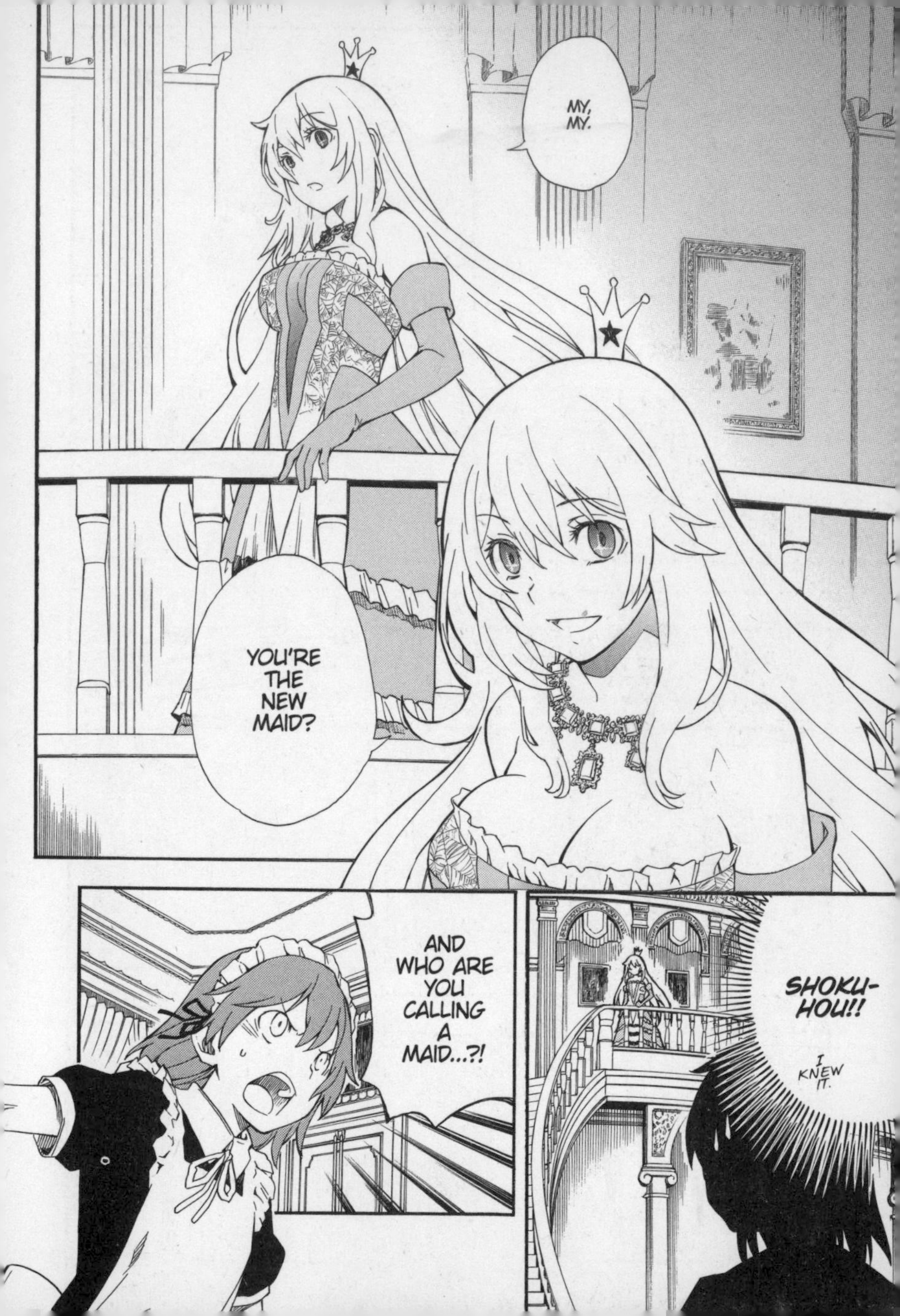
MY, MY.
YOU'RE THE NEW MAID?
SHOKU-HOU!!
I KNEW IT.
AND WHO ARE YOU CALLING A MAID...?!

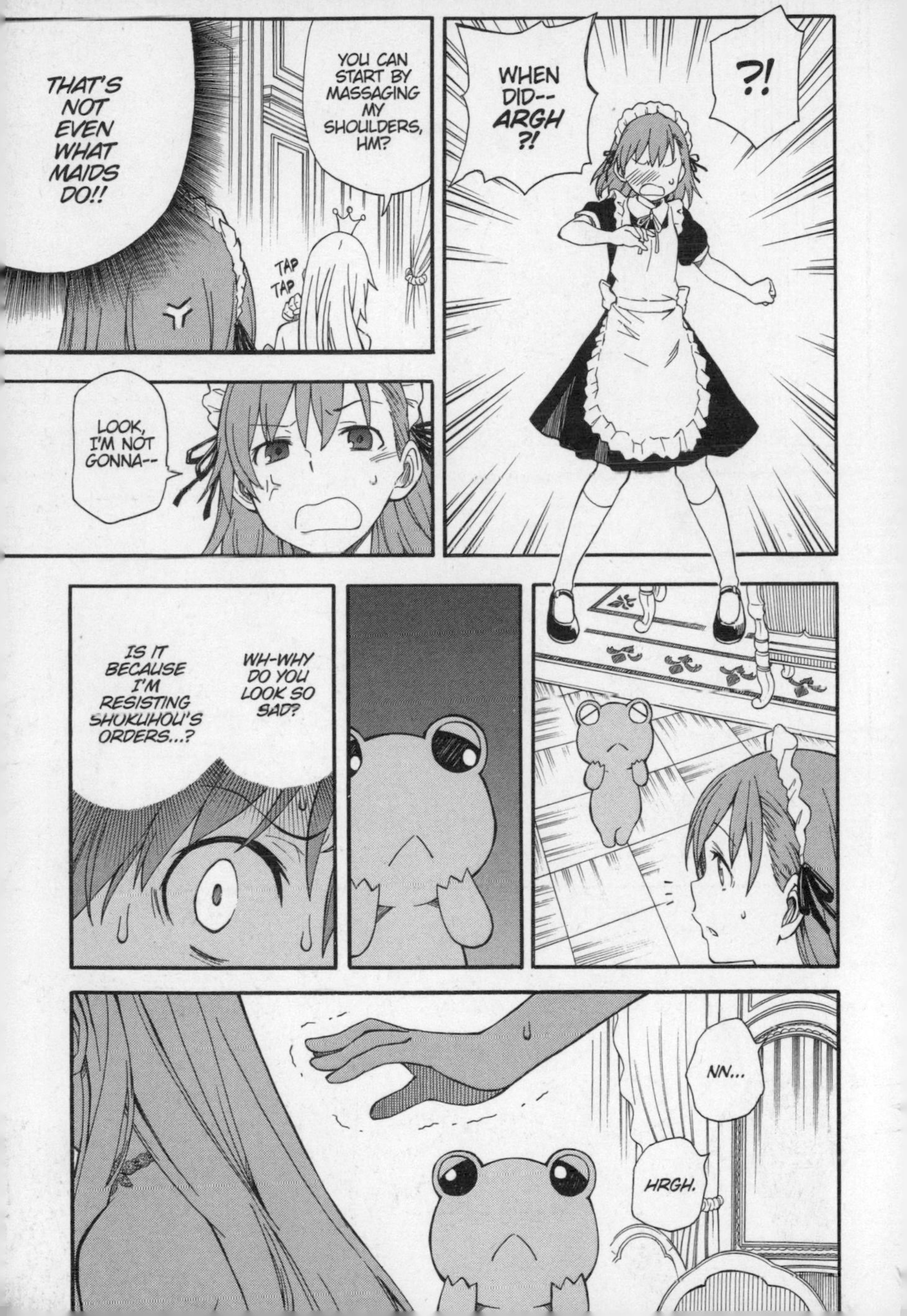
?!
WHEN DID-- ARGH ?!
YOU CAN START BY MASSAGING MY SHOULDERS, HM?
TAP TAP
THAT'S NOT EVEN WHAT MAIDS DO!!
LOOK, I'M NOT GONNA--
WH-WHY DO YOU LOOK SO SAD?
IS IT BECAUSE I'M RESISTING SHOKUHOU'S ORDERS...?
NN...
HRGH.

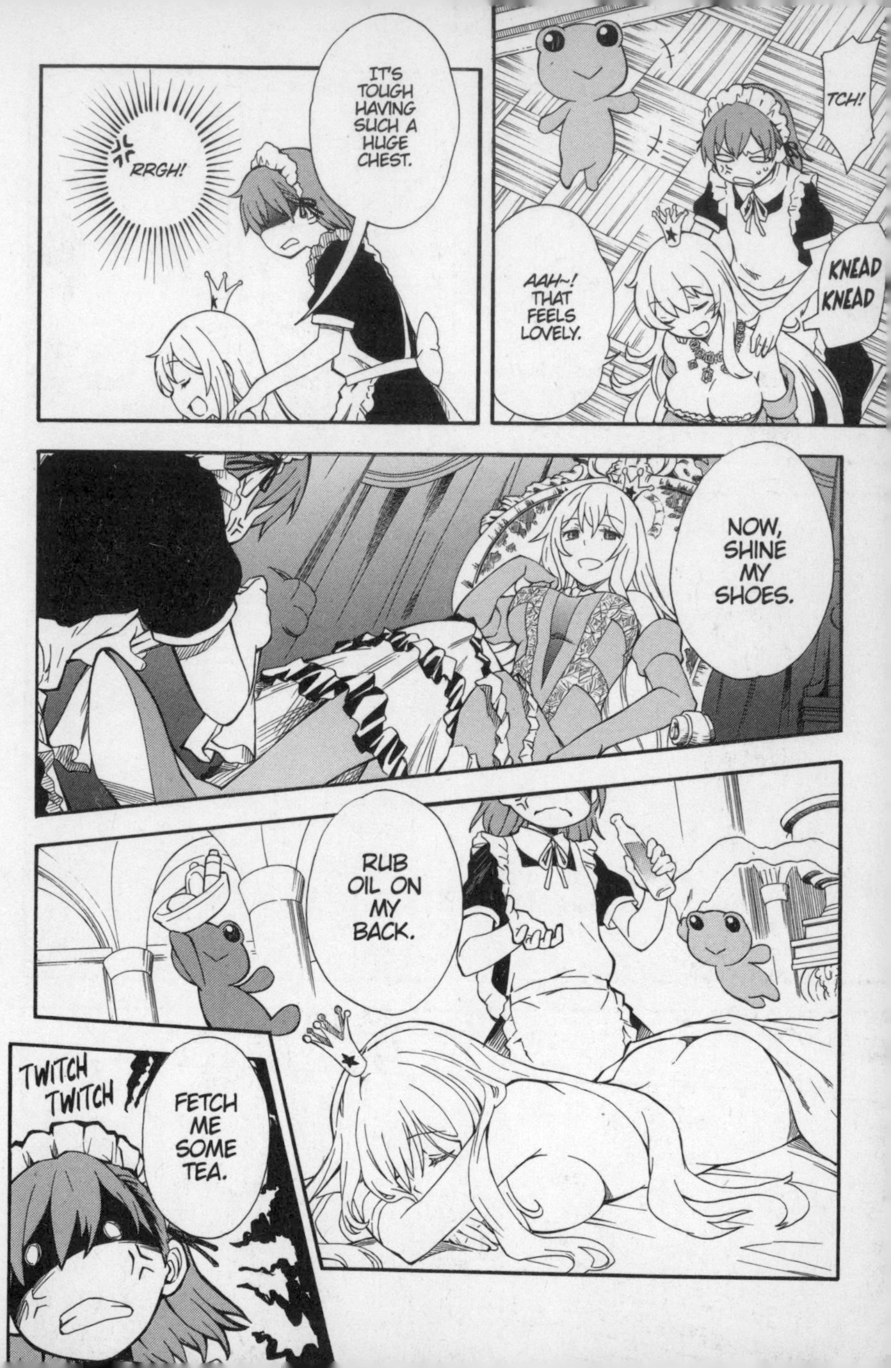
TCH!
KNEAD KNEAD
AAH~! THAT FEELS LOVELY.
IT'S TOUGH HAVING SUCH A HUGE CHEST.
RRGH!
NOW, SHINE MY SHOES.
RUB OIL ON MY BACK.
FETCH ME SOME TEA.
TWITCH TWITCH

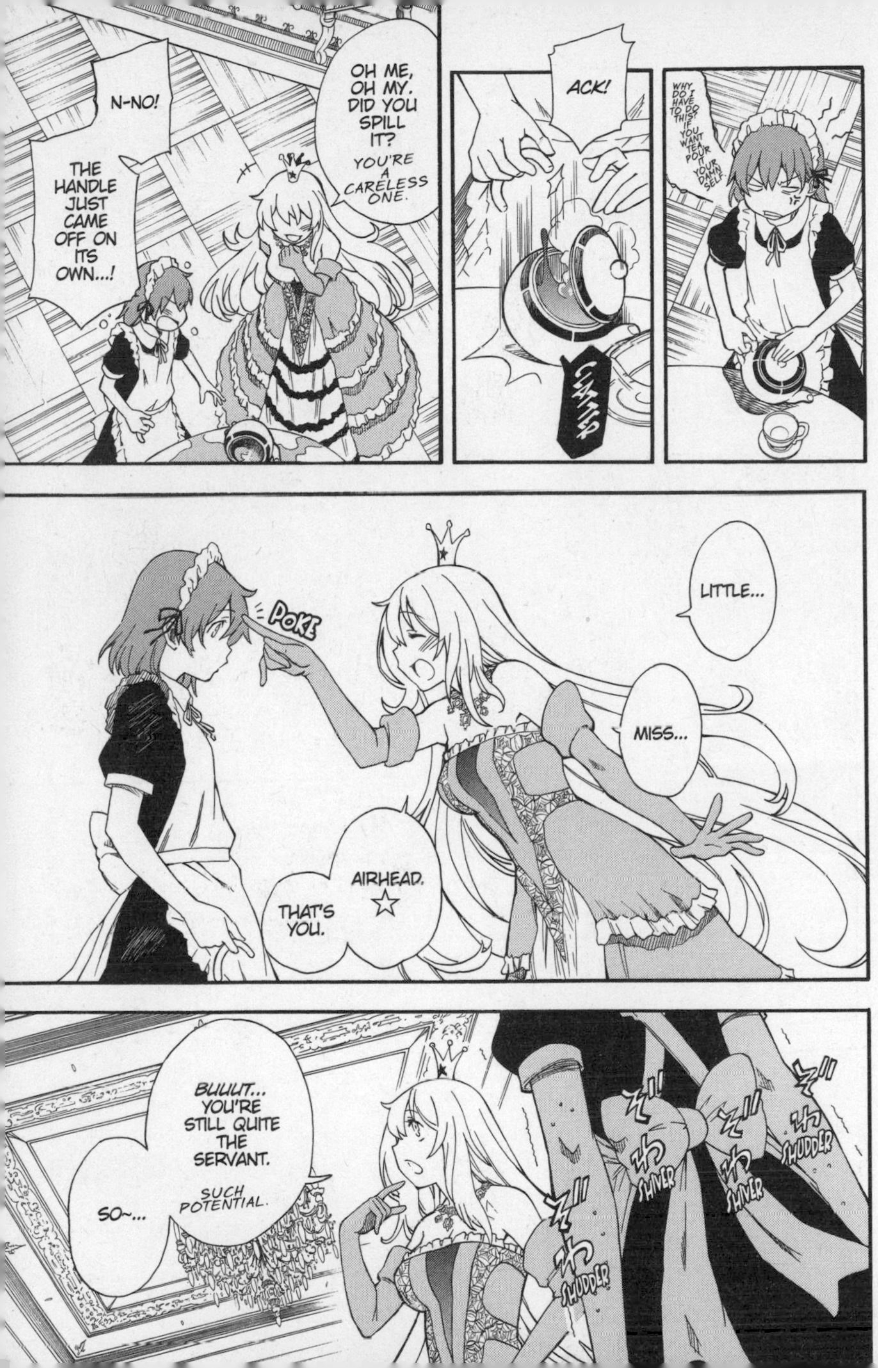
WHY DO I HAVE TO DO THIS? IF YOU WANT TEA, POUR IT YOUR DAMN SELF.
ACK!
CLATTER
OH ME, OH MY. DID YOU SPILL IT?
YOU'RE A CARELESS ONE.
N-NO!
THE HANDLE JUST CAME OFF ON ITS OWN...!
LITTLE...
POKE
MISS...
AIRHEAD. ☆
THAT'S YOU.
SHUDDER
SHIVER
SHIVER
SHUDDER
BUUUT... YOU'RE STILL QUITE THE SERVANT.
SUCH POTENTIAL.
SO~...

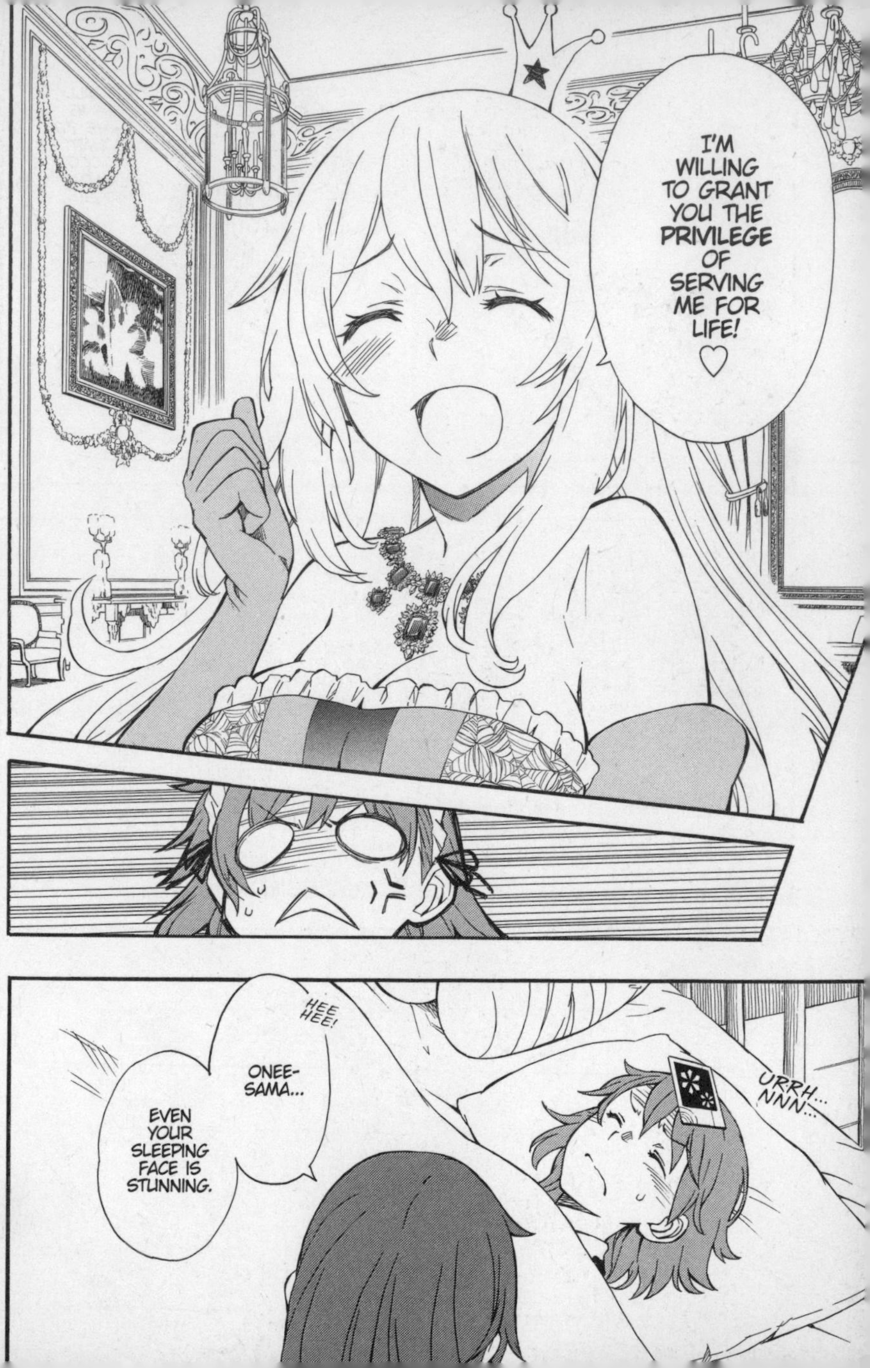
I'M WILLING TO GRANT YOU THE PRIVILEGE OF SERVING ME FOR LIFE! ♡
URRH... NNN...
HEE HEE!
ONEE-SAMA...
EVEN YOUR SLEEPING FACE IS STUNNING.

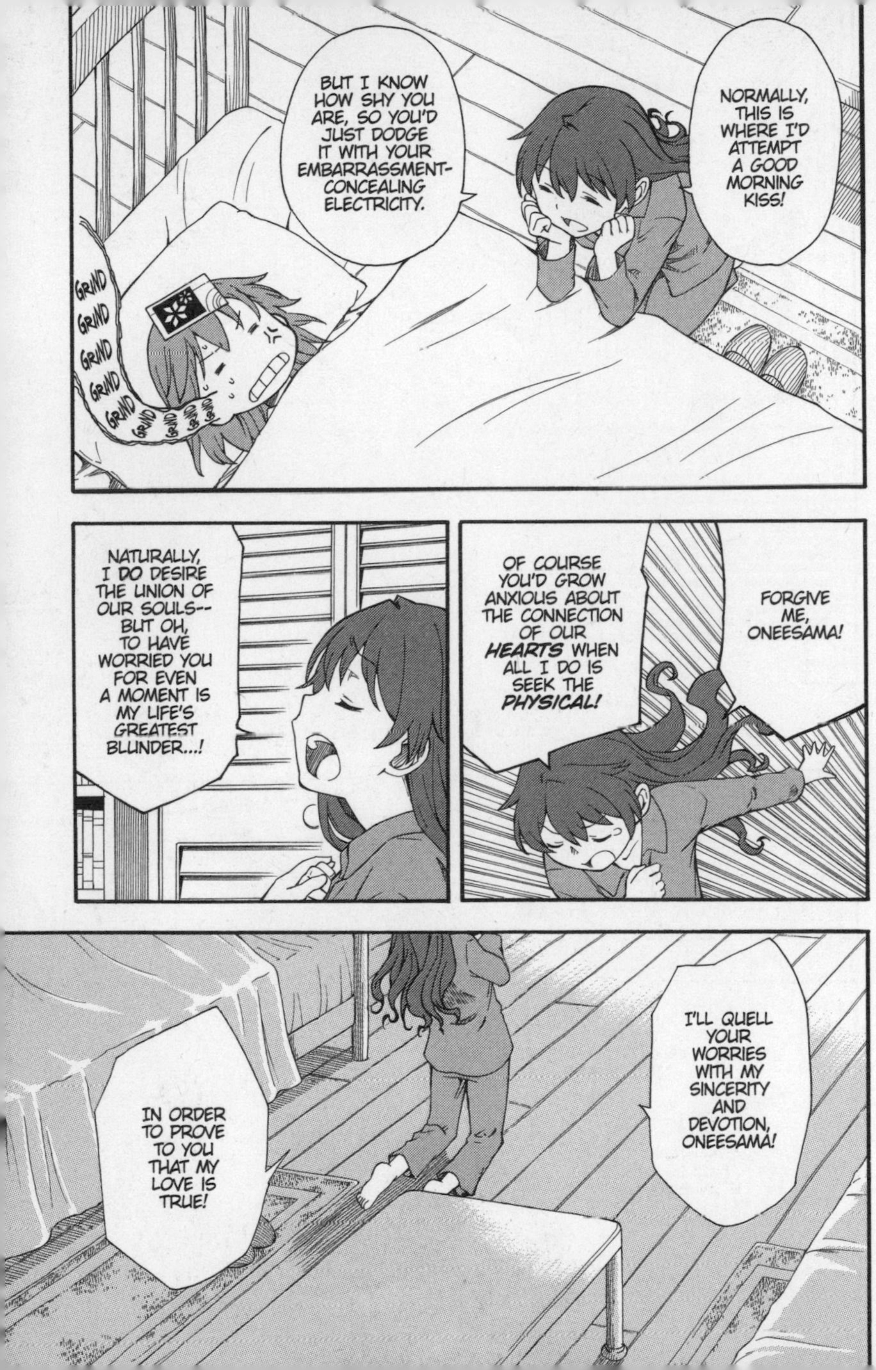
NORMALLY, THIS IS WHERE I'D ATTEMPT A GOOD MORNING KISS!
BUT I KNOW HOW SHY YOU ARE, SO YOU'D JUST DODGE IT WITH YOUR EMBARRASSMENT-CONCEALING ELECTRICITY.
GRIND GRIND GRIND GRIND GRIND GRIND GRIND GRIND
FORGIVE ME, ONEESAMA!
OF COURSE YOU'D GROW ANXIOUS ABOUT THE CONNECTION OF OUR ***HEARTS*** WHEN ALL I DO IS SEEK THE ***PHYSICAL!***
NATURALLY, I DO DESIRE THE UNION OF OUR SOULS-- BUT OH, TO HAVE WORRIED YOU FOR EVEN A MOMENT IS MY LIFE'S GREATEST BLUNDER...!
I'LL QUELL YOUR WORRIES WITH MY SINCERITY AND DEVOTION, ONEESAMA!
IN ORDER TO PROVE TO YOU THAT MY LOVE IS TRUE!

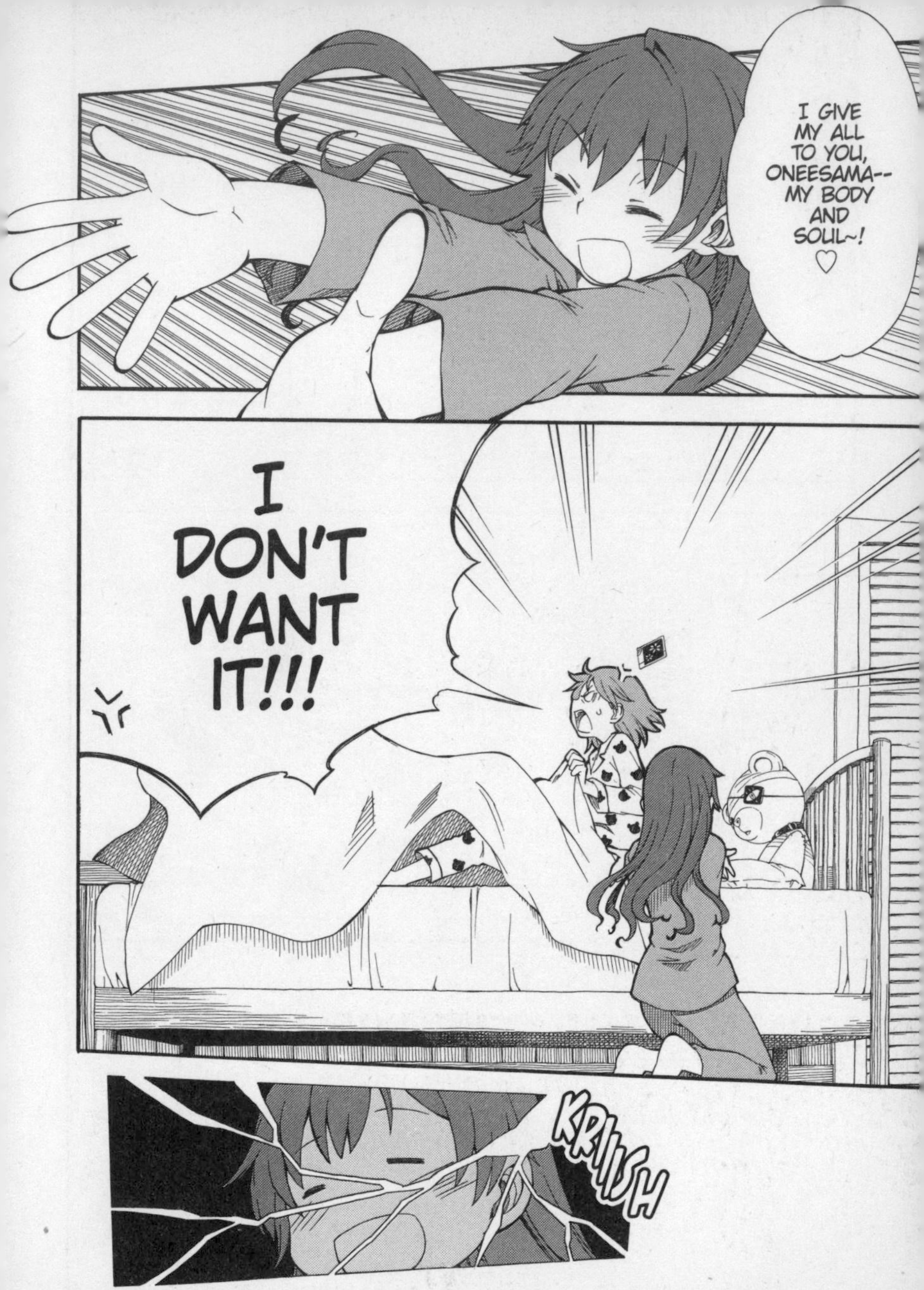
I GIVE MY ALL TO YOU, ONEESAMA-- MY BODY AND SOUL~! ♡
I DON'T WANT IT!!!
KRIISH

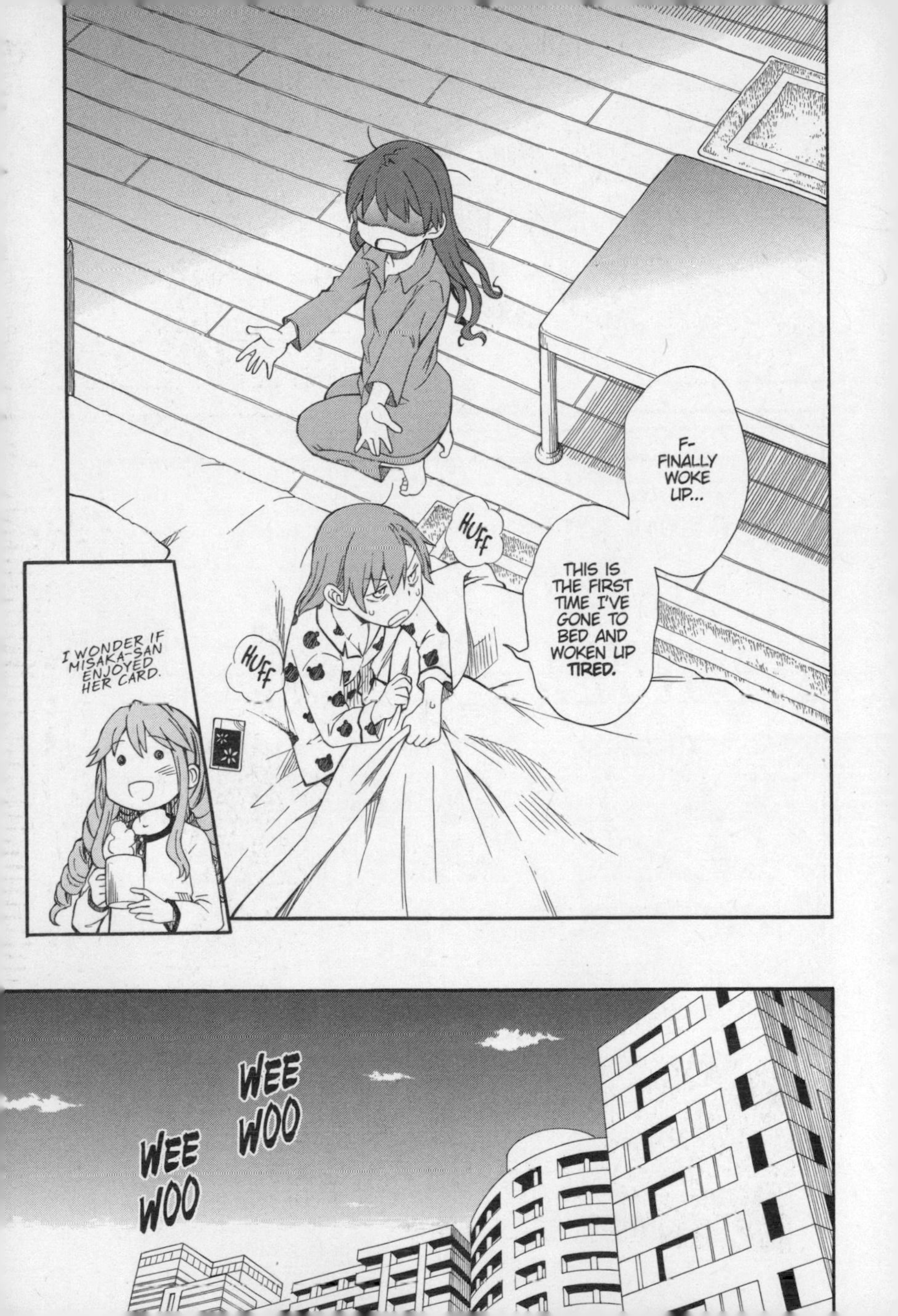
F-FINALLY WOKE UP...
HUFF
THIS IS THE FIRST TIME I'VE GONE TO BED AND WOKEN UP TIRED.
HUFF
I WONDER IF MISAKA-SAN ENJOYED HER CARD.
WEE WOO
WEE WOO

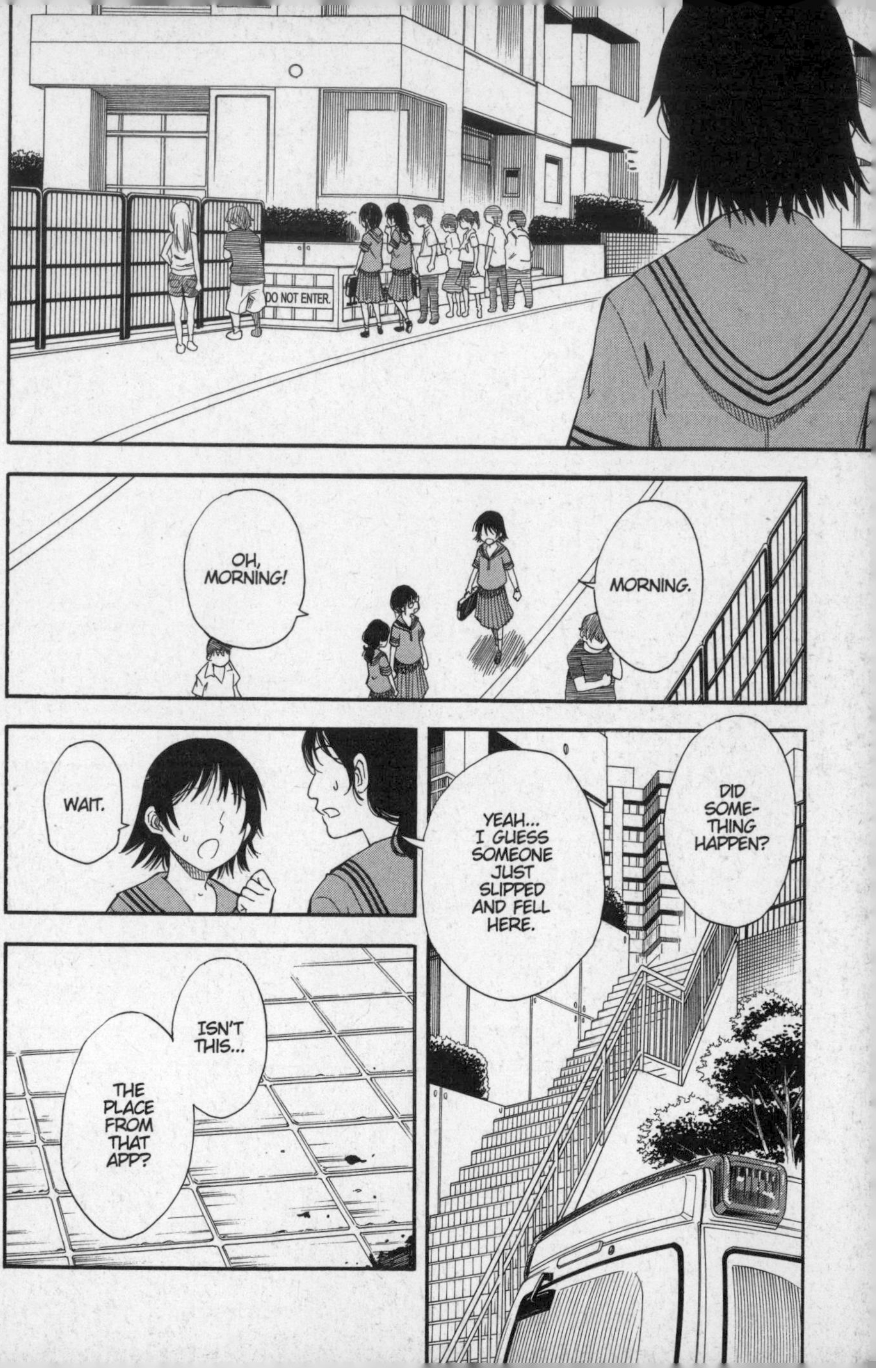
DO NOT ENTER.
MORNING.
OH, MORNING!
DID SOMETHING-THING HAPPEN?
YEAH... I GUESS SOMEONE JUST SLIPPED AND FELL HERE.
WAIT.
ISN'T THIS...
THE PLACE FROM THAT APP?

A Certain SCIENTIFIC Railgun

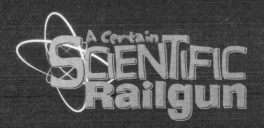

A Certain SCIENTIFIC Railgun

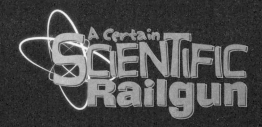

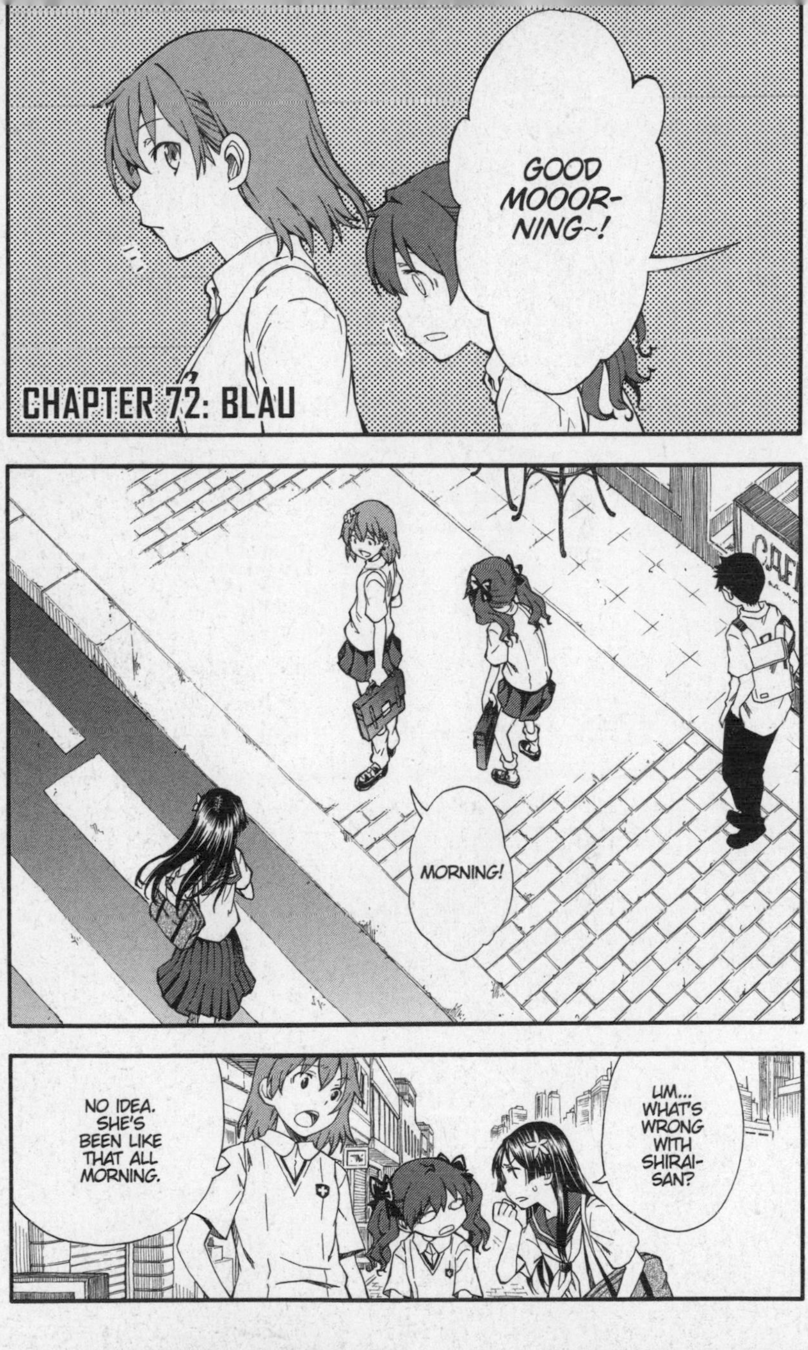
GOOD MOOOR-NING~!
CHAPTER 72: BLAU
MORNING!
UM... WHAT'S WRONG WITH SHIRAI-SAN?
NO IDEA. SHE'S BEEN LIKE THAT ALL MORNING.

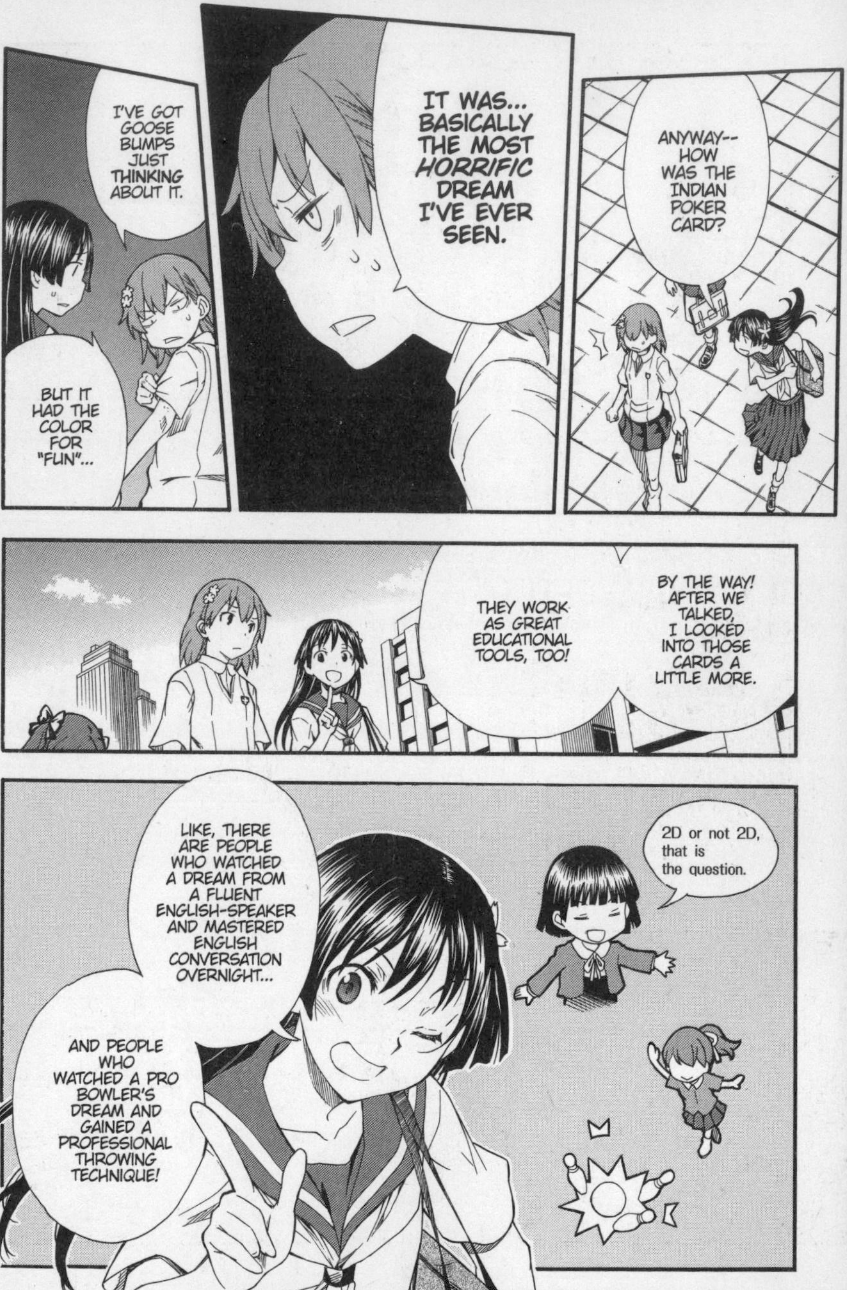
ANYWAY-- HOW WAS THE INDIAN POKER CARD?
IT WAS... BASICALLY THE MOST *HORRIFIC* DREAM I'VE EVER SEEN.
I'VE GOT GOOSE BUMPS JUST THINKING ABOUT IT.
BUT IT HAD THE COLOR FOR "FUN"...
BY THE WAY! AFTER WE TALKED, I LOOKED INTO THOSE CARDS A LITTLE MORE.
THEY WORK AS GREAT EDUCATIONAL TOOLS, TOO!
2D or not 2D, that is the question.
LIKE, THERE ARE PEOPLE WHO WATCHED A DREAM FROM A FLUENT ENGLISH-SPEAKER AND MASTERED ENGLISH CONVERSATION OVERNIGHT...
AND PEOPLE WHO WATCHED A PRO BOWLER'S DREAM AND GAINED A PROFESSIONAL THROWING TECHNIQUE!

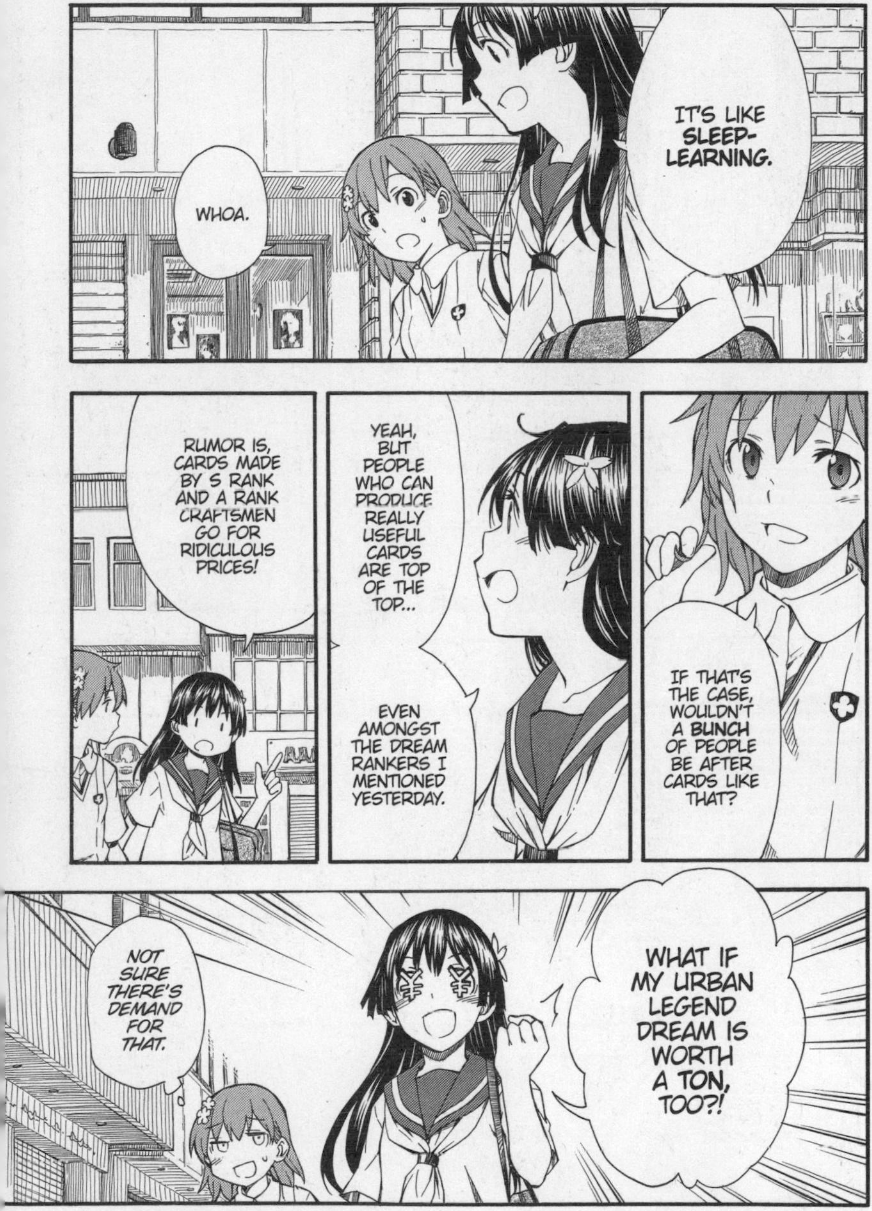
IT'S LIKE SLEEP-LEARNING.
WHOA.
IF THAT'S THE CASE, WOULDN'T A BUNCH OF PEOPLE BE AFTER CARDS LIKE THAT?
YEAH, BUT PEOPLE WHO CAN PRODUCE REALLY USEFUL CARDS ARE TOP OF THE TOP...
EVEN AMONGST THE DREAM RANKERS I MENTIONED YESTERDAY.
RUMOR IS, CARDS MADE BY S RANK AND A RANK CRAFTSMEN GO FOR RIDICULOUS PRICES!
WHAT IF MY URBAN LEGEND DREAM IS WORTH A TON, TOO?!
NOT SURE THERE'S DEMAND FOR THAT.

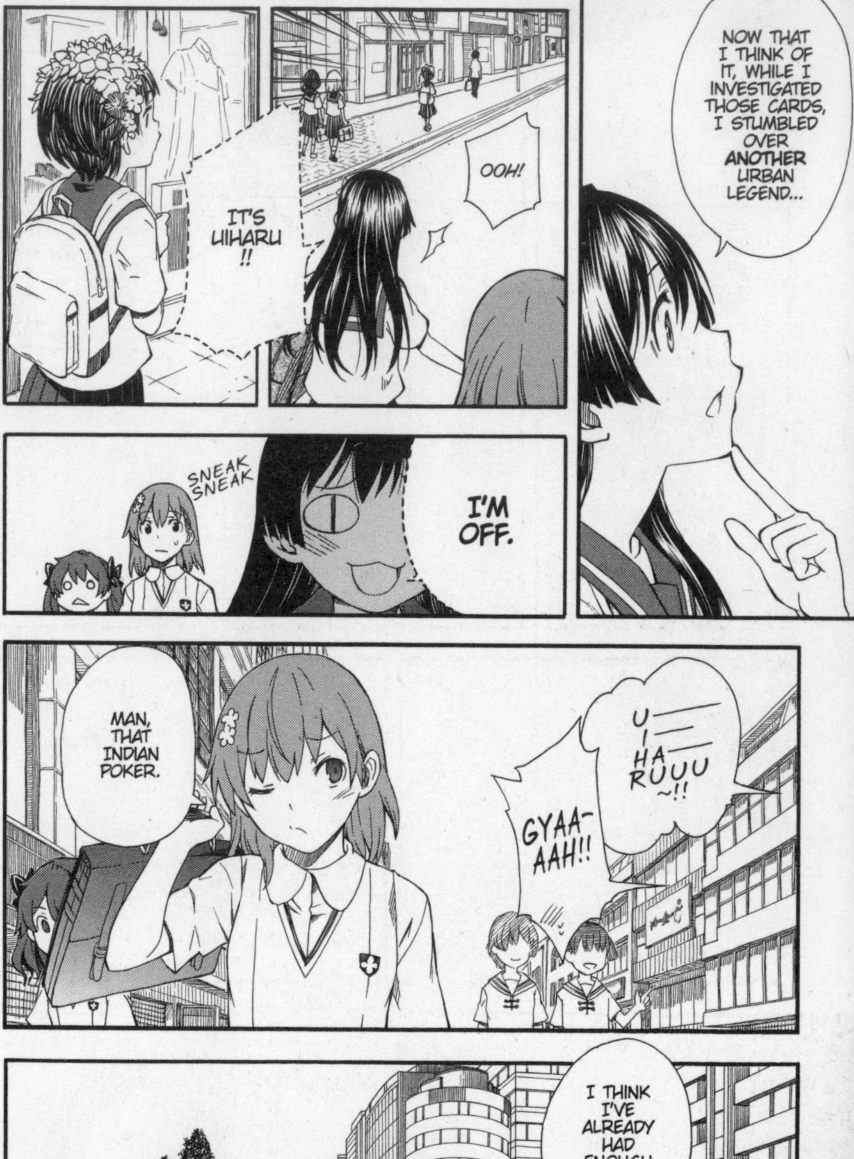
NOW THAT I THINK OF IT, WHILE I INVESTIGATED THOSE CARDS, I STUMBLED OVER **ANOTHER** URBAN LEGEND...
OOH!
IT'S UIHARU !!
I'M OFF.
SNEAK SNEAK
U—I—HA—RUUU ~!!
GYAA-AAH!!
MAN, THAT INDIAN POKER.
I THINK I'VE ALREADY HAD ENOUGH OF IT.

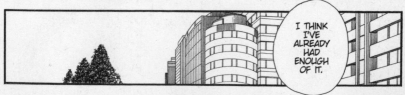

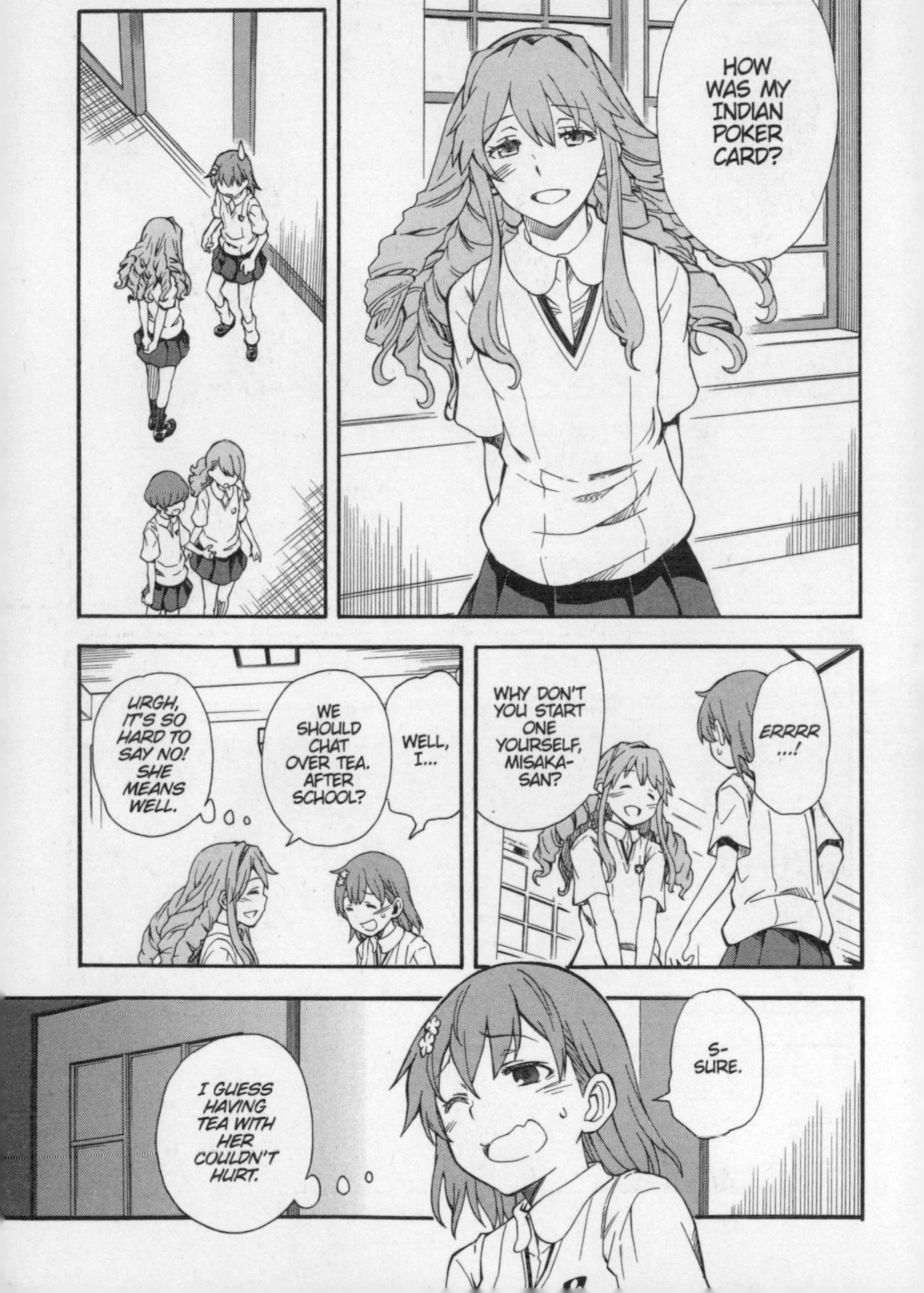
HOW WAS MY INDIAN POKER CARD?
WHY DON'T YOU START ONE YOURSELF, MISAKA-SAN?
ERRRR ...!
WE SHOULD CHAT OVER TEA. AFTER SCHOOL?
WELL, I...
URGH, IT'S SO HARD TO SAY NO! SHE MEANS WELL.
S-SURE.
I GUESS HAVING TEA WITH HER COULDN'T HURT.

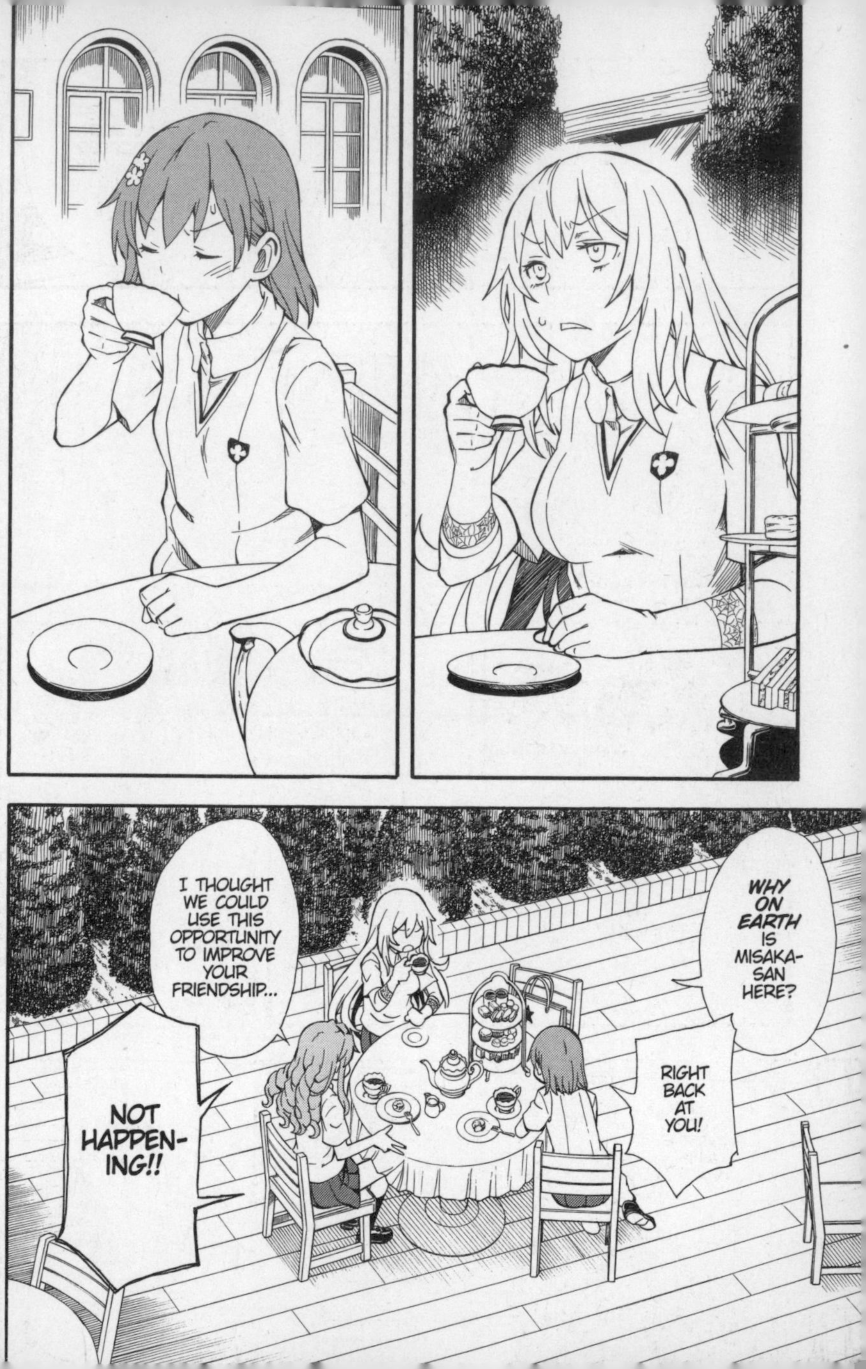
WHY ON EARTH IS MISAKA-SAN HERE?
RIGHT BACK AT YOU!
I THOUGHT WE COULD USE THIS OPPORTUNITY TO IMPROVE YOUR FRIENDSHIP...
NOT HAPPEN-ING!!

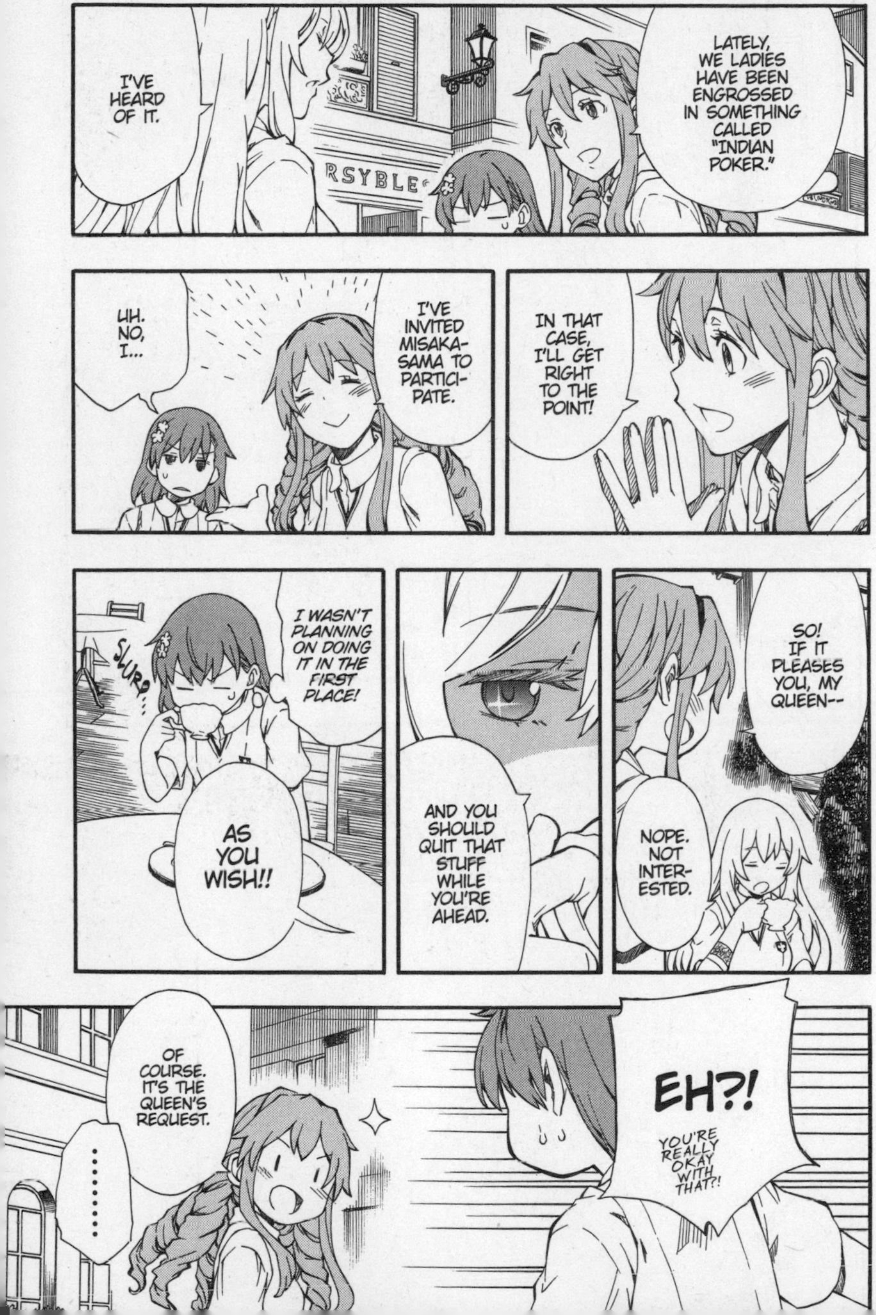
LATELY, WE LADIES HAVE BEEN ENGROSSED IN SOMETHING CALLED "INDIAN POKER."
I'VE HEARD OF IT.
RSYBLE
IN THAT CASE, I'LL GET RIGHT TO THE POINT!
I'VE INVITED MISAKA-SAMA TO PARTICIPATE.
UH. NO, I...
SO! IF IT PLEASES YOU, MY QUEEN--
NOPE. NOT INTERESTED.
AND YOU SHOULD QUIT THAT STUFF WHILE YOU'RE AHEAD.
I WASN'T PLANNING ON DOING IT IN THE FIRST PLACE!
SLURP...
AS YOU WISH!!
EH?!
YOU'RE REALLY OKAY WITH THAT?!
OF COURSE. IT'S THE QUEEN'S REQUEST.
......

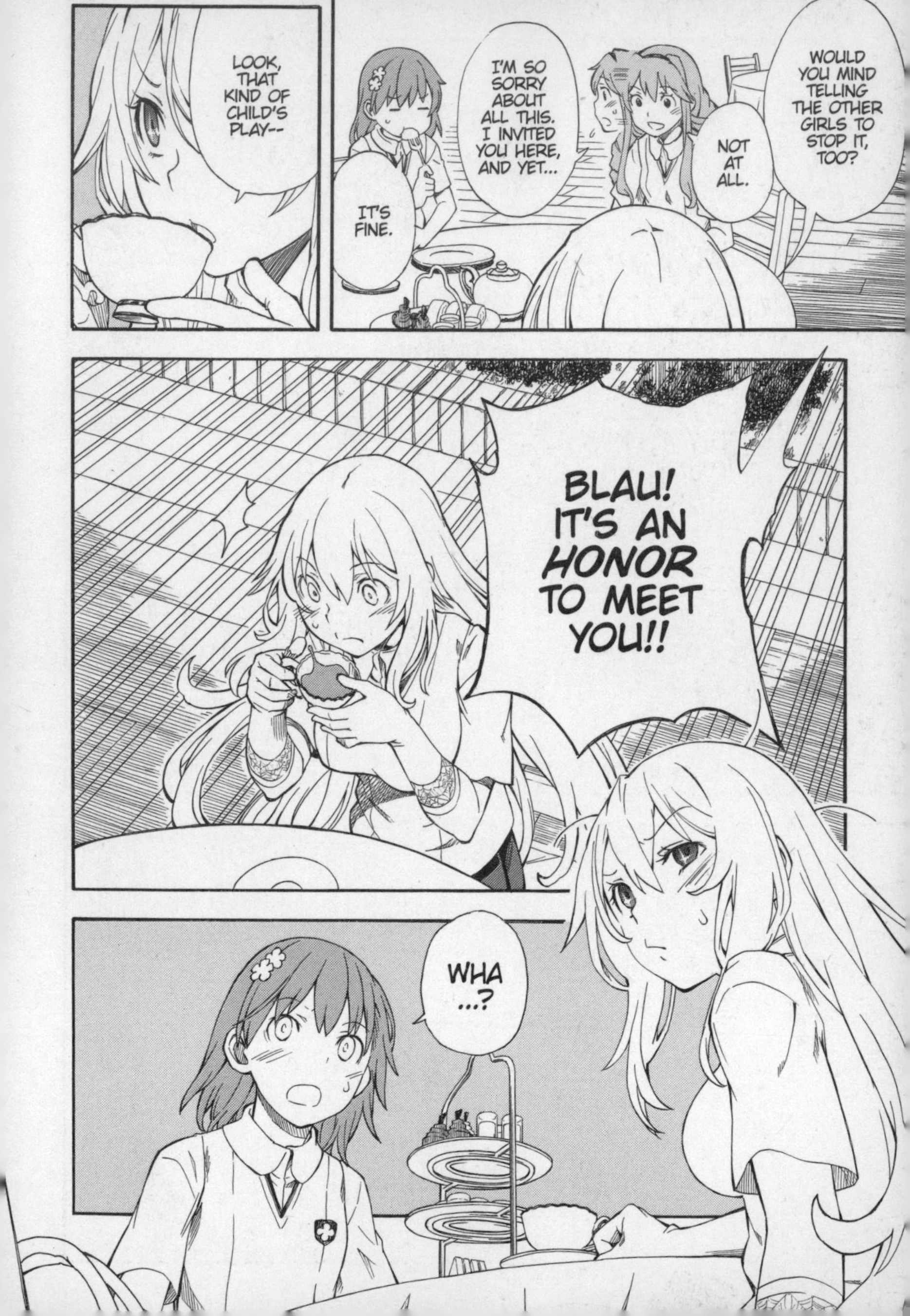
WOULD YOU MIND TELLING THE OTHER GIRLS TO STOP IT, TOO?
NOT AT ALL.
I'M SO SORRY ABOUT ALL THIS. I INVITED YOU HERE, AND YET...
IT'S FINE.
LOOK, THAT KIND OF CHILD'S PLAY--
BLAU! IT'S AN HONOR TO MEET YOU!!
WHA ...?

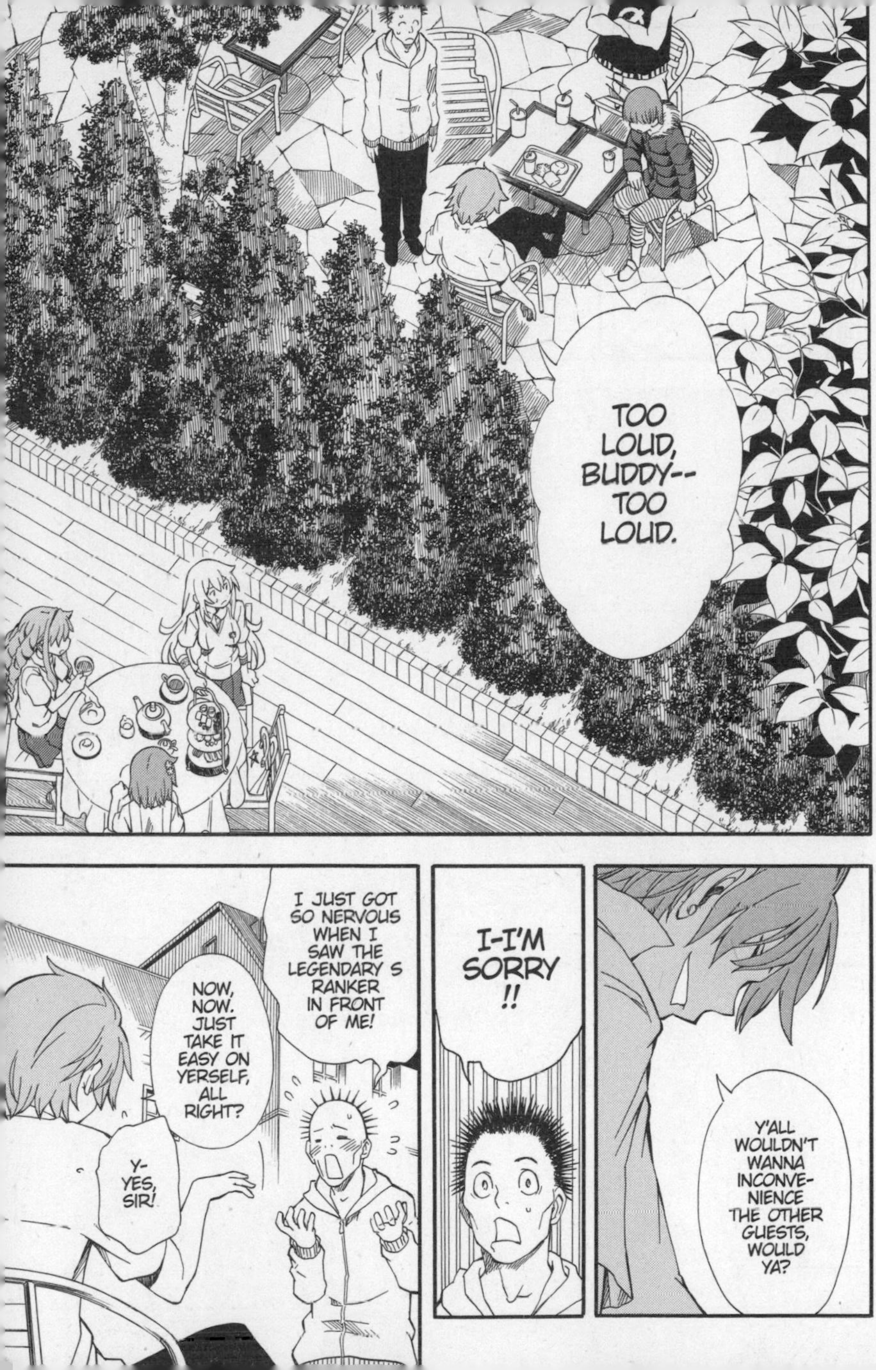
TOO LOUD, BUDDY-- TOO LOUD.
Y'ALL WOULDN'T WANNA INCONVE-NIENCE THE OTHER GUESTS, WOULD YA?
I-I'M SORRY!!
I JUST GOT SO NERVOUS WHEN I SAW THE LEGENDARY S RANKER IN FRONT OF ME!
NOW, NOW. JUST TAKE IT EASY ON YERSELF, ALL RIGHT?
Y-YES, SIR!

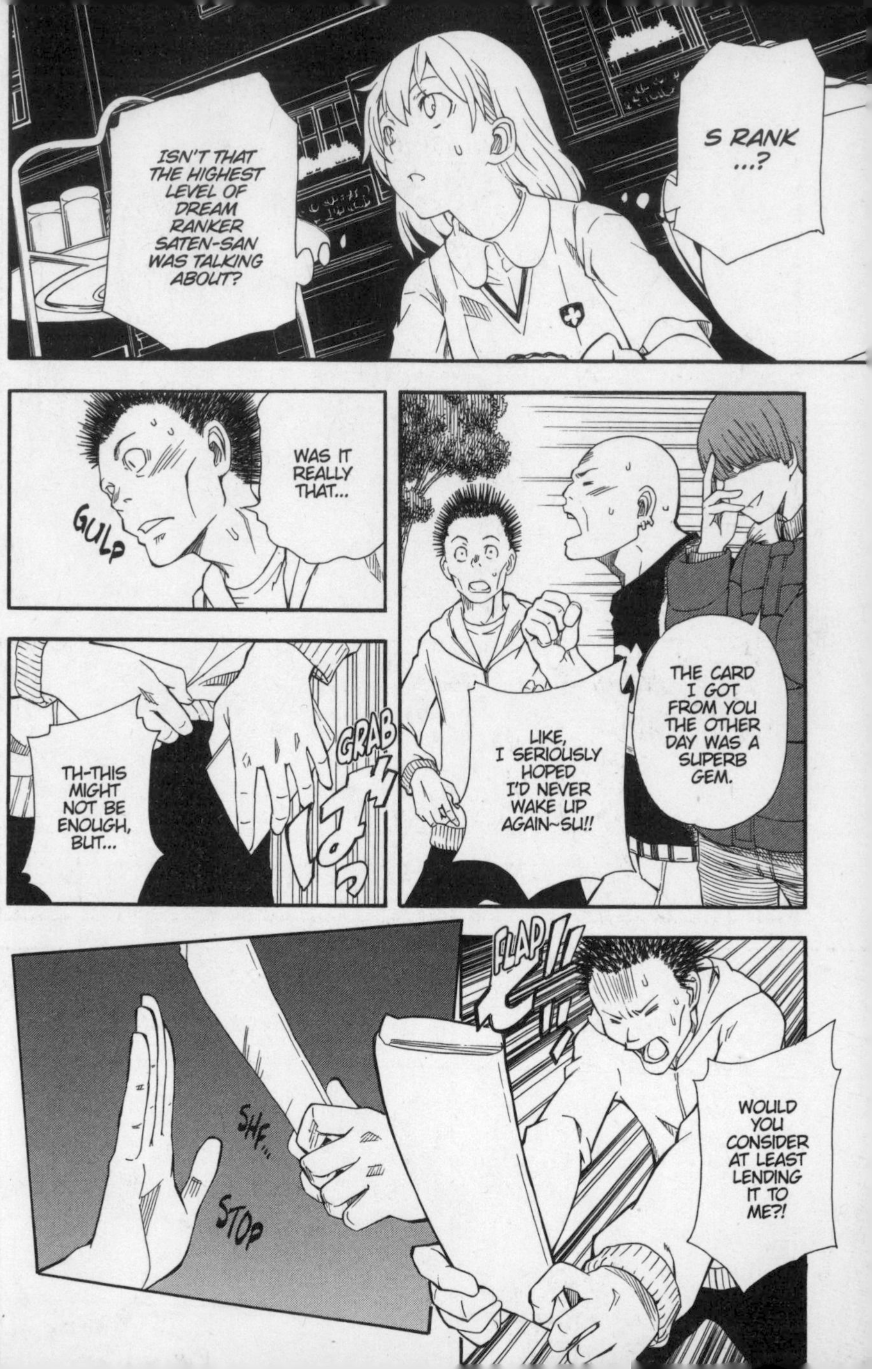
S RANK ...?
ISN'T THAT THE HIGHEST LEVEL OF DREAM RANKER SATEN-SAN WAS TALKING ABOUT?
THE CARD I GOT FROM YOU THE OTHER DAY WAS A SUPERB GEM.
LIKE, I SERIOUSLY HOPED I'D NEVER WAKE UP AGAIN~SU!!
WAS IT REALLY THAT...
GULP
GRAB
TH-THIS MIGHT NOT BE ENOUGH, BUT...
FLAP!!
WOULD YOU CONSIDER AT LEAST LENDING IT TO ME?!
SHF...
STOP

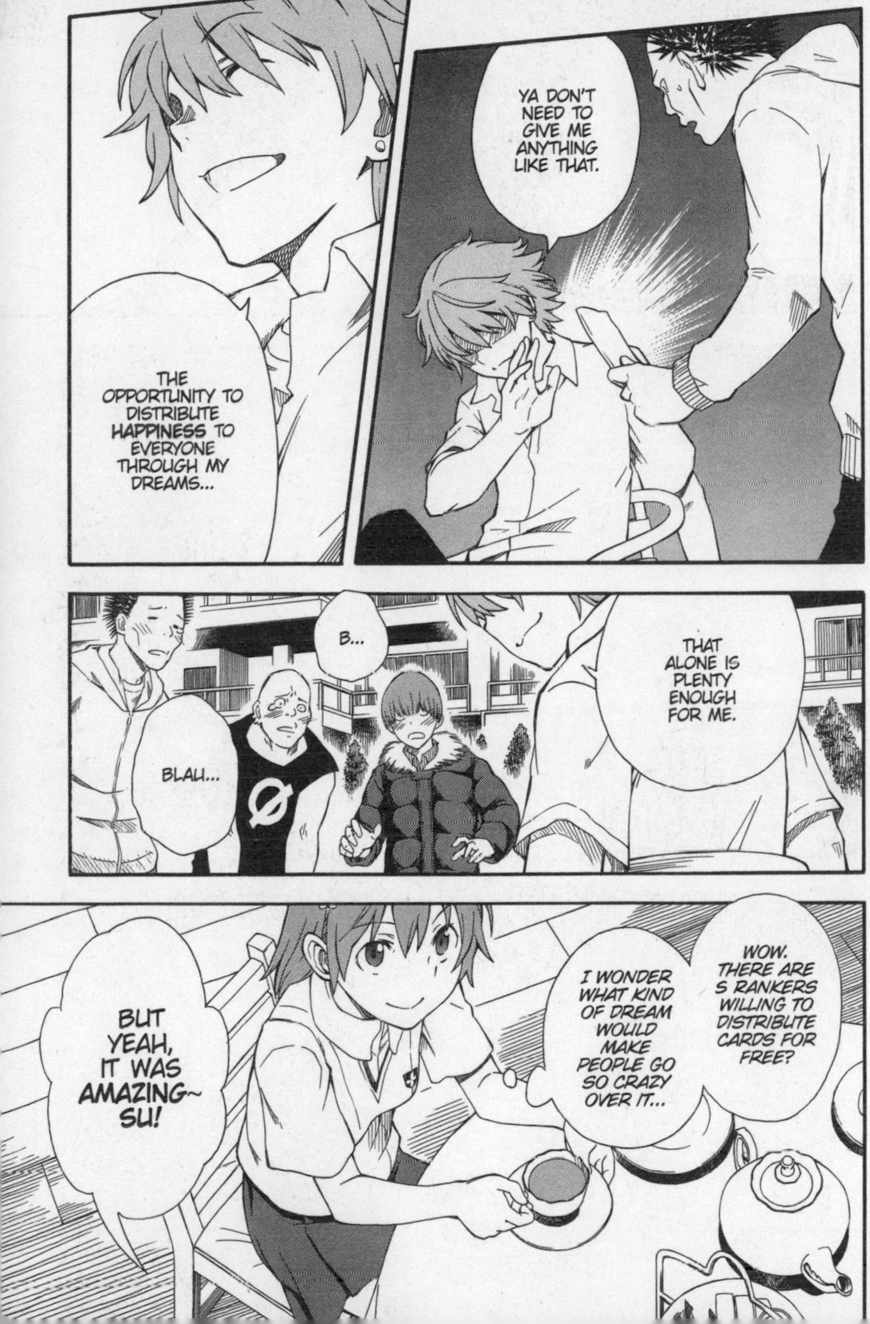
YA DON'T NEED TO GIVE ME ANYTHING LIKE THAT.
THE OPPORTUNITY TO DISTRIBUTE HAPPINESS TO EVERYONE THROUGH MY DREAMS...
THAT ALONE IS PLENTY ENOUGH FOR ME.
B...
BLAU...
WOW. THERE ARE S RANKERS WILLING TO DISTRIBUTE CARDS FOR FREE?
I WONDER WHAT KIND OF DREAM WOULD MAKE PEOPLE GO SO CRAZY OVER IT...
BUT YEAH, IT WAS AMAZING~ SU!

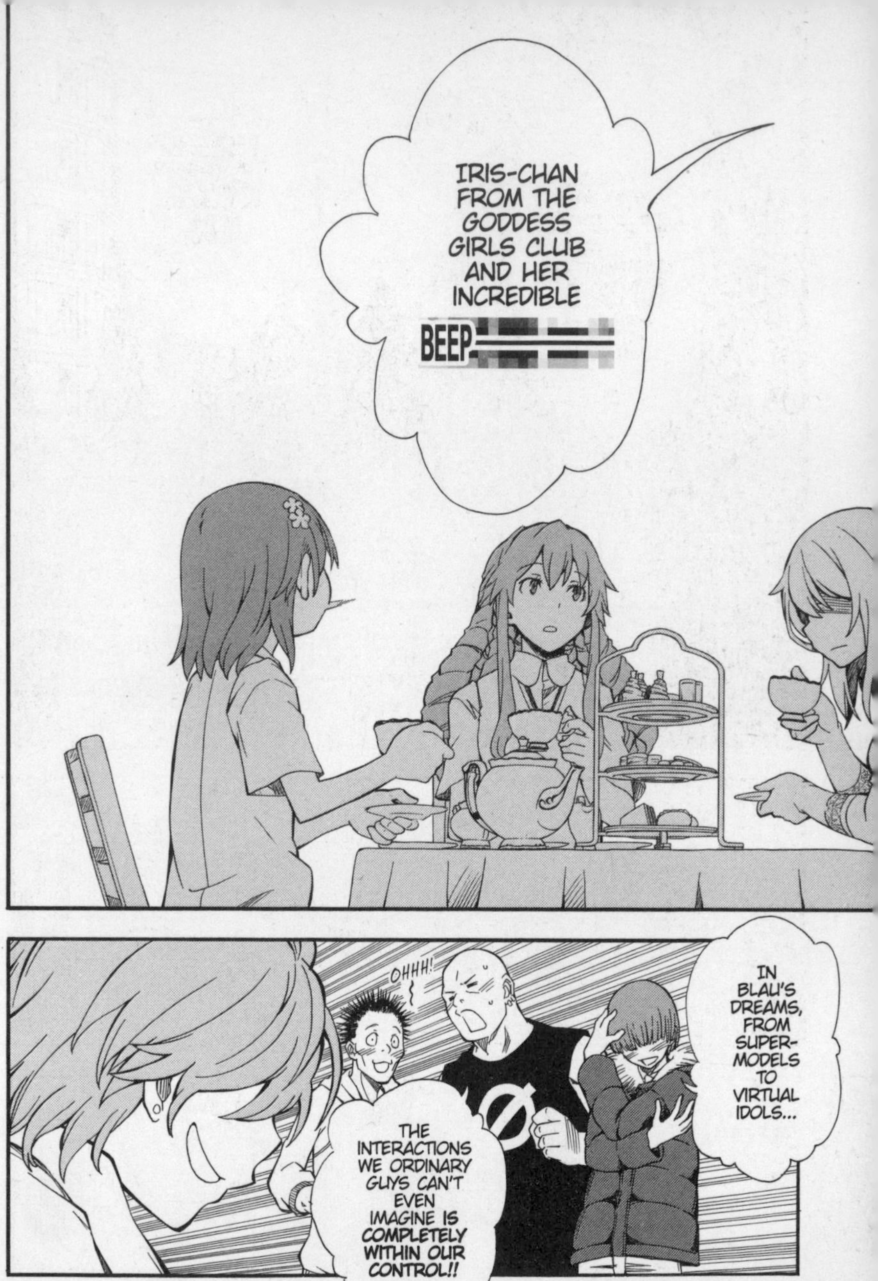
IRIS-CHAN FROM THE GODDESS GIRLS CLUB AND HER INCREDIBLE
BEEP
IN BLAU'S DREAMS, FROM SUPER-MODELS TO VIRTUAL IDOLS...
OHHHH!
THE INTERACTIONS WE ORDINARY GUYS CAN'T EVEN IMAGINE IS COMPLETELY WITHIN OUR CONTROL!!

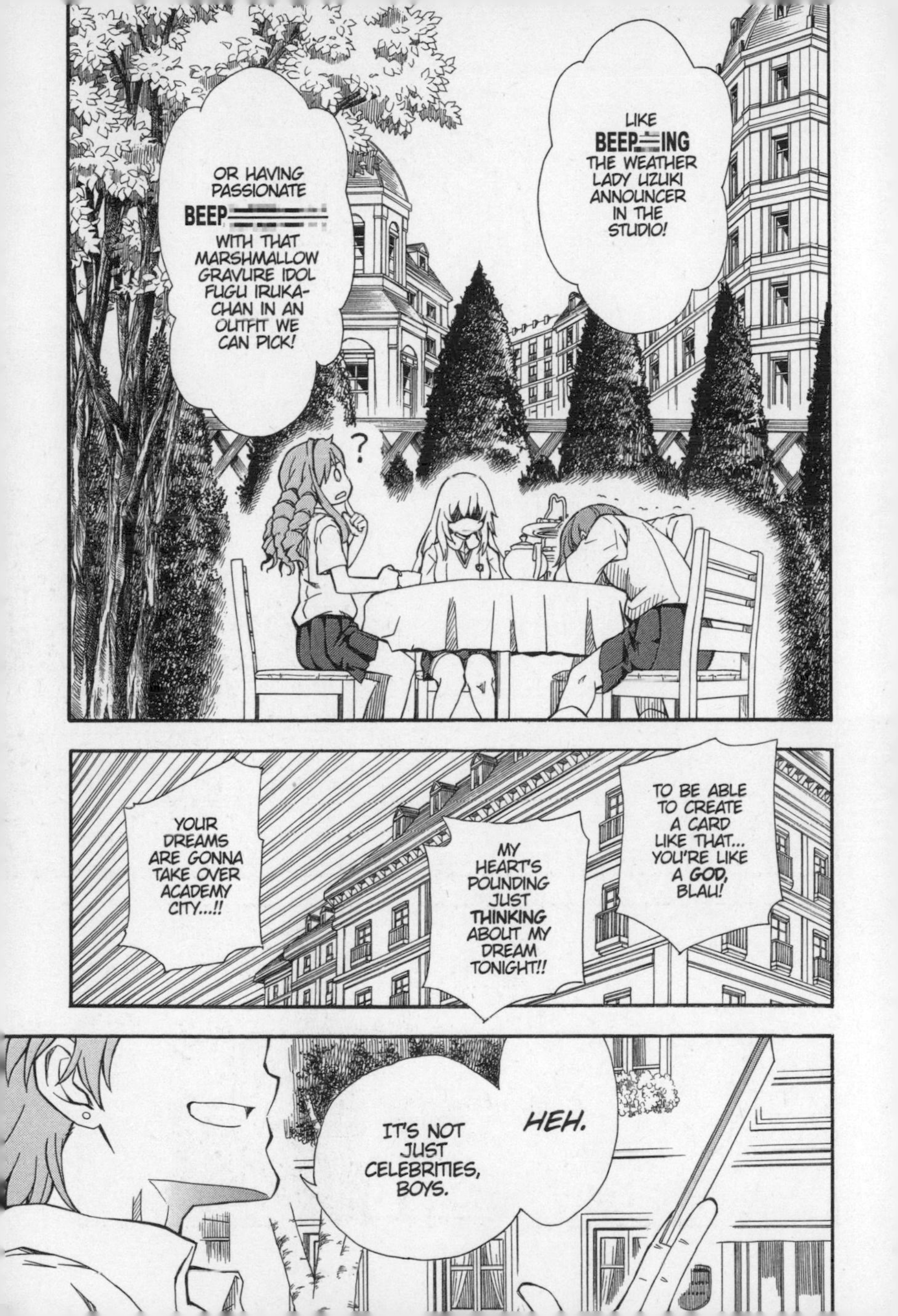
LIKE BEEP-ING THE WEATHER LADY UZUKI ANNOUNCER IN THE STUDIO!
OR HAVING PASSIONATE BEEP WITH THAT MARSHMALLOW GRAVURE IDOL FUGU IRUKA-CHAN IN AN OUTFIT WE CAN PICK!
?
TO BE ABLE TO CREATE A CARD LIKE THAT... YOU'RE LIKE A GOD, BLAU!
MY HEART'S POUNDING JUST THINKING ABOUT MY DREAM TONIGHT!!
YOUR DREAMS ARE GONNA TAKE OVER ACADEMY CITY...!!
HEH.
IT'S NOT JUST CELEBRITIES, BOYS.

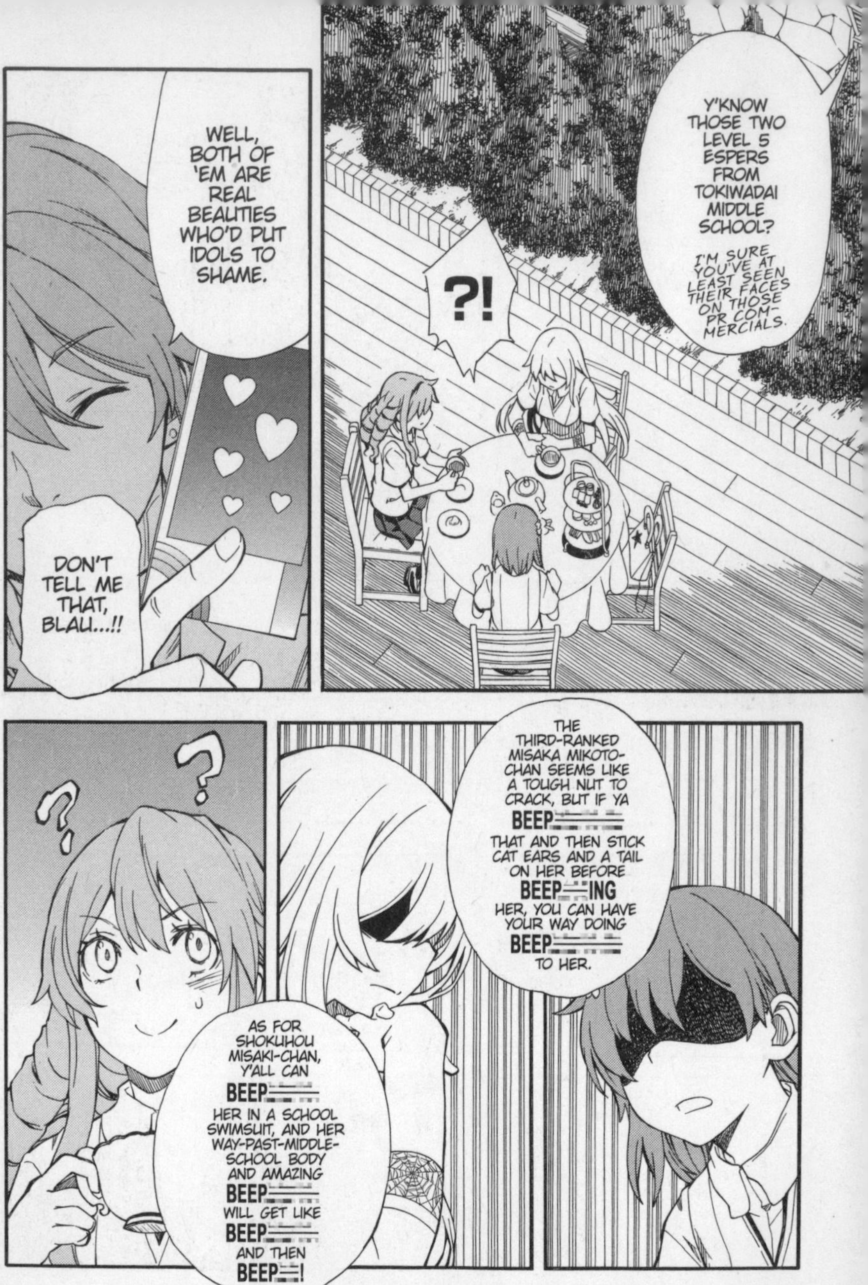
Y'KNOW THOSE TWO LEVEL 5 ESPERS FROM TOKIWADAI MIDDLE SCHOOL?
I'M SURE YOU'VE AT LEAST SEEN THEIR FACES ON THOSE PR COMMERCIALS.
?!
WELL, BOTH OF 'EM ARE REAL BEAUTIES WHO'D PUT IDOLS TO SHAME.
DON'T TELL ME THAT, BLAU...!!
THE THIRD-RANKED MISAKA MIKOTO-CHAN SEEMS LIKE A TOUGH NUT TO CRACK, BUT IF YA BEEP THAT AND THEN STICK CAT EARS AND A TAIL ON HER BEFORE BEEPING HER, YOU CAN HAVE YOUR WAY DOING BEEP TO HER.
AS FOR SHOKUHOU MISAKI-CHAN, Y'ALL CAN BEEP HER IN A SCHOOL SWIMSUIT, AND HER WAY-PAST-MIDDLE-SCHOOL BODY AND AMAZING BEEP WILL GET LIKE BEEP AND THEN BEEP!

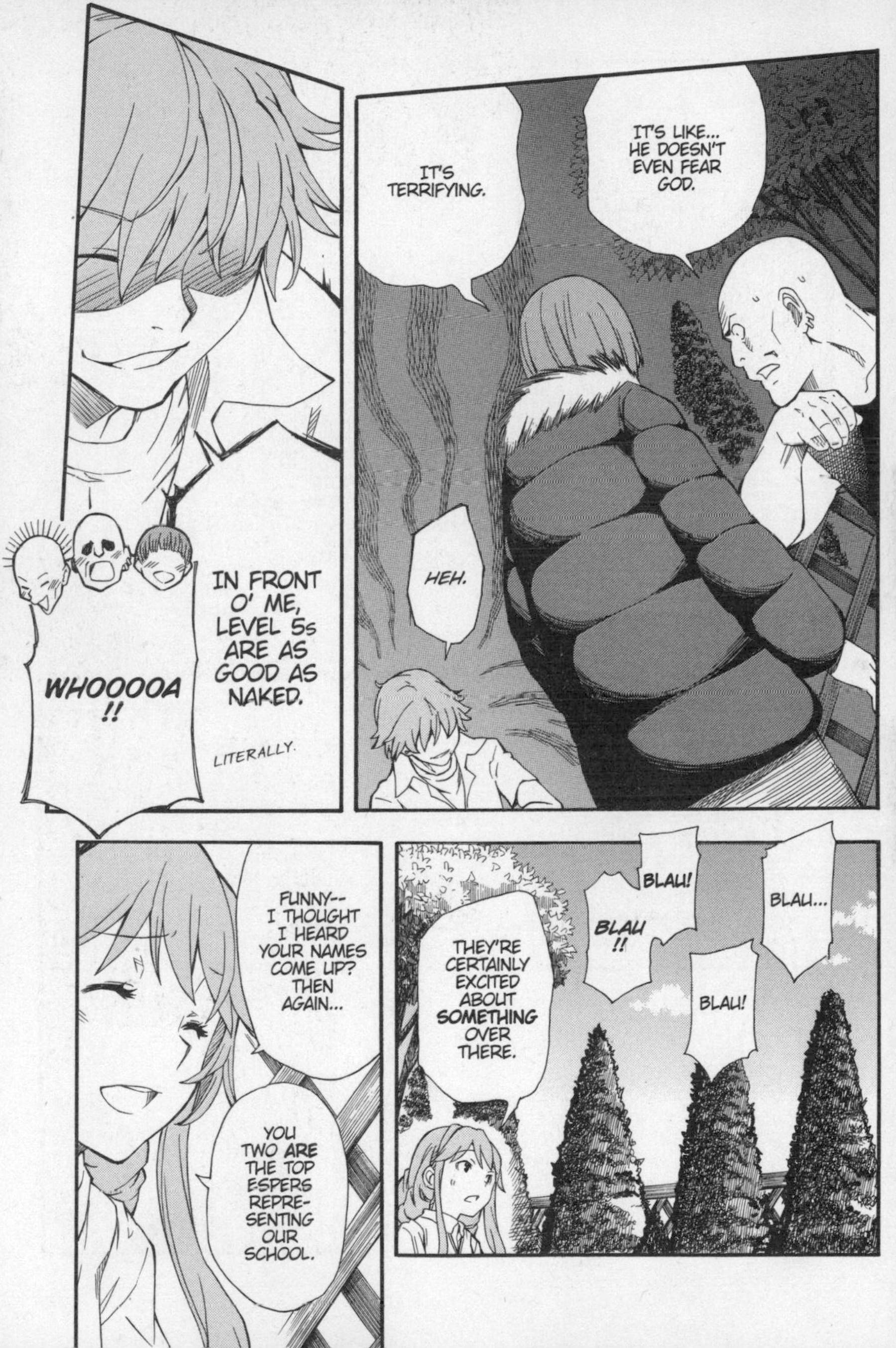
IT'S LIKE... HE DOESN'T EVEN FEAR GOD.
IT'S TERRIFYING.
HEH.
IN FRONT O' ME, LEVEL 5s ARE AS GOOD AS NAKED.
WHOOOOA!!
LITERALLY.
BLAU...
BLAU!
BLAU!!
BLAU!
THEY'RE CERTAINLY EXCITED ABOUT SOMETHING OVER THERE.
FUNNY-- I THOUGHT I HEARD YOUR NAMES COME UP? THEN AGAIN...
YOU TWO ARE THE TOP ESPERS REPRE-SENTING OUR SCHOOL.

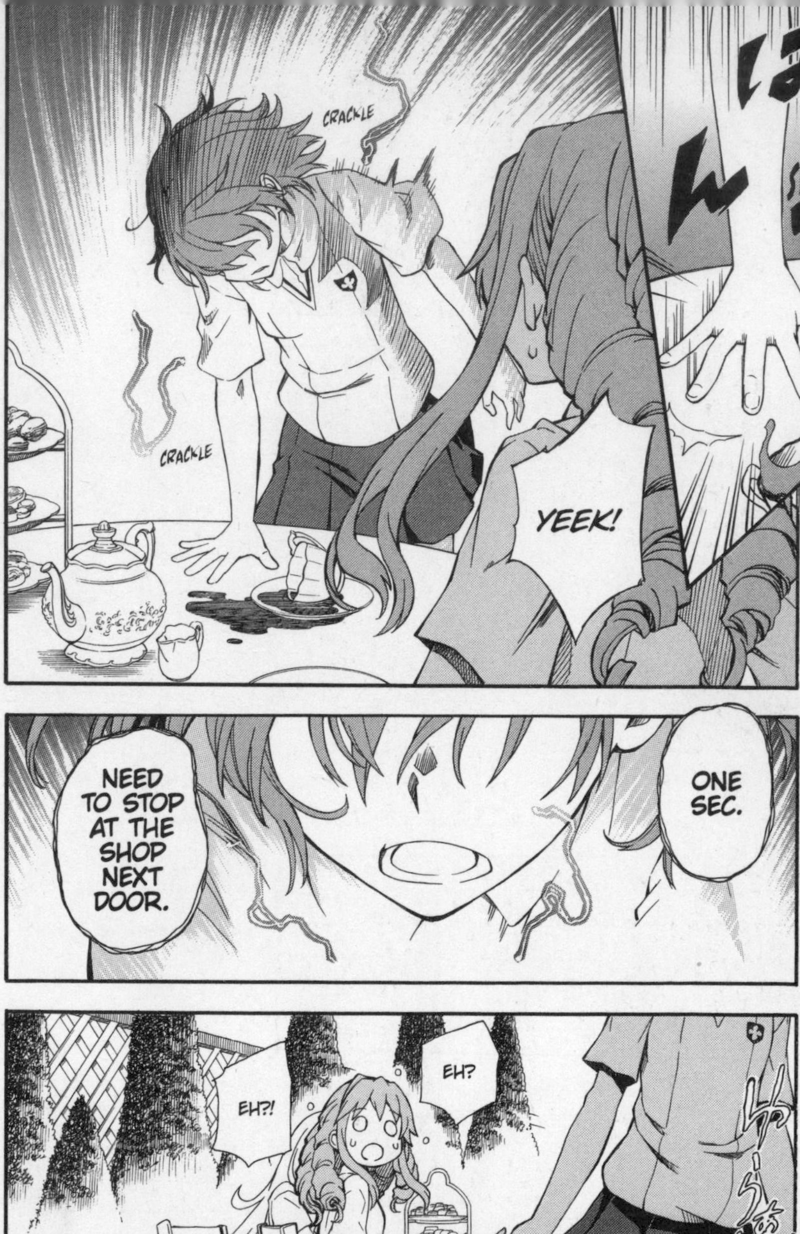
ばん
SLAM
CRACKLE
YEEK!
CRACKLE
ONE SEC.
NEED TO STOP AT THE SHOP NEXT DOOR.
SWAY
EH?
EH?!

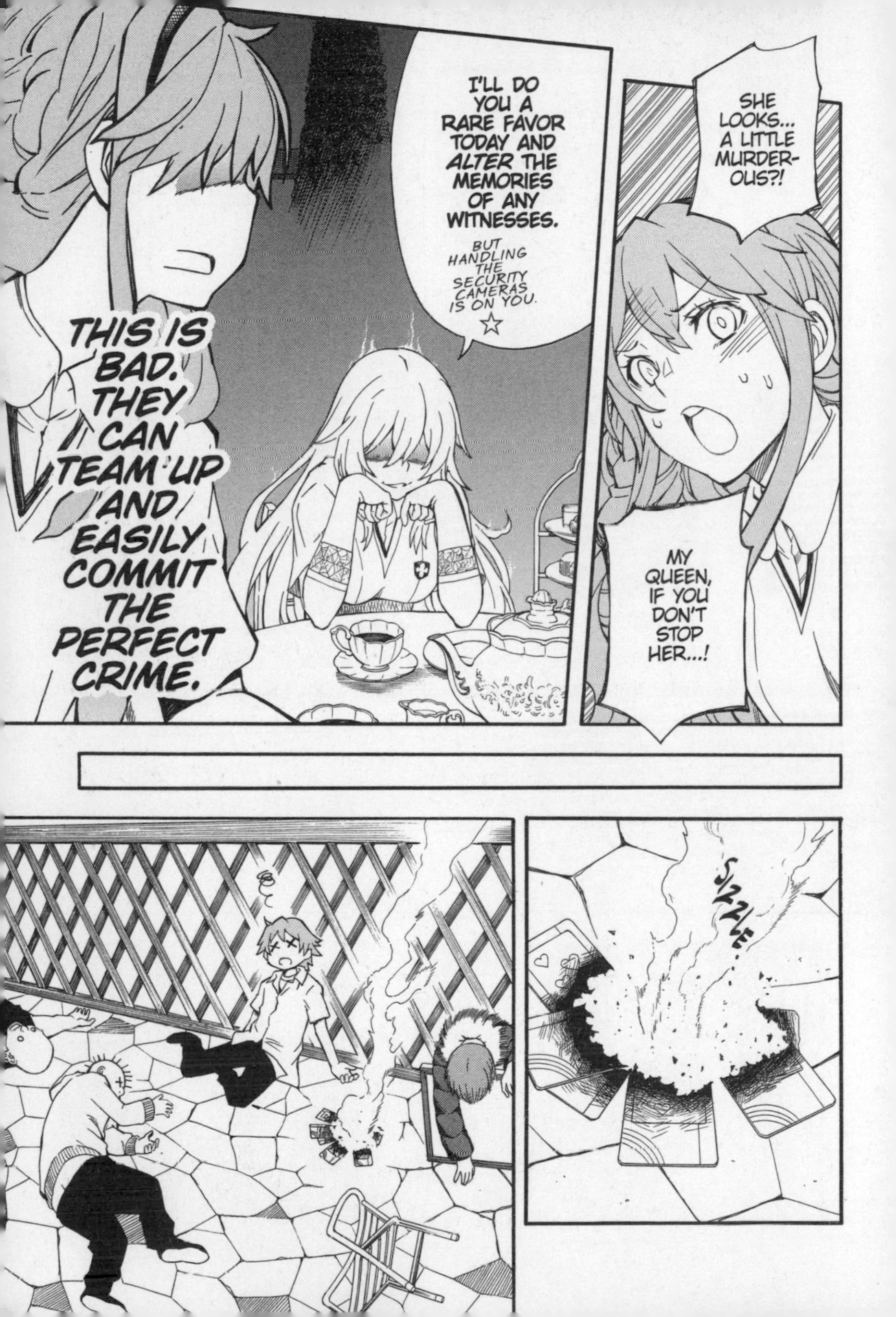
SHE LOOKS... A LITTLE MURDER-OUS?!
MY QUEEN, IF YOU DON'T STOP HER...!
I'LL DO YOU A RARE FAVOR TODAY AND ALTER THE MEMORIES OF ANY WITNESSES.
BUT HANDLING THE SECURITY CAMERAS IS ON YOU. ☆
THIS IS BAD. THEY CAN TEAM UP AND EASILY COMMIT THE PERFECT CRIME.
SIZZLE

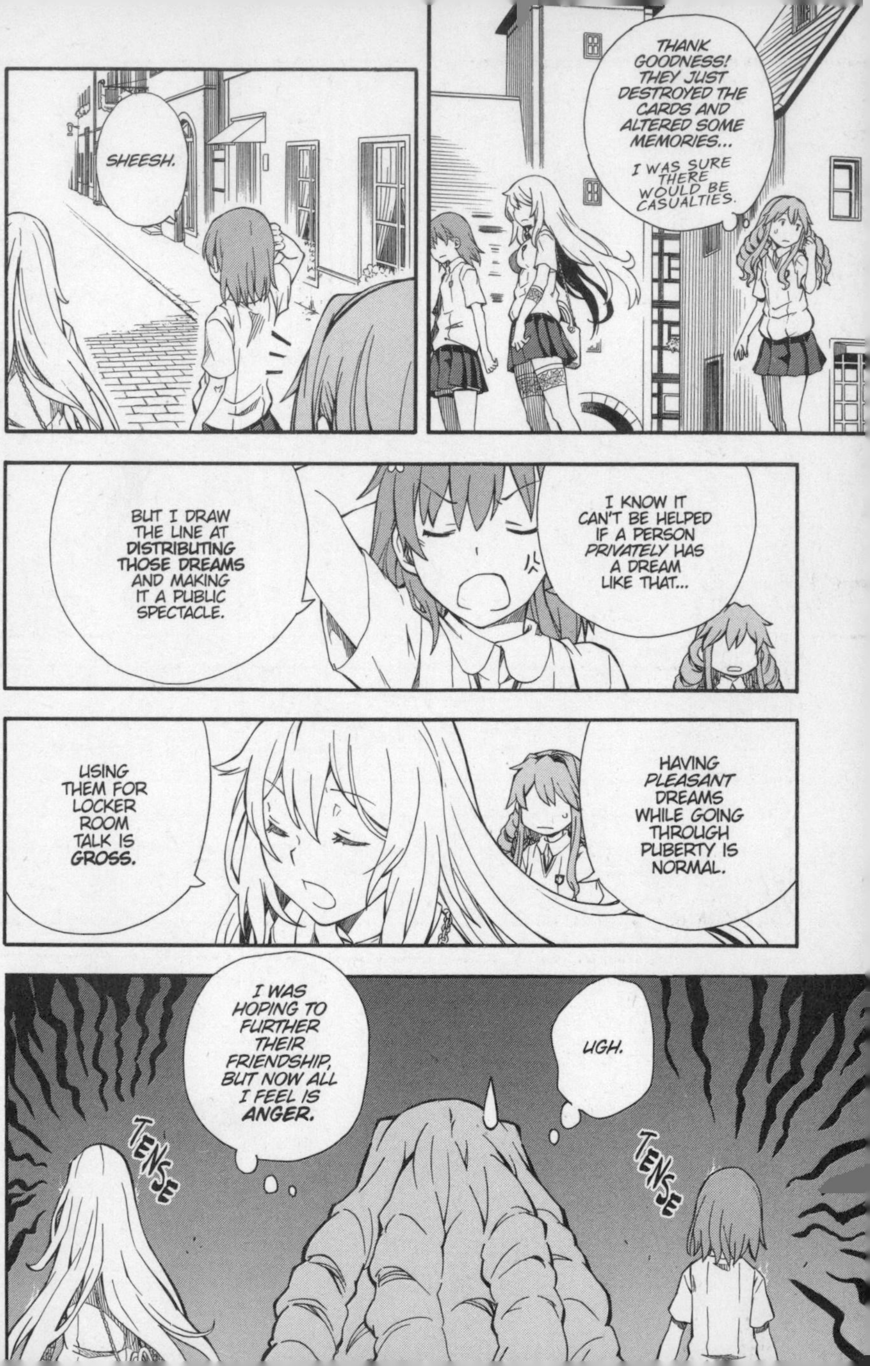
THANK GOODNESS! THEY JUST DESTROYED THE CARDS AND ALTERED SOME MEMORIES...
I WAS SURE THERE WOULD BE CASUALTIES.
SHEESH.
I KNOW IT CAN'T BE HELPED IF A PERSON *PRIVATELY* HAS A DREAM LIKE THAT...
BUT I DRAW THE LINE AT DISTRIBUTING THOSE DREAMS AND MAKING IT A PUBLIC SPECTACLE.
HAVING *PLEASANT* DREAMS WHILE GOING THROUGH PUBERTY IS NORMAL.
USING THEM FOR LOCKER ROOM TALK IS **GROSS.**
UGH.
I WAS HOPING TO FURTHER THEIR FRIENDSHIP, BUT NOW ALL I FEEL IS **ANGER.**
TENSE
TENSE

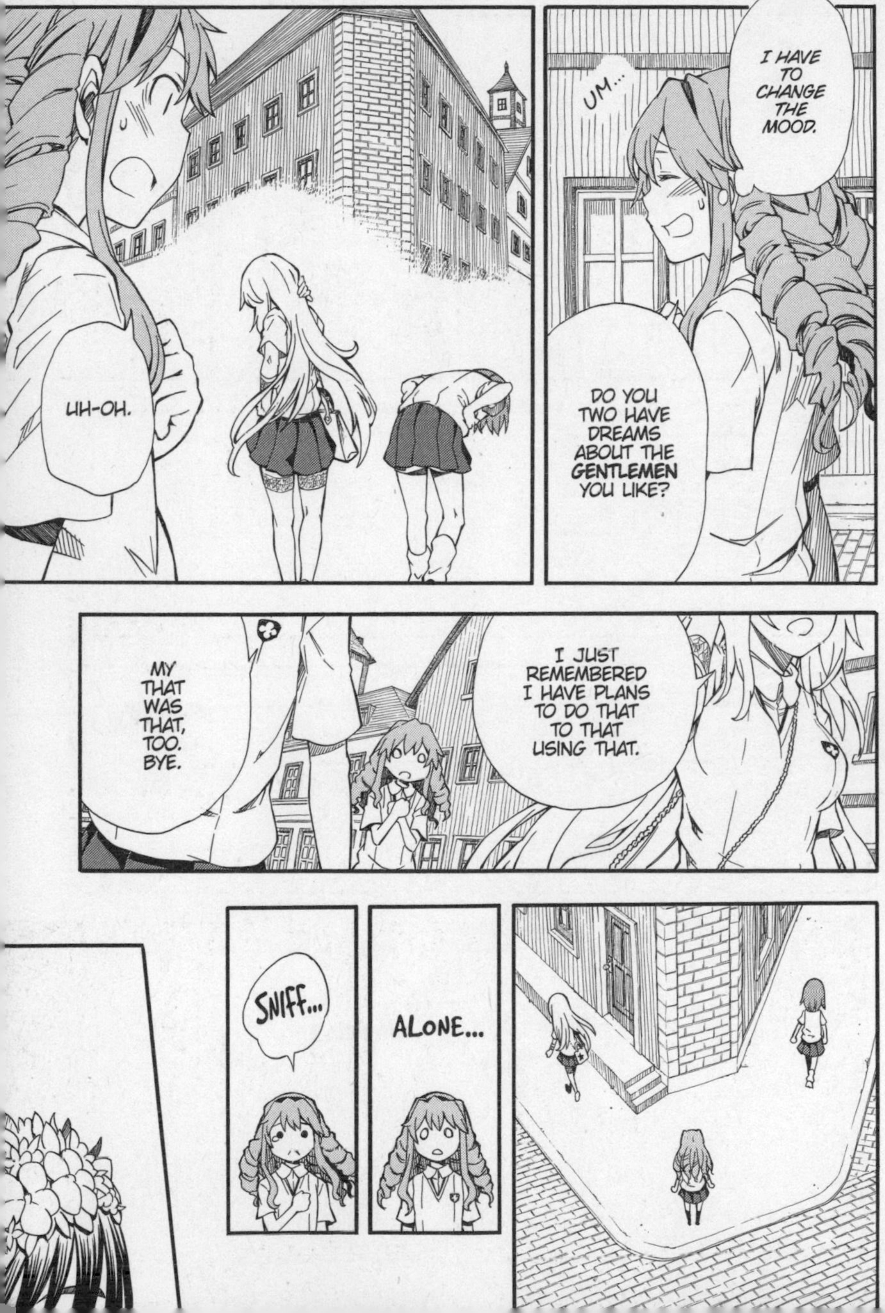
I HAVE TO CHANGE THE MOOD.
UM...
DO YOU TWO HAVE DREAMS ABOUT THE GENTLEMEN YOU LIKE?
UH-OH.
I JUST REMEMBERED I HAVE PLANS TO DO THAT TO THAT USING THAT.
MY THAT WAS THAT, TOO. BYE.
ALONE...
SNIFF...

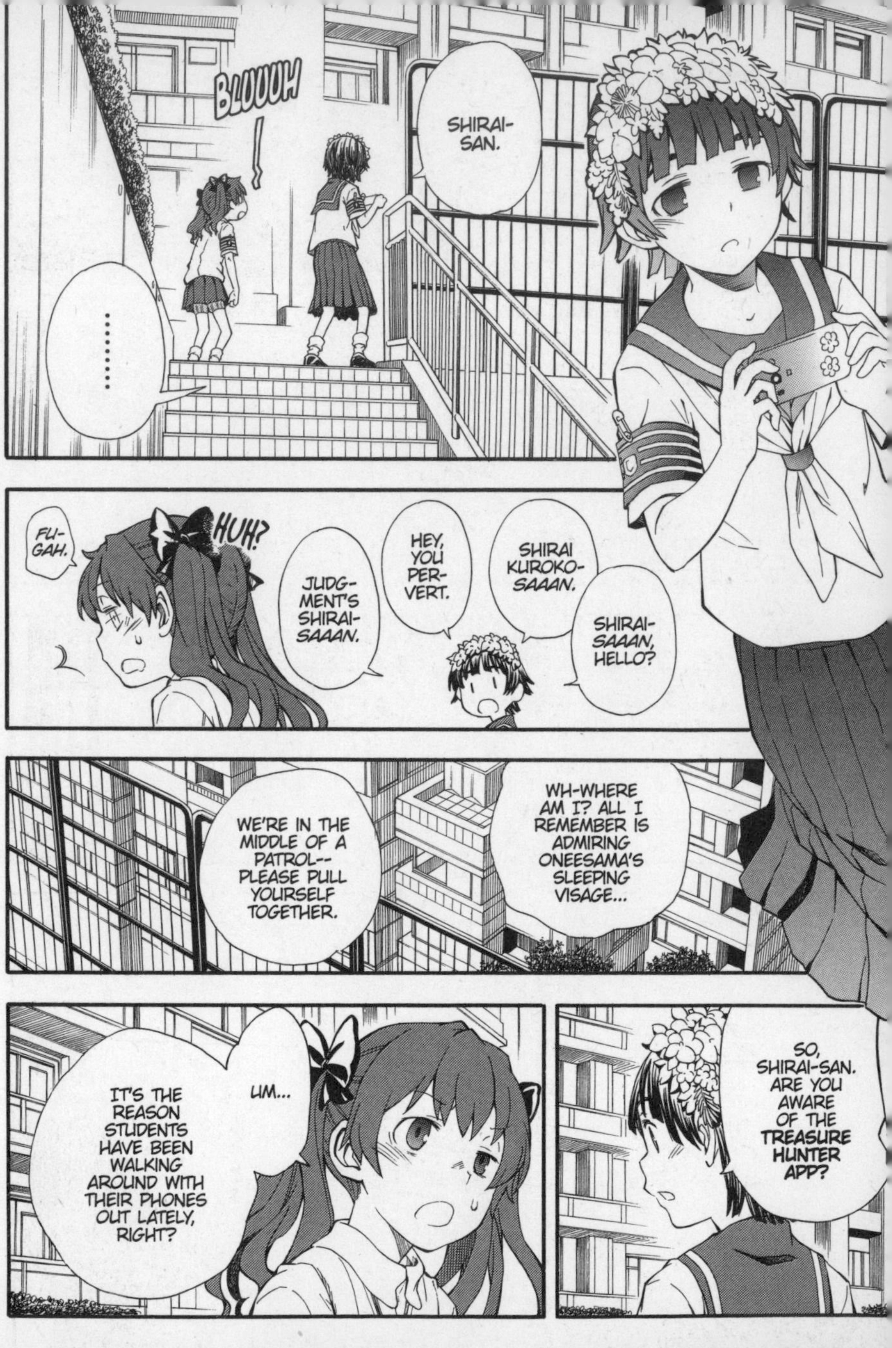
SHIRAI-SAN.
BLUUUH
......
SHIRAI KUROKO-SAAAN.
SHIRAI-SAAAN, HELLO?
HEY, YOU PERVERT.
JUDGMENT'S SHIRAI-SAAAN.
HUH?
FU-GAH.
WH-WHERE AM I? ALL I REMEMBER IS ADMIRING ONEESAMA'S SLEEPING VISAGE...
WE'RE IN THE MIDDLE OF A PATROL--PLEASE PULL YOURSELF TOGETHER.
SO, SHIRAI-SAN. ARE YOU AWARE OF THE TREASURE HUNTER APP?
UM...
IT'S THE REASON STUDENTS HAVE BEEN WALKING AROUND WITH THEIR PHONES OUT LATELY, RIGHT?

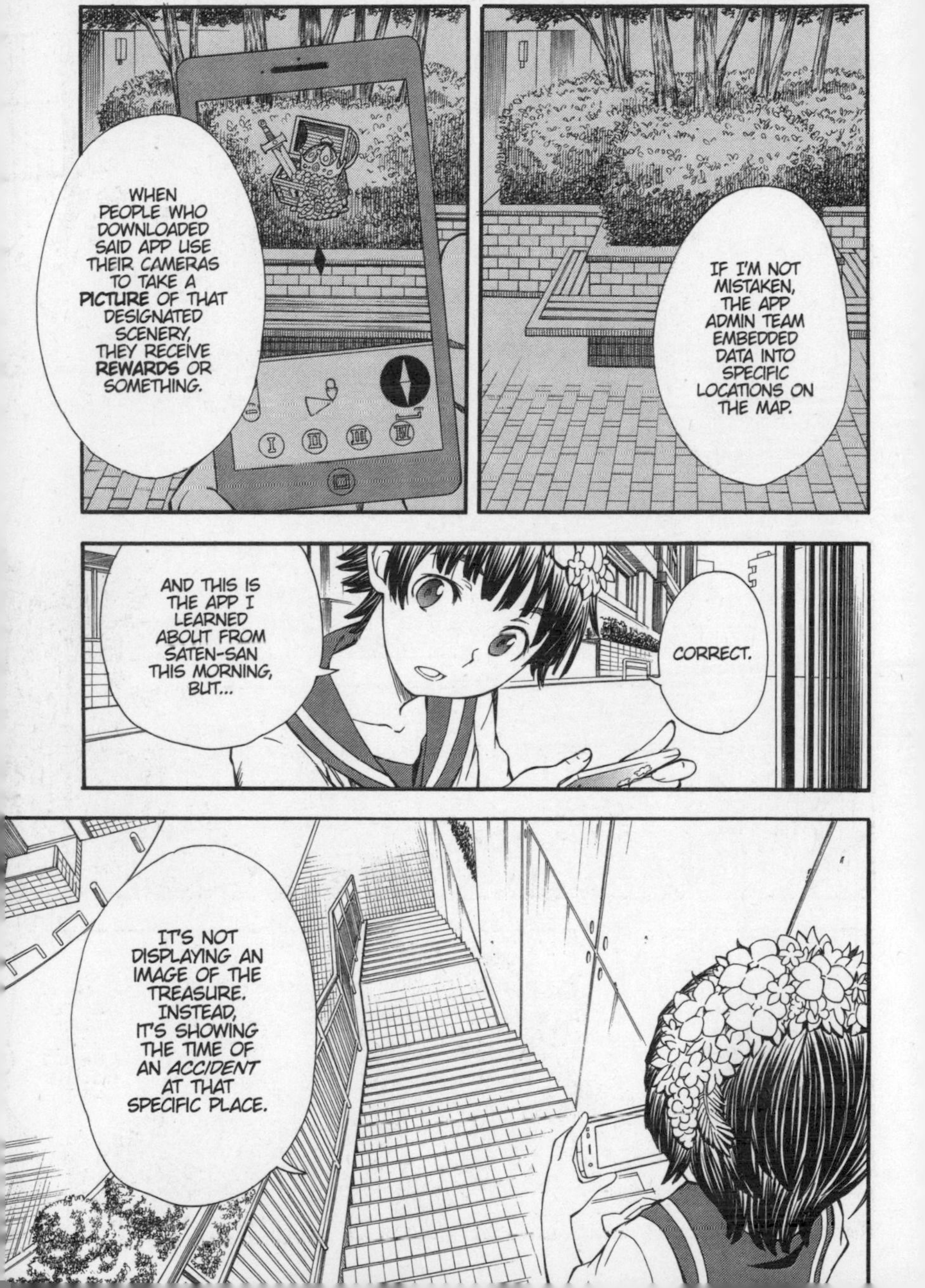
IF I'M NOT MISTAKEN, THE APP ADMIN TEAM EMBEDDED DATA INTO SPECIFIC LOCATIONS ON THE MAP.
WHEN PEOPLE WHO DOWNLOADED SAID APP USE THEIR CAMERAS TO TAKE A **PICTURE** OF THAT DESIGNATED SCENERY, THEY RECEIVE **REWARDS** OR SOMETHING.
CORRECT.
AND THIS IS THE APP I LEARNED ABOUT FROM SATEN-SAN THIS MORNING, BUT...
IT'S NOT DISPLAYING AN IMAGE OF THE TREASURE. INSTEAD, IT'S SHOWING THE TIME OF AN *ACCIDENT* AT THAT SPECIFIC PLACE.

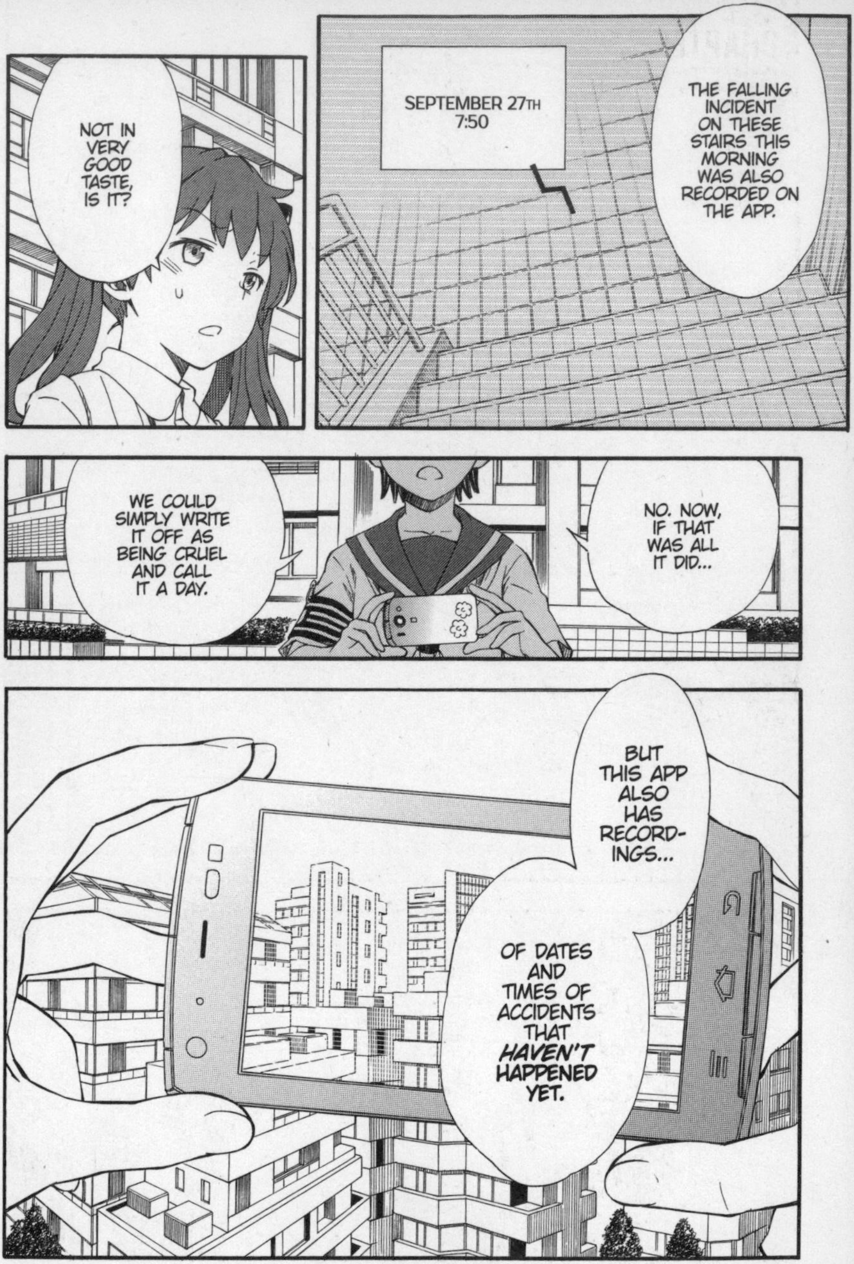
SEPTEMBER 27TH 7:50
THE FALLING INCIDENT ON THESE STAIRS THIS MORNING WAS ALSO RECORDED ON THE APP.
NOT IN VERY GOOD TASTE, IS IT?
NO. NOW, IF THAT WAS ALL IT DID...
WE COULD SIMPLY WRITE IT OFF AS BEING CRUEL AND CALL IT A DAY.
BUT THIS APP ALSO HAS RECORD-INGS...
OF DATES AND TIMES OF ACCIDENTS THAT *HAVEN'T* HAPPENED YET.

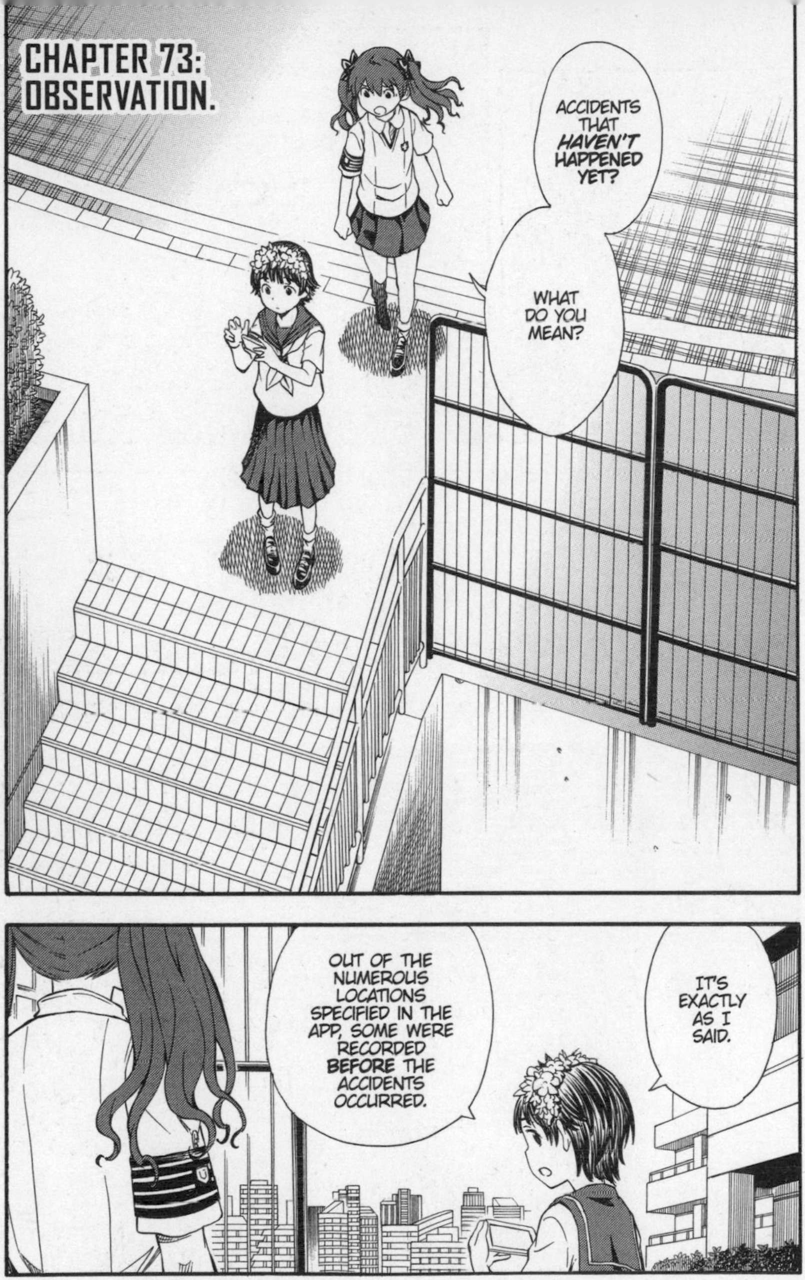
CHAPTER 73: OBSERVATION.
ACCIDENTS THAT *HAVEN'T* HAPPENED YET?
WHAT DO YOU MEAN?
IT'S EXACTLY AS I SAID.
OUT OF THE NUMEROUS LOCATIONS SPECIFIED IN THE APP, SOME WERE RECORDED **BEFORE** THE ACCIDENTS OCCURRED.

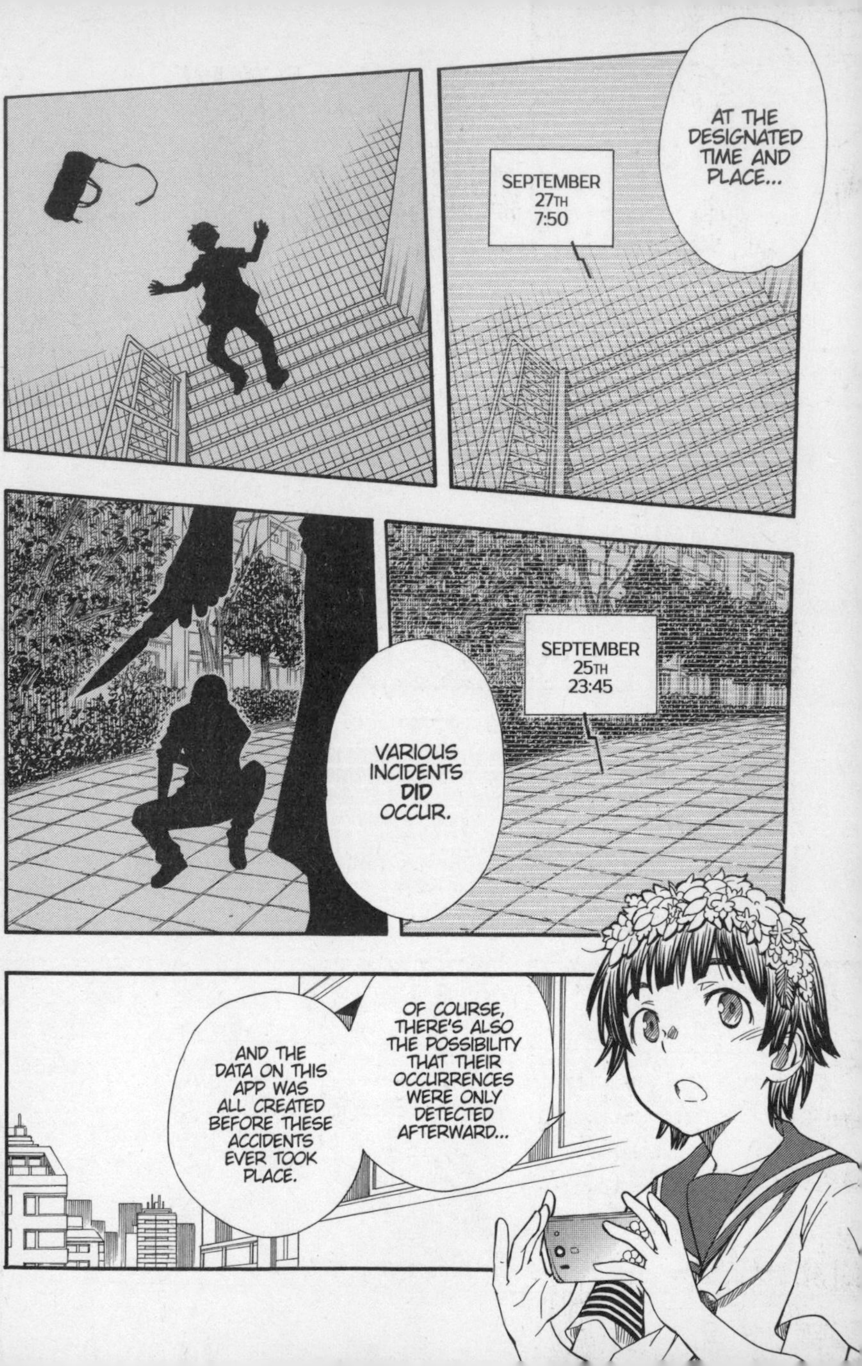
AT THE DESIGNATED TIME AND PLACE...
SEPTEMBER 27TH 7:50
SEPTEMBER 25TH 23:45
VARIOUS INCIDENTS DID OCCUR.
OF COURSE, THERE'S ALSO THE POSSIBILITY THAT THEIR OCCURRENCES WERE ONLY DETECTED AFTERWARD...
AND THE DATA ON THIS APP WAS ALL CREATED BEFORE THESE ACCIDENTS EVER TOOK PLACE.

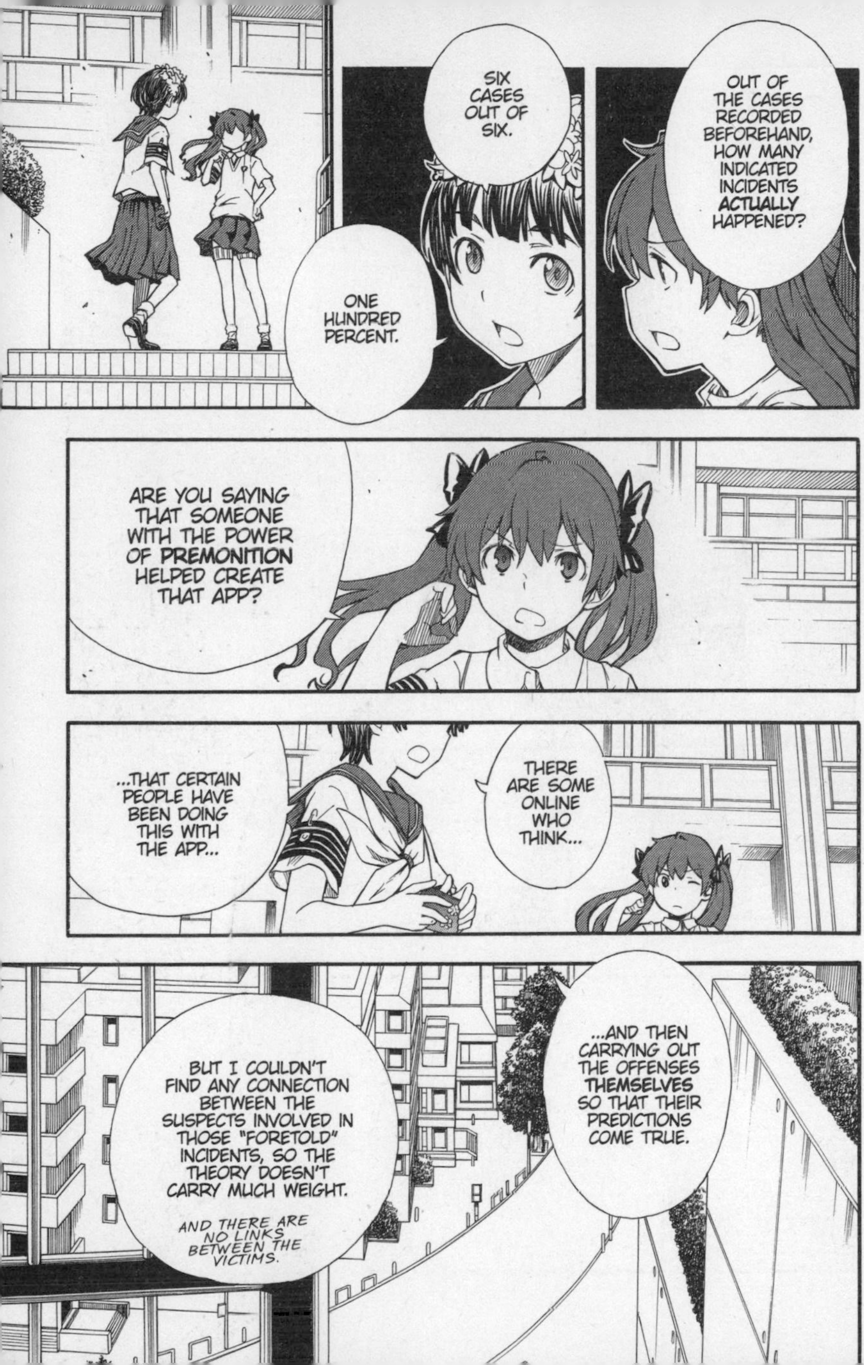
OUT OF THE CASES RECORDED BEFOREHAND, HOW MANY INDICATED INCIDENTS **ACTUALLY** HAPPENED?
SIX CASES OUT OF SIX.
ONE HUNDRED PERCENT.
ARE YOU SAYING THAT SOMEONE WITH THE POWER OF **PREMONITION** HELPED CREATE THAT APP?
THERE ARE SOME ONLINE WHO THINK...
...THAT CERTAIN PEOPLE HAVE BEEN DOING THIS WITH THE APP...
...AND THEN CARRYING OUT THE OFFENSES **THEMSELVES** SO THAT THEIR PREDICTIONS COME TRUE.
BUT I COULDN'T FIND ANY CONNECTION BETWEEN THE SUSPECTS INVOLVED IN THOSE "FORETOLD" INCIDENTS, SO THE THEORY DOESN'T CARRY MUCH WEIGHT.
AND THERE ARE NO LINKS BETWEEN THE VICTIMS.

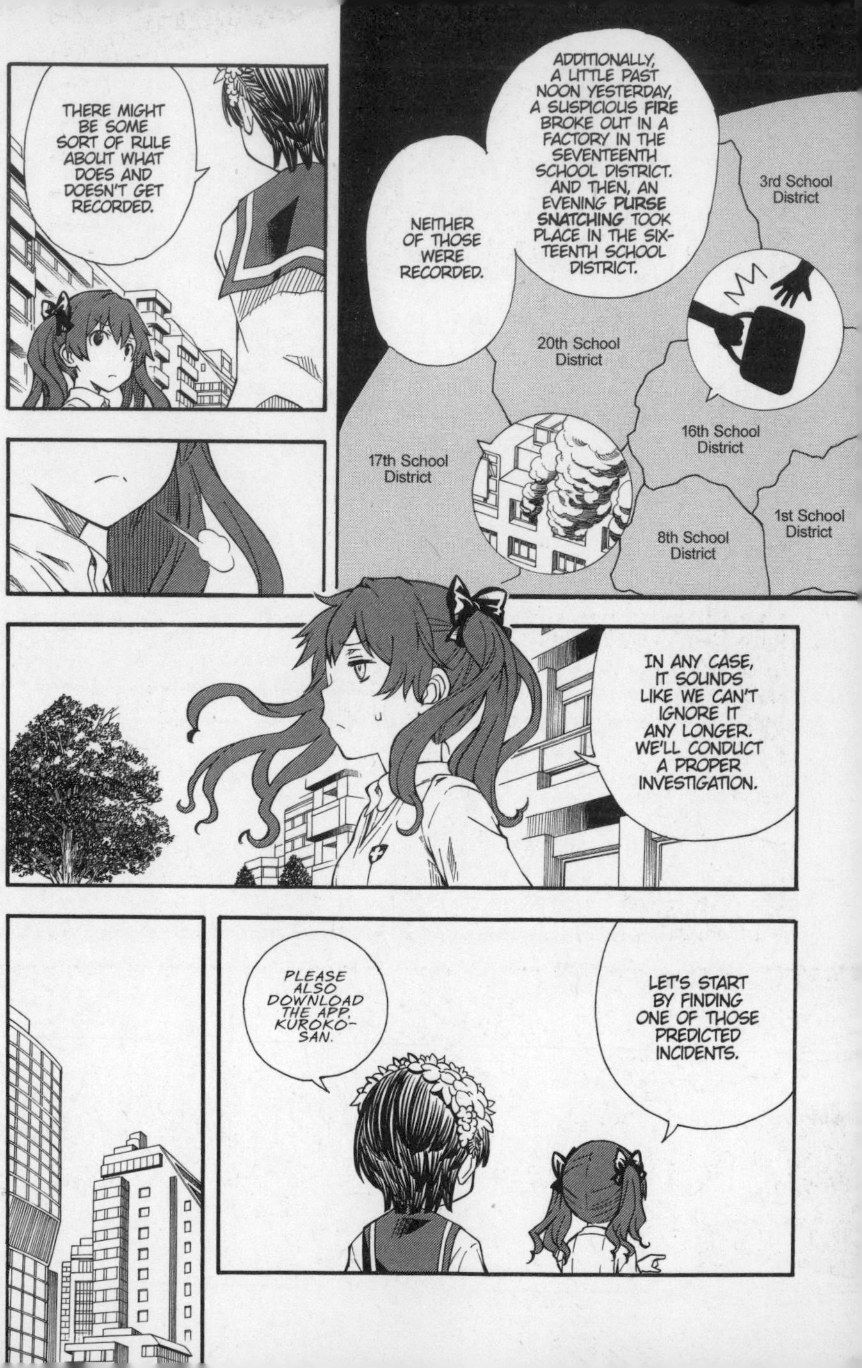
ADDITIONALLY, A LITTLE PAST NOON YESTERDAY, A SUSPICIOUS FIRE BROKE OUT IN A FACTORY IN THE SEVENTEENTH SCHOOL DISTRICT. AND THEN, AN EVENING PURSE SNATCHING TOOK PLACE IN THE SIXTEENTH SCHOOL DISTRICT.
NEITHER OF THOSE WERE RECORDED.
3rd School District
20th School District
16th School District
17th School District
1st School District
8th School District
THERE MIGHT BE SOME SORT OF RULE ABOUT WHAT DOES AND DOESN'T GET RECORDED.
IN ANY CASE, IT SOUNDS LIKE WE CAN'T IGNORE IT ANY LONGER. WE'LL CONDUCT A PROPER INVESTIGATION.
LET'S START BY FINDING ONE OF THOSE PREDICTED INCIDENTS.
PLEASE ALSO DOWNLOAD THE APP, KUROKO-SAN.

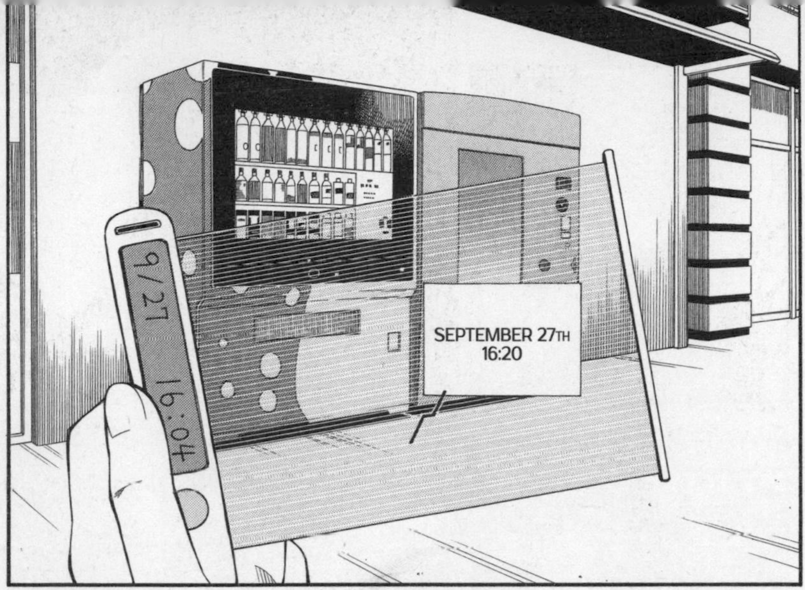
SEPTEMBER 27TH 16:20
9/27 16:04

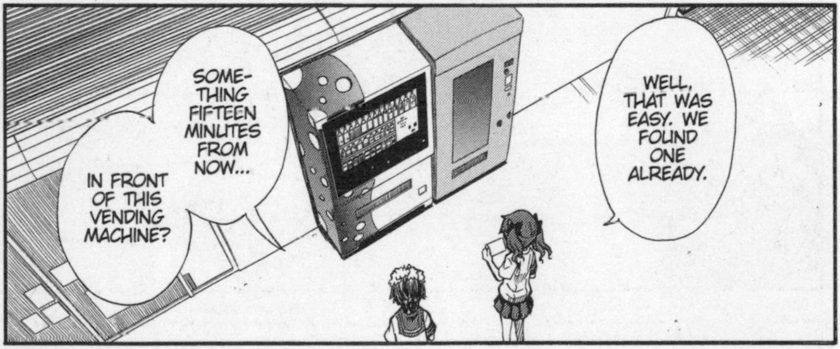
WELL, THAT WAS EASY. WE FOUND ONE ALREADY.
SOME-THING FIFTEEN MINUTES FROM NOW...
IN FRONT OF THIS VENDING MACHINE?

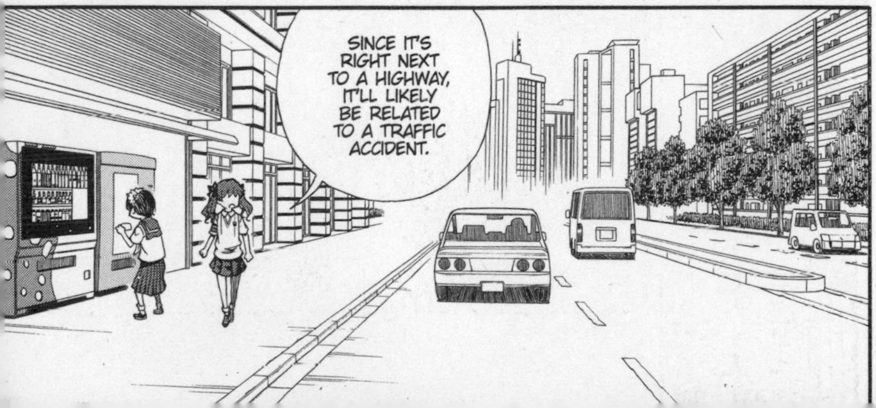
SINCE IT'S RIGHT NEXT TO A HIGHWAY, IT'LL LIKELY BE RELATED TO A TRAFFIC ACCIDENT.

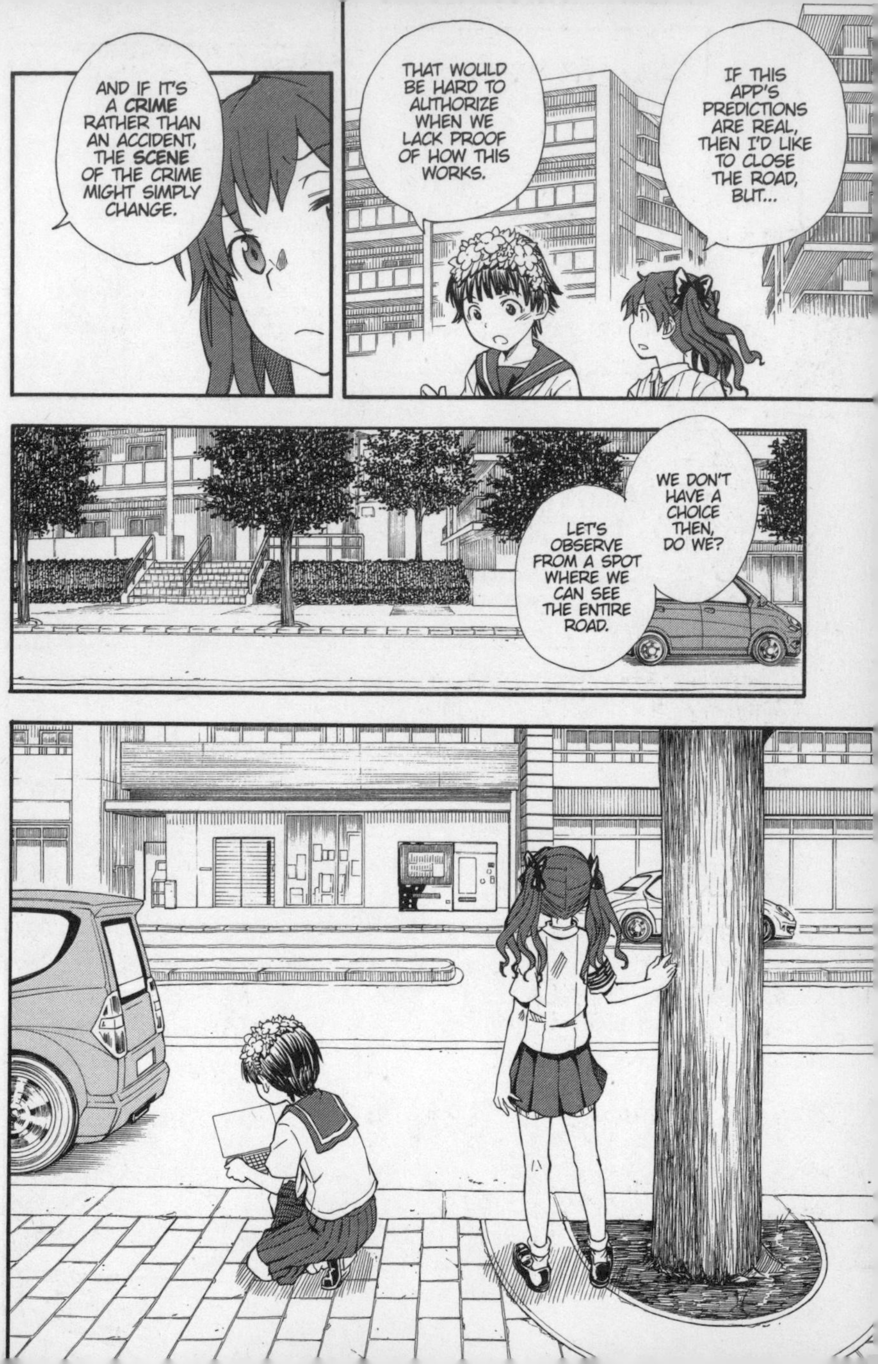
IF THIS APP'S PREDICTIONS ARE REAL, THEN I'D LIKE TO CLOSE THE ROAD, BUT...
THAT WOULD BE HARD TO AUTHORIZE WHEN WE LACK PROOF OF HOW THIS WORKS.
AND IF IT'S A CRIME RATHER THAN AN ACCIDENT, THE SCENE OF THE CRIME MIGHT SIMPLY CHANGE.
WE DON'T HAVE A CHOICE THEN, DO WE?
LET'S OBSERVE FROM A SPOT WHERE WE CAN SEE THE ENTIRE ROAD.

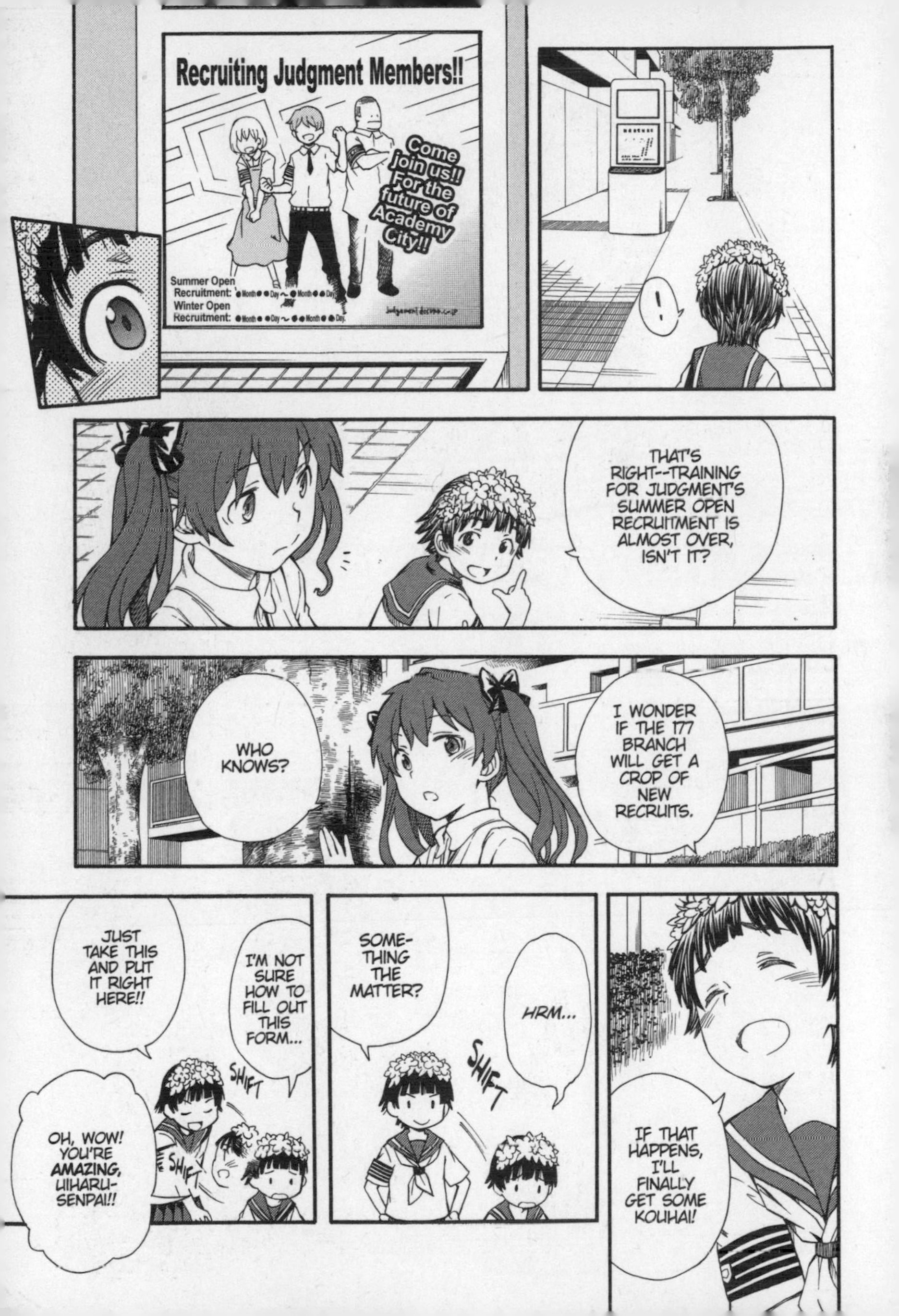
!
Recruiting Judgment Members!!
Come join us!! For the future of Academy City!!
Summer Open Recruitment: ●Month●●Day～●●Month●●Day.
Winter Open Recruitment: ●Month●●Day～●●Month●●Day.
THAT'S RIGHT--TRAINING FOR JUDGMENT'S SUMMER OPEN RECRUITMENT IS ALMOST OVER, ISN'T IT?
I WONDER IF THE 177 BRANCH WILL GET A CROP OF NEW RECRUITS.
WHO KNOWS?
IF THAT HAPPENS, I'LL FINALLY GET SOME KOUHAI!
HRM...
SOME-THING THE MATTER?
SHIFT
I'M NOT SURE HOW TO FILL OUT THIS FORM...
JUST TAKE THIS AND PUT IT RIGHT HERE!!
SHIFT
SHIFT
OH, WOW! YOU'RE AMAZING, UIHARU-SENPAI!!

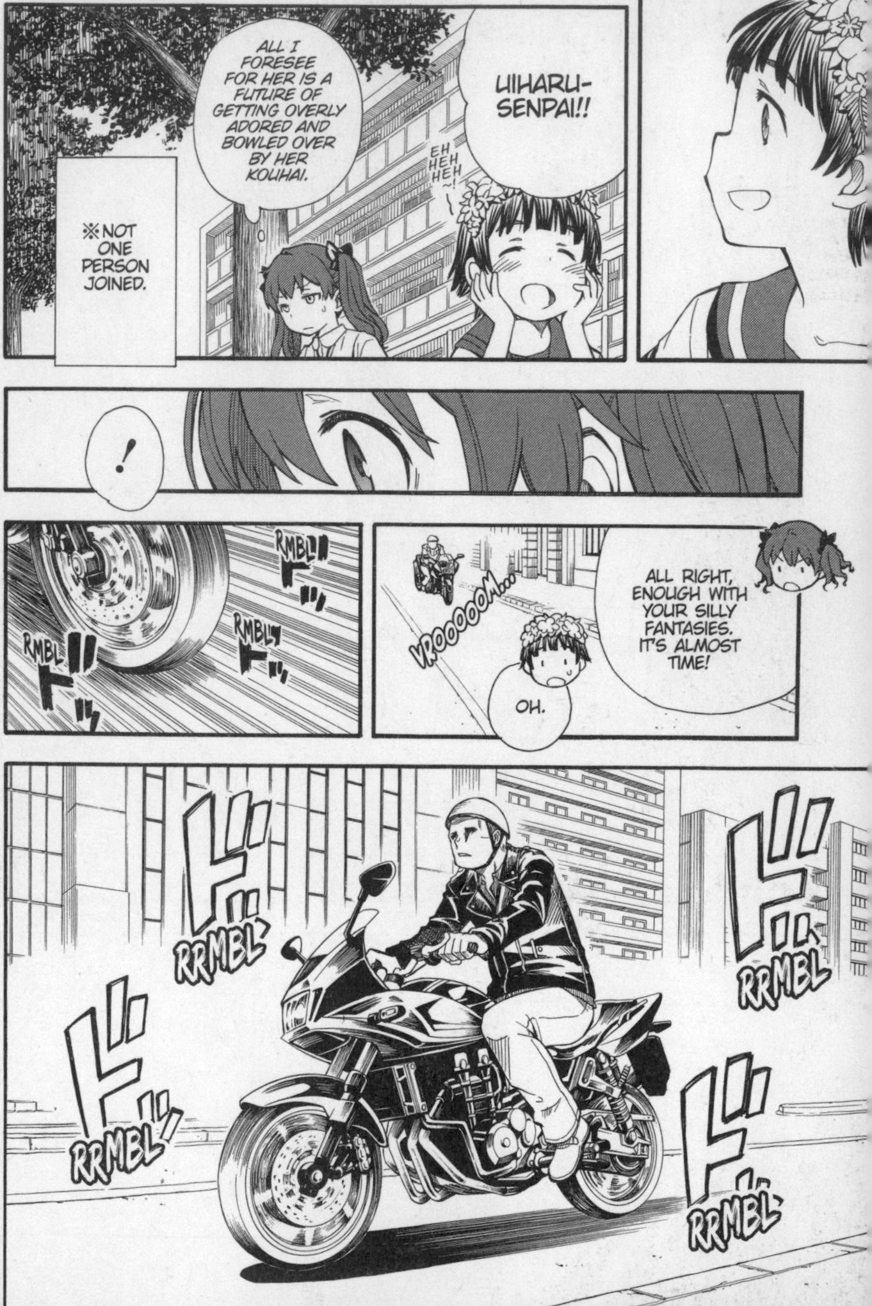
UIHARU-SENPAI!!
EH HEH HEH ~!
ALL I FORESEE FOR HER IS A FUTURE OF GETTING OVERLY ADORED AND BOWLED OVER BY HER KOUHAI.
※NOT ONE PERSON JOINED.
!
ALL RIGHT, ENOUGH WITH YOUR SILLY FANTASIES. IT'S ALMOST TIME!
VROOOOOM...
OH.
RMBL
RMBL
RMBL
RRMBL
RRMBL
RRMBL
RRMBL

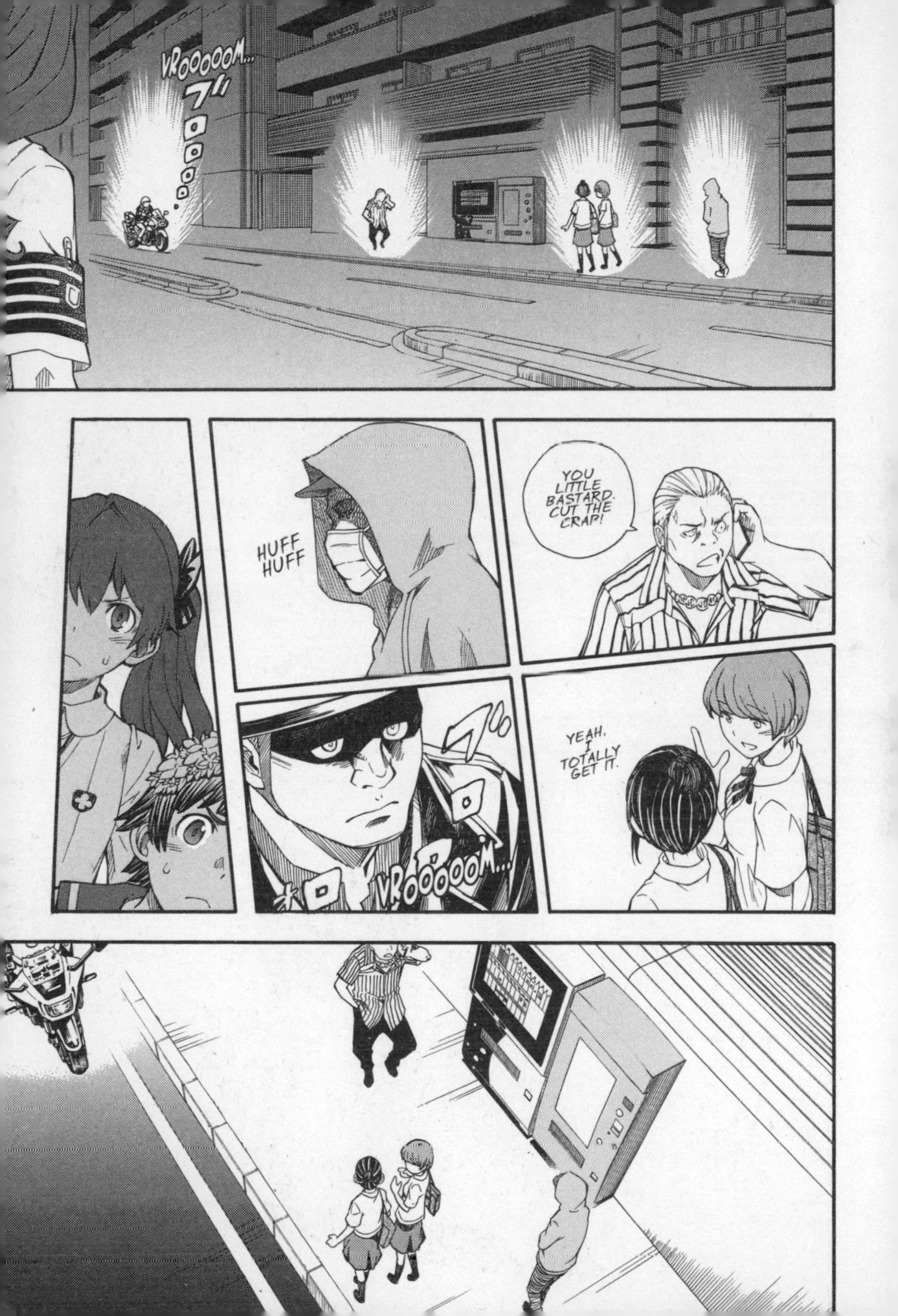
VROOOOOM...
YOU LITTLE BASTARD. CUT THE CRAP!
HUFF HUFF
YEAH, I TOTALLY GET IT.
VROOOOOM...

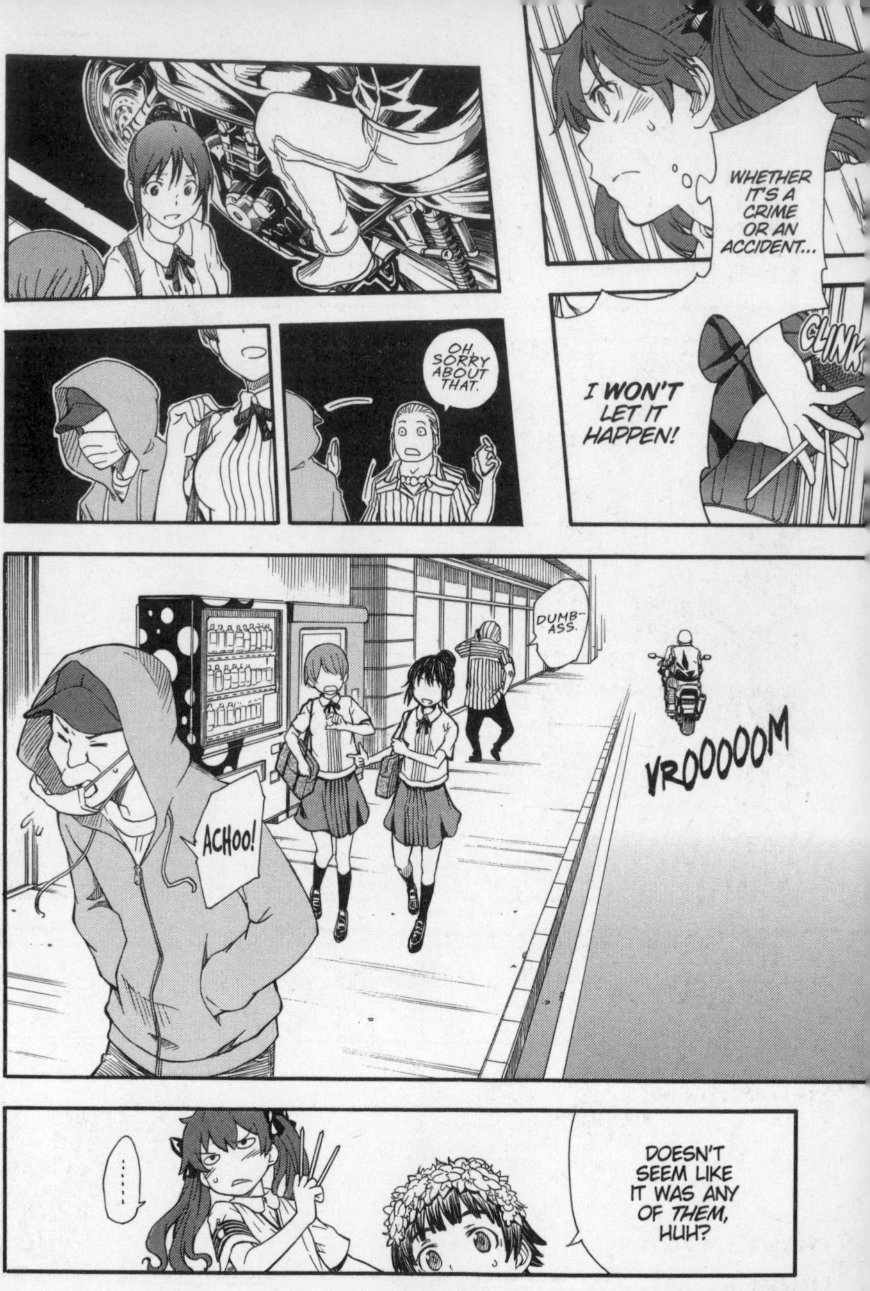
WHETHER IT'S A CRIME OR AN ACCIDENT...
CLINK
I WON'T LET IT HAPPEN!
OH, SORRY ABOUT THAT.
DUMB-ASS.
VROOOOOM
ACHOO!
DOESN'T SEEM LIKE IT WAS ANY OF THEM, HUH?
......

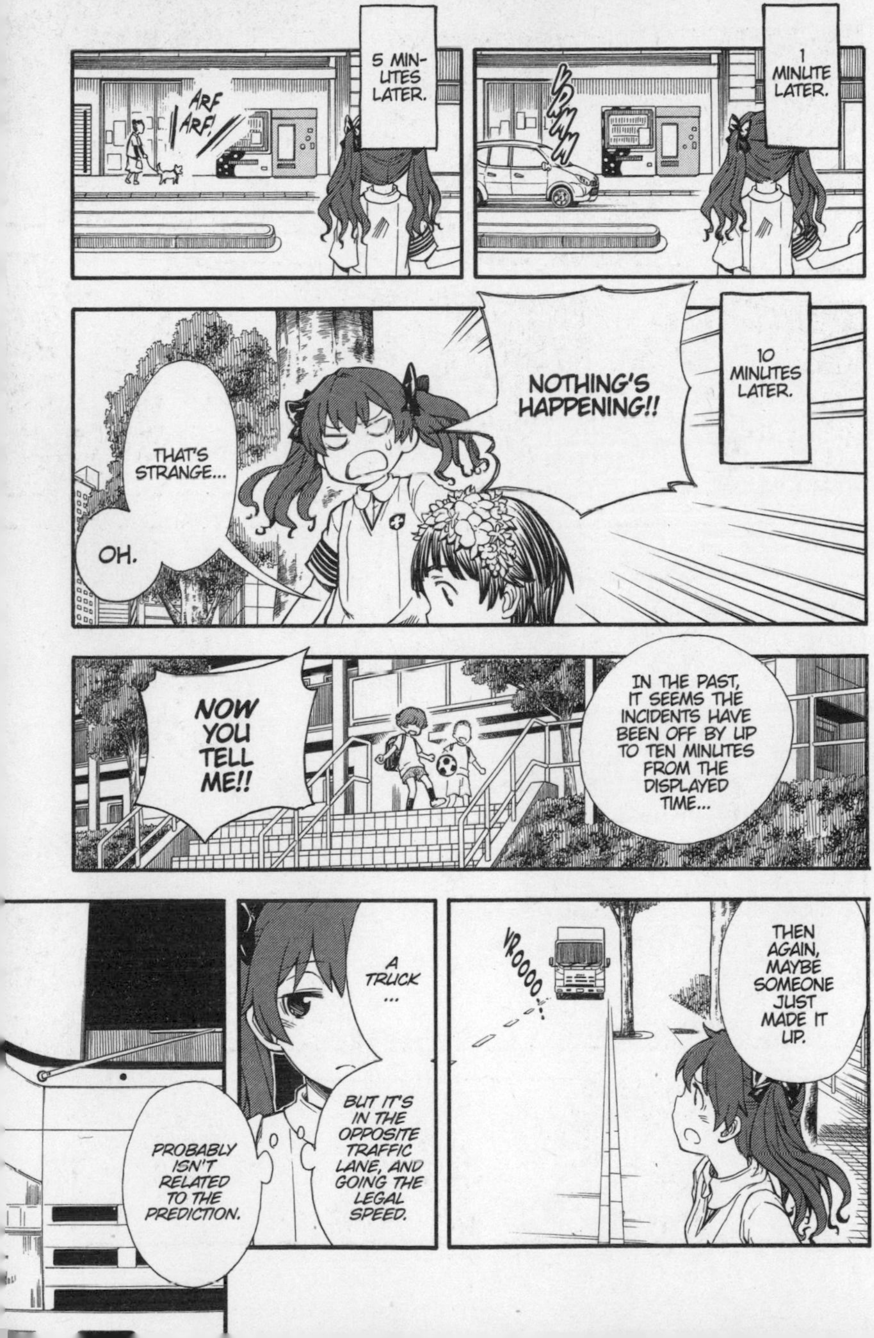
1 MINUTE LATER.
VRMM
5 MIN-UTES LATER.
ARF ARF!
10 MINUTES LATER.
NOTHING'S HAPPENING!!
THAT'S STRANGE...
OH.
IN THE PAST, IT SEEMS THE INCIDENTS HAVE BEEN OFF BY UP TO TEN MINUTES FROM THE DISPLAYED TIME...
NOW YOU TELL ME!!
VROOOO...
THEN AGAIN, MAYBE SOMEONE JUST MADE IT UP.
A TRUCK ...
BUT IT'S IN THE OPPOSITE TRAFFIC LANE, AND GOING THE LEGAL SPEED.
PROBABLY ISN'T RELATED TO THE PREDICTION.

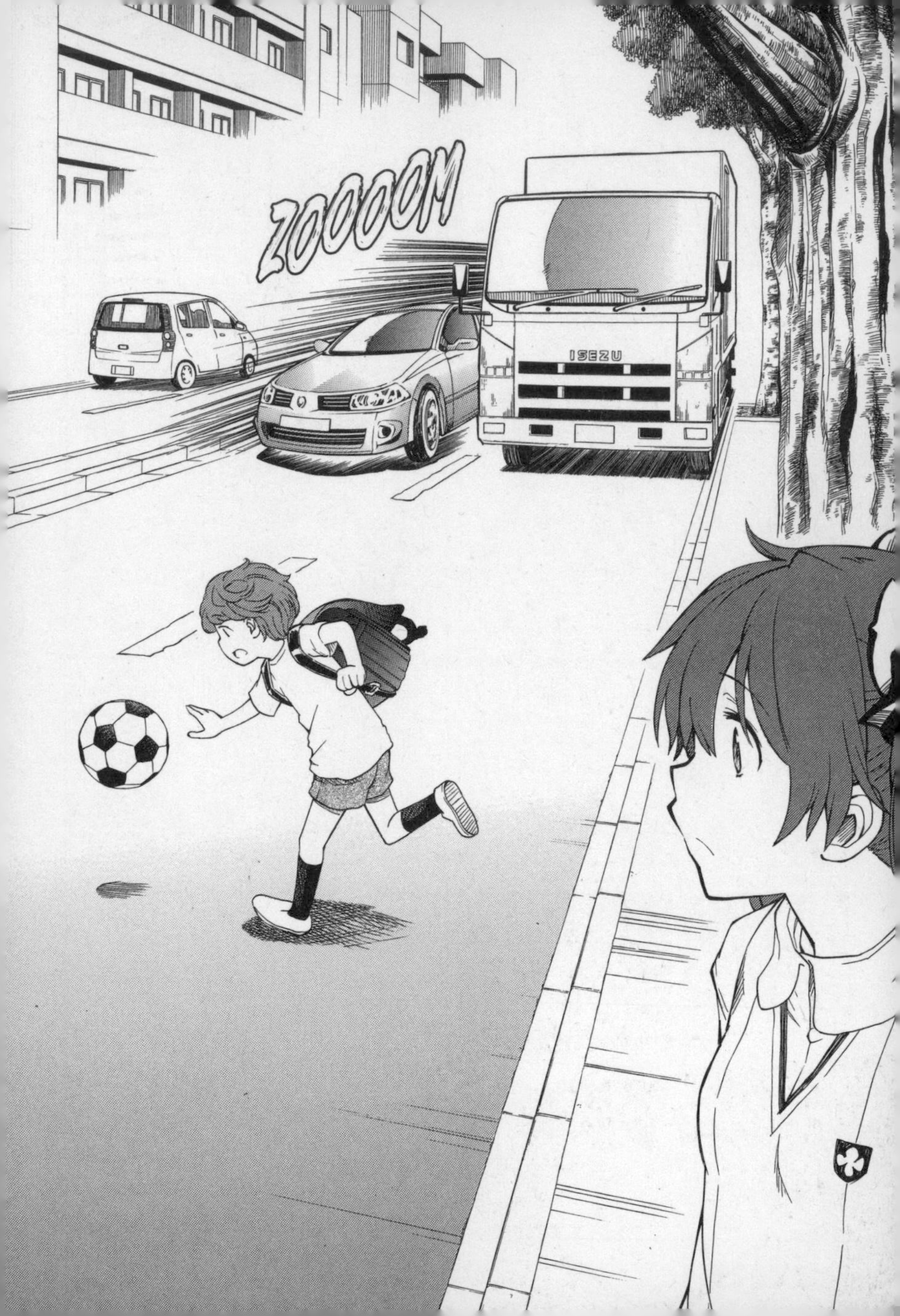
ZOOOOM
ISEZU

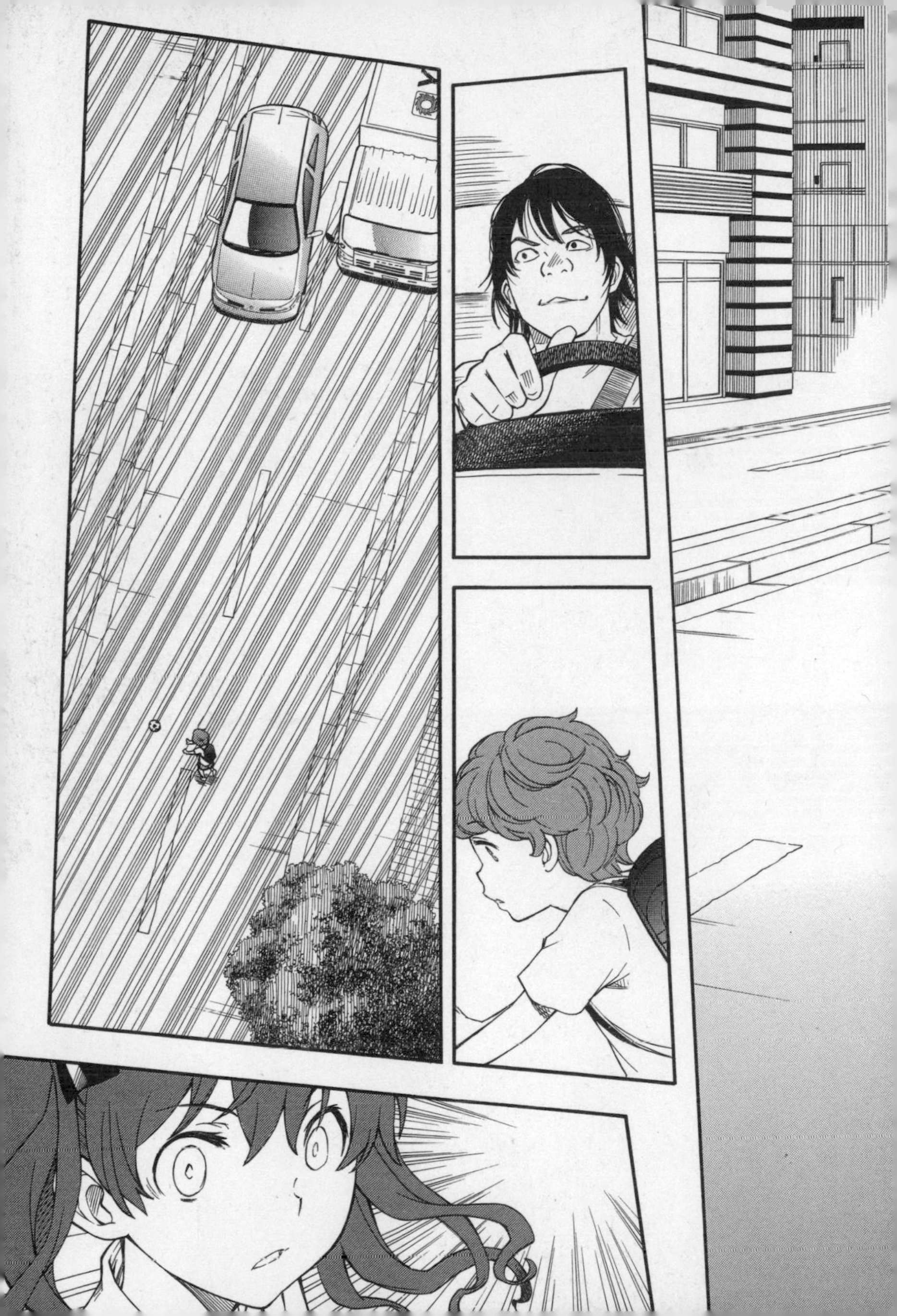

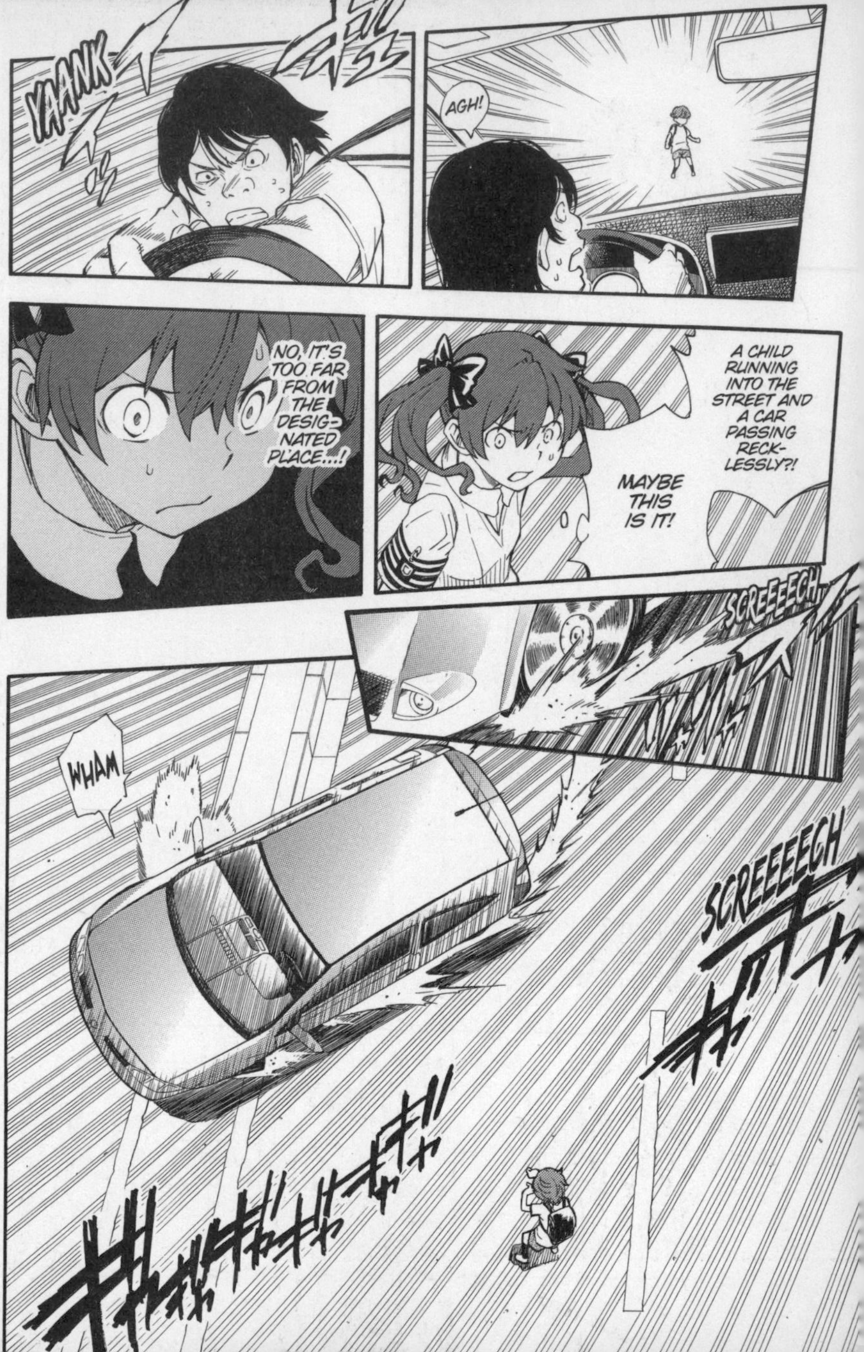
AGH!
YAANK
A CHILD RUNNING INTO THE STREET AND A CAR PASSING RECK-LESSLY?!
MAYBE THIS IS IT!
NO, IT'S TOO FAR FROM THE DESIG-NATED PLACE...!
SCREEEECH
WHAM
SCREEEECH

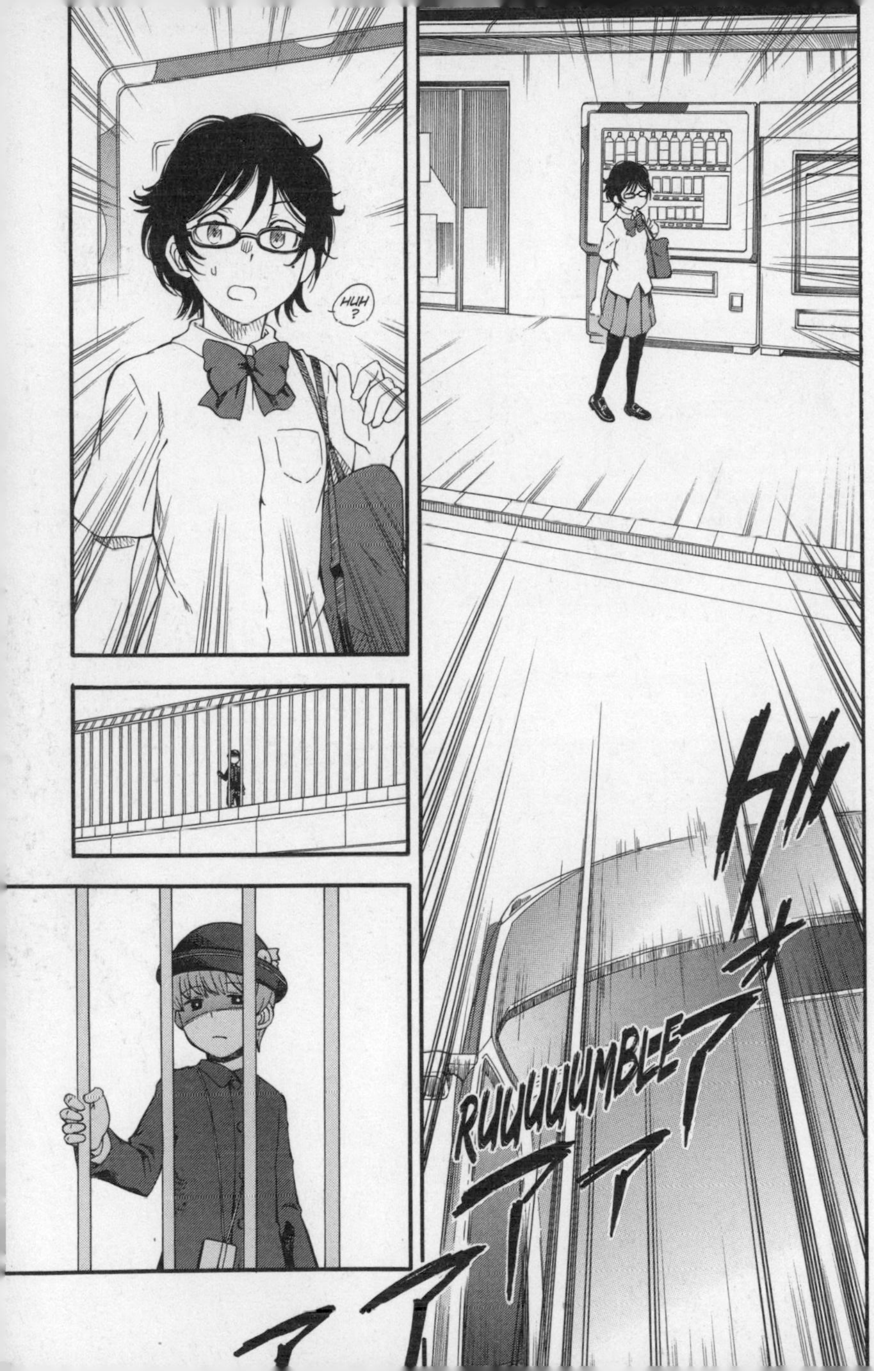
RUUUUUMBLE
HUH ?

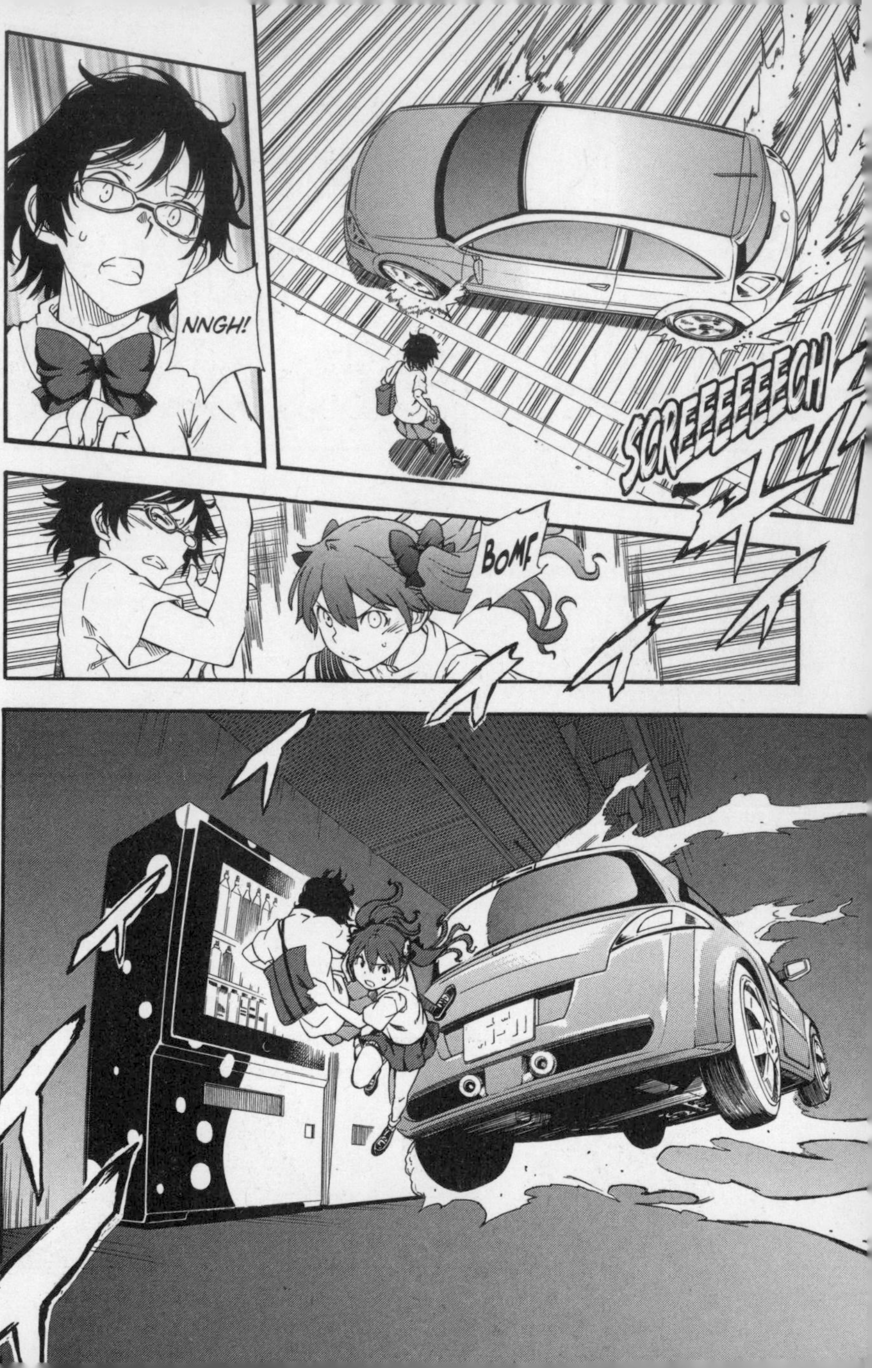
SCREEEEEECH
NNGH!
BOMF

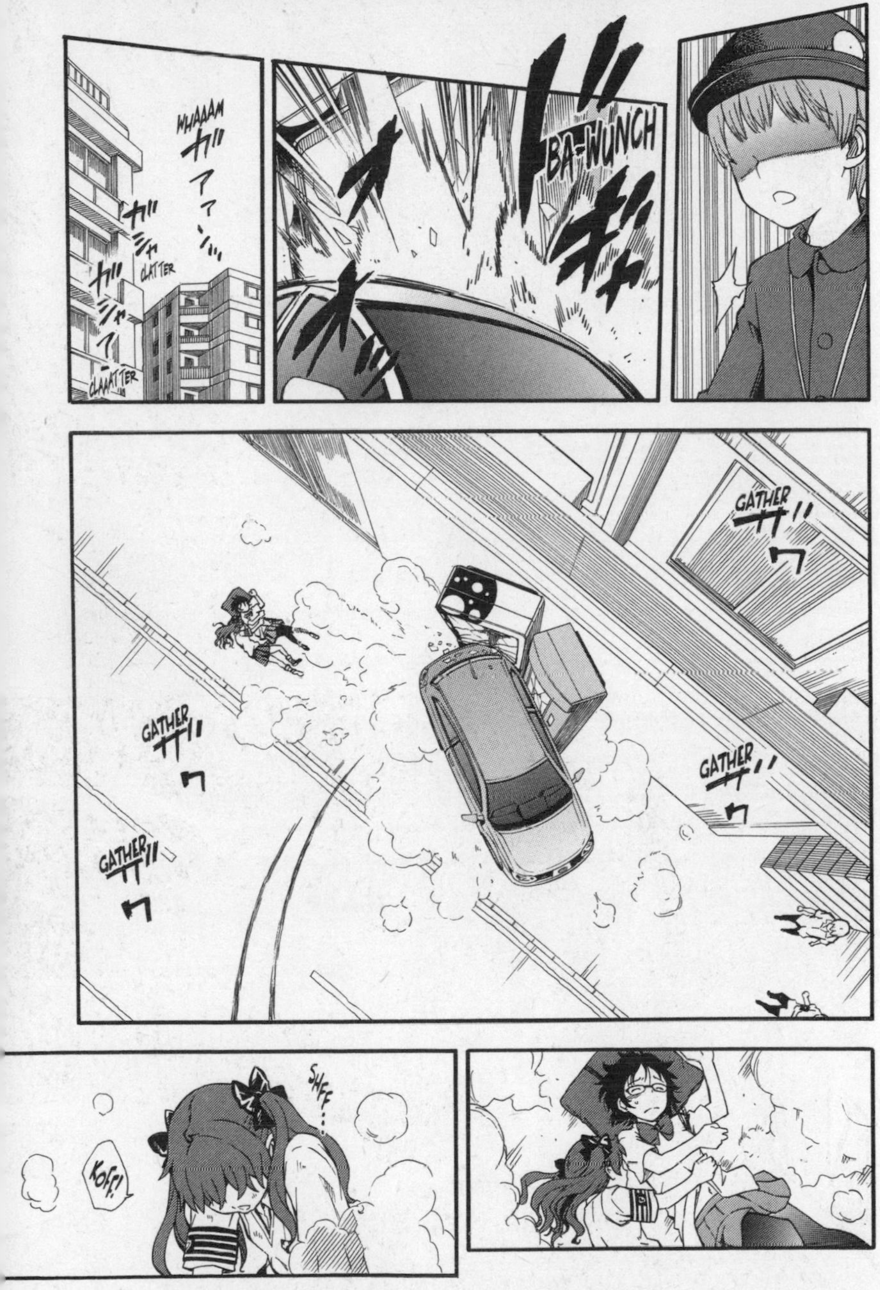

BA-WUNCH
WHAAAM
CLATTER
CLAAATTER
GATHER
GATHER
GATHER
GATHER
SHFF...
KOFF!

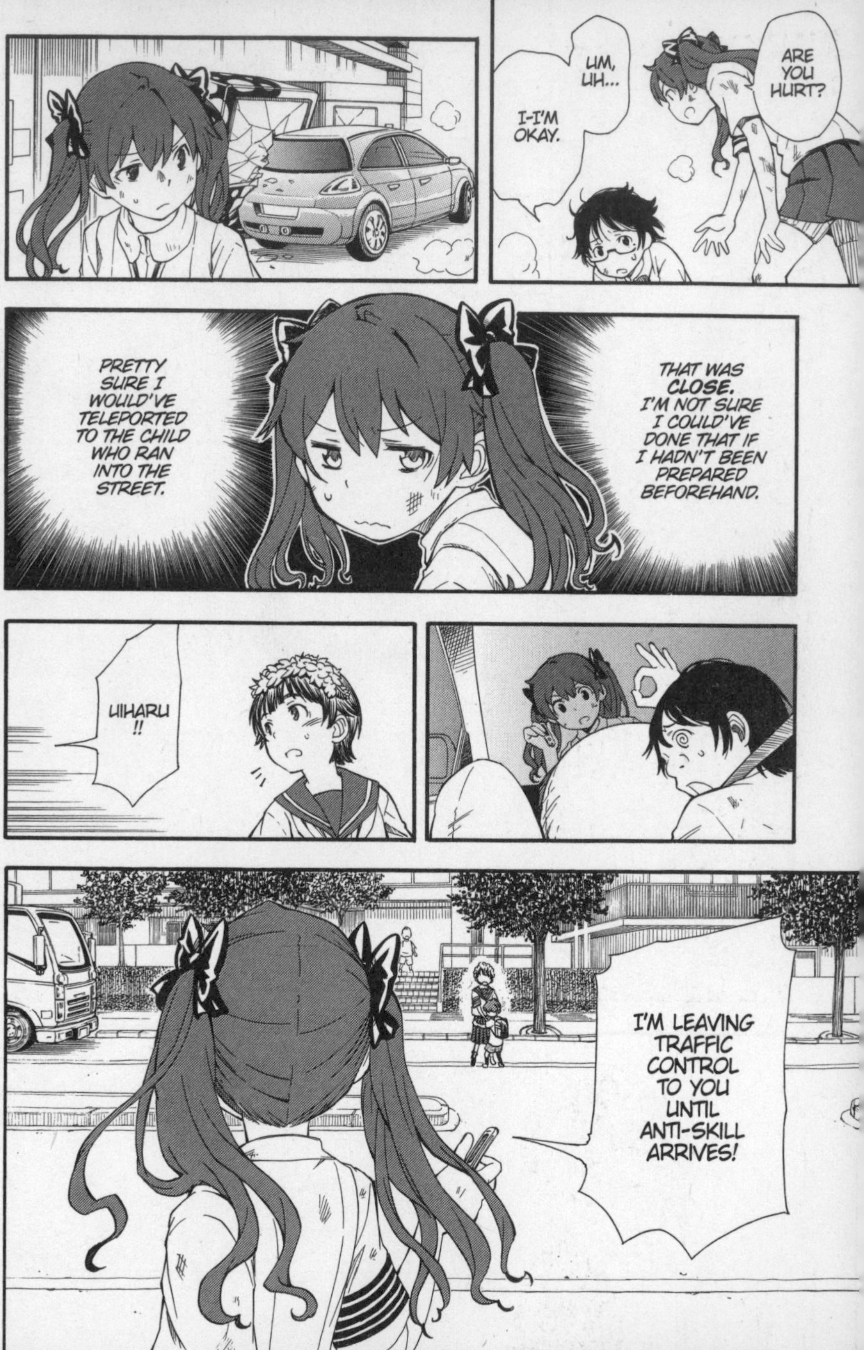
ARE YOU HURT?
UM, UH...
I-I'M OKAY.
THAT WAS CLOSE. I'M NOT SURE I COULD'VE DONE THAT IF I HADN'T BEEN PREPARED BEFOREHAND.
PRETTY SURE I WOULD'VE TELEPORTED TO THE CHILD WHO RAN INTO THE STREET.
UIHARU !!
I'M LEAVING TRAFFIC CONTROL TO YOU UNTIL ANTI-SKILL ARRIVES!

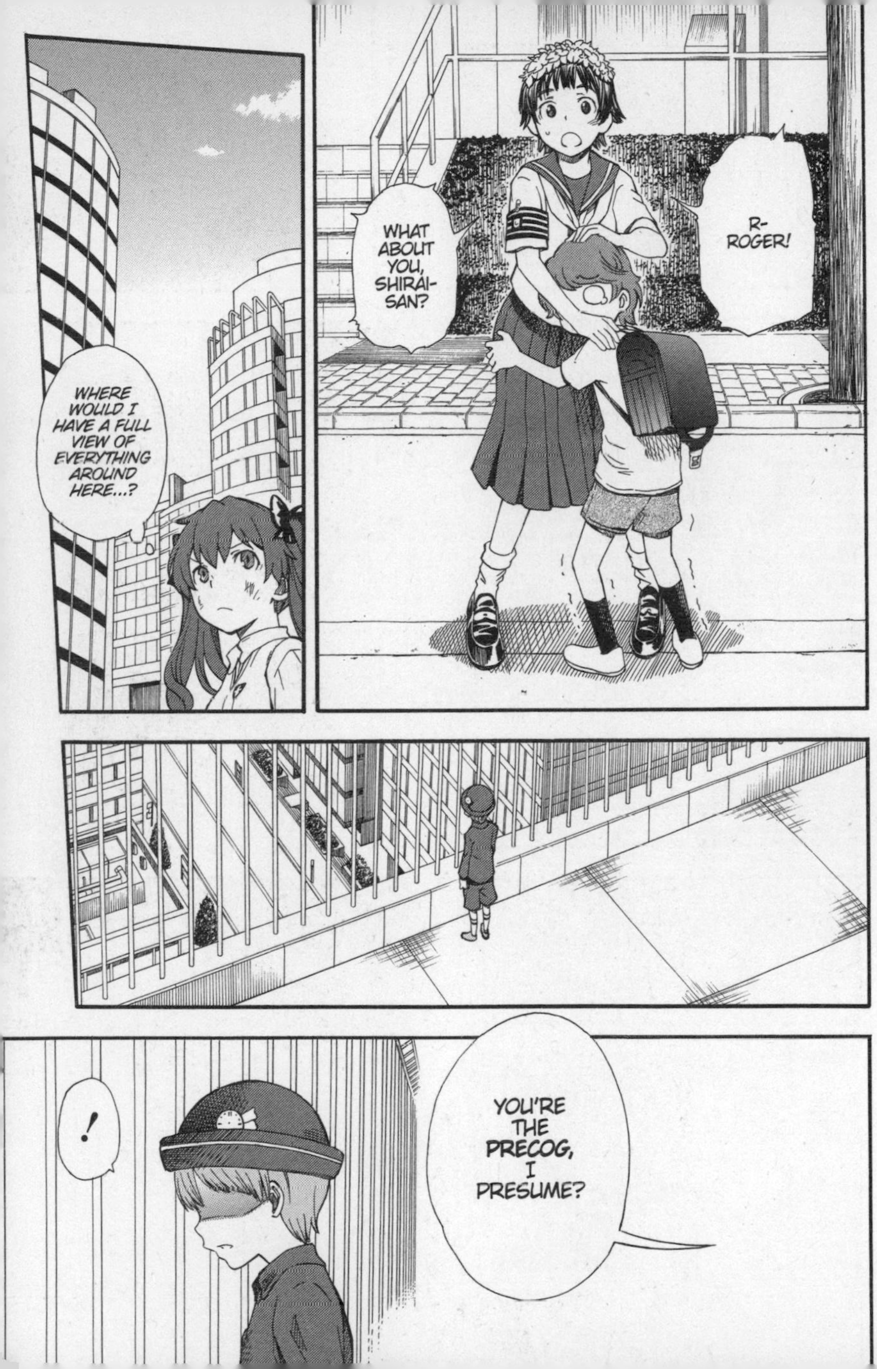
R-ROGER!
WHAT ABOUT YOU, SHIRAI-SAN?
WHERE WOULD I HAVE A FULL VIEW OF EVERYTHING AROUND HERE...?
YOU'RE THE PRECOG, I PRESUME?
!

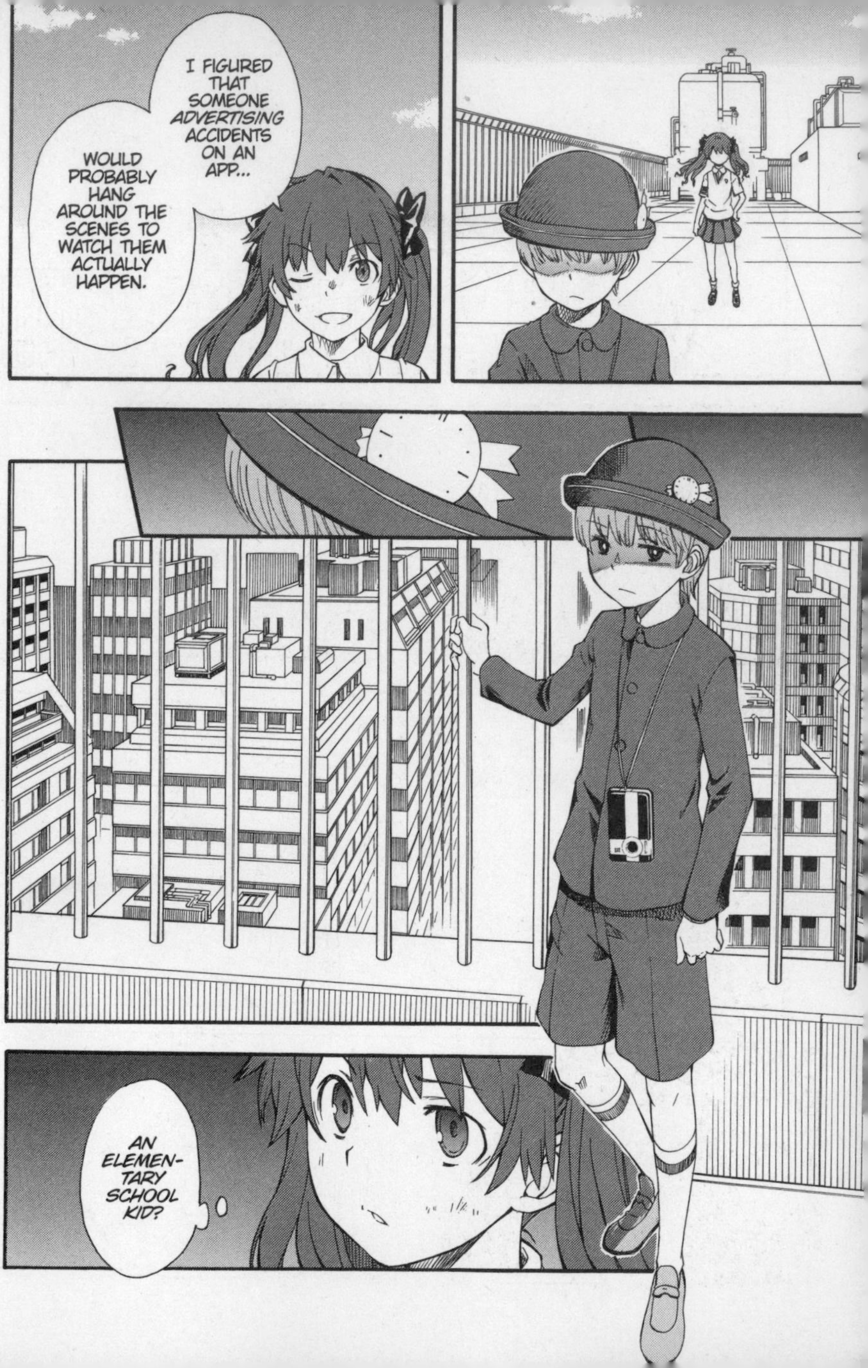
I FIGURED THAT SOMEONE *ADVERTISING* ACCIDENTS ON AN APP...
WOULD PROBABLY HANG AROUND THE SCENES TO WATCH THEM ACTUALLY HAPPEN.
AN ELEMEN-TARY SCHOOL KID?

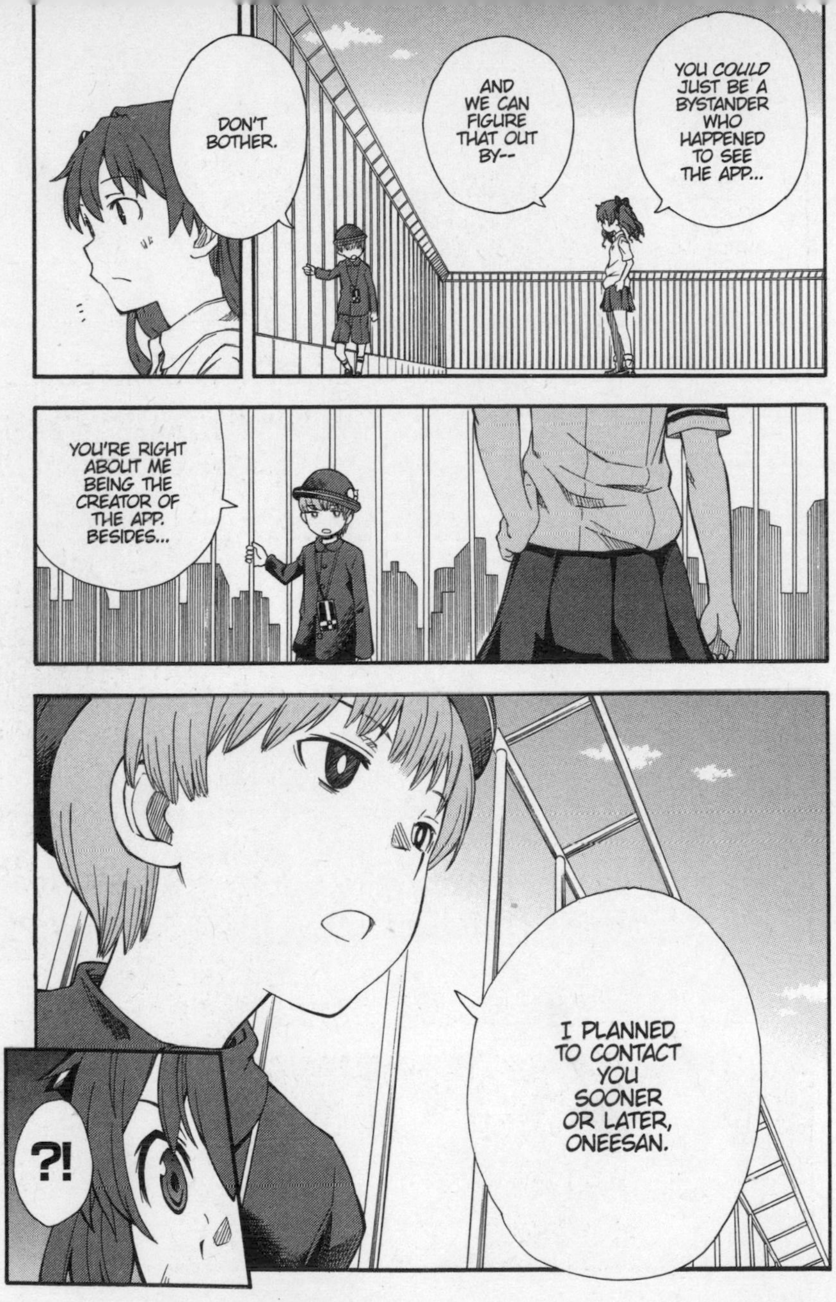
YOU COULD JUST BE A BYSTANDER WHO HAPPENED TO SEE THE APP...
AND WE CAN FIGURE THAT OUT BY--
DON'T BOTHER.
YOU'RE RIGHT ABOUT ME BEING THE CREATOR OF THE APP. BESIDES...
I PLANNED TO CONTACT YOU SOONER OR LATER, ONEESAN.
?!

A Certain SCIENTIFIC Railgun

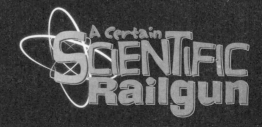

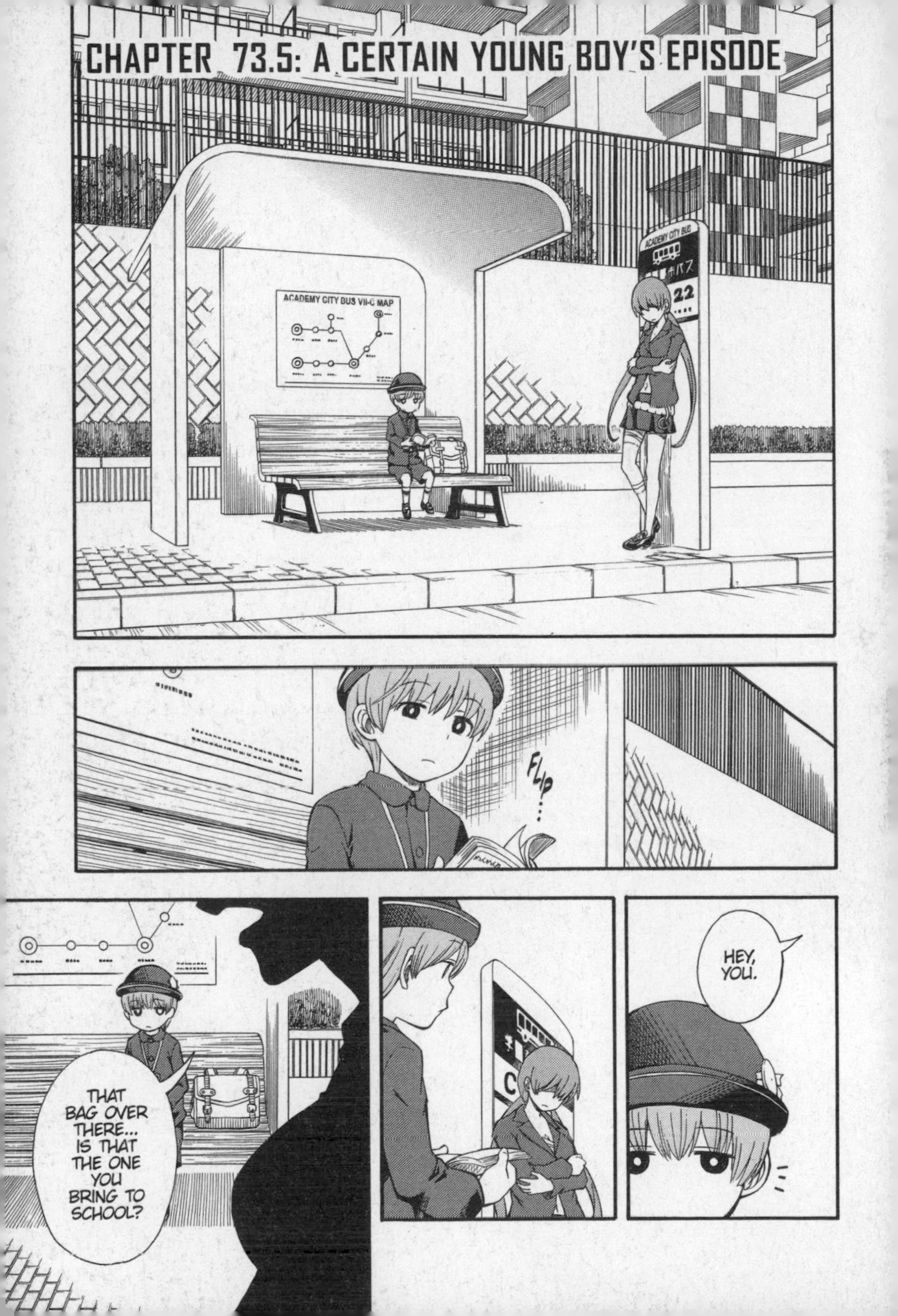
CHAPTER 73.5: A CERTAIN YOUNG BOY'S EPISODE
ACADEMY CITY BUS VII-C MAP
ACADEMY CITY BUS
22
FLIP...
HEY, YOU.
THAT BAG OVER THERE... IS THAT THE ONE YOU BRING TO SCHOOL?

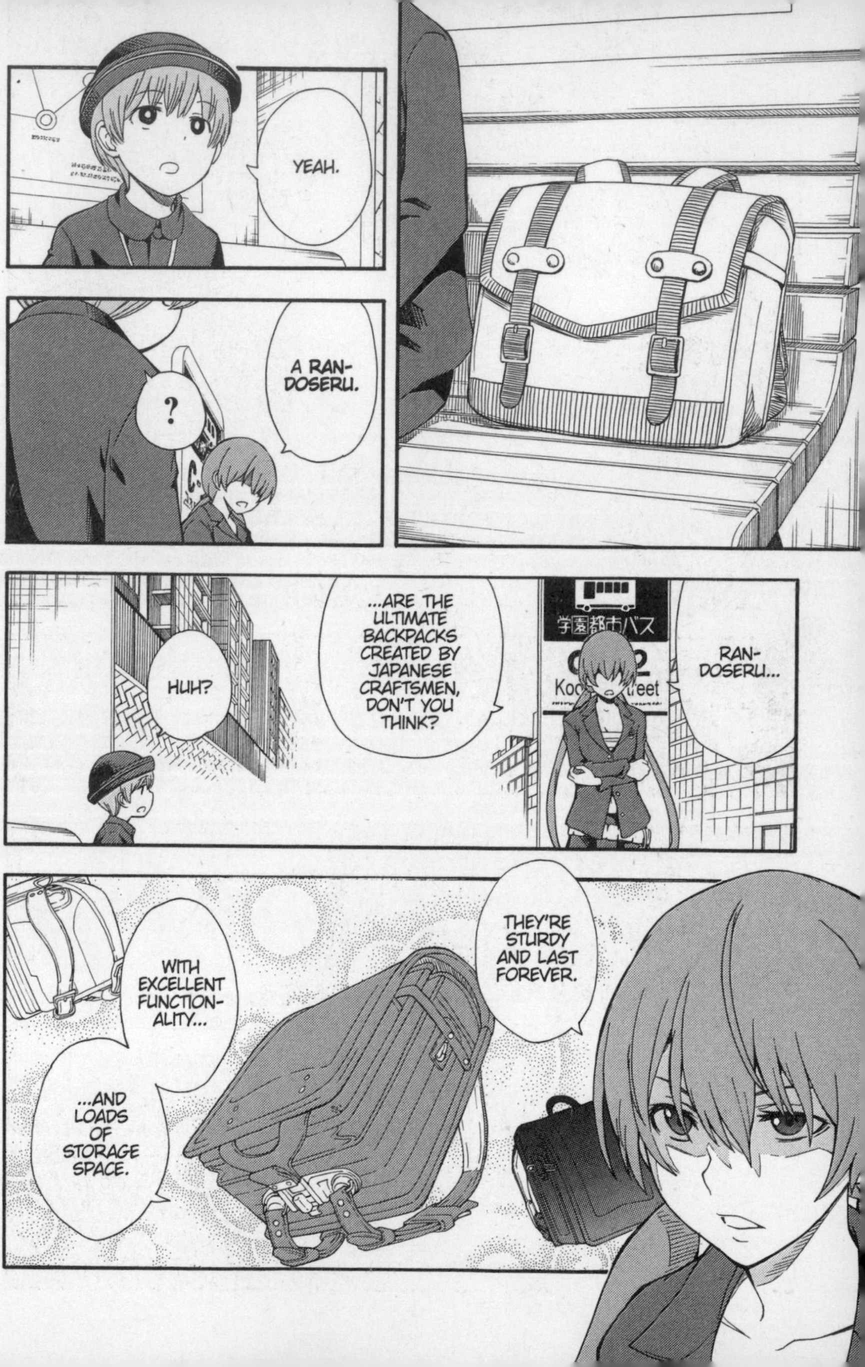
YEAH.
A RAN-DOSERU.
?
RAN-DOSERU...
学園都市バス
...ARE THE ULTIMATE BACKPACKS CREATED BY JAPANESE CRAFTSMEN, DON'T YOU THINK?
HUH?
THEY'RE STURDY AND LAST FOREVER.
WITH EXCELLENT FUNCTION-ALITY...
...AND LOADS OF STORAGE SPACE.

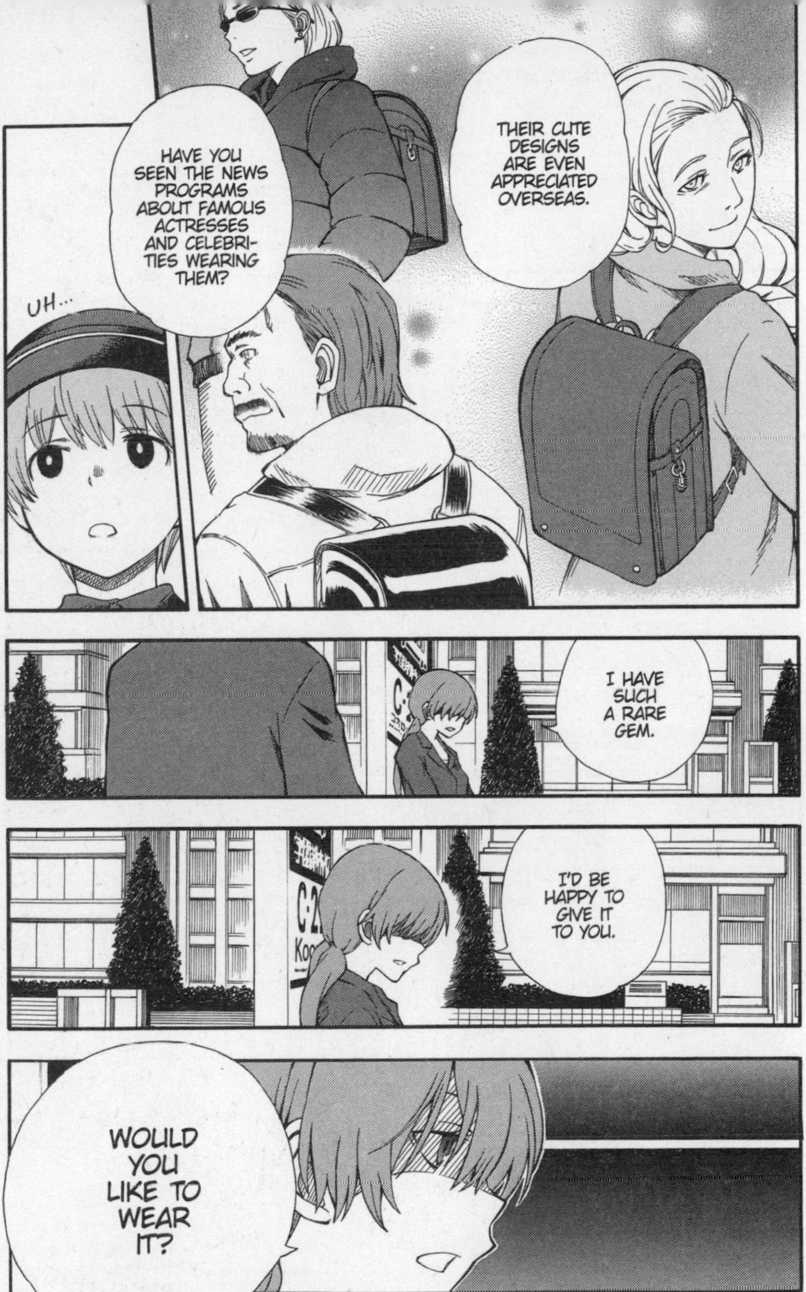
THEIR CUTE DESIGNS ARE EVEN APPRECIATED OVERSEAS.
HAVE YOU SEEN THE NEWS PROGRAMS ABOUT FAMOUS ACTRESSES AND CELEBRI-TIES WEARING THEM?
UH...
I HAVE SUCH A RARE GEM.
I'D BE HAPPY TO GIVE IT TO YOU.
WOULD YOU LIKE TO WEAR IT?

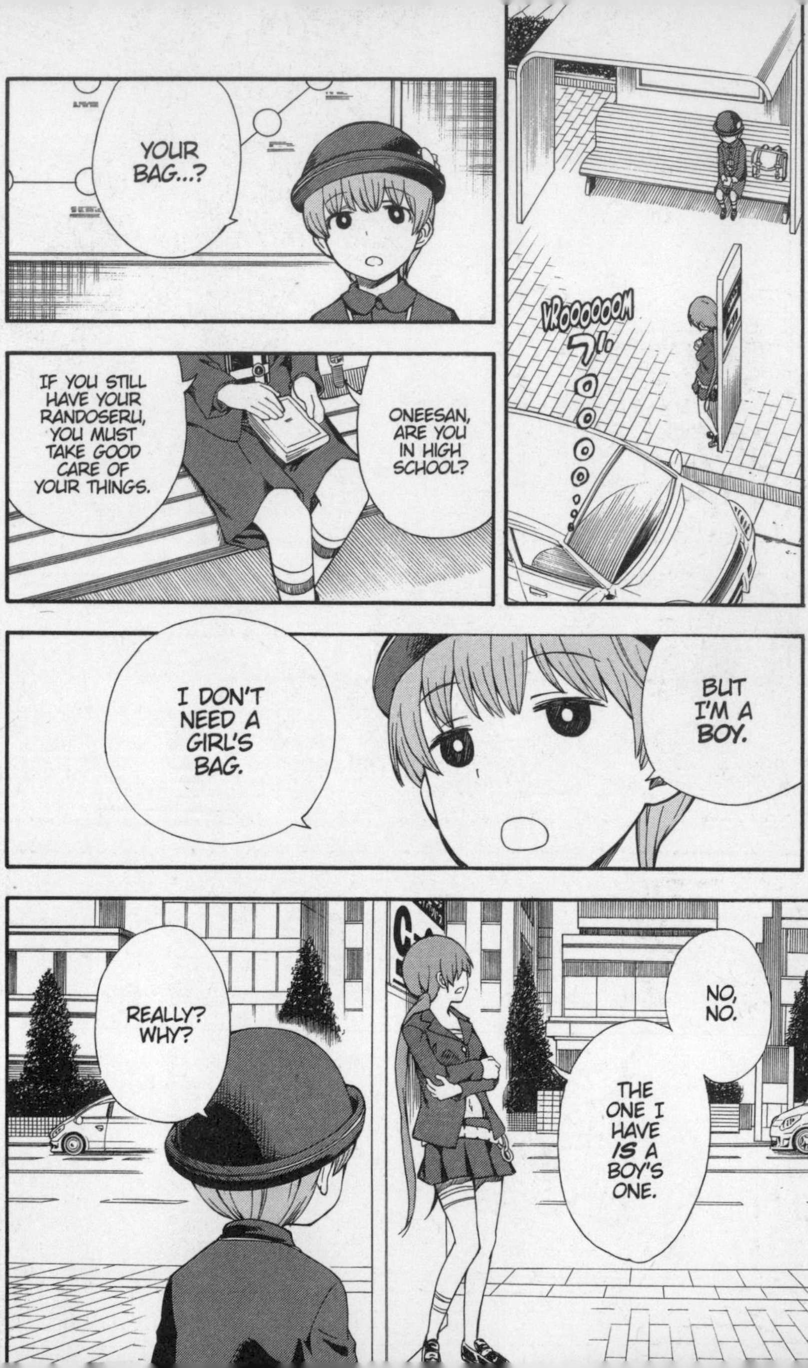
VROOOOOOM
YOUR BAG...?
ONEESAN, ARE YOU IN HIGH SCHOOL?
IF YOU STILL HAVE YOUR RANDOSERU, YOU MUST TAKE GOOD CARE OF YOUR THINGS.
BUT I'M A BOY.
I DON'T NEED A GIRL'S BAG.
NO, NO.
THE ONE I HAVE *IS* A BOY'S ONE.
REALLY? WHY?

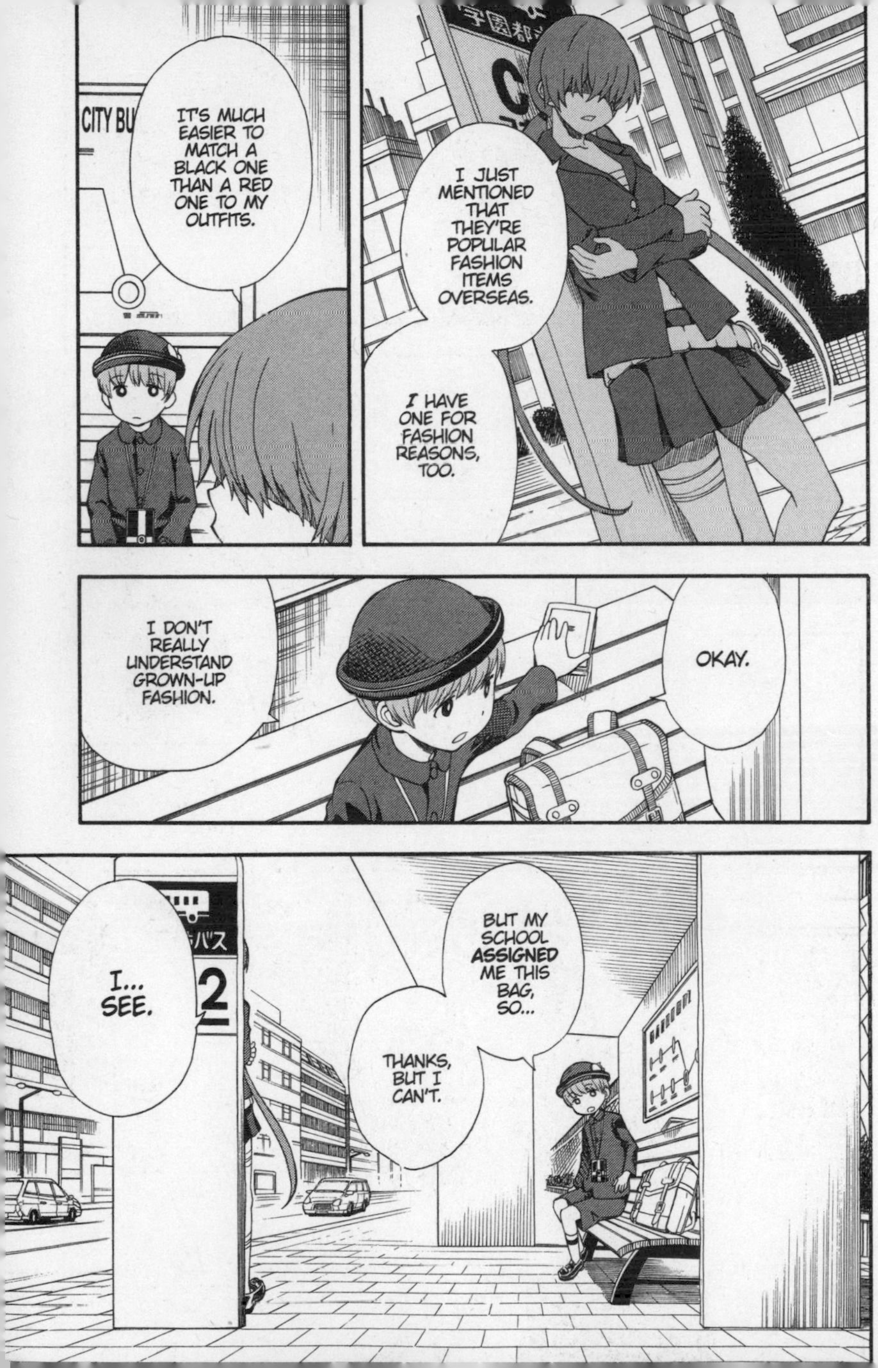
学園都
I JUST MENTIONED THAT THEY'RE POPULAR FASHION ITEMS OVERSEAS.
I HAVE ONE FOR FASHION REASONS, TOO.
CITY BU
IT'S MUCH EASIER TO MATCH A BLACK ONE THAN A RED ONE TO MY OUTFITS.
OKAY.
I DON'T REALLY UNDERSTAND GROWN-UP FASHION.
BUT MY SCHOOL ASSIGNED ME THIS BAG, SO...
THANKS, BUT I CAN'T.
バス
2
I... SEE.

OH.

AND THIS ONE'S PRETTY USEFUL, IF YOU ASK ME.

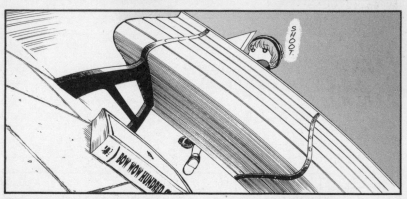

SHOOT.

BOW WOW HUNDRED

NN ....!

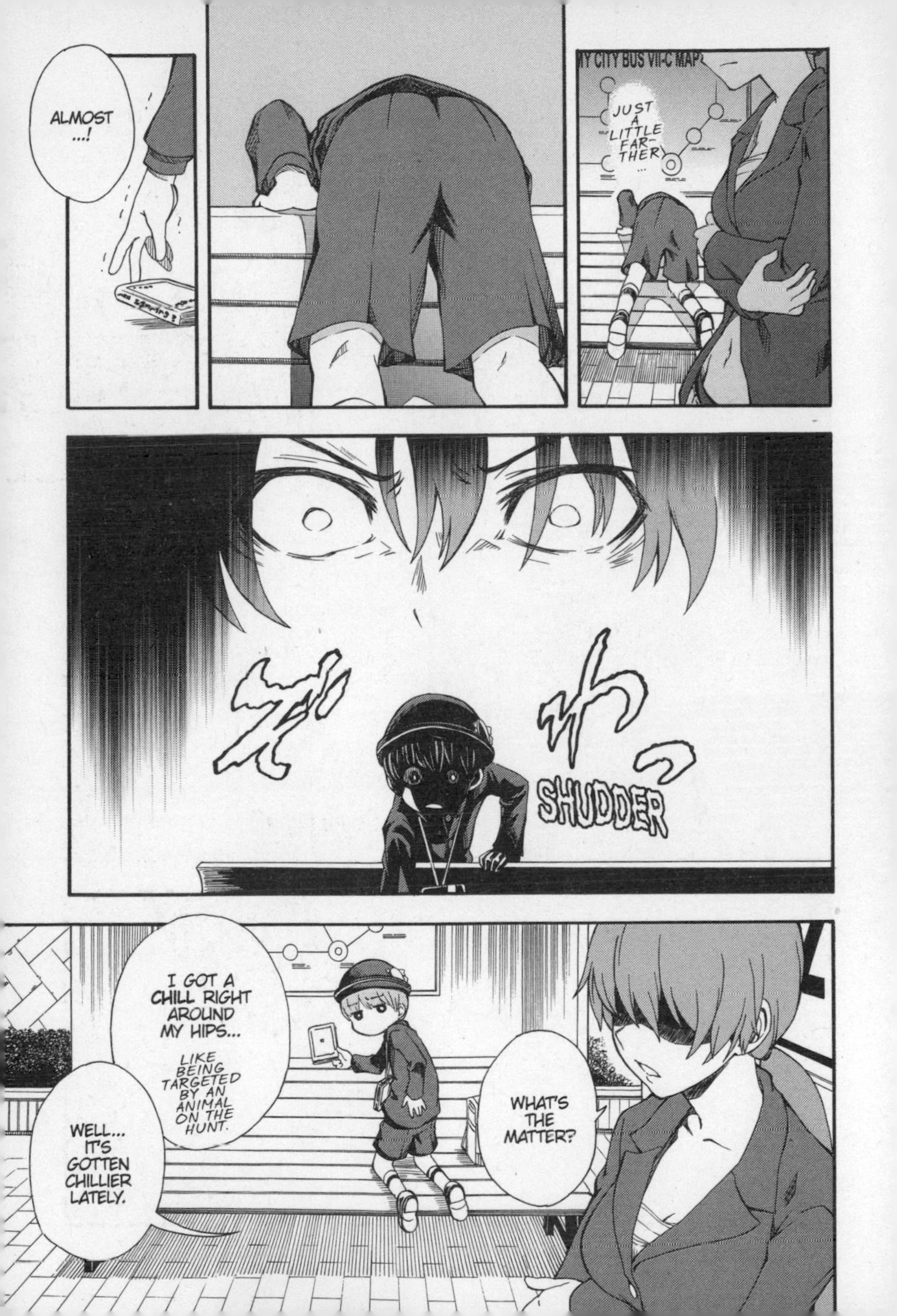
MY CITY BUS VII-C MAP
JUST A LITTLE FAR-THER ...
ALMOST ...!
ぞわっ
SHUDDER
WHAT'S THE MATTER?
I GOT A CHILL RIGHT AROUND MY HIPS...
LIKE BEING TARGETED BY AN ANIMAL ON THE HUNT.
WELL... IT'S GOTTEN CHILLIER LATELY.

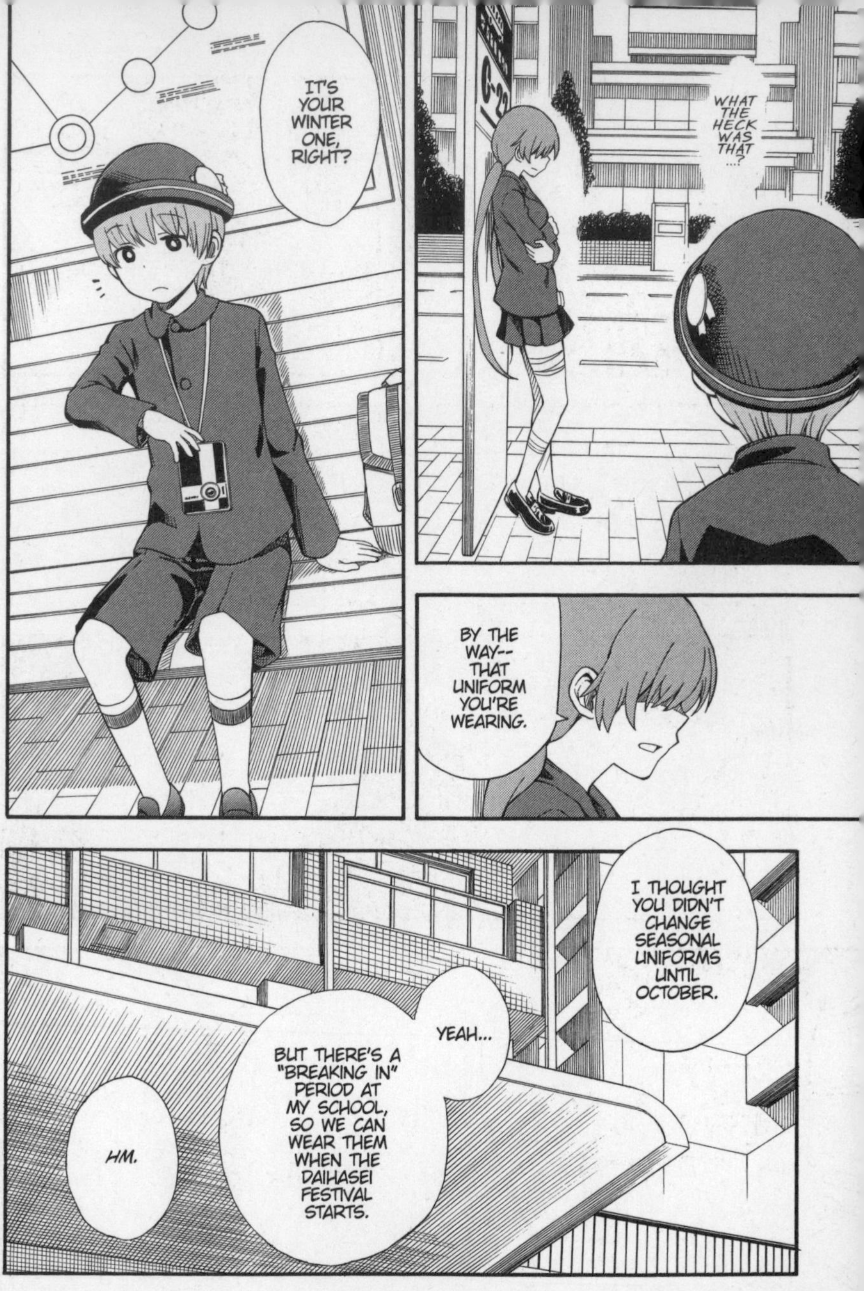
WHAT THE HECK WAS THAT ...?
BY THE WAY-- THAT UNIFORM YOU'RE WEARING.
IT'S YOUR WINTER ONE, RIGHT?
I THOUGHT YOU DIDN'T CHANGE SEASONAL UNIFORMS UNTIL OCTOBER.
YEAH...
BUT THERE'S A "BREAKING IN" PERIOD AT MY SCHOOL, SO WE CAN WEAR THEM WHEN THE DAIHASEI FESTIVAL STARTS.
HM.

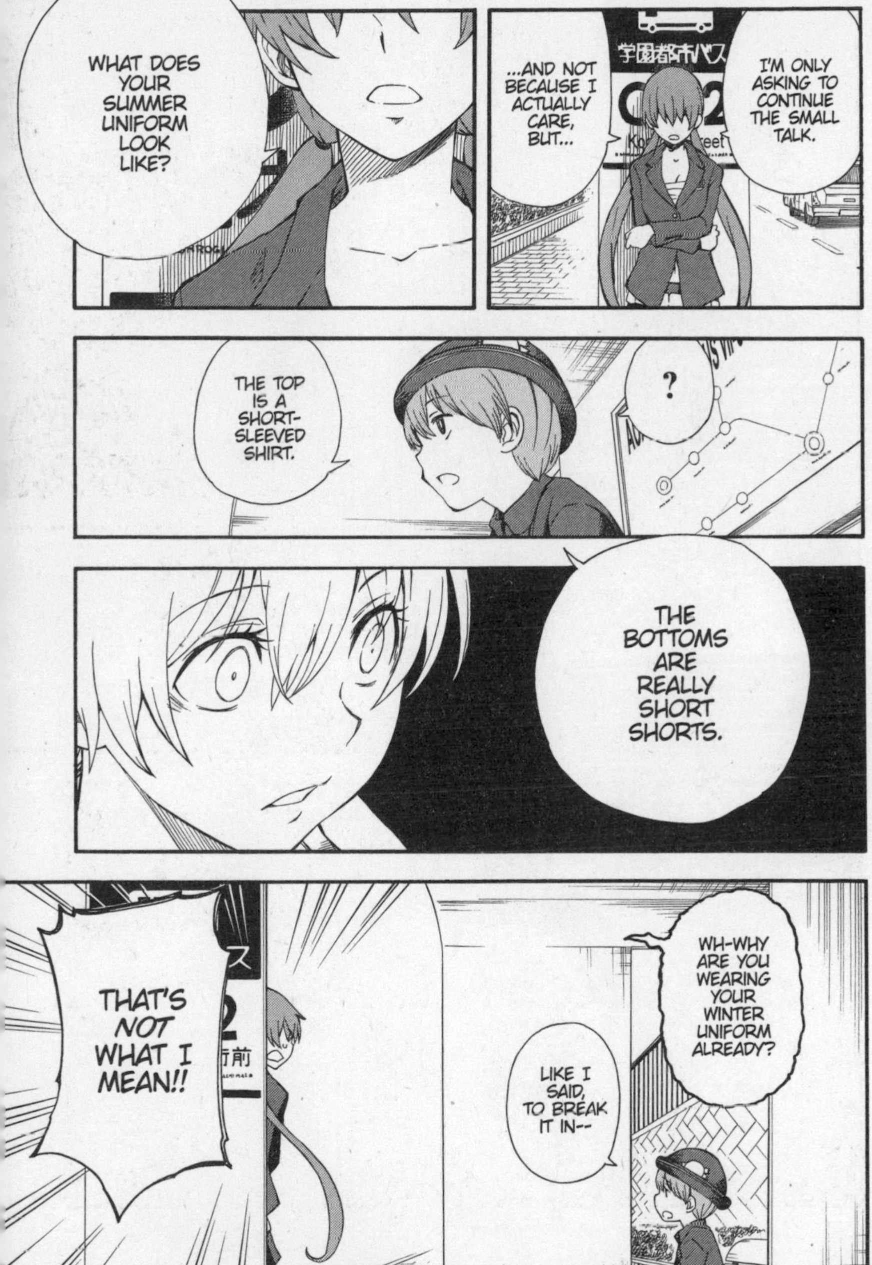

学園都市バス
I'M ONLY ASKING TO CONTINUE THE SMALL TALK.
...AND NOT BECAUSE I ACTUALLY CARE, BUT...
WHAT DOES YOUR SUMMER UNIFORM LOOK LIKE?
?
THE TOP IS A SHORT-SLEEVED SHIRT.
THE BOTTOMS ARE REALLY SHORT SHORTS.
WH-WHY ARE YOU WEARING YOUR WINTER UNIFORM ALREADY?
LIKE I SAID, TO BREAK IT IN--
THAT'S *NOT* WHAT I MEAN!!

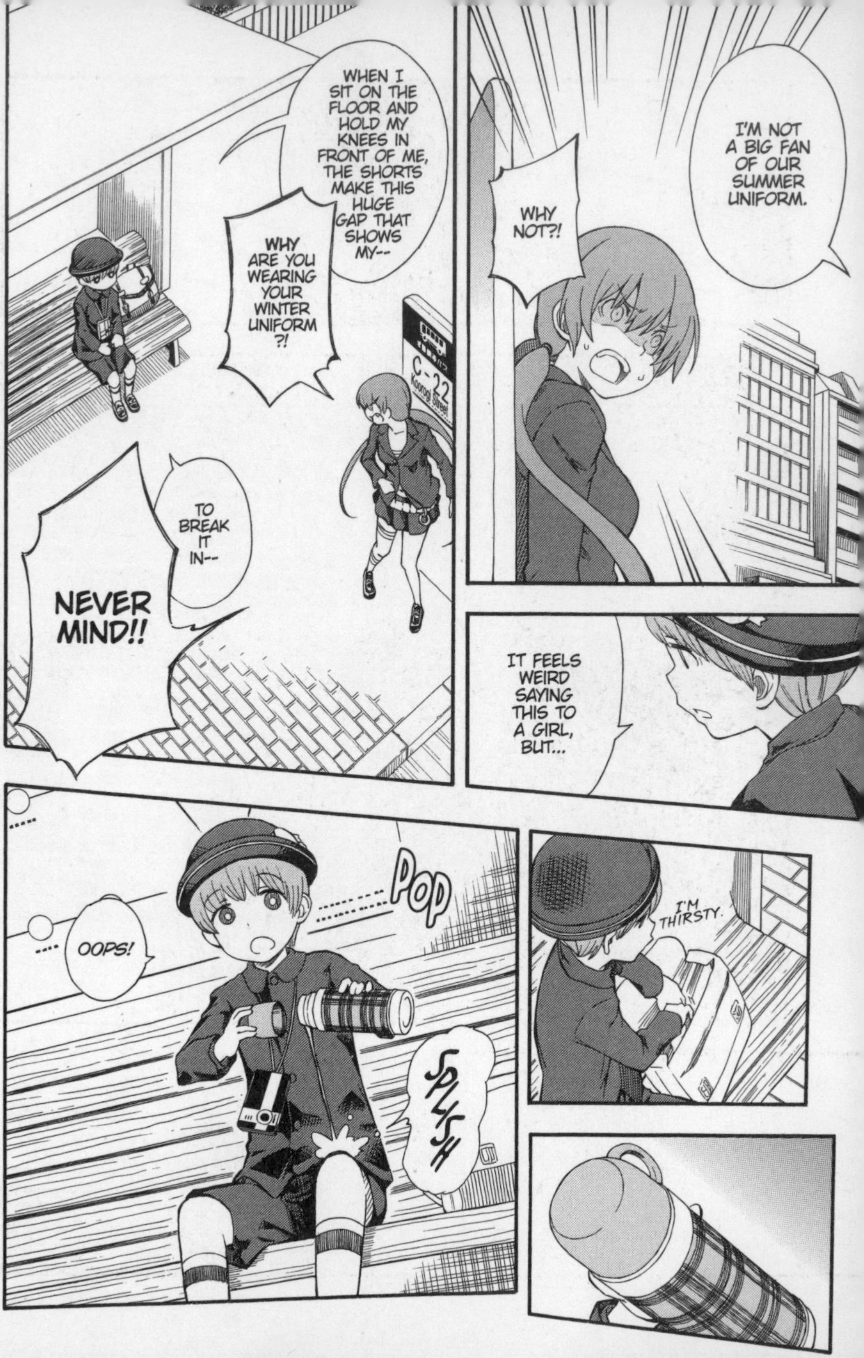
I'M NOT A BIG FAN OF OUR SUMMER UNIFORM.
WHY NOT?!
IT FEELS WEIRD SAYING THIS TO A GIRL, BUT...
WHEN I SIT ON THE FLOOR AND HOLD MY KNEES IN FRONT OF ME, THE SHORTS MAKE THIS HUGE GAP THAT SHOWS MY--
WHY ARE YOU WEARING YOUR WINTER UNIFORM?!
C-22
Koorogi Street
TO BREAK IT IN--
NEVER MIND!!
I'M THIRSTY.
POP
SPLSH
OOPS!

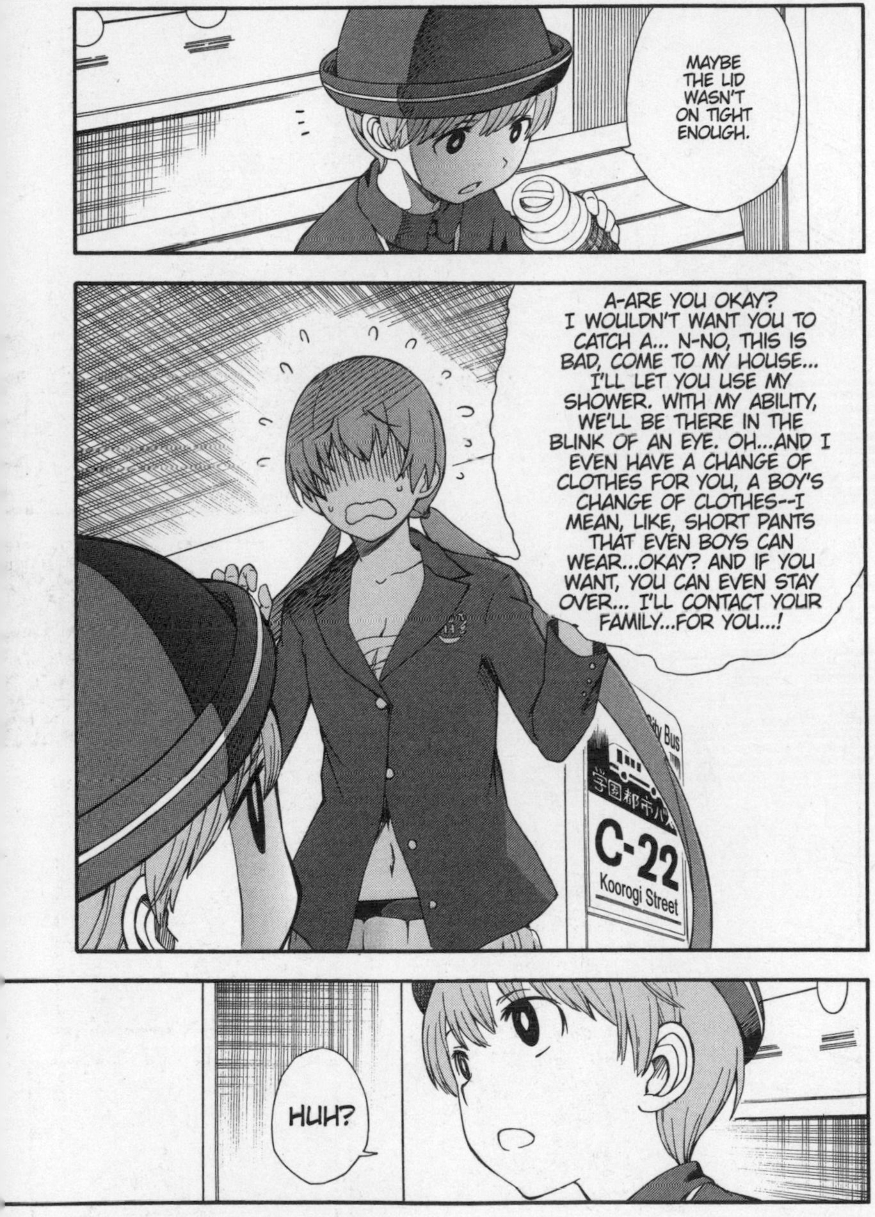
MAYBE THE LID WASN'T ON TIGHT ENOUGH.
A-ARE YOU OKAY? I WOULDN'T WANT YOU TO CATCH A... N-NO, THIS IS BAD, COME TO MY HOUSE... I'LL LET YOU USE MY SHOWER. WITH MY ABILITY, WE'LL BE THERE IN THE BLINK OF AN EYE. OH...AND I EVEN HAVE A CHANGE OF CLOTHES FOR YOU, A BOY'S CHANGE OF CLOTHES--I MEAN, LIKE, SHORT PANTS THAT EVEN BOYS CAN WEAR...OKAY? AND IF YOU WANT, YOU CAN EVEN STAY OVER... I'LL CONTACT YOUR FAMILY...FOR YOU...!
C-22
Koorogi Street
HUH?

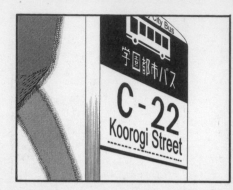

学園都市バス
C-22
Koorogi Street
City Bus
学園都市バス
C-22
Koorogi Street
IS THIS BUS STOP C-22?
I WAS SUPPOSED TO RIDE FROM C-12 TO GET TO THE NEXT PREDICTED SITE.
THIS IS THE WRONG STOP, OOF.
Academy City Bus
学園都市バス
C-22
Koorogi Street

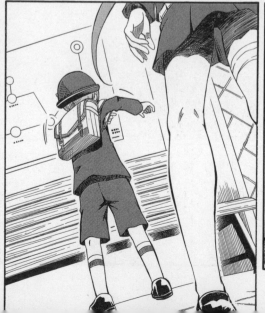

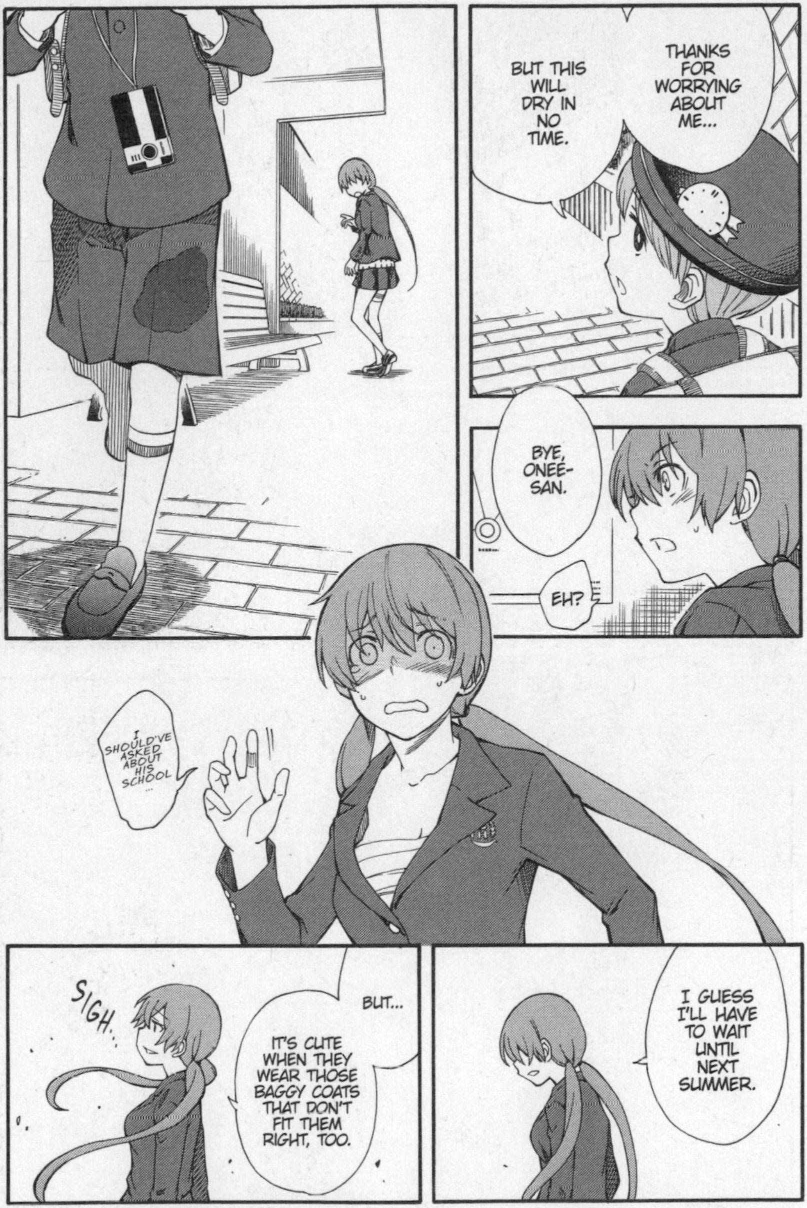
THANKS FOR WORRYING ABOUT ME...
BUT THIS WILL DRY IN NO TIME.
BYE, ONEE-SAN.
EH?
I SHOULD'VE ASKED ABOUT HIS SCHOOL...
I GUESS I'LL HAVE TO WAIT UNTIL NEXT SUMMER.
SIGH...
BUT...
IT'S CUTE WHEN THEY WEAR THOSE BAGGY COATS THAT DON'T FIT THEM RIGHT, TOO.

A Certain SCIENTIFIC Railgun

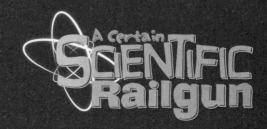

CHAPTER 74: PRECOGNITION

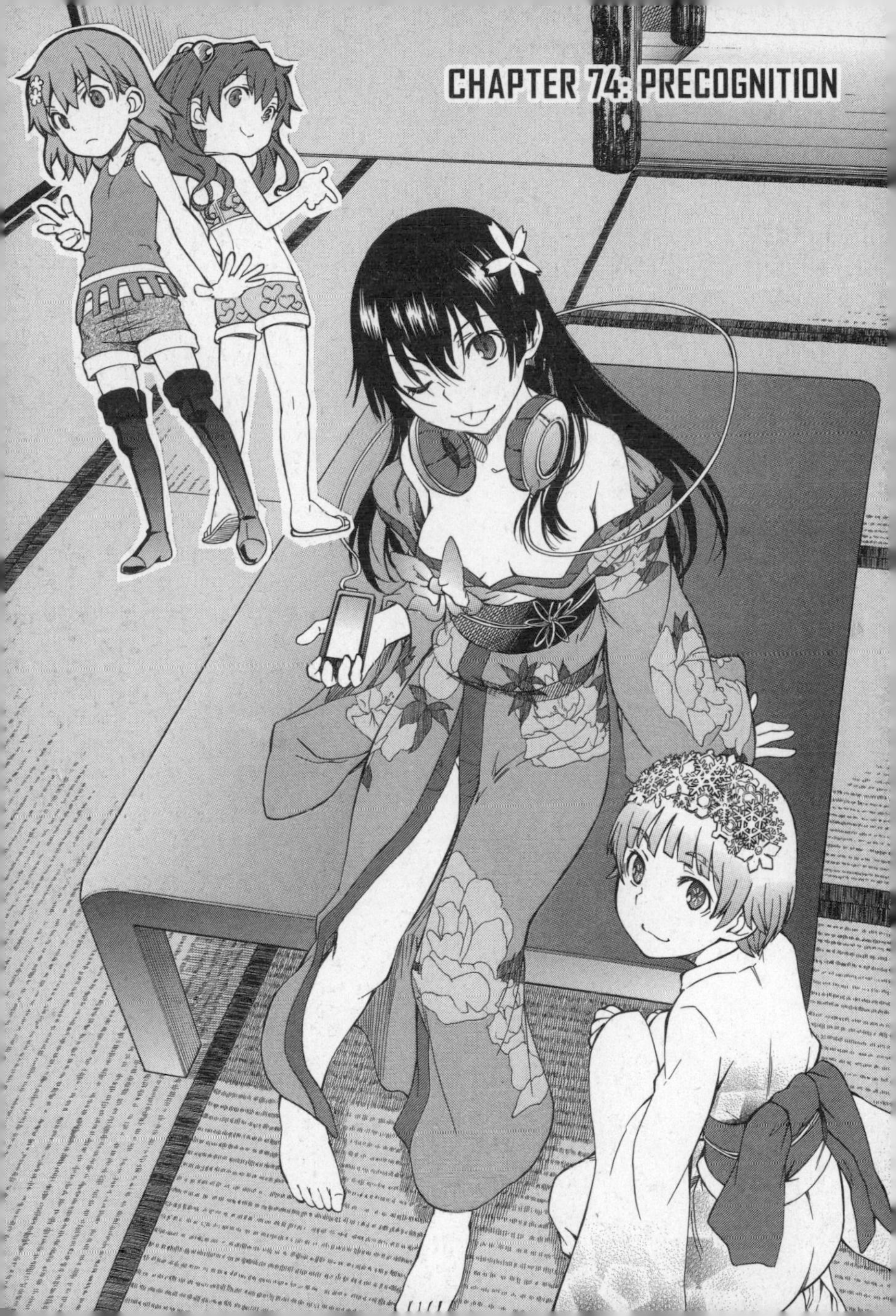

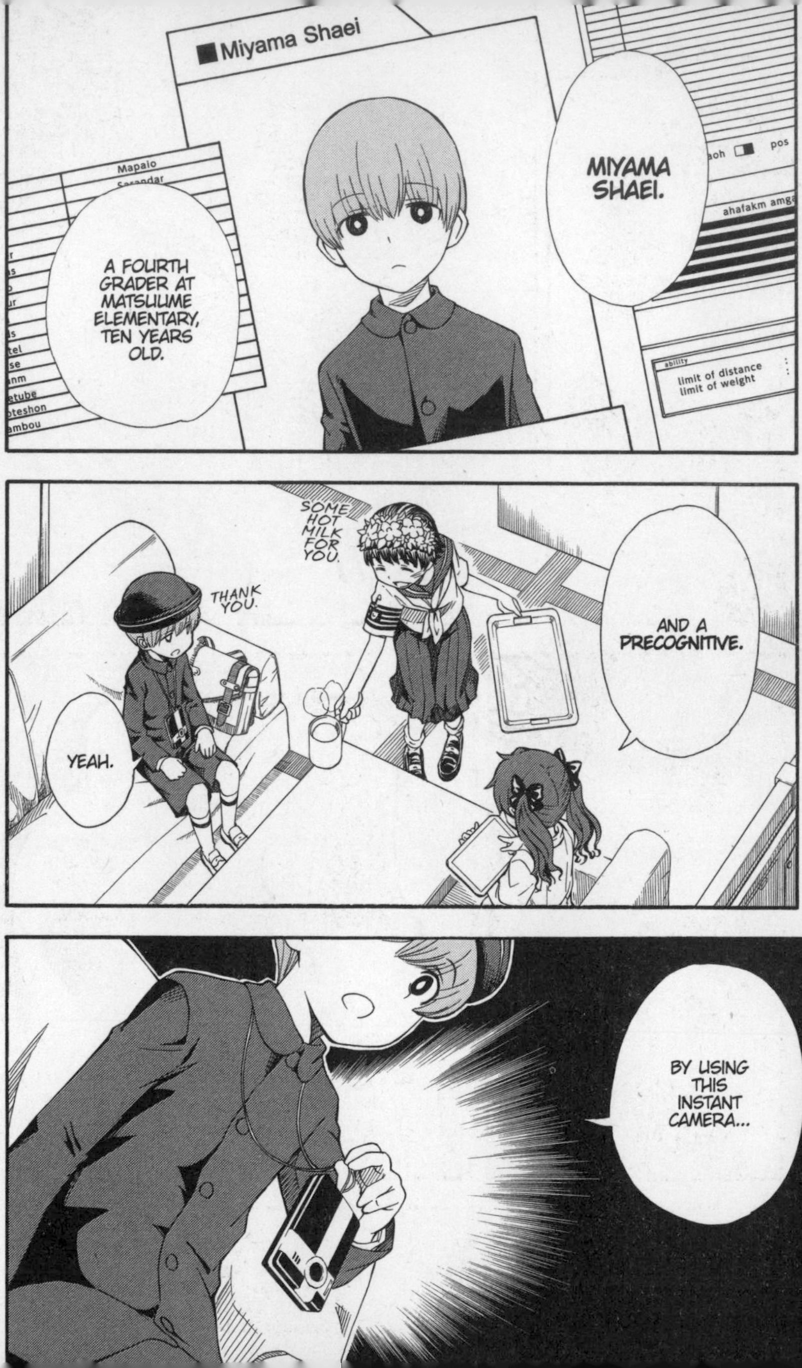
Miyama Shaei
MIYAMA SHAEI.
A FOURTH GRADER AT MATSUUME ELEMENTARY, TEN YEARS OLD.
ability
limit of distance
limit of weight
AND A PRECOGNITIVE.
SOME HOT MILK FOR YOU.
THANK YOU.
YEAH.
BY USING THIS INSTANT CAMERA...

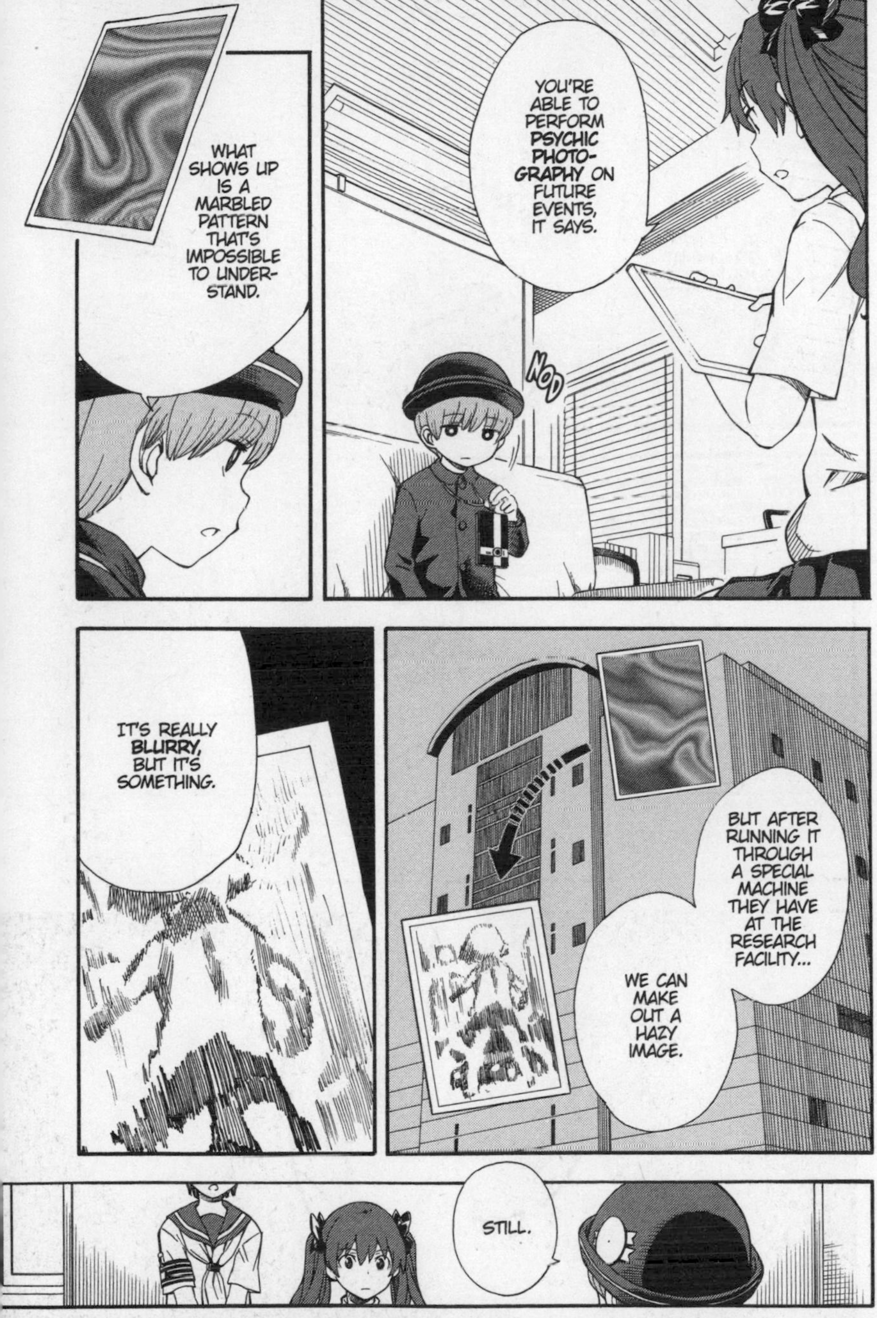
YOU'RE ABLE TO PERFORM PSYCHIC PHOTOGRAPHY ON FUTURE EVENTS, IT SAYS.
NOD
WHAT SHOWS UP IS A MARBLED PATTERN THAT'S IMPOSSIBLE TO UNDERSTAND.
BUT AFTER RUNNING IT THROUGH A SPECIAL MACHINE THEY HAVE AT THE RESEARCH FACILITY...
WE CAN MAKE OUT A HAZY IMAGE.
IT'S REALLY BLURRY, BUT IT'S SOMETHING.
STILL.

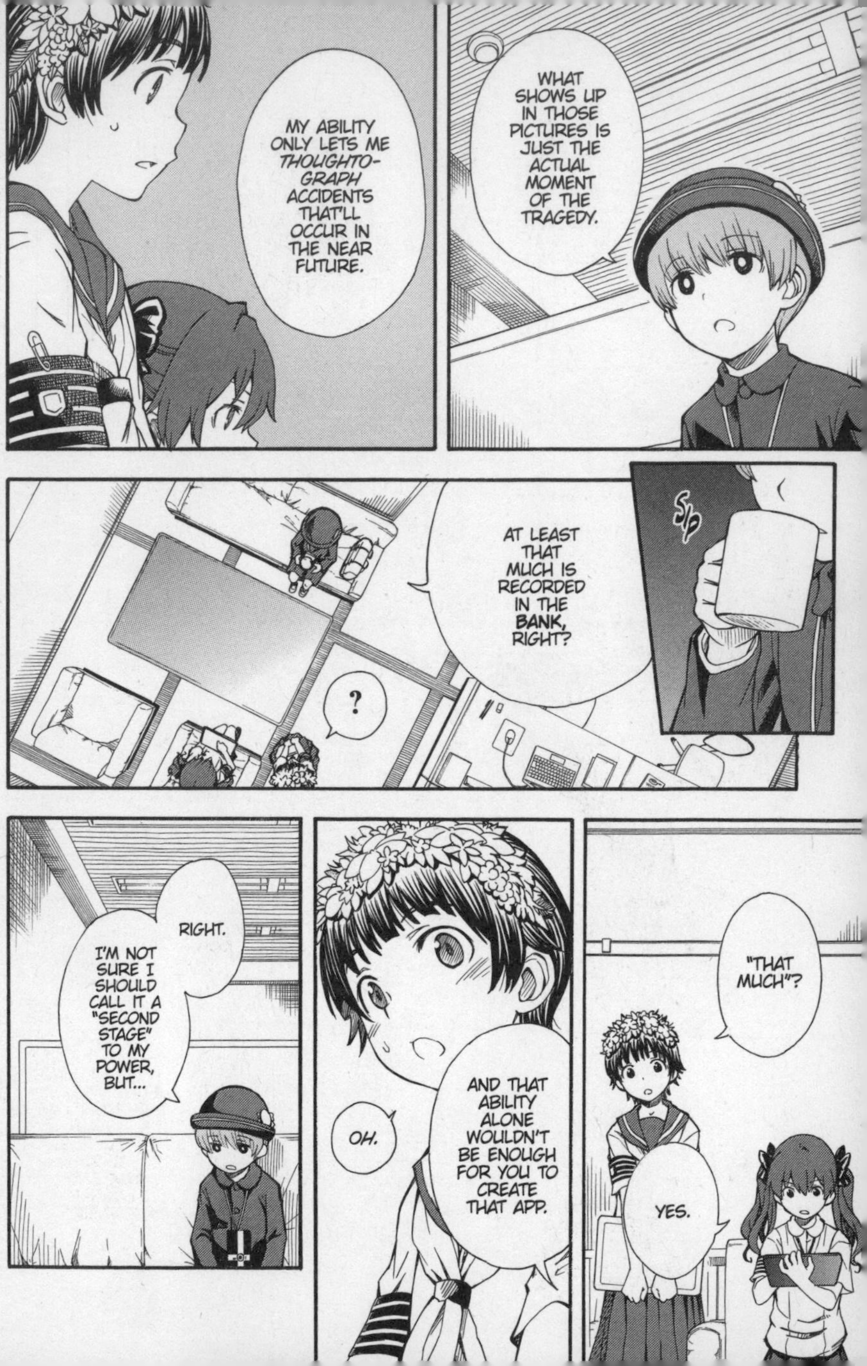
WHAT SHOWS UP IN THOSE PICTURES IS JUST THE ACTUAL MOMENT OF THE TRAGEDY.
MY ABILITY ONLY LETS ME *THOUGHTOGRAPH* ACCIDENTS THAT'LL OCCUR IN THE NEAR FUTURE.
SIP
AT LEAST THAT MUCH IS RECORDED IN THE **BANK**, RIGHT?
?
"THAT MUCH"?
YES.
AND THAT ABILITY ALONE WOULDN'T BE ENOUGH FOR YOU TO CREATE THAT APP.
OH.
RIGHT.
I'M NOT SURE I SHOULD CALL IT A "SECOND STAGE" TO MY POWER, BUT...

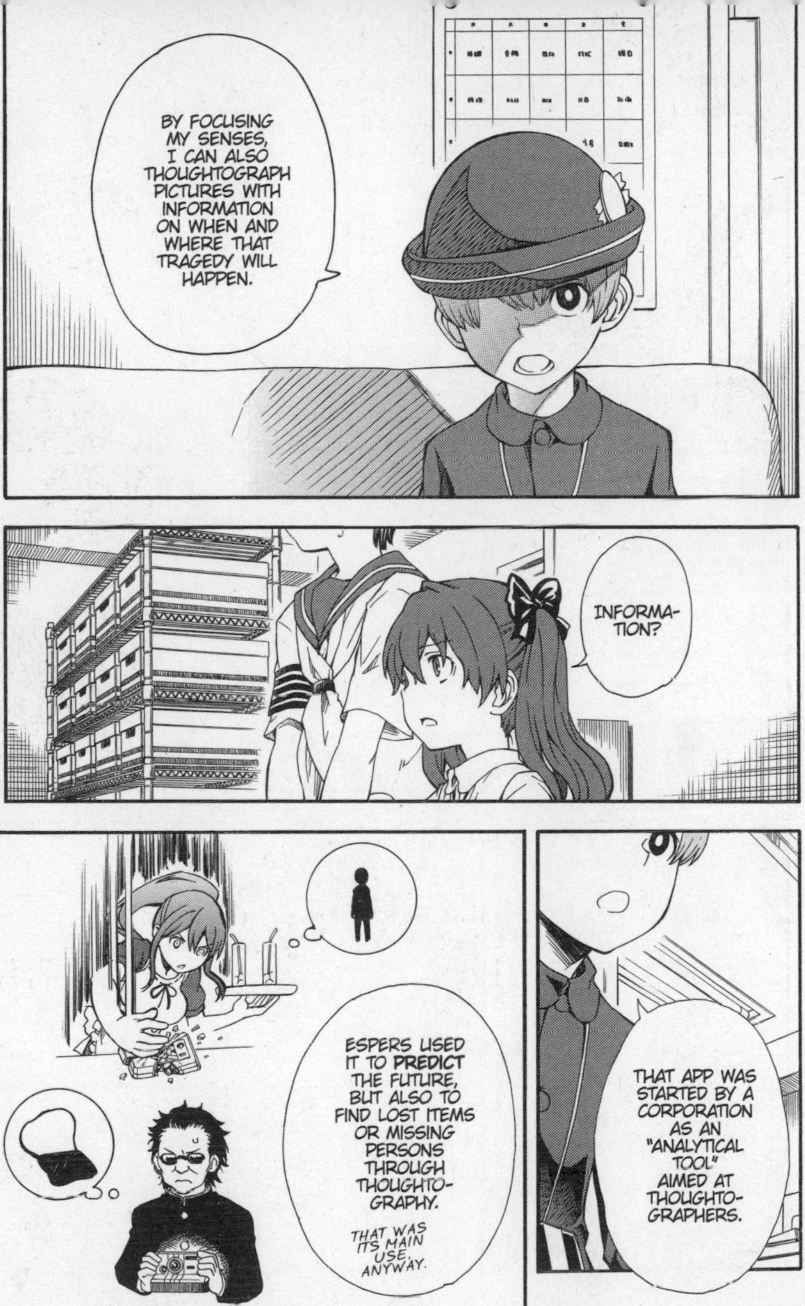
BY FOCUSING MY SENSES, I CAN ALSO THOUGHTOGRAPH PICTURES WITH INFORMATION ON WHEN AND WHERE THAT TRAGEDY WILL HAPPEN.
INFORMATION?
THAT APP WAS STARTED BY A CORPORATION AS AN "ANALYTICAL TOOL" AIMED AT THOUGHTOGRAPHERS.
ESPERS USED IT TO PREDICT THE FUTURE, BUT ALSO TO FIND LOST ITEMS OR MISSING PERSONS THROUGH THOUGHTOGRAPHY.
THAT WAS ITS MAIN USE, ANYWAY.

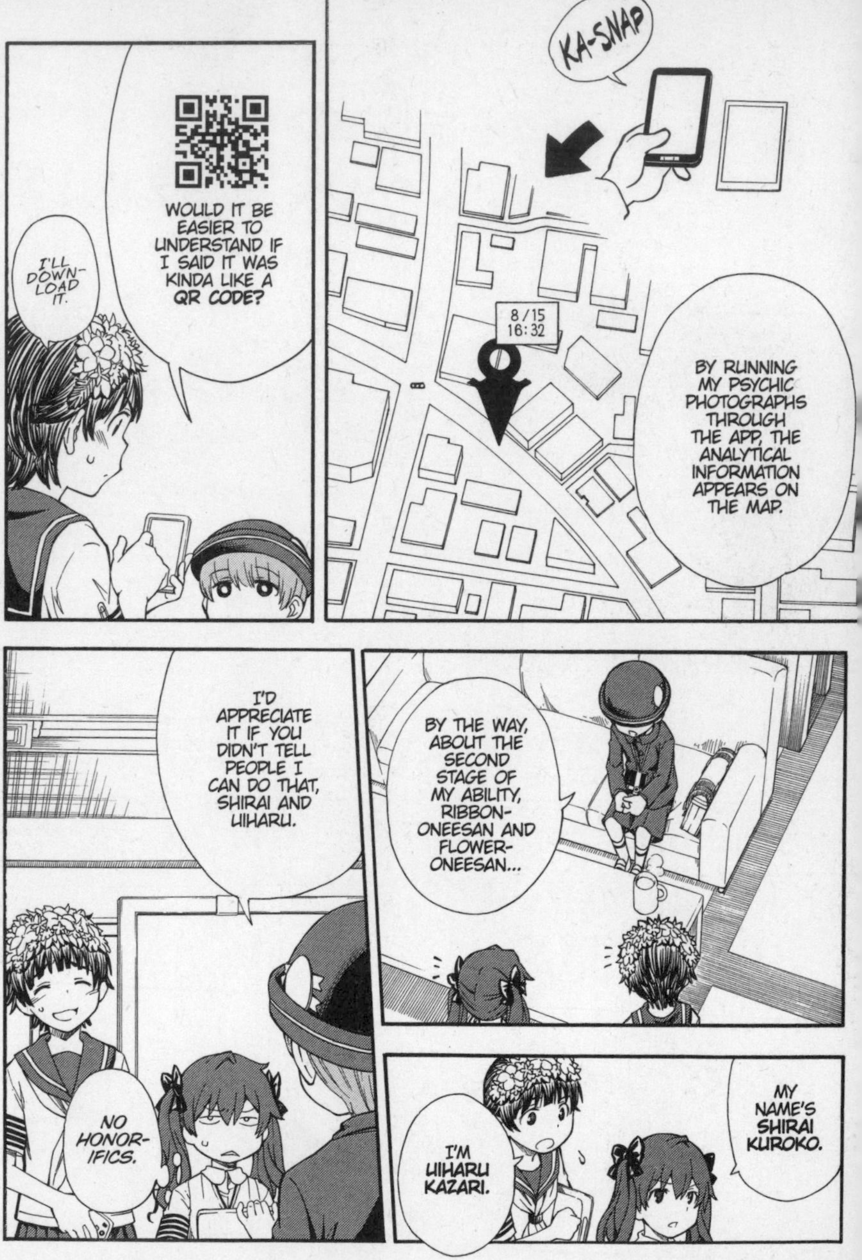
KA-SNAP
8/15 16:32
BY RUNNING MY PSYCHIC PHOTOGRAPHS THROUGH THE APP, THE ANALYTICAL INFORMATION APPEARS ON THE MAP.
WOULD IT BE EASIER TO UNDERSTAND IF I SAID IT WAS KINDA LIKE A QR CODE?
I'LL DOWN-LOAD IT.
BY THE WAY, ABOUT THE SECOND STAGE OF MY ABILITY, RIBBON-ONEESAN AND FLOWER-ONEESAN...
MY NAME'S SHIRAI KUROKO.
I'M UIHARU KAZARI.
I'D APPRECIATE IT IF YOU DIDN'T TELL PEOPLE I CAN DO THAT, SHIRAI AND UIHARU.
NO HONOR-IFICS.

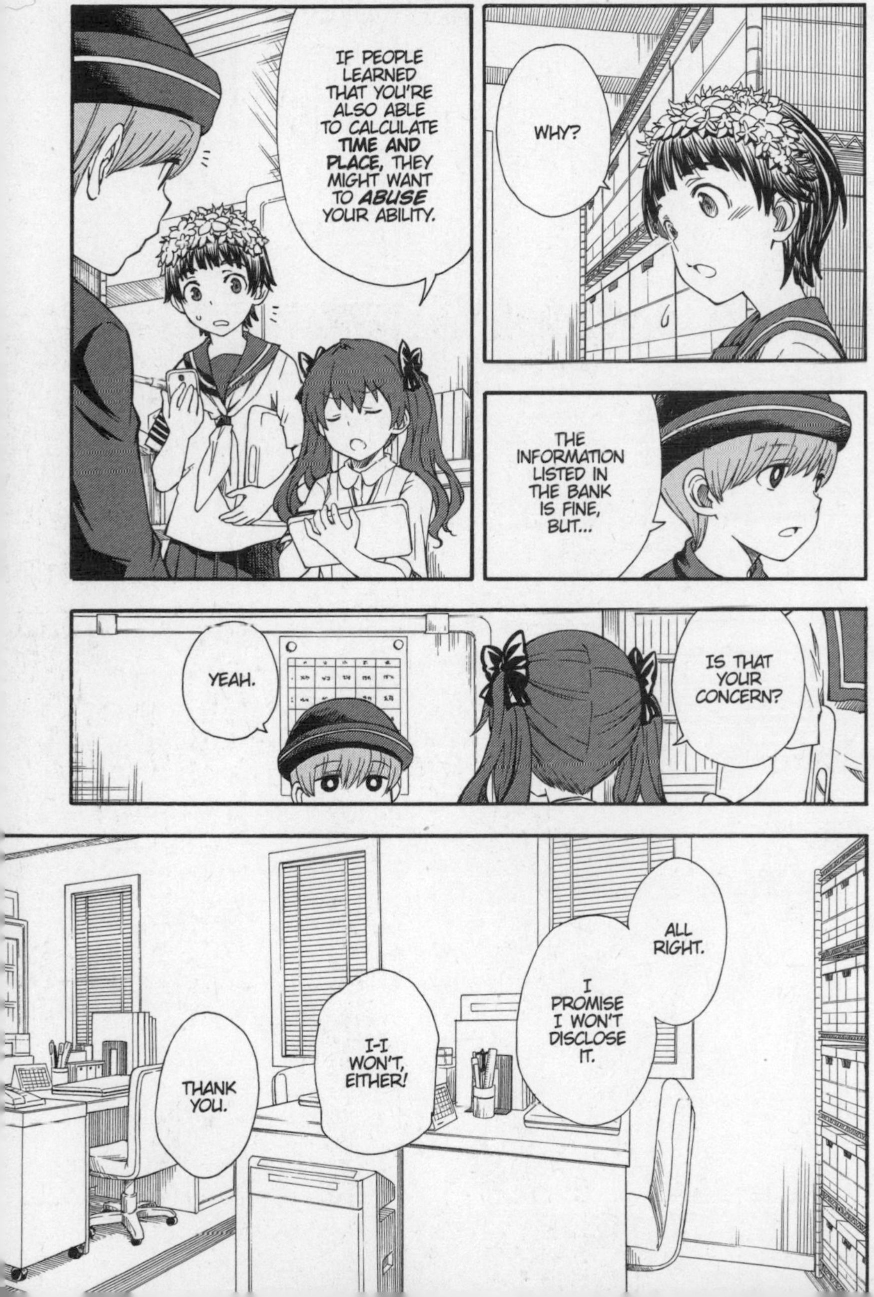
WHY?
THE INFORMATION LISTED IN THE BANK IS FINE, BUT...
IF PEOPLE LEARNED THAT YOU'RE ALSO ABLE TO CALCULATE **TIME AND PLACE,** THEY MIGHT WANT TO ***ABUSE*** YOUR ABILITY.
IS THAT YOUR CONCERN?
YEAH.
ALL RIGHT.
I PROMISE I WON'T DISCLOSE IT.
I-I WON'T, EITHER!
THANK YOU.

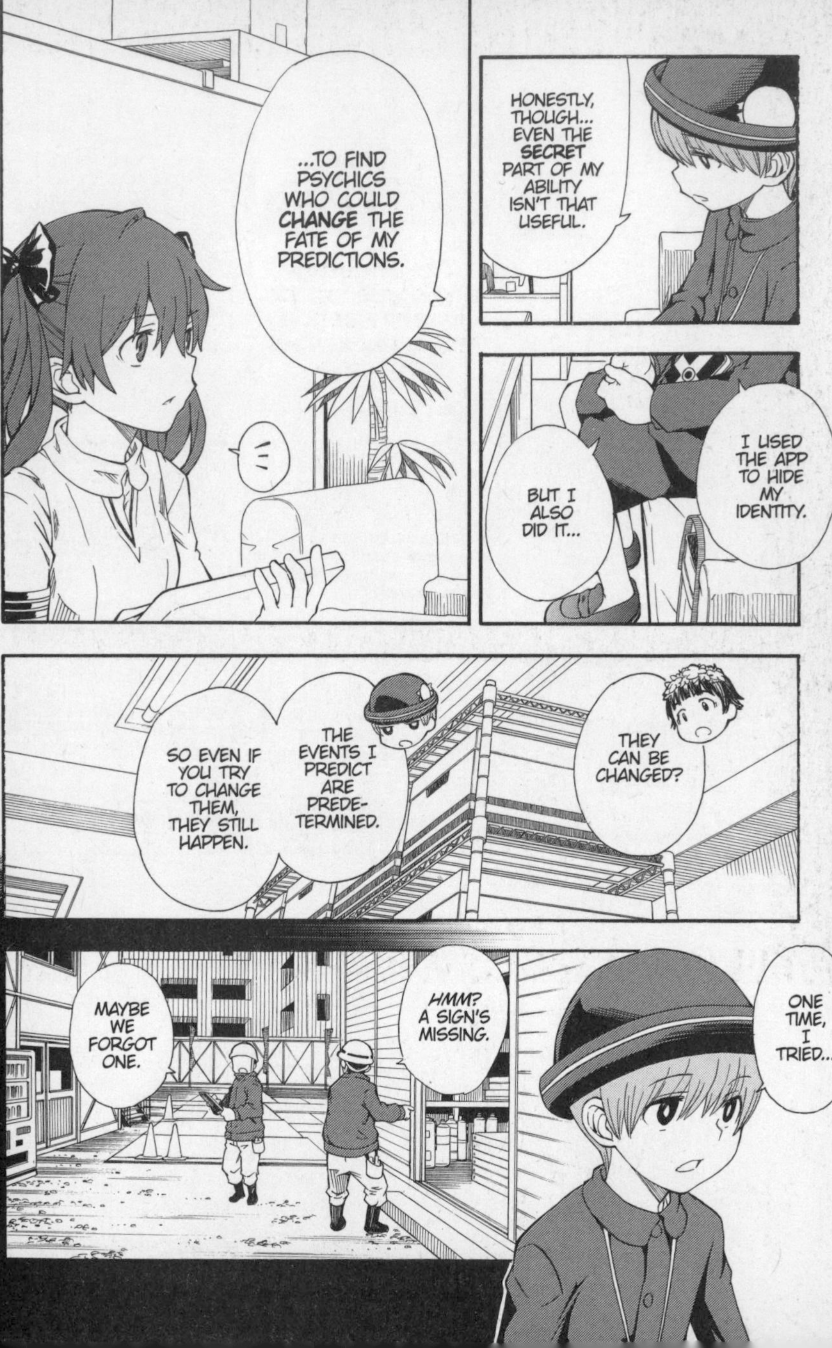
HONESTLY, THOUGH... EVEN THE **SECRET** PART OF MY ABILITY ISN'T THAT USEFUL.
I USED THE APP TO HIDE MY IDENTITY.
BUT I ALSO DID IT...
...TO FIND PSYCHICS WHO COULD **CHANGE** THE FATE OF MY PREDICTIONS.
THEY CAN BE CHANGED?
THE EVENTS I PREDICT ARE PREDE-TERMINED.
SO EVEN IF YOU TRY TO CHANGE THEM, THEY STILL HAPPEN.
ONE TIME, I TRIED...
HMM? A SIGN'S MISSING.
MAYBE WE FORGOT ONE.

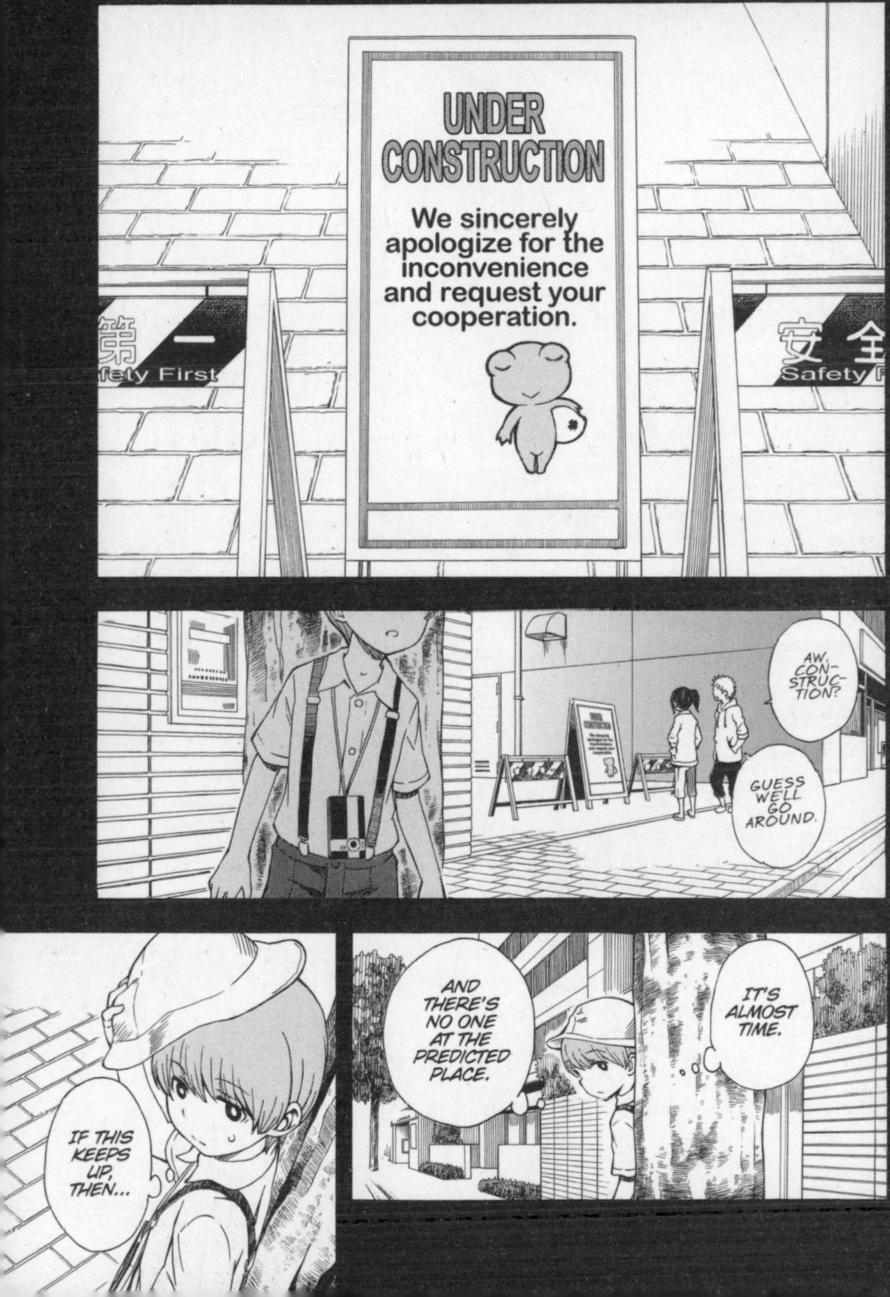
UNDER CONSTRUCTION
We sincerely apologize for the inconvenience and request your cooperation.
AW, CON-STRUC-TION?
GUESS WE'LL GO AROUND.
IT'S ALMOST TIME.
AND THERE'S NO ONE AT THE PREDICTED PLACE.
IF THIS KEEPS UP, THEN...

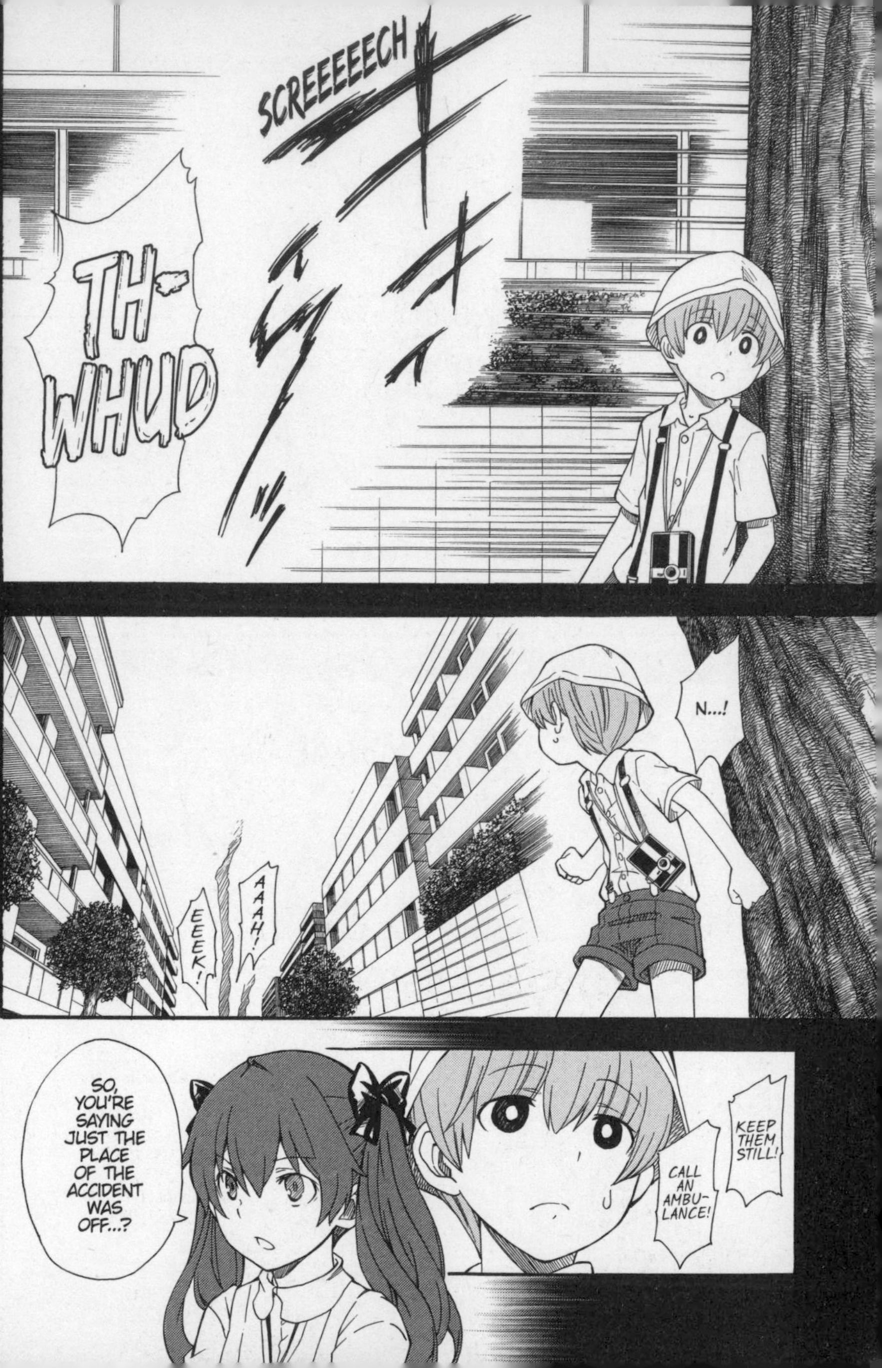
SCREEEEECH
TH-WHUD
N...!
AAAAH!
EEEEK!
KEEP THEM STILL!
CALL AN AMBULANCE!
SO, YOU'RE SAYING JUST THE PLACE OF THE ACCIDENT WAS OFF...?

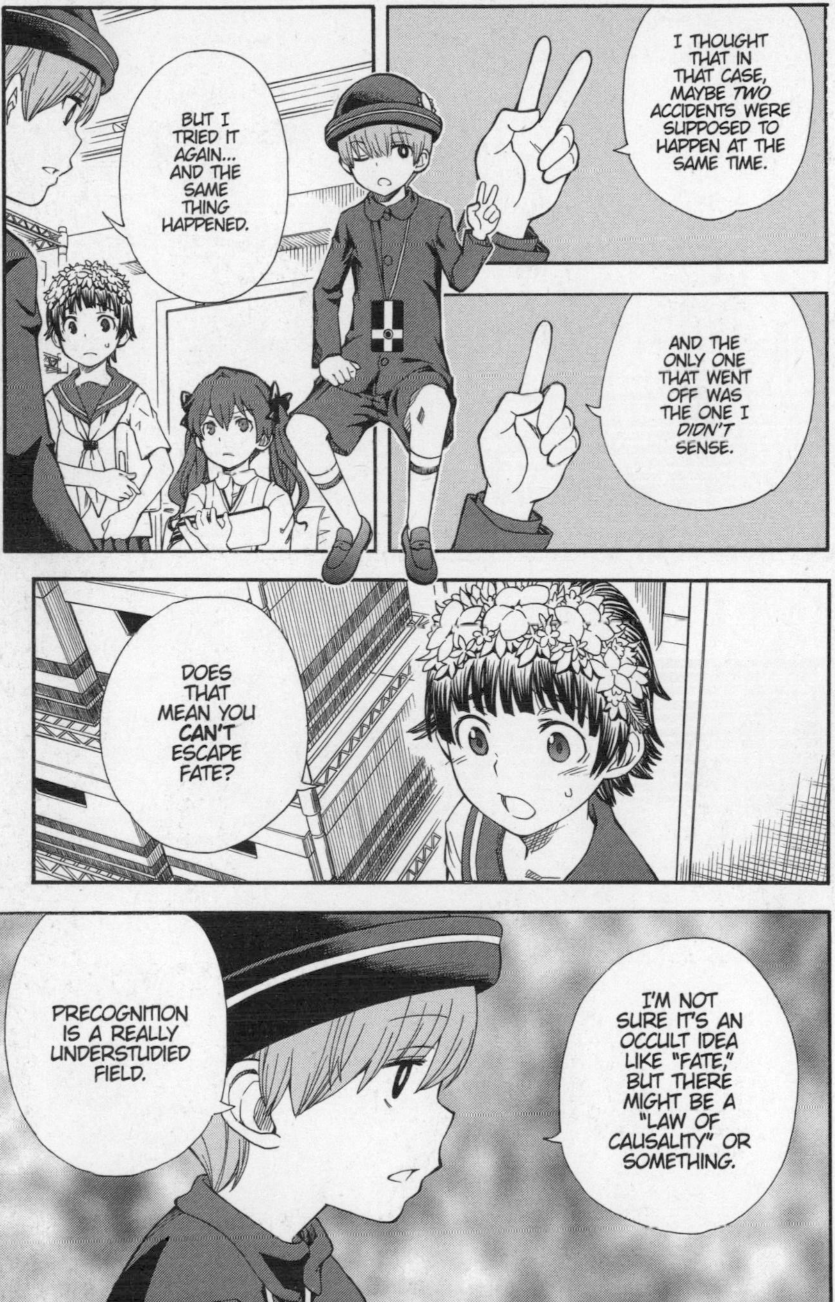
I THOUGHT THAT IN THAT CASE, MAYBE *TWO* ACCIDENTS WERE SUPPOSED TO HAPPEN AT THE SAME TIME.
AND THE ONLY ONE THAT WENT OFF WAS THE ONE I *DIDN'T* SENSE.
BUT I TRIED IT AGAIN... AND THE SAME THING HAPPENED.
DOES THAT MEAN YOU **CAN'T** ESCAPE FATE?
I'M NOT SURE IT'S AN OCCULT IDEA LIKE "FATE," BUT THERE MIGHT BE A "LAW OF CAUSALITY" OR SOMETHING.
PRECOGNITION IS A REALLY UNDERSTUDIED FIELD.

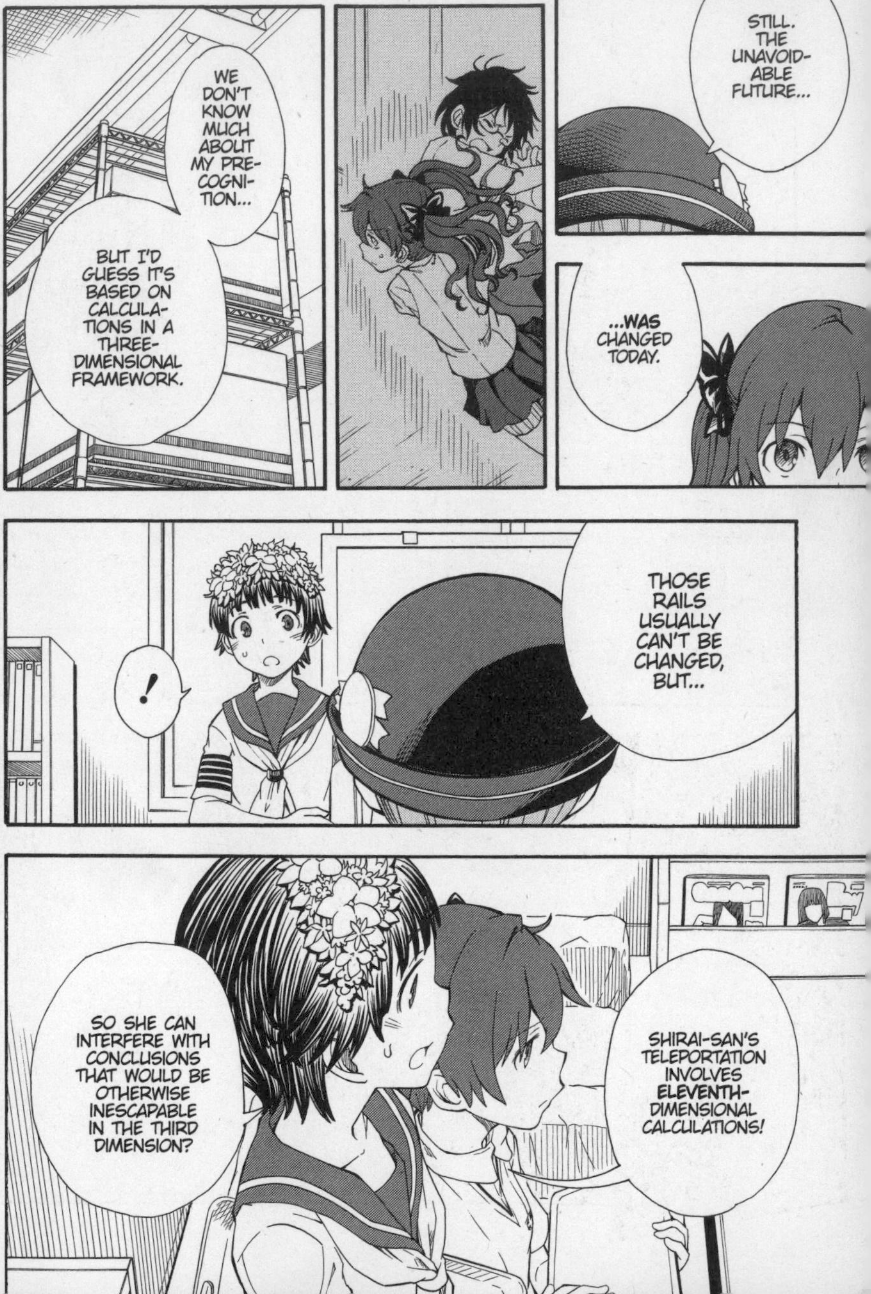
STILL. THE UNAVOID-ABLE FUTURE...
...WAS CHANGED TODAY.
WE DON'T KNOW MUCH ABOUT MY PRE-COGNI-TION...
BUT I'D GUESS IT'S BASED ON CALCULA-TIONS IN A THREE-DIMENSIONAL FRAMEWORK.
THOSE RAILS USUALLY CAN'T BE CHANGED, BUT...
!
SHIRAI-SAN'S TELEPORTATION INVOLVES **ELEVENTH-**DIMENSIONAL CALCULATIONS!
SO SHE CAN INTERFERE WITH CONCLUSIONS THAT WOULD BE OTHERWISE INESCAPABLE IN THE THIRD DIMENSION?

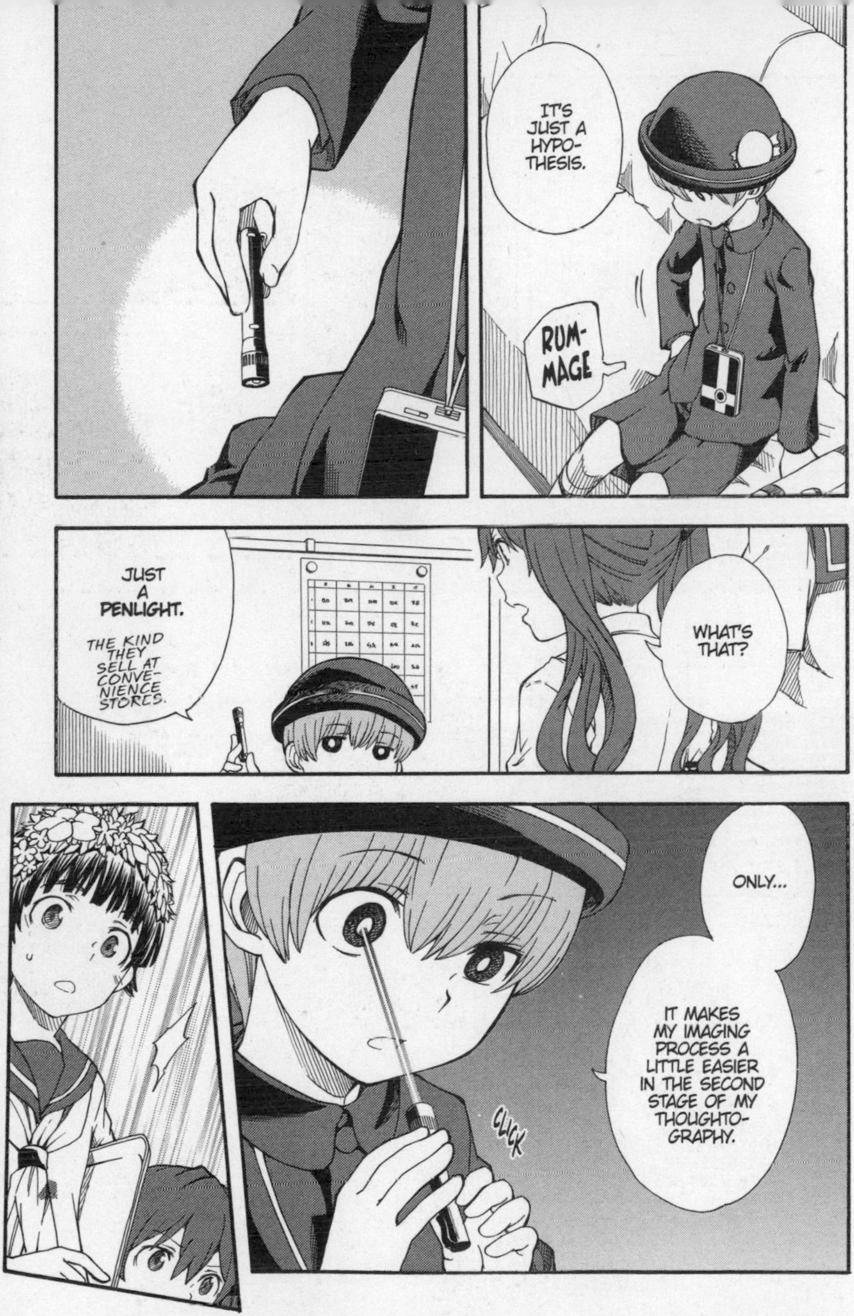
IT'S JUST A HYPO-THESIS.
RUM-MAGE
WHAT'S THAT?
JUST A PENLIGHT.
THE KIND THEY SELL AT CONVE-NIENCE STORES.
ONLY...
IT MAKES MY IMAGING PROCESS A LITTLE EASIER IN THE SECOND STAGE OF MY THOUGHTOG-RAPHY.
CLICK

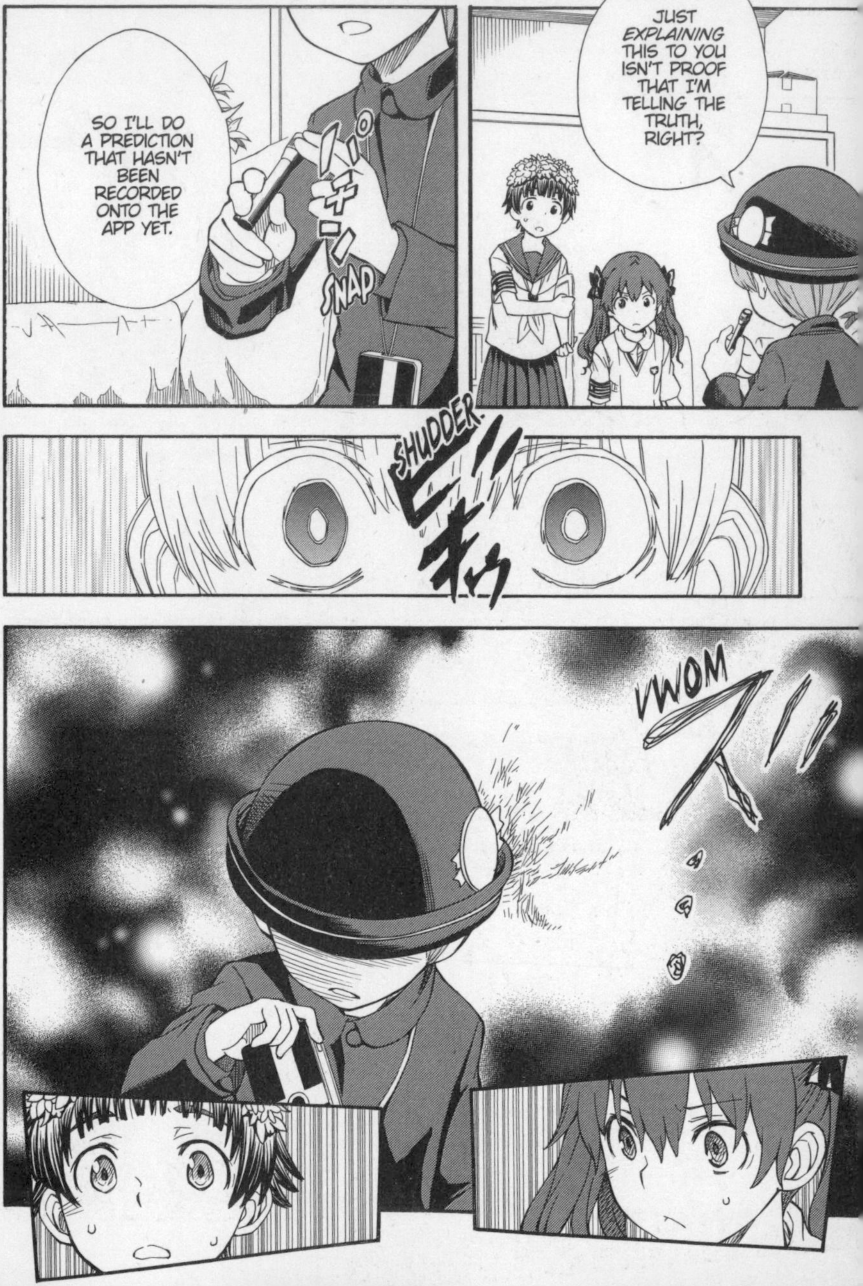
JUST EXPLAINING THIS TO YOU ISN'T PROOF THAT I'M TELLING THE TRUTH, RIGHT?
SO I'LL DO A PREDICTION THAT HASN'T BEEN RECORDED ONTO THE APP YET.
SNAP
SHUDDER
VWOM

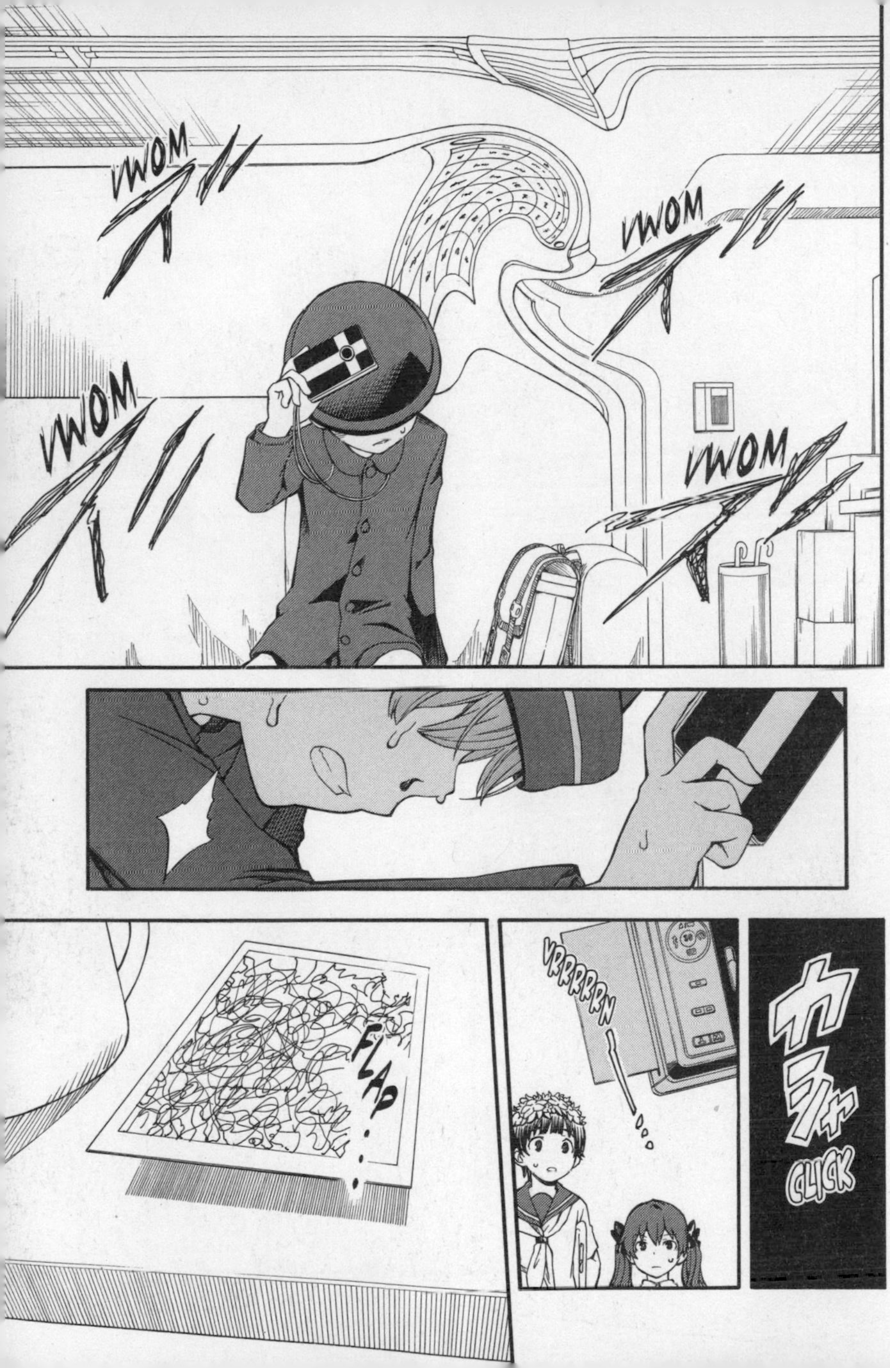
VWOM
VWOM
VWOM
VWOM
カシャ
CLICK
VRRRRRN
FLAP

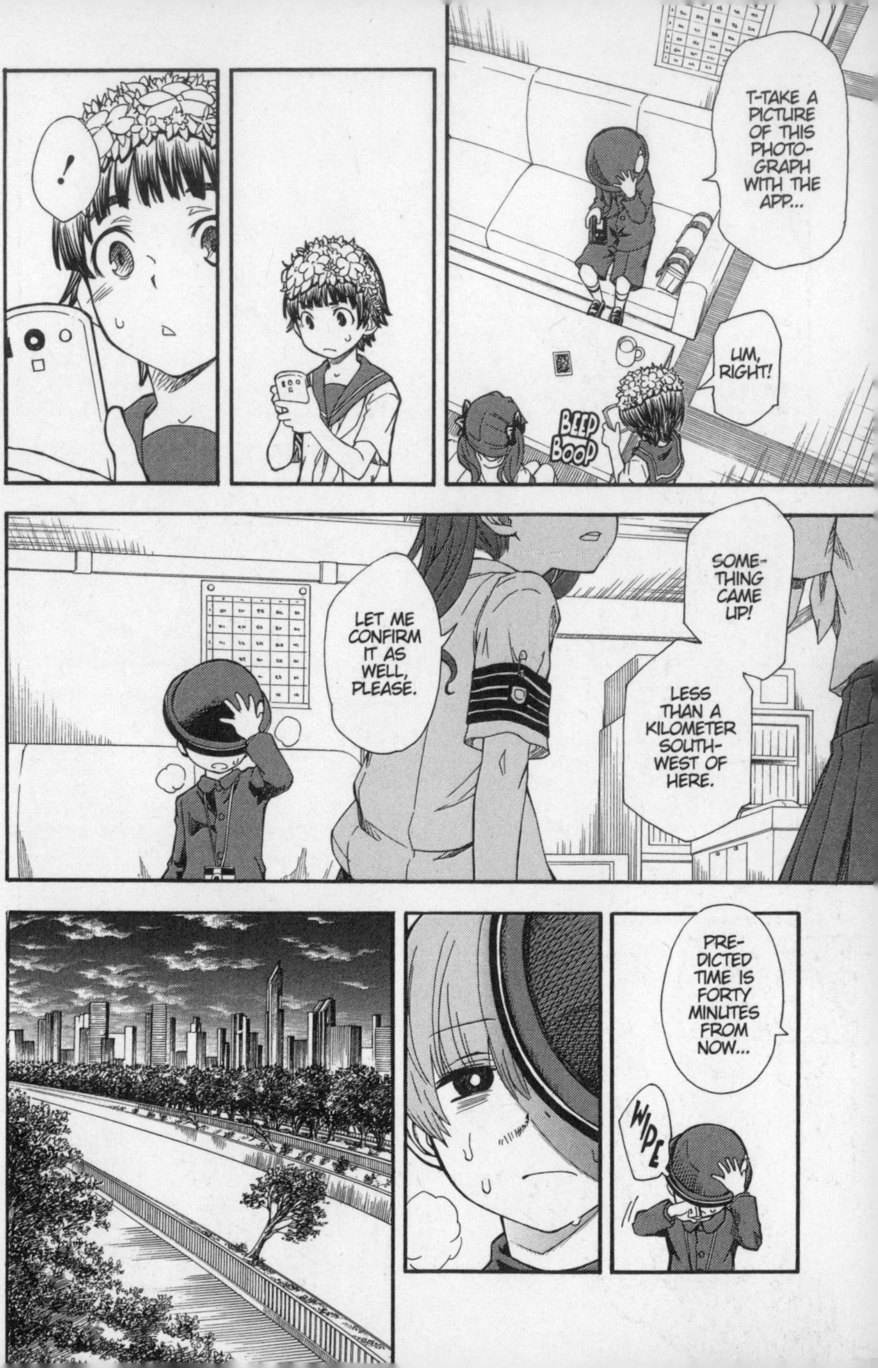
T-TAKE A PICTURE OF THIS PHOTOGRAPH WITH THE APP...
UM, RIGHT!
BEEP BOOP
!
SOMETHING CAME UP!
LESS THAN A KILOMETER SOUTHWEST OF HERE.
LET ME CONFIRM IT AS WELL, PLEASE.
PREDICTED TIME IS FORTY MINUTES FROM NOW...
WIPE

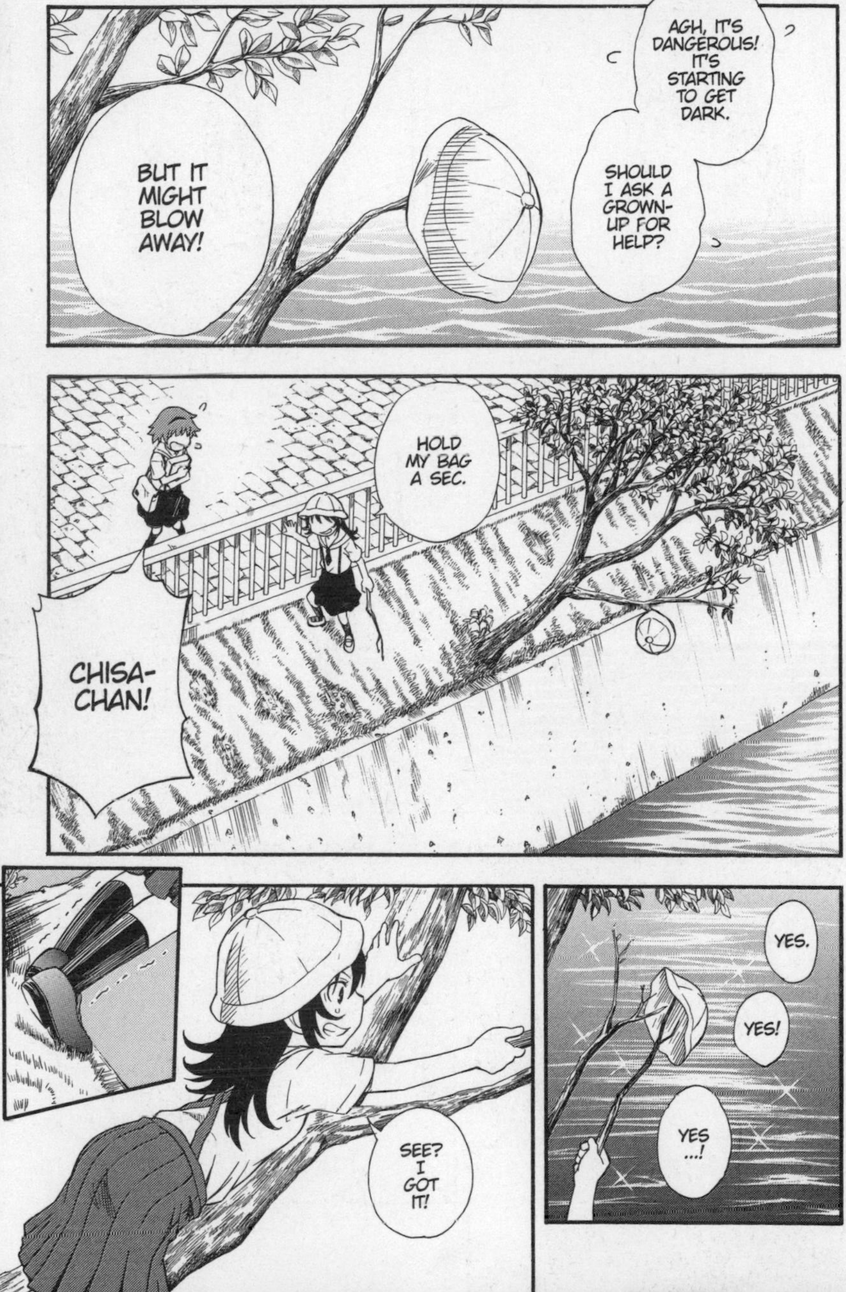
AGH, IT'S DANGEROUS! IT'S STARTING TO GET DARK.
SHOULD I ASK A GROWN-UP FOR HELP?
BUT IT MIGHT BLOW AWAY!
HOLD MY BAG A SEC.
CHISA-CHAN!
YES.
YES!
YES ...!
SEE? I GOT IT!

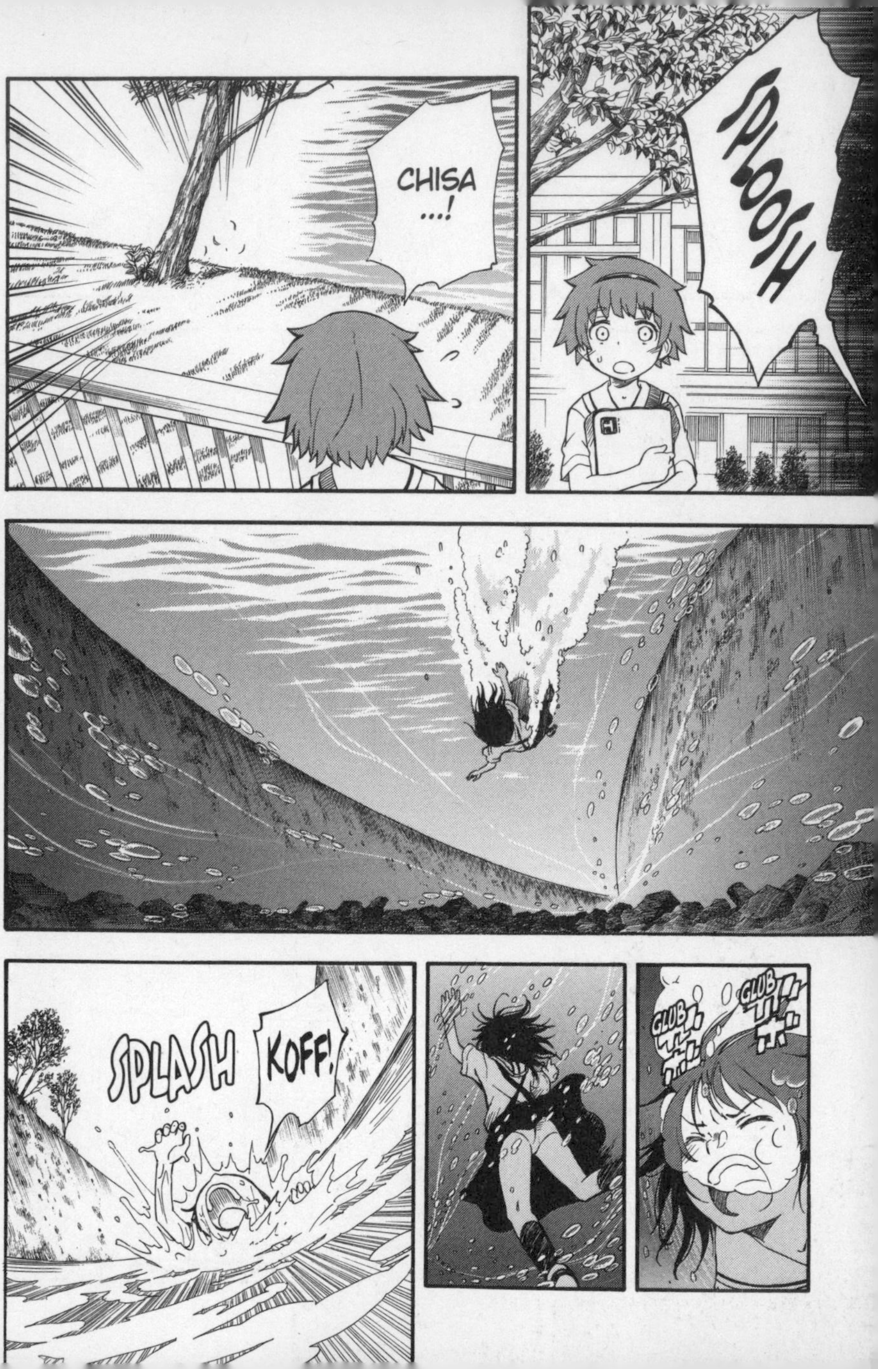
PLOOSH
CHISA ...!
GLUB
GLUB
SPLASH
KOFF!

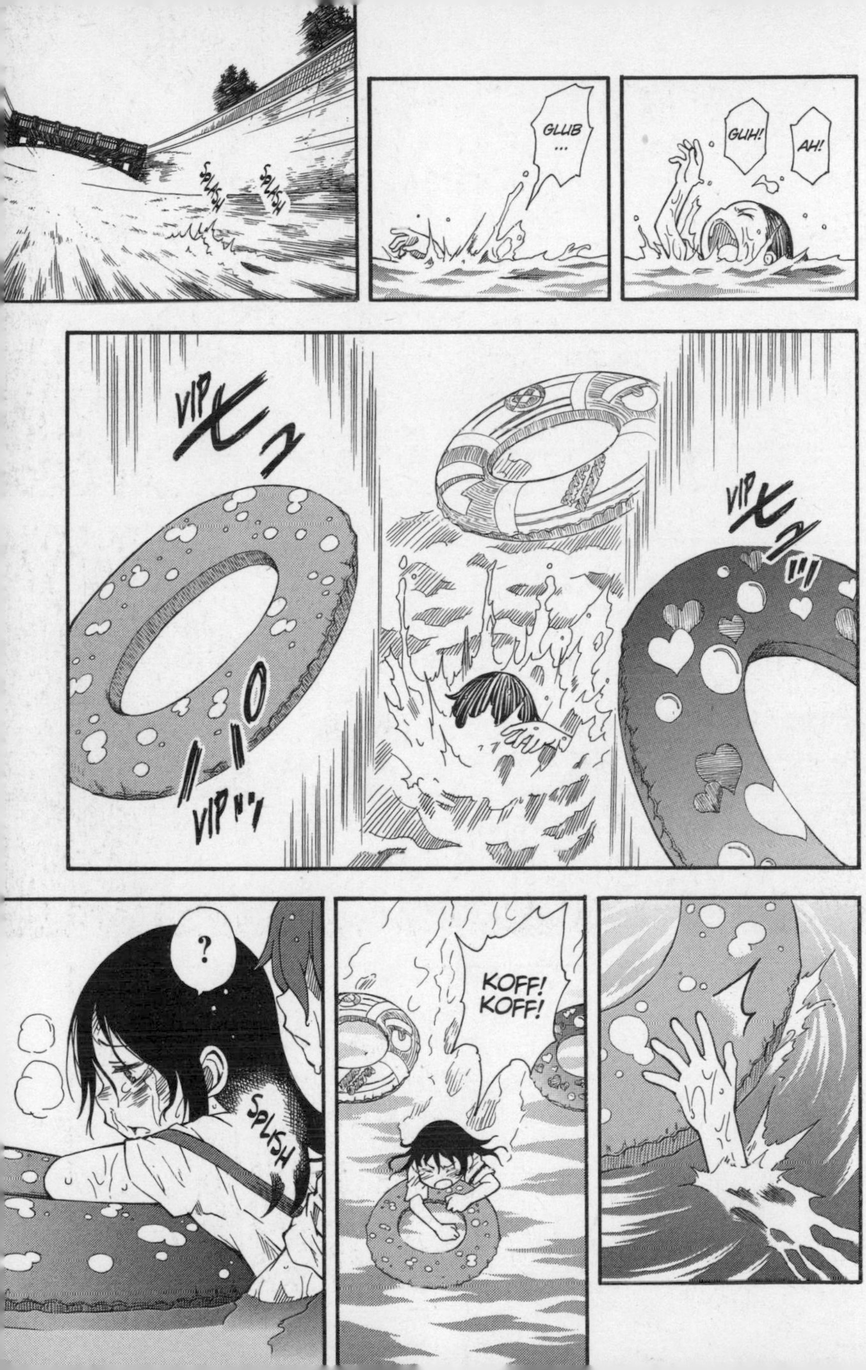

GUH!
AH!
GLUB ...
SPLASH
SPLASH
VIP
VIP
VIP
KOFF! KOFF!
?
SPLASH

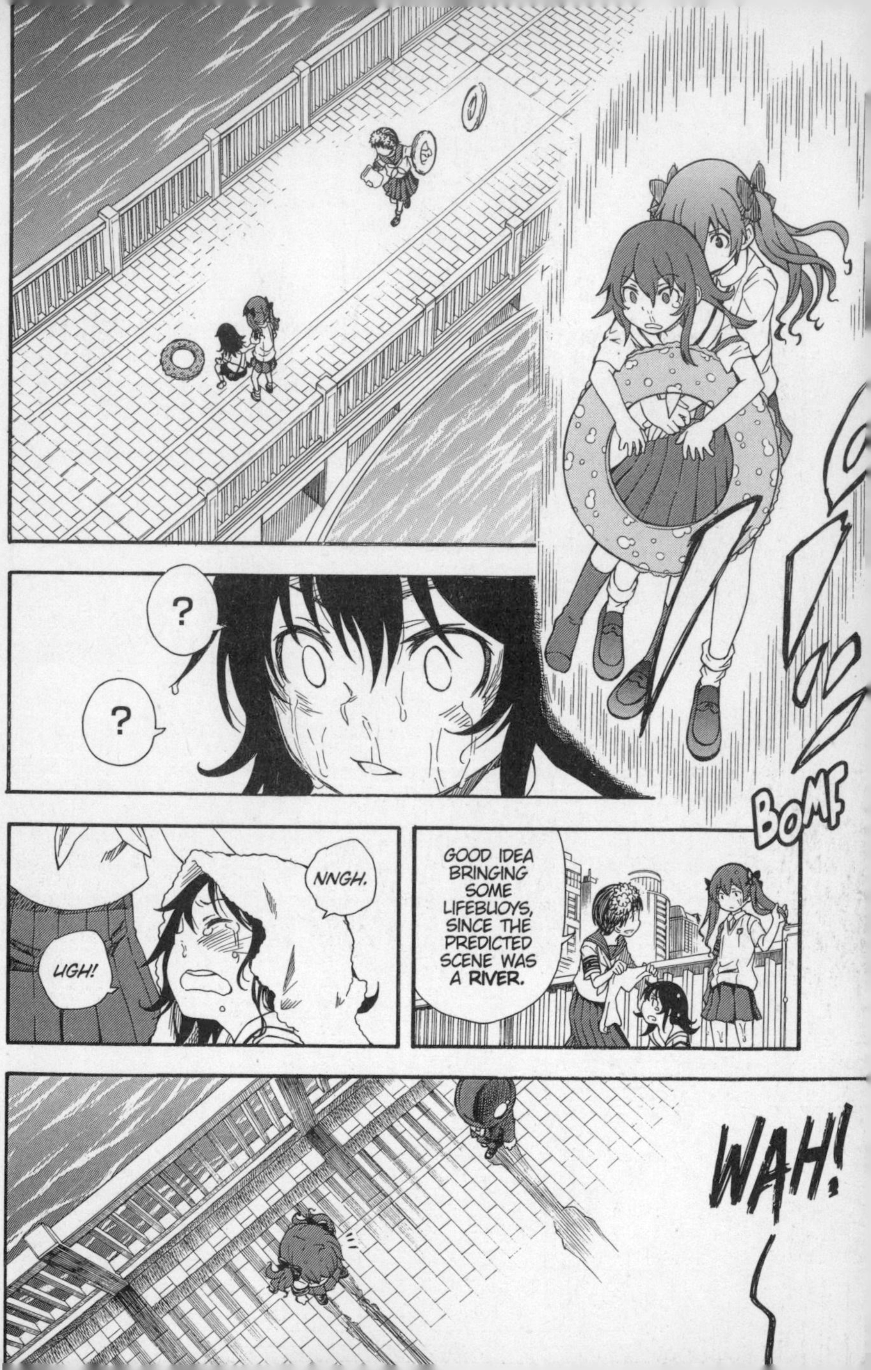

BOMF
?
?
GOOD IDEA BRINGING SOME LIFEBUOYS, SINCE THE PREDICTED SCENE WAS A **RIVER**.
NNGH.
UGH!
WAH!

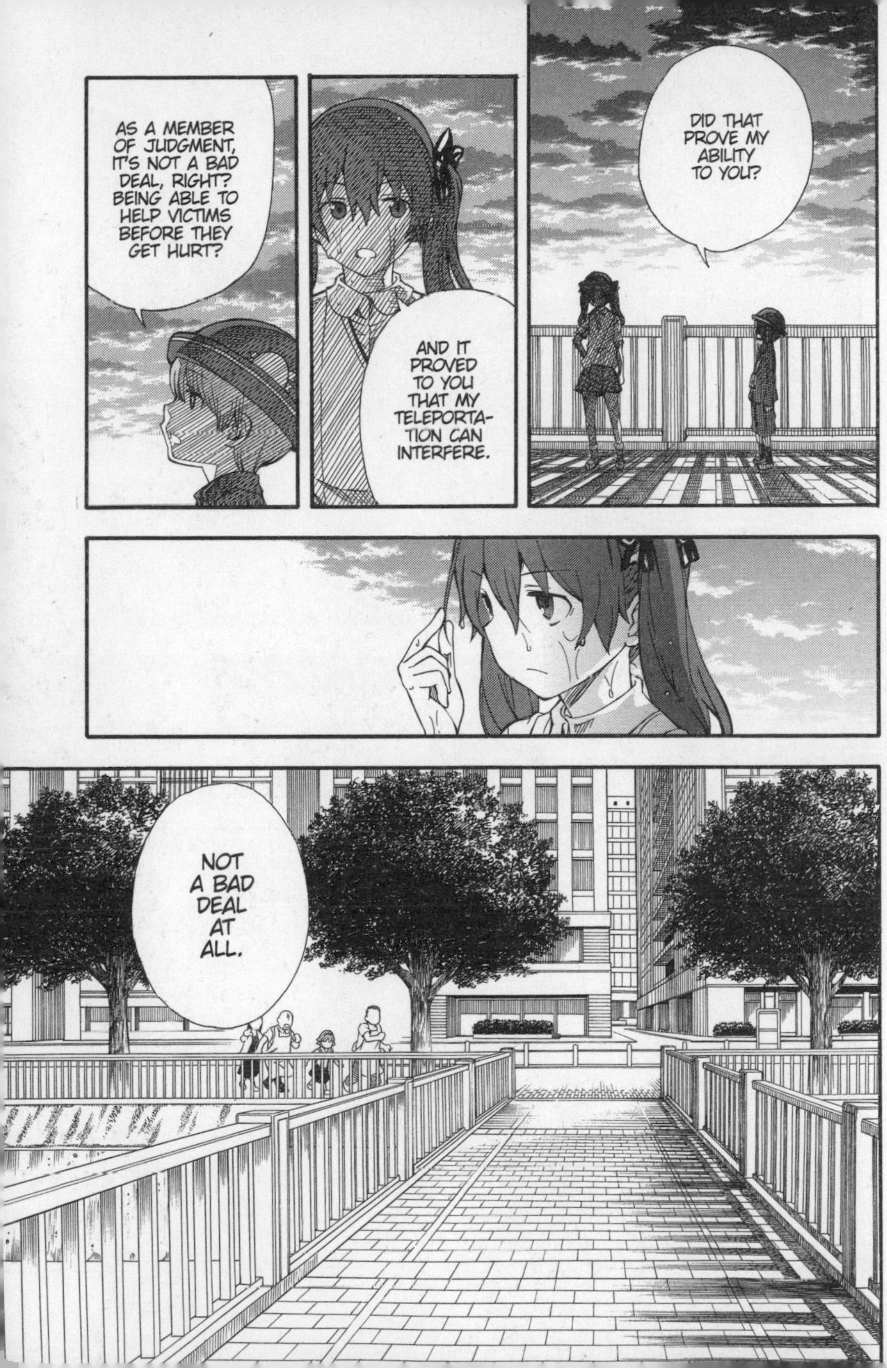
DID THAT PROVE MY ABILITY TO YOU?
AND IT PROVED TO YOU THAT MY TELEPORTATION CAN INTERFERE.
AS A MEMBER OF JUDGMENT, IT'S NOT A BAD DEAL, RIGHT? BEING ABLE TO HELP VICTIMS BEFORE THEY GET HURT?
NOT A BAD DEAL AT ALL.

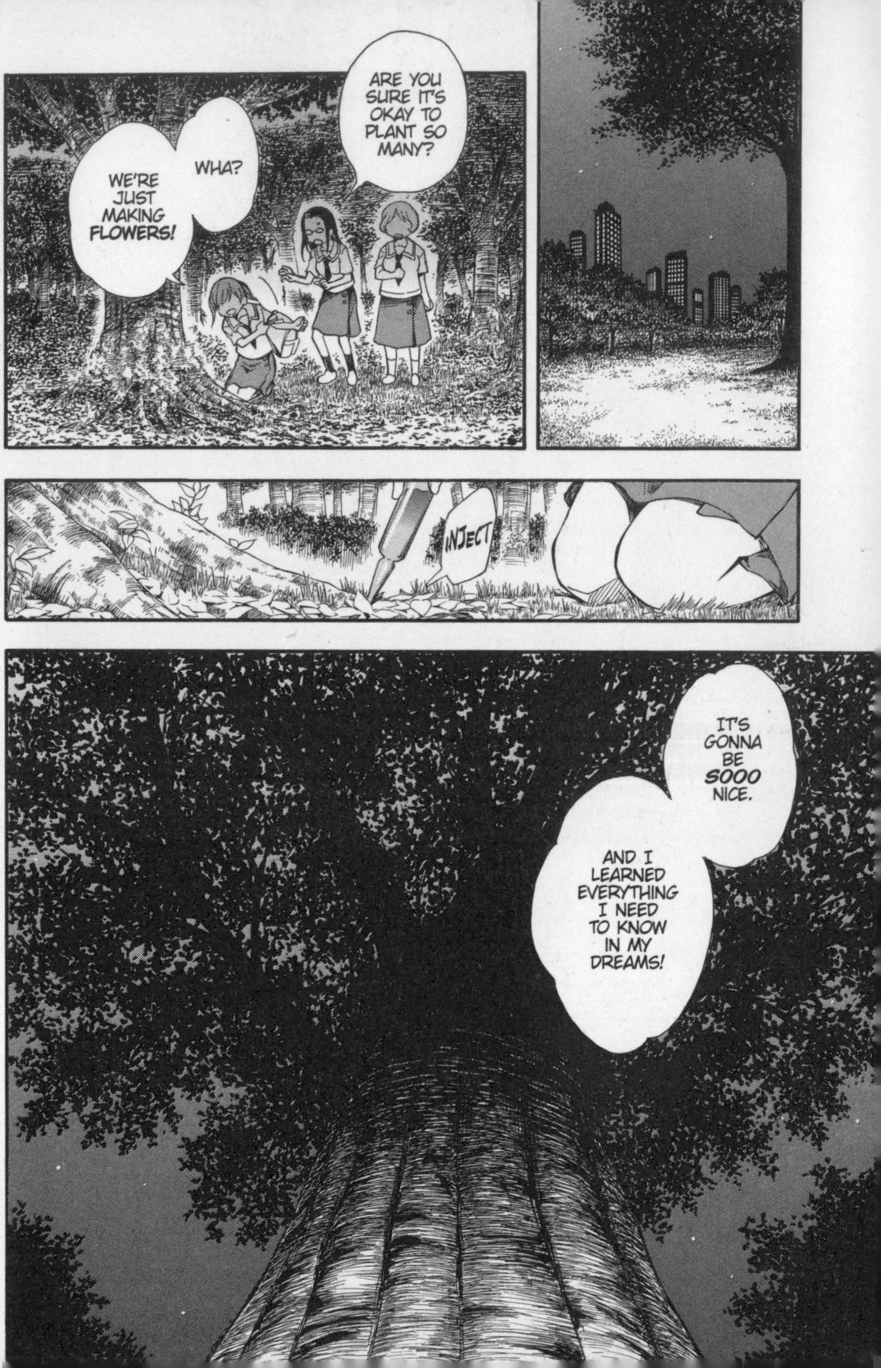
ARE YOU SURE IT'S OKAY TO PLANT SO MANY?
WHA?
WE'RE JUST MAKING FLOWERS!
INJECT
IT'S GONNA BE SOOO NICE.
AND I LEARNED EVERYTHING I NEED TO KNOW IN MY DREAMS!

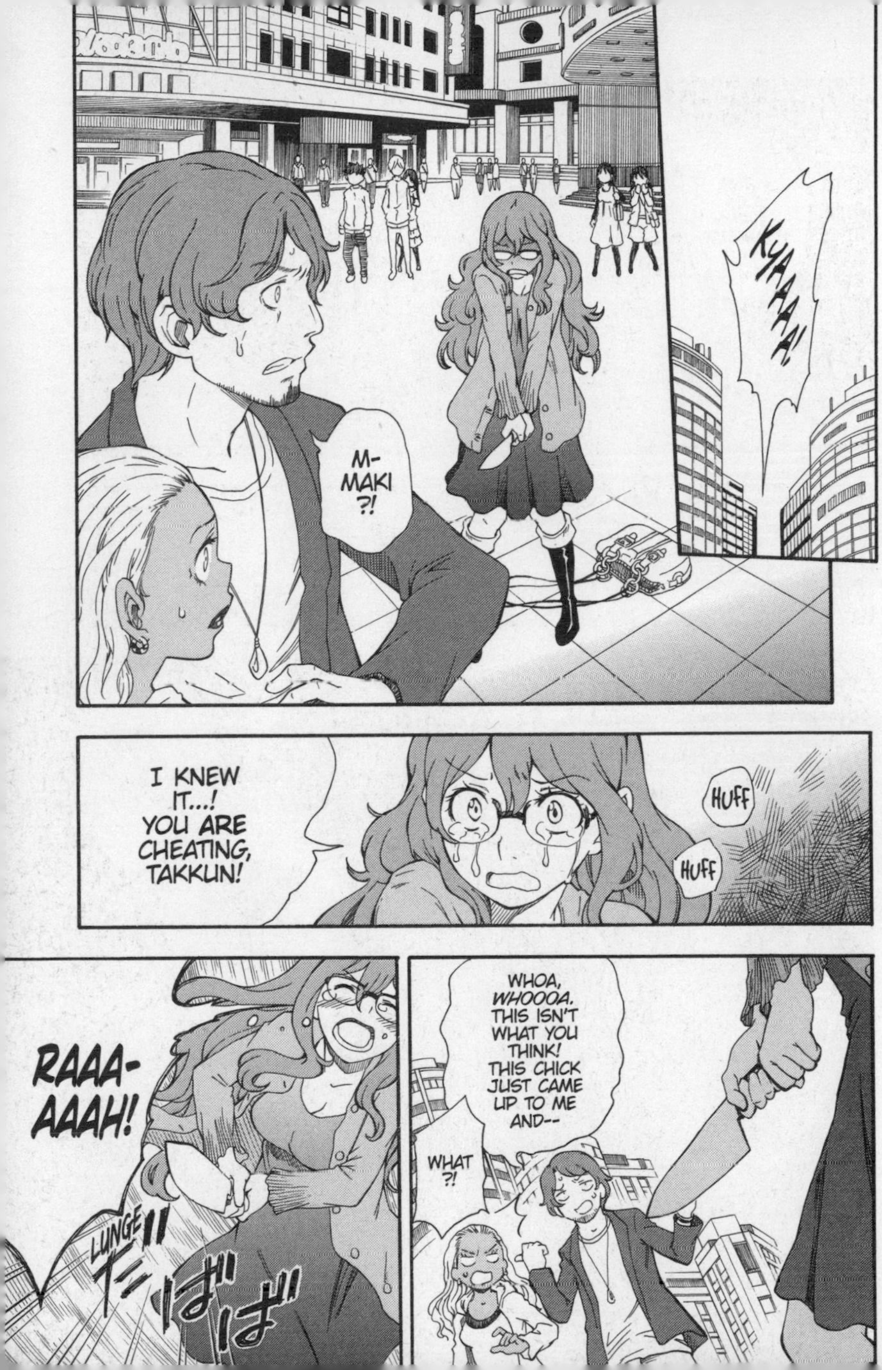
KYAAAA!
M-MAKI?!
HUFF
HUFF
I KNEW IT...! YOU ARE CHEATING, TAKKUN!
WHOA, WHOOOA. THIS ISN'T WHAT YOU THINK! THIS CHICK JUST CAME UP TO ME AND--
WHAT?!
RAAA-AAAH!
LUNGE

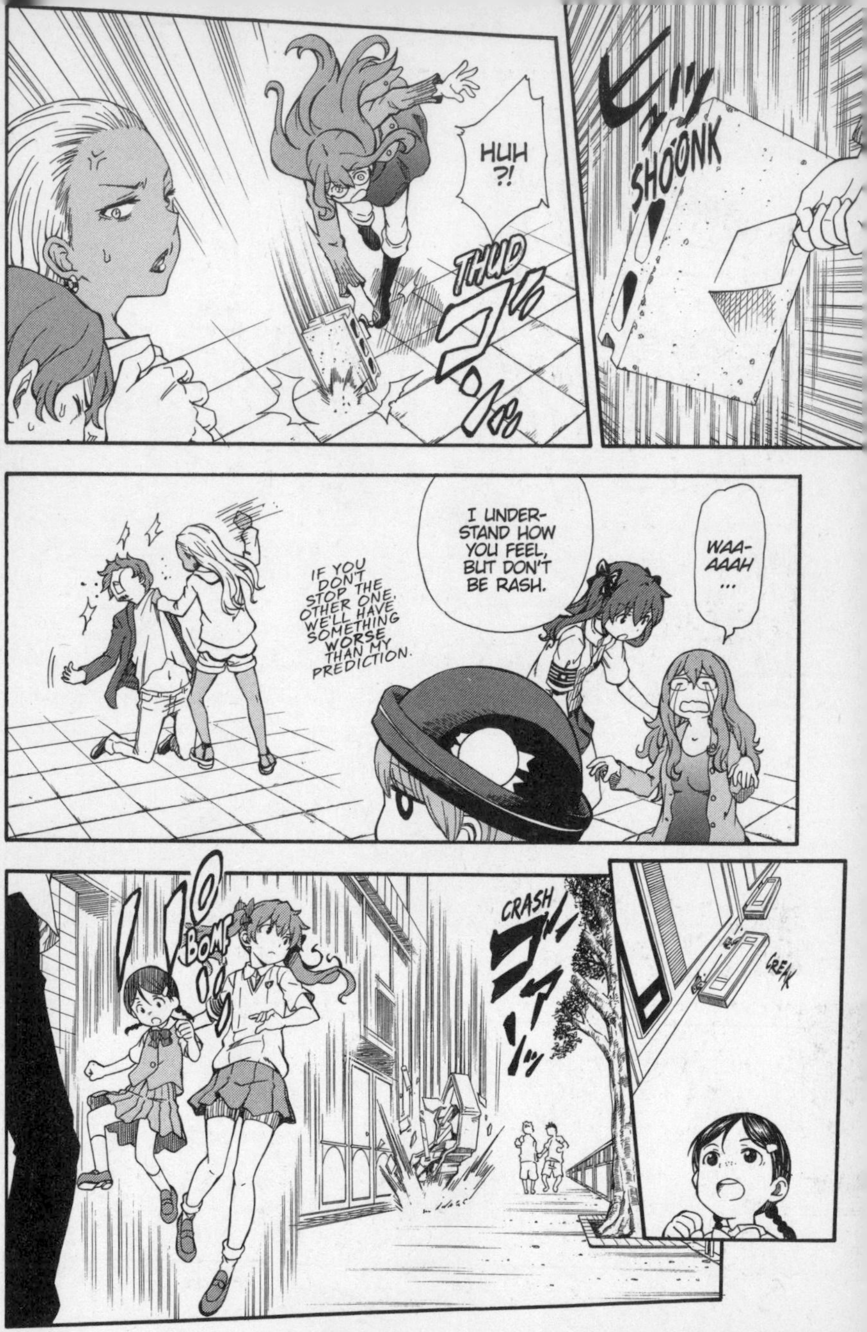
SHOONK
HUH ?!
THUD
WAA-AAAH ...
I UNDER-STAND HOW YOU FEEL, BUT DON'T BE RASH.
IF YOU DON'T STOP THE OTHER ONE, WE'LL HAVE SOMETHING WORSE THAN MY PREDICTION.
CREAK
CRASH
BOMF

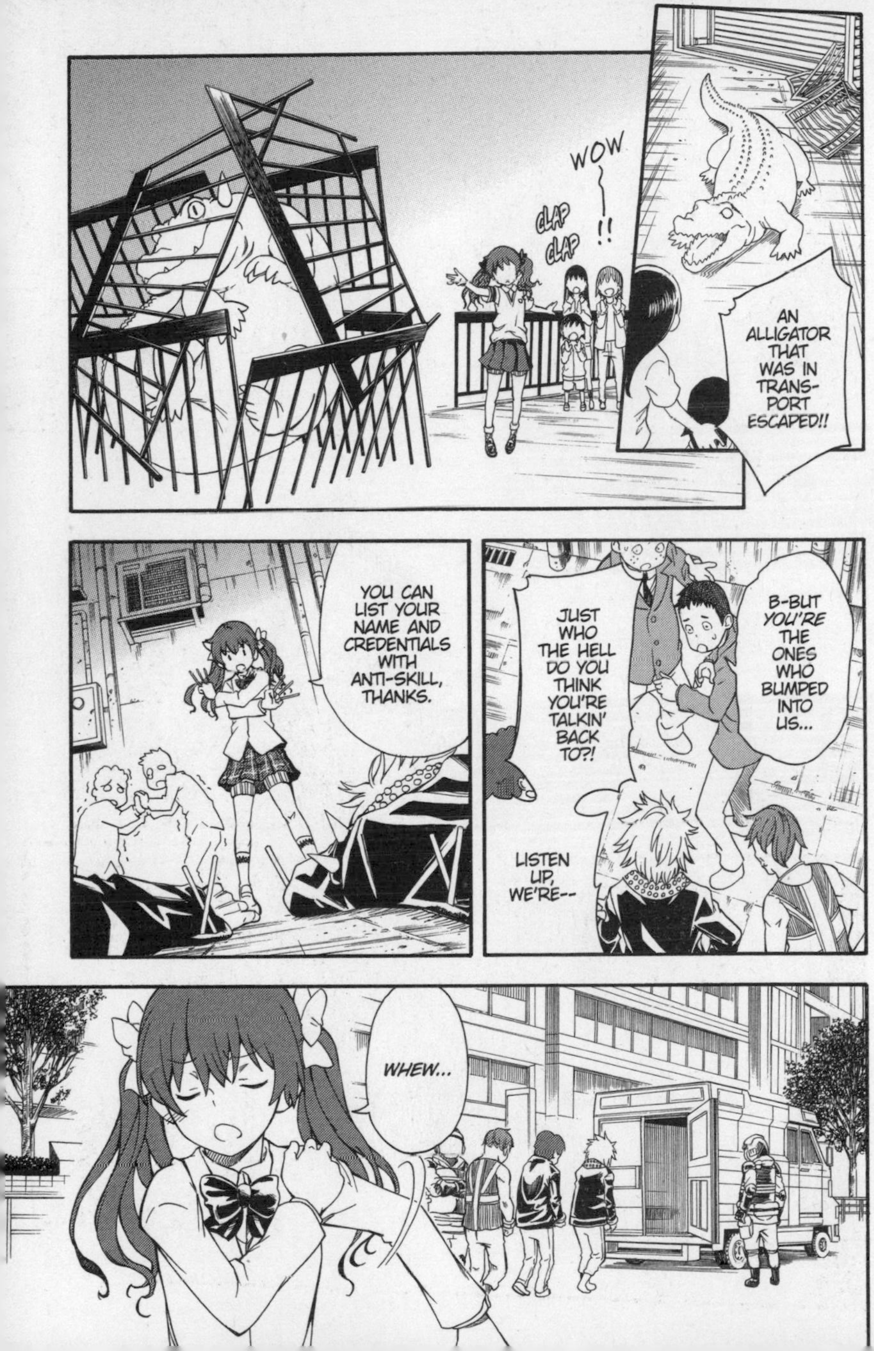
AN ALLIGATOR THAT WAS IN TRANSPORT ESCAPED!!
WOW ~ !!
CLAP CLAP
B-BUT *YOU'RE* THE ONES WHO BUMPED INTO US...
JUST WHO THE HELL DO YOU THINK YOU'RE TALKIN' BACK TO?!
LISTEN UP, WE'RE--
YOU CAN LIST YOUR NAME AND CREDENTIALS WITH ANTI-SKILL, THANKS.
WHEW...

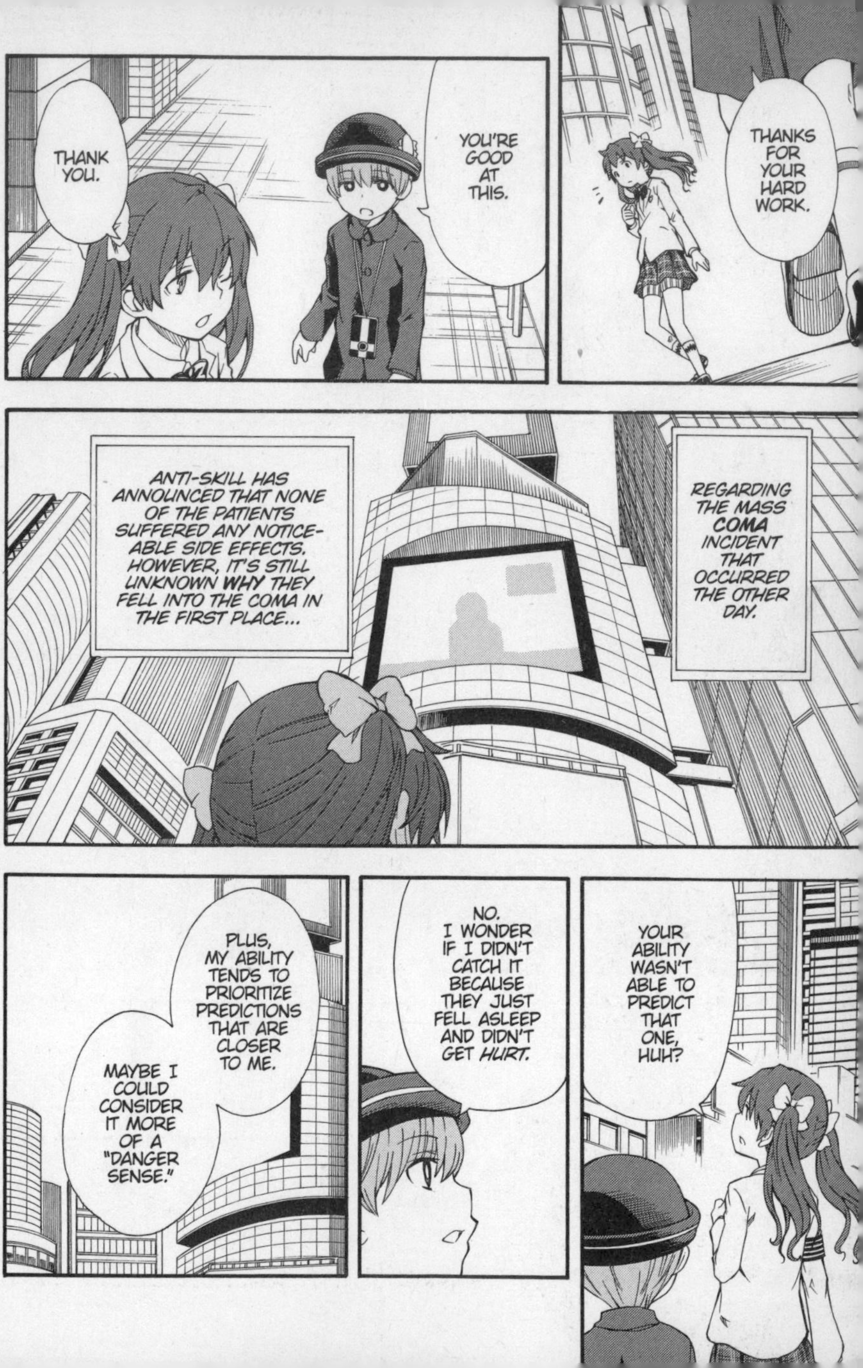
THANKS FOR YOUR HARD WORK.
YOU'RE GOOD AT THIS.
THANK YOU.
REGARDING THE MASS COMA INCIDENT THAT OCCURRED THE OTHER DAY.
ANTI-SKILL HAS ANNOUNCED THAT NONE OF THE PATIENTS SUFFERED ANY NOTICEABLE SIDE EFFECTS. HOWEVER, IT'S STILL UNKNOWN WHY THEY FELL INTO THE COMA IN THE FIRST PLACE...
YOUR ABILITY WASN'T ABLE TO PREDICT THAT ONE, HUH?
NO. I WONDER IF I DIDN'T CATCH IT BECAUSE THEY JUST FELL ASLEEP AND DIDN'T GET HURT.
PLUS, MY ABILITY TENDS TO PRIORITIZE PREDICTIONS THAT ARE CLOSER TO ME.
MAYBE I COULD CONSIDER IT MORE OF A "DANGER SENSE."

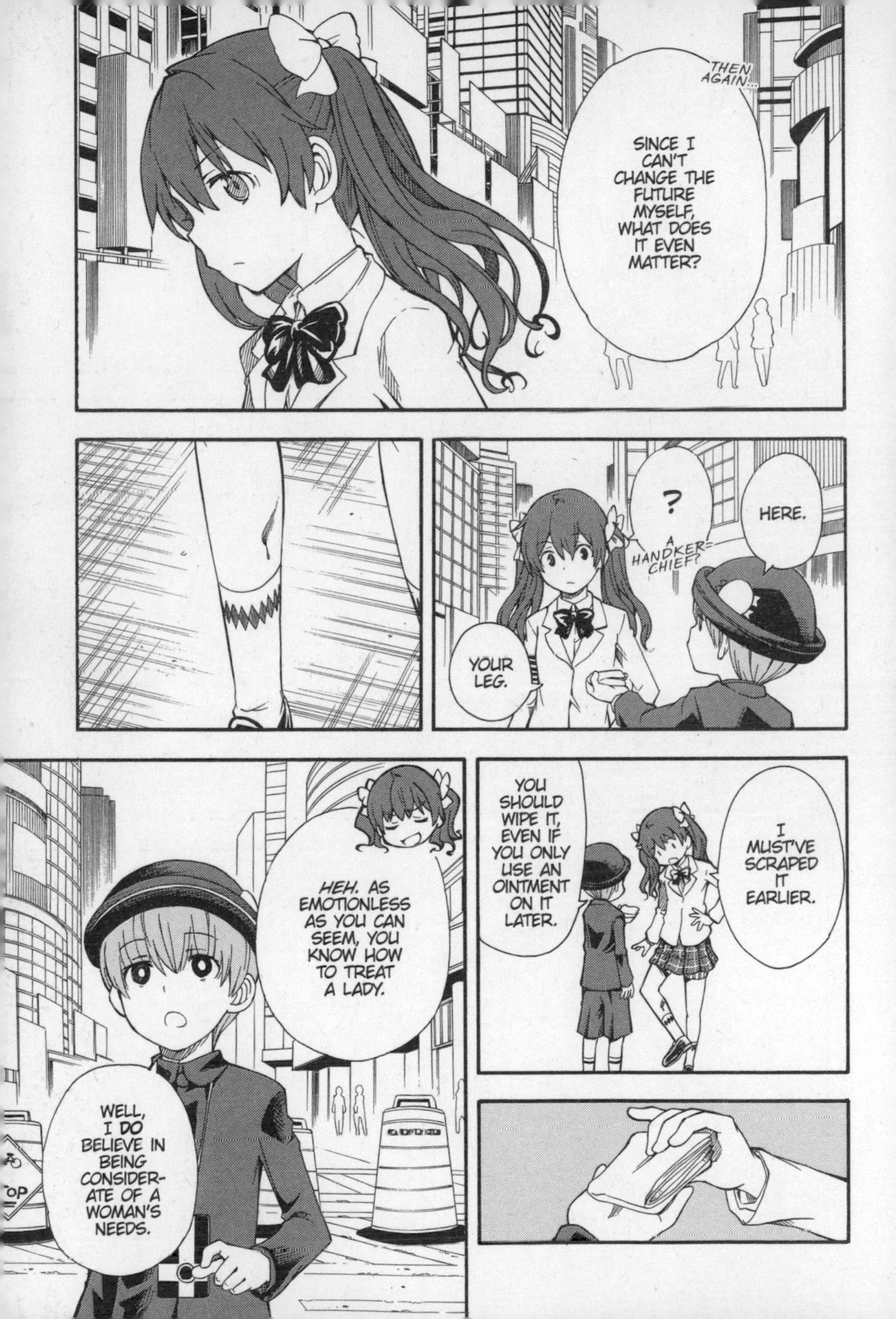
THEN AGAIN...
SINCE I CAN'T CHANGE THE FUTURE MYSELF, WHAT DOES IT EVEN MATTER?
HERE.
?
A HANDKER-CHIEF?
YOUR LEG.
I MUST'VE SCRAPED IT EARLIER.
YOU SHOULD WIPE IT, EVEN IF YOU ONLY USE AN OINTMENT ON IT LATER.
HEH. AS EMOTIONLESS AS YOU CAN SEEM, YOU KNOW HOW TO TREAT A LADY.
WELL, I DO BELIEVE IN BEING CONSIDER-ATE OF A WOMAN'S NEEDS.

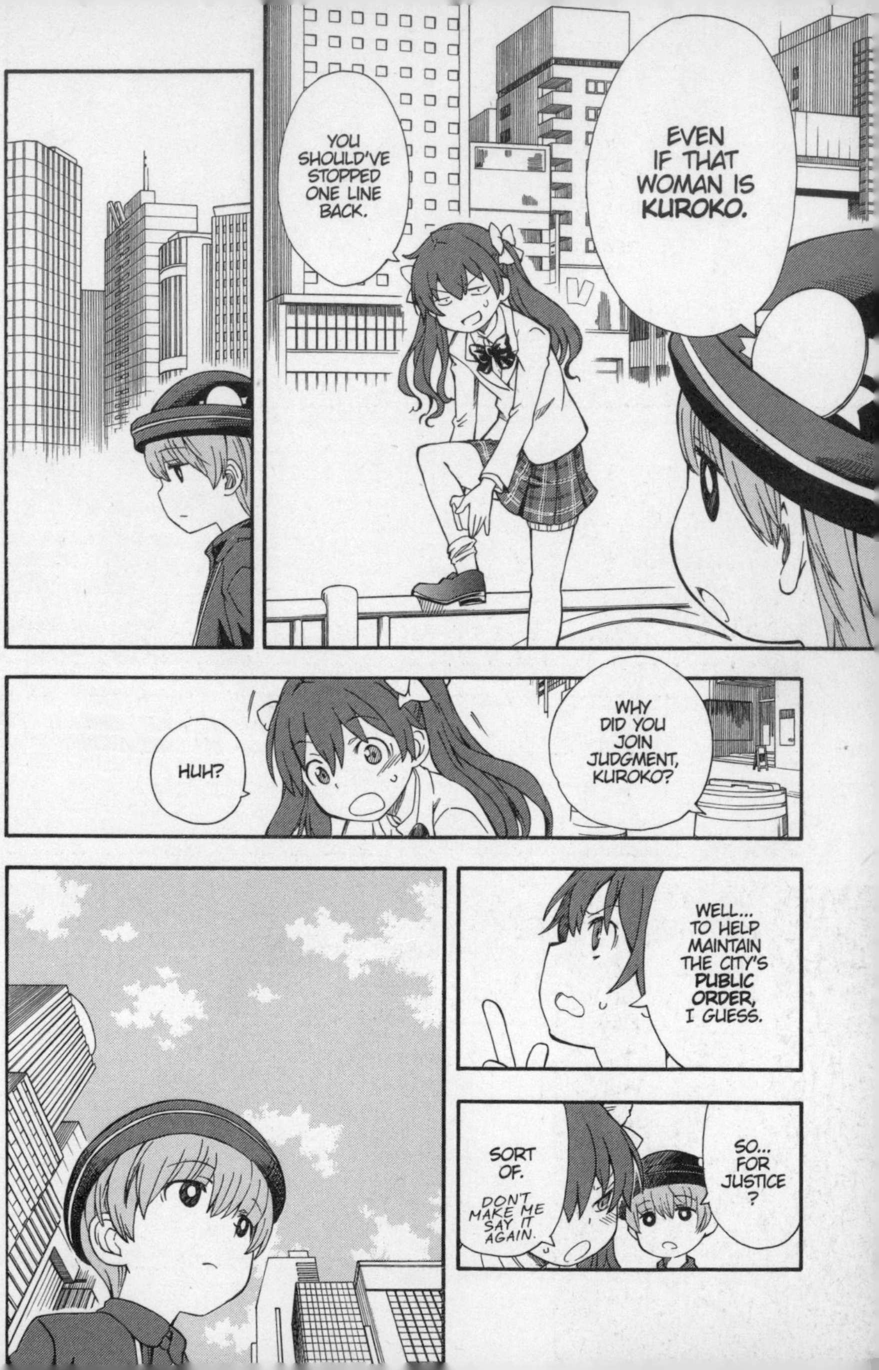
EVEN IF THAT WOMAN IS KUROKO.
YOU SHOULD'VE STOPPED ONE LINE BACK.
WHY DID YOU JOIN JUDGMENT, KUROKO?
HUH?
WELL... TO HELP MAINTAIN THE CITY'S PUBLIC ORDER, I GUESS.
SO... FOR JUSTICE?
SORT OF.
DON'T MAKE ME SAY IT AGAIN.

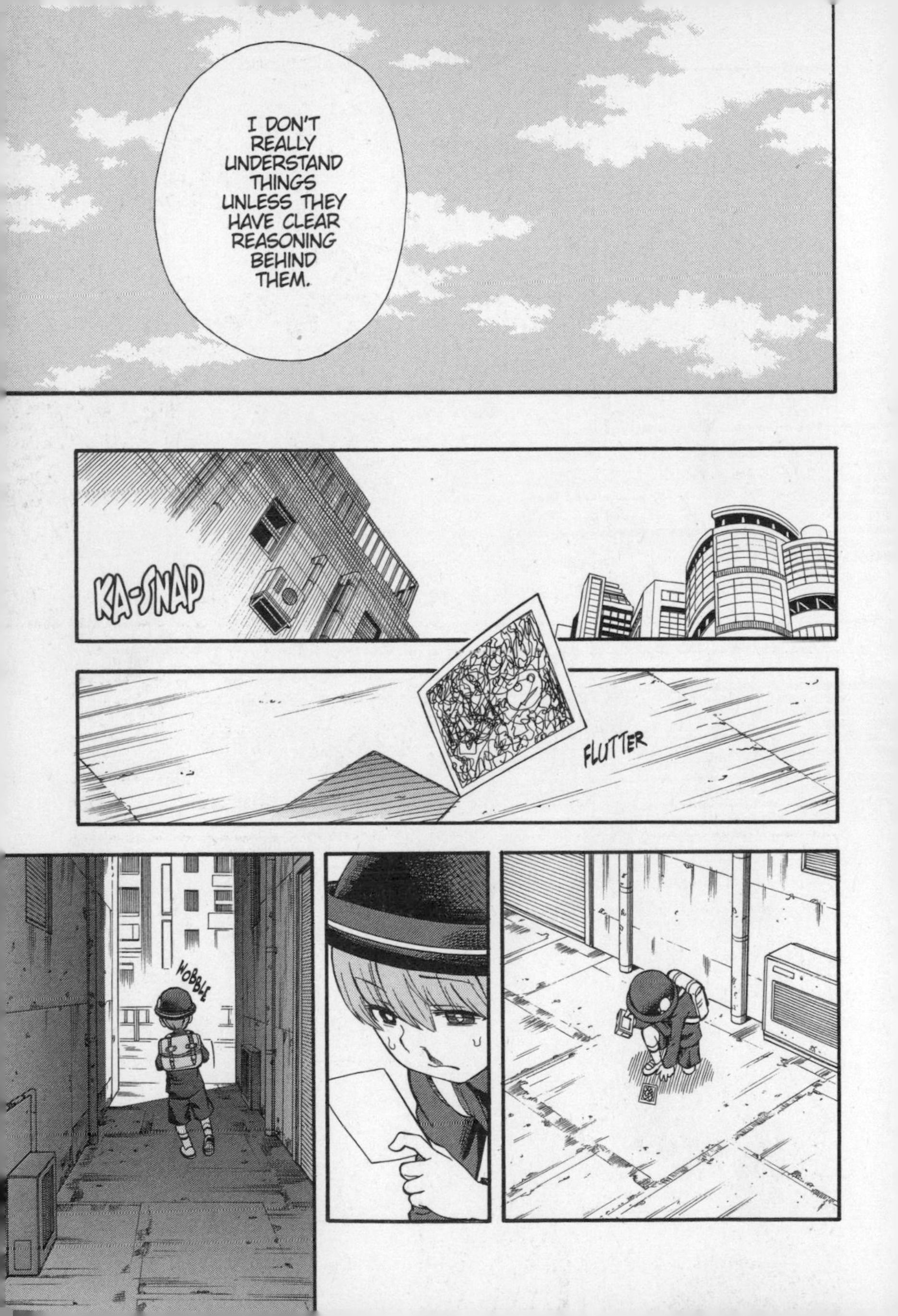
I DON'T REALLY UNDERSTAND THINGS UNLESS THEY HAVE CLEAR REASONING BEHIND THEM.
KA-SNAP
FLUTTER
WOBBLE

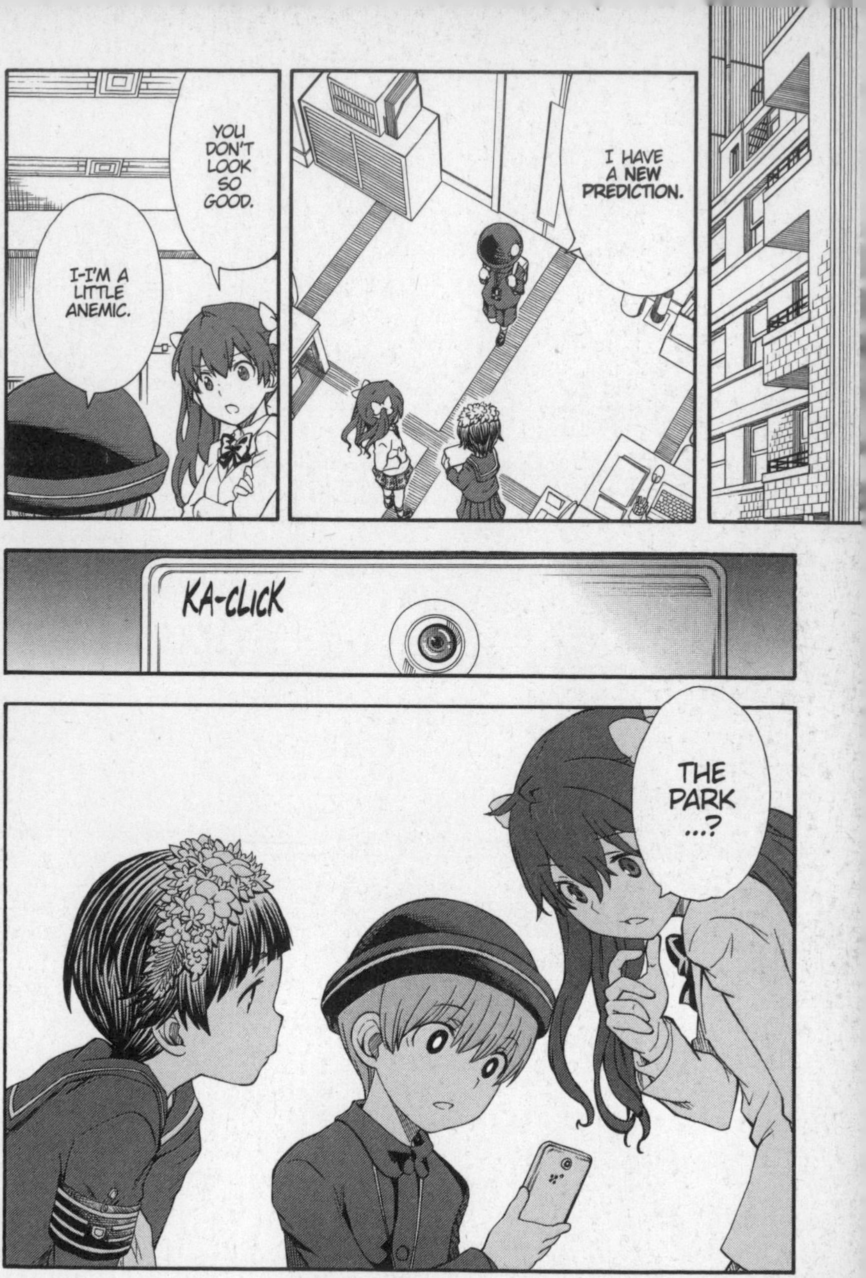
I HAVE A NEW PREDICTION.
YOU DON'T LOOK SO GOOD.
I-I'M A LITTLE ANEMIC.
KA-CLICK
THE PARK ...?

A Certain
SCIENTIFIC
Railgun

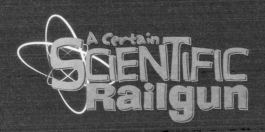

A Certain SCIENTIFIC Railgun

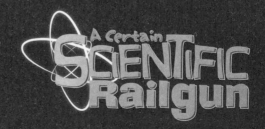

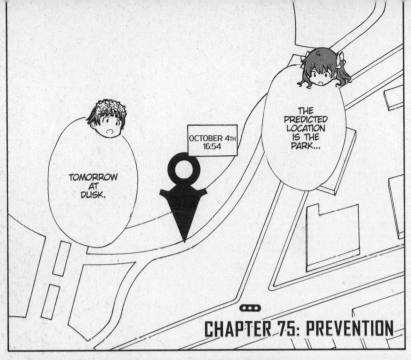

THE PREDICTED LOCATION IS THE PARK...

OCTOBER 4TH 16:54

TOMORROW AT DUSK.

CHAPTER 75: PREVENTION

LOOK.

WHAT'S WRONG, MIYAMA?

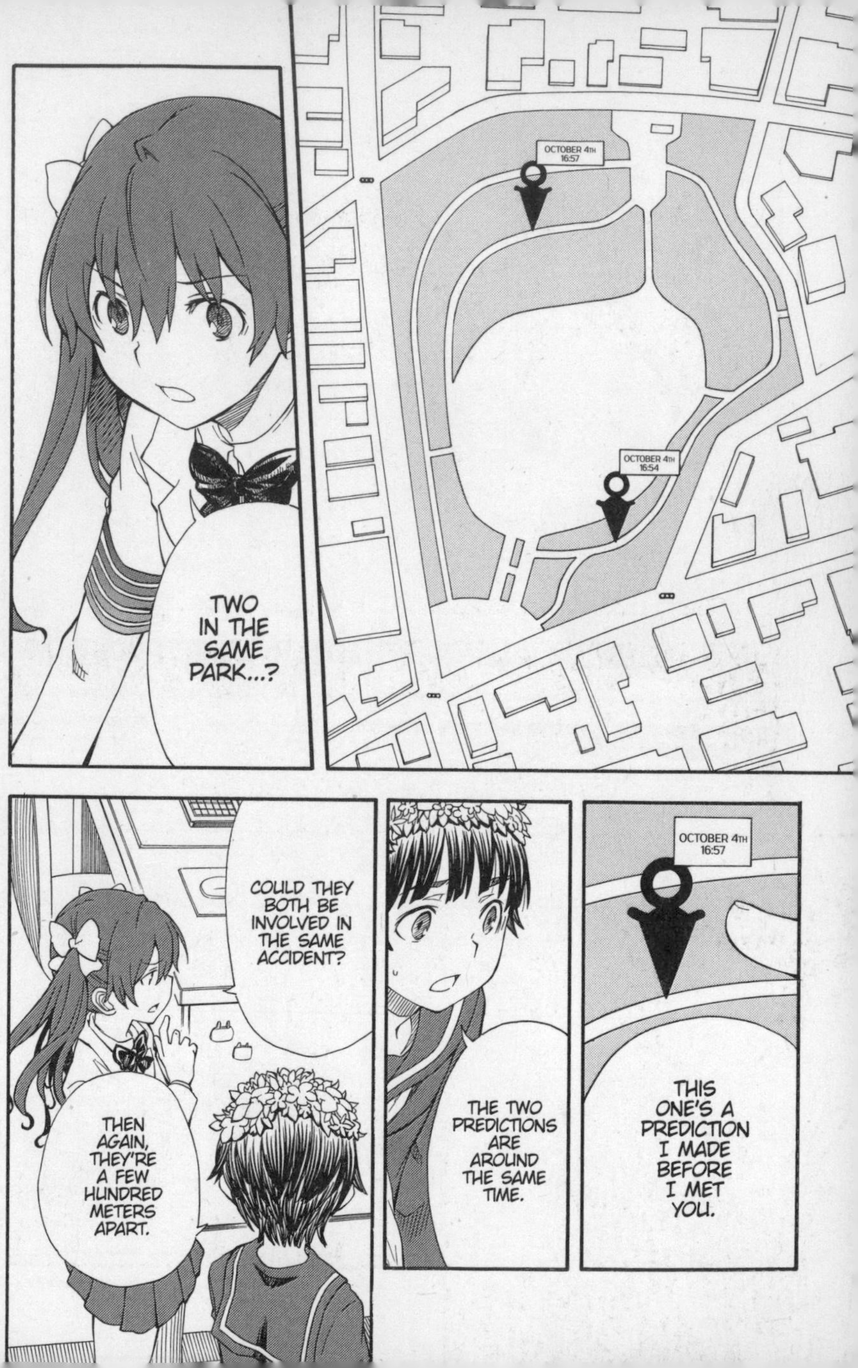
OCTOBER 4TH 16:57
OCTOBER 4TH 16:54
TWO IN THE SAME PARK...?
OCTOBER 4TH 16:57
THIS ONE'S A PREDICTION I MADE BEFORE I MET YOU.
THE TWO PREDICTIONS ARE AROUND THE SAME TIME.
COULD THEY BOTH BE INVOLVED IN THE SAME ACCIDENT?
THEN AGAIN, THEY'RE A FEW HUNDRED METERS APART.

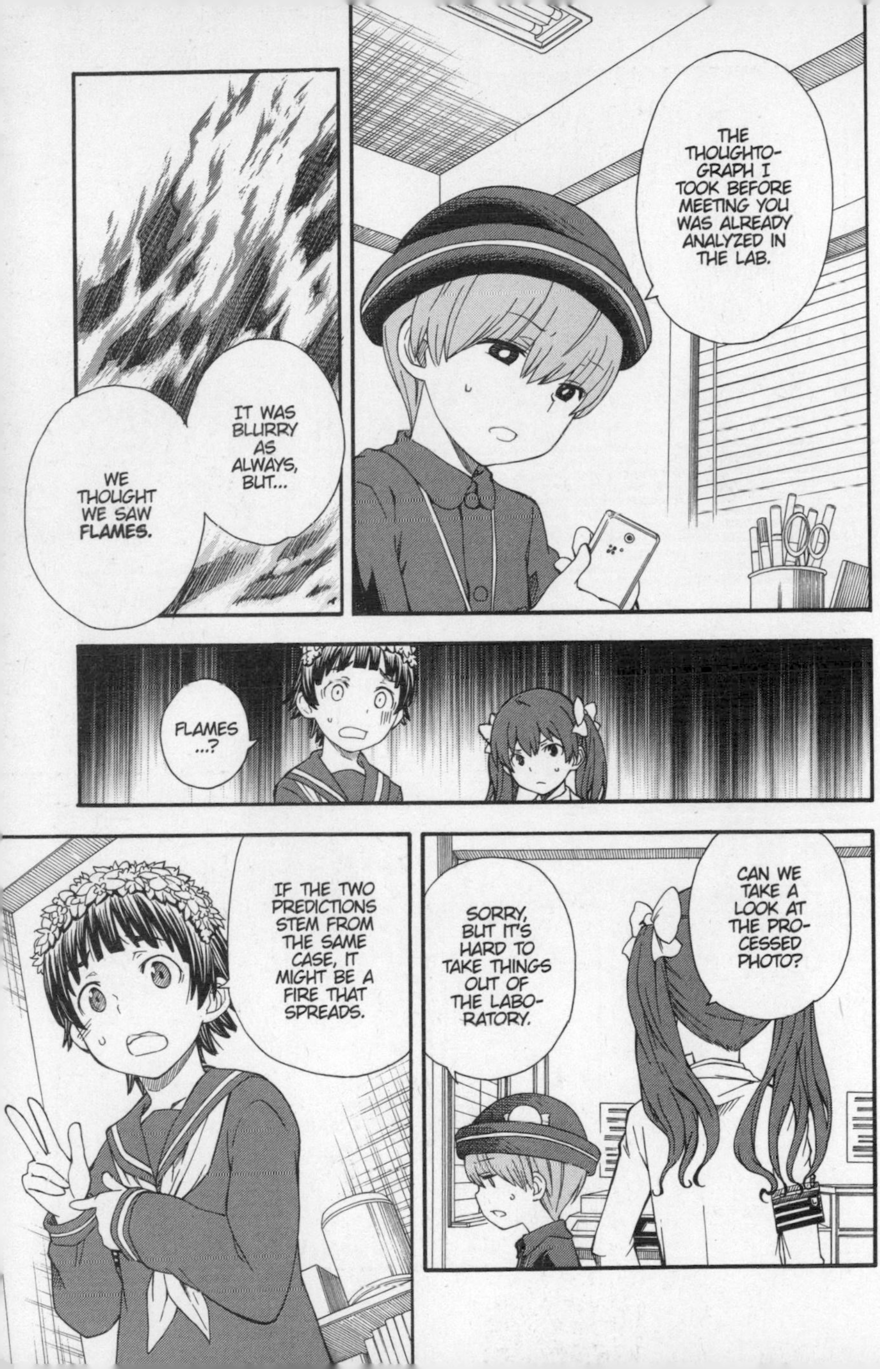
THE THOUGHTOGRAPH I TOOK BEFORE MEETING YOU WAS ALREADY ANALYZED IN THE LAB.
IT WAS BLURRY AS ALWAYS, BUT...
WE THOUGHT WE SAW FLAMES.
FLAMES ...?
CAN WE TAKE A LOOK AT THE PROCESSED PHOTO?
SORRY, BUT IT'S HARD TO TAKE THINGS OUT OF THE LABORATORY.
IF THE TWO PREDICTIONS STEM FROM THE SAME CASE, IT MIGHT BE A FIRE THAT SPREADS.

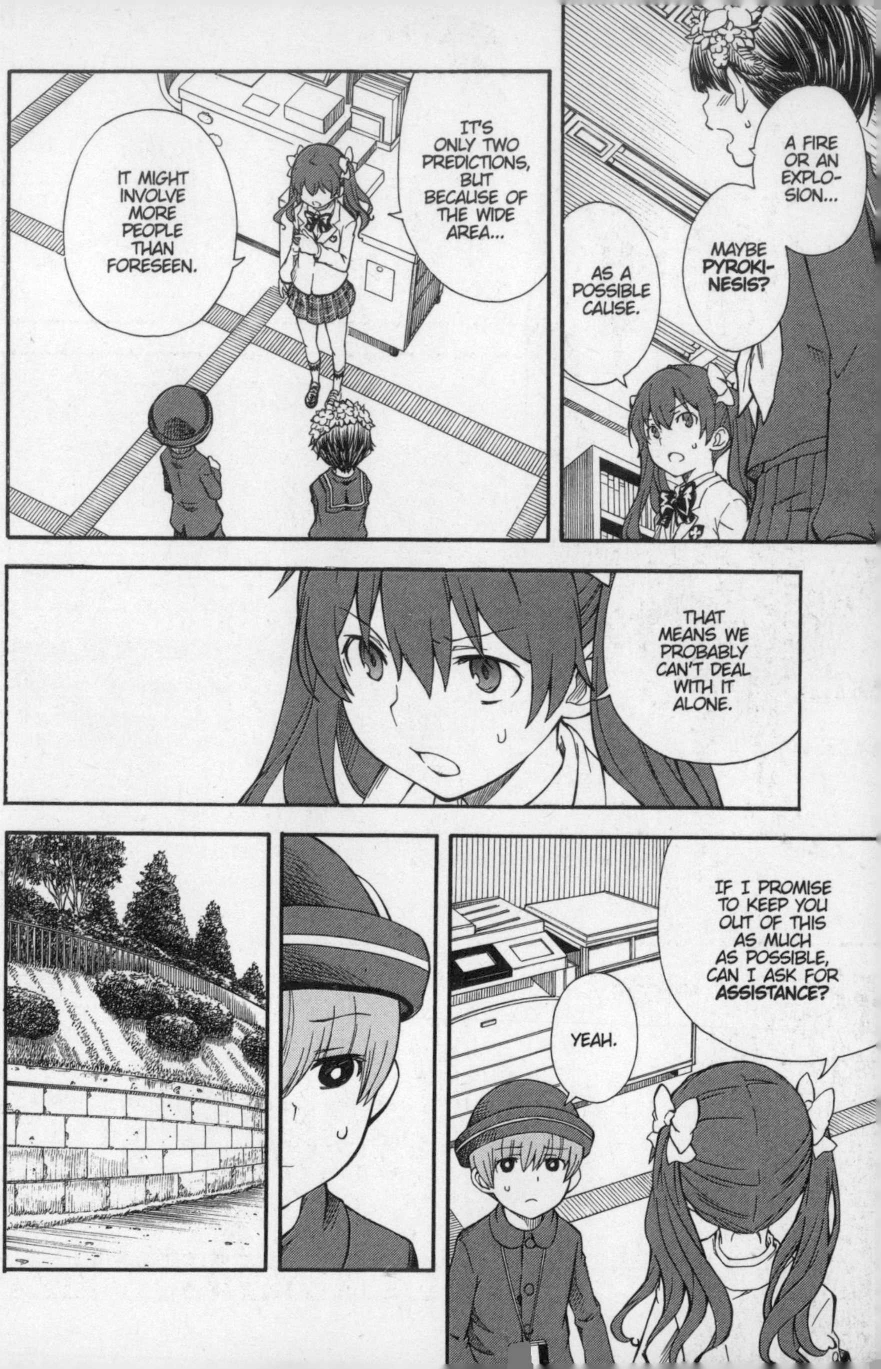
A FIRE OR AN EXPLOSION...
MAYBE PYROKINESIS?
AS A POSSIBLE CAUSE.
IT'S ONLY TWO PREDICTIONS, BUT BECAUSE OF THE WIDE AREA...
IT MIGHT INVOLVE MORE PEOPLE THAN FORESEEN.
THAT MEANS WE PROBABLY CAN'T DEAL WITH IT ALONE.
IF I PROMISE TO KEEP YOU OUT OF THIS AS MUCH AS POSSIBLE, CAN I ASK FOR ASSISTANCE?
YEAH.

EXCUSE ME~!

IT'S CRIME PREVENTION MONTH, SO~...

MAY WE PLEASE SEE YOUR STUDENT I.D.?

THANK YOU VERY MUCH.

HERE.

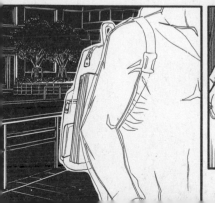

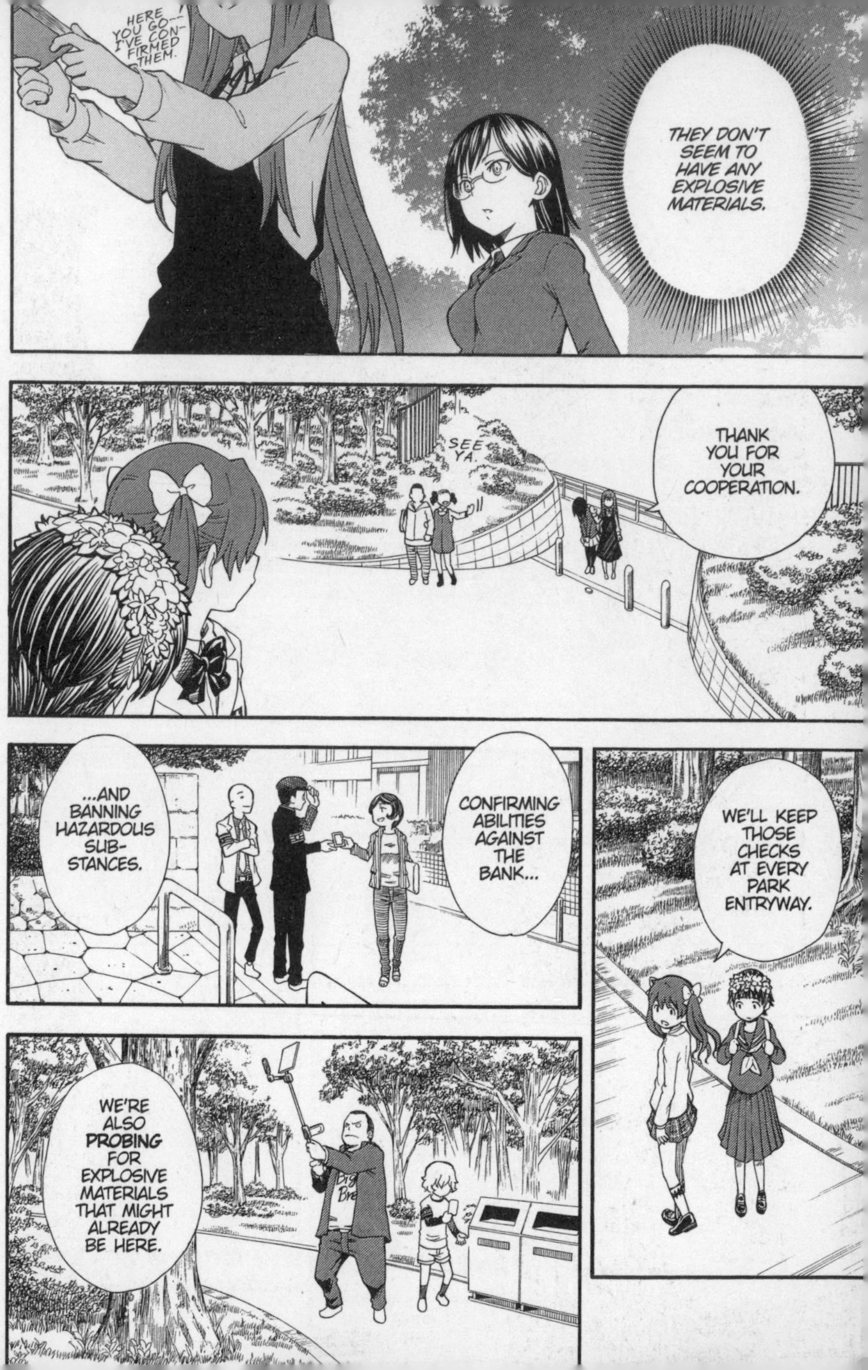
HERE YOU GO-- I'VE CONFIRMED THEM.
THEY DON'T SEEM TO HAVE ANY EXPLOSIVE MATERIALS.
THANK YOU FOR YOUR COOPERATION.
SEE YA.
WE'LL KEEP THOSE CHECKS AT EVERY PARK ENTRYWAY.
CONFIRMING ABILITIES AGAINST THE BANK...
...AND BANNING HAZARDOUS SUBSTANCES.
WE'RE ALSO PROBING FOR EXPLOSIVE MATERIALS THAT MIGHT ALREADY BE HERE.

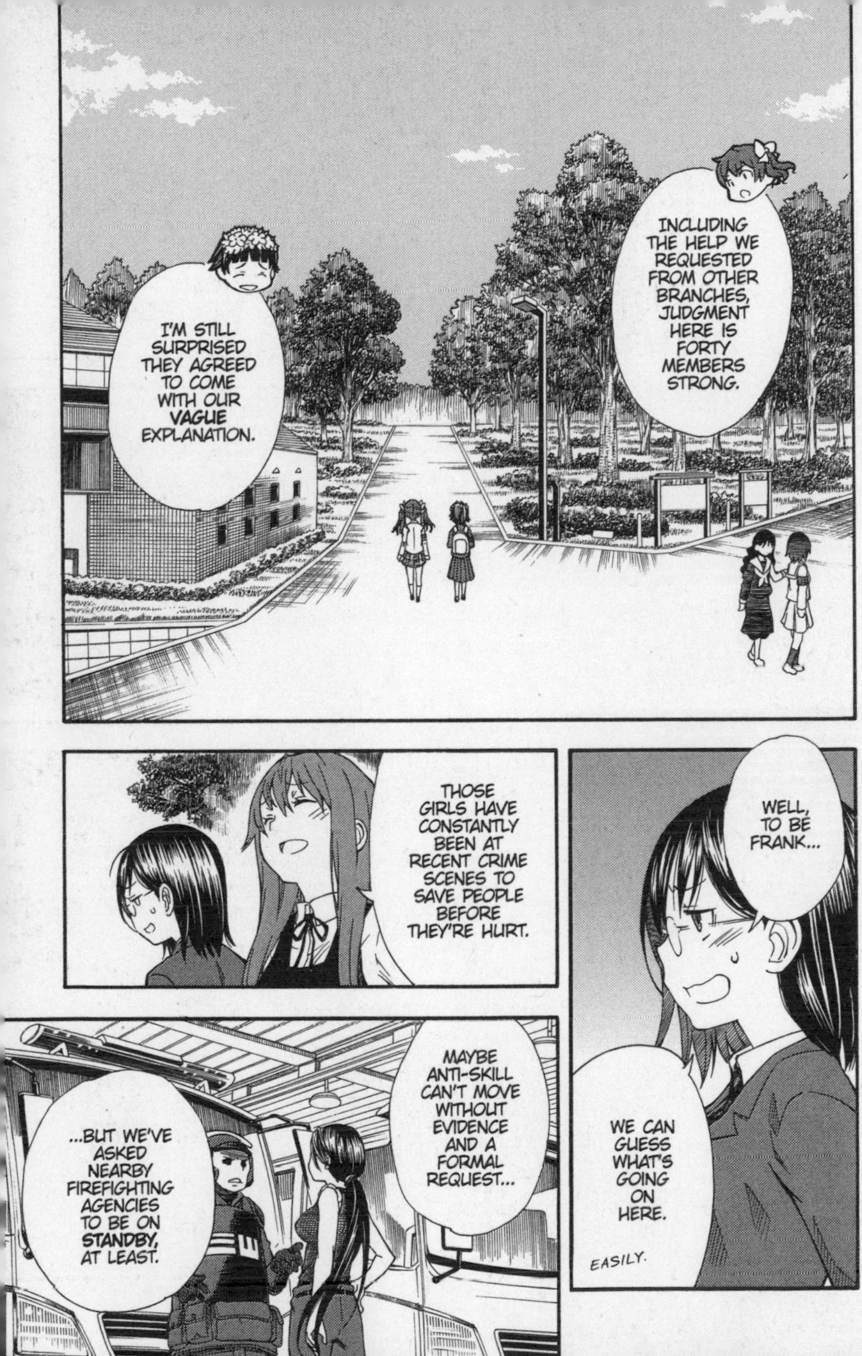
INCLUDING THE HELP WE REQUESTED FROM OTHER BRANCHES, JUDGMENT HERE IS FORTY MEMBERS STRONG.
I'M STILL SURPRISED THEY AGREED TO COME WITH OUR VAGUE EXPLANATION.
WELL, TO BE FRANK...
WE CAN GUESS WHAT'S GOING ON HERE.
EASILY.
THOSE GIRLS HAVE CONSTANTLY BEEN AT RECENT CRIME SCENES TO SAVE PEOPLE BEFORE THEY'RE HURT.
MAYBE ANTI-SKILL CAN'T MOVE WITHOUT EVIDENCE AND A FORMAL REQUEST...
...BUT WE'VE ASKED NEARBY FIREFIGHTING AGENCIES TO BE ON STANDBY, AT LEAST.

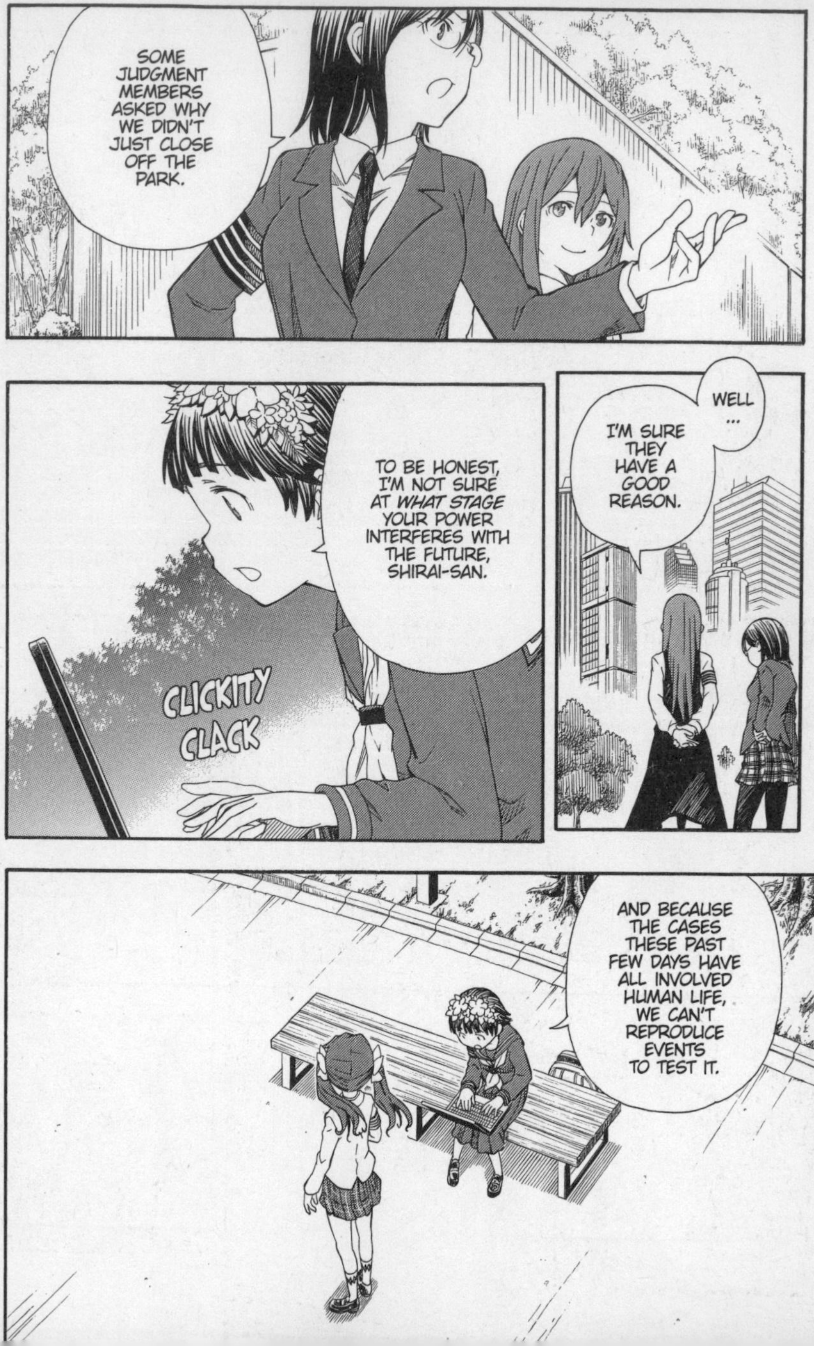
SOME JUDGMENT MEMBERS ASKED WHY WE DIDN'T JUST CLOSE OFF THE PARK.
WELL ...
I'M SURE THEY HAVE A GOOD REASON.
TO BE HONEST, I'M NOT SURE AT *WHAT STAGE* YOUR POWER INTERFERES WITH THE FUTURE, SHIRAI-SAN.
CLICKITY CLACK
AND BECAUSE THE CASES THESE PAST FEW DAYS HAVE ALL INVOLVED HUMAN LIFE, WE CAN'T REPRODUCE EVENTS TO TEST IT.

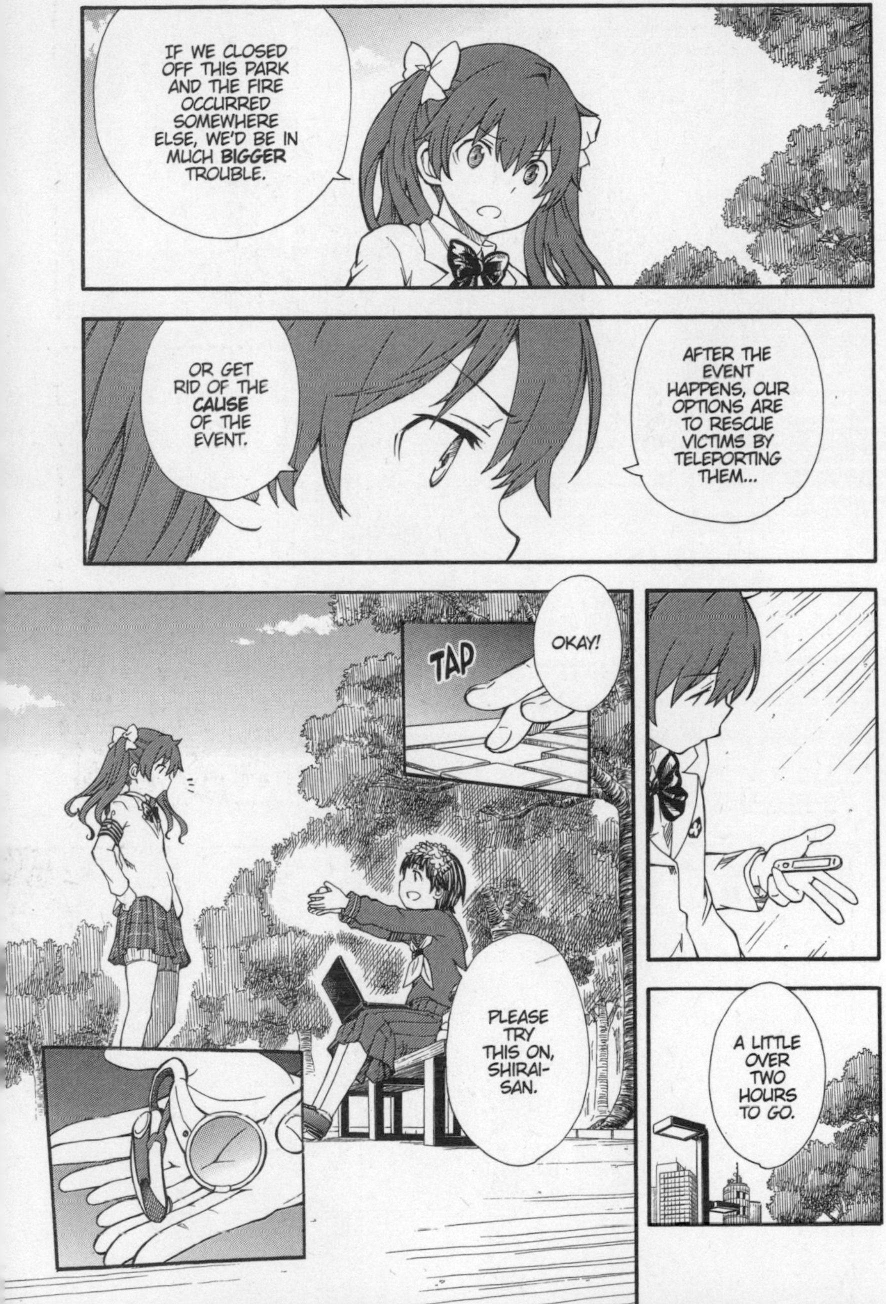
IF WE CLOSED OFF THIS PARK AND THE FIRE OCCURRED SOMEWHERE ELSE, WE'D BE IN MUCH BIGGER TROUBLE.
AFTER THE EVENT HAPPENS, OUR OPTIONS ARE TO RESCUE VICTIMS BY TELEPORTING THEM...
OR GET RID OF THE CAUSE OF THE EVENT.
A LITTLE OVER TWO HOURS TO GO.
OKAY!
TAP
PLEASE TRY THIS ON, SHIRAI-SAN.

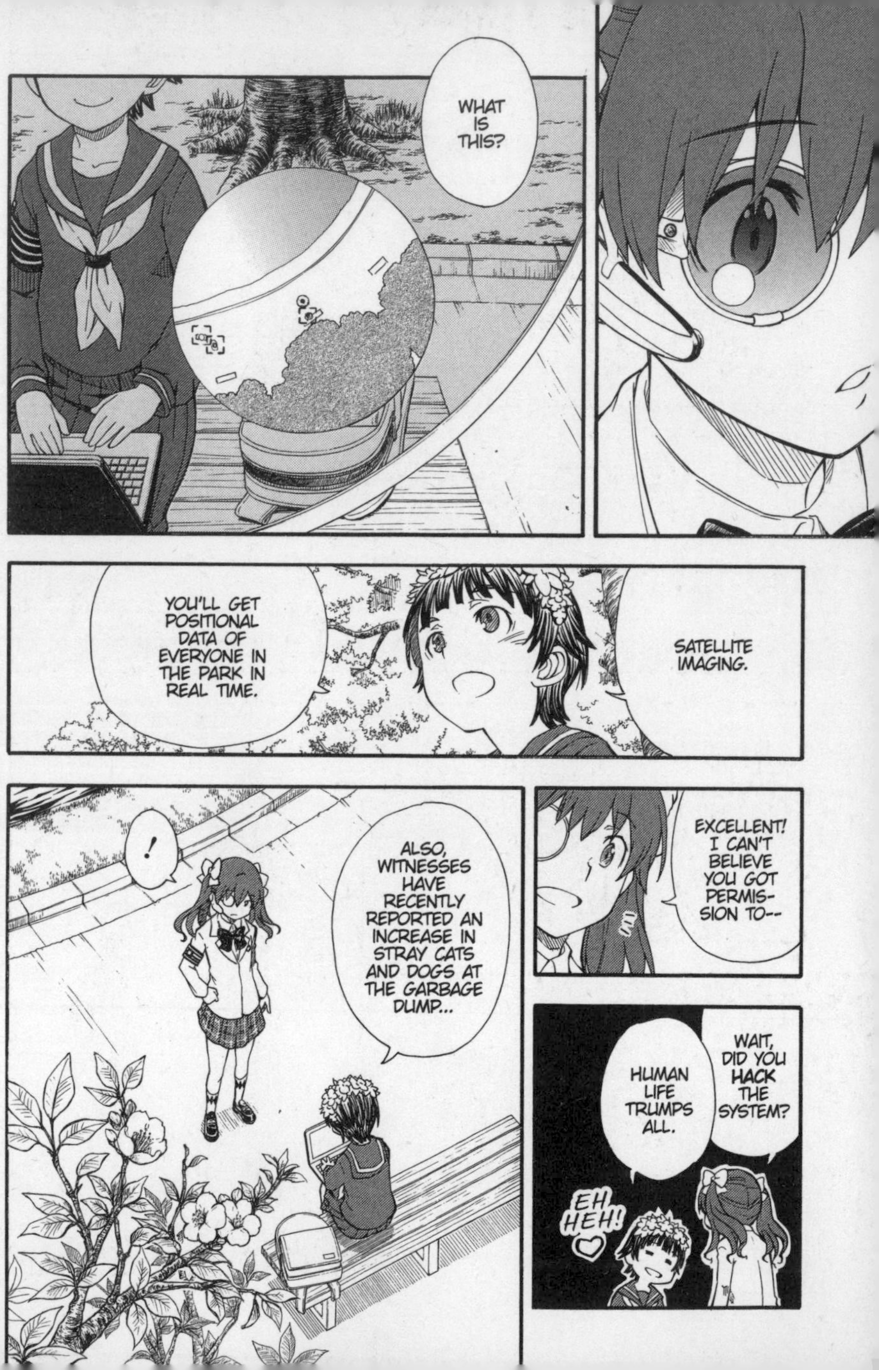
WHAT IS THIS?
SATELLITE IMAGING.
YOU'LL GET POSITIONAL DATA OF EVERYONE IN THE PARK IN REAL TIME.
EXCELLENT! I CAN'T BELIEVE YOU GOT PERMIS-SION TO--
WAIT, DID YOU HACK THE SYSTEM?
HUMAN LIFE TRUMPS ALL.
EH HEH!
ALSO, WITNESSES HAVE RECENTLY REPORTED AN INCREASE IN STRAY CATS AND DOGS AT THE GARBAGE DUMP...
!

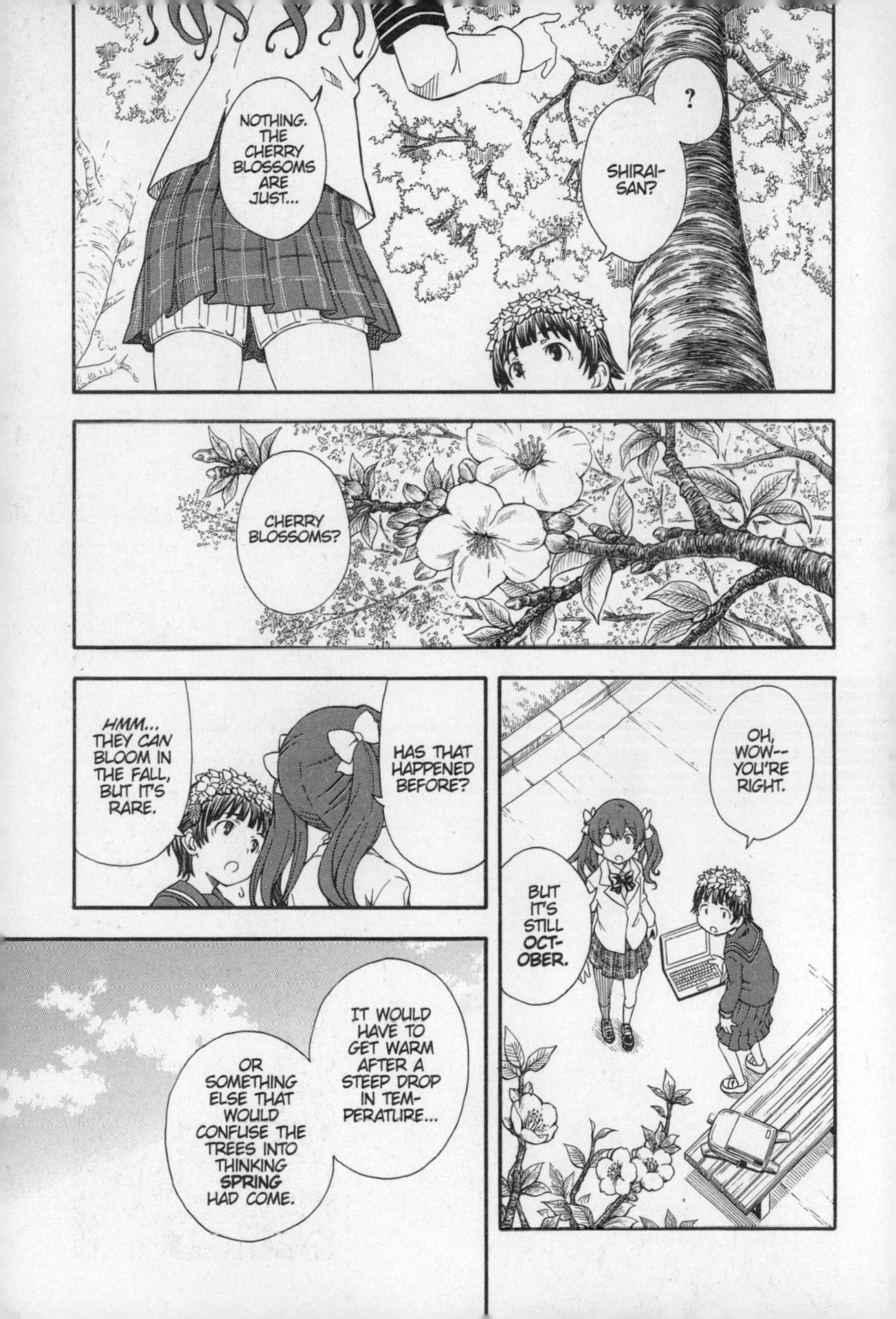
?
SHIRAI-SAN?
NOTHING. THE CHERRY BLOSSOMS ARE JUST...
CHERRY BLOSSOMS?
OH, WOW-- YOU'RE RIGHT.
BUT IT'S STILL OCT-OBER.
HAS THAT HAPPENED BEFORE?
HMM... THEY CAN BLOOM IN THE FALL, BUT IT'S RARE.
IT WOULD HAVE TO GET WARM AFTER A STEEP DROP IN TEM-PERATURE...
OR SOMETHING ELSE THAT WOULD CONFUSE THE TREES INTO THINKING SPRING HAD COME.

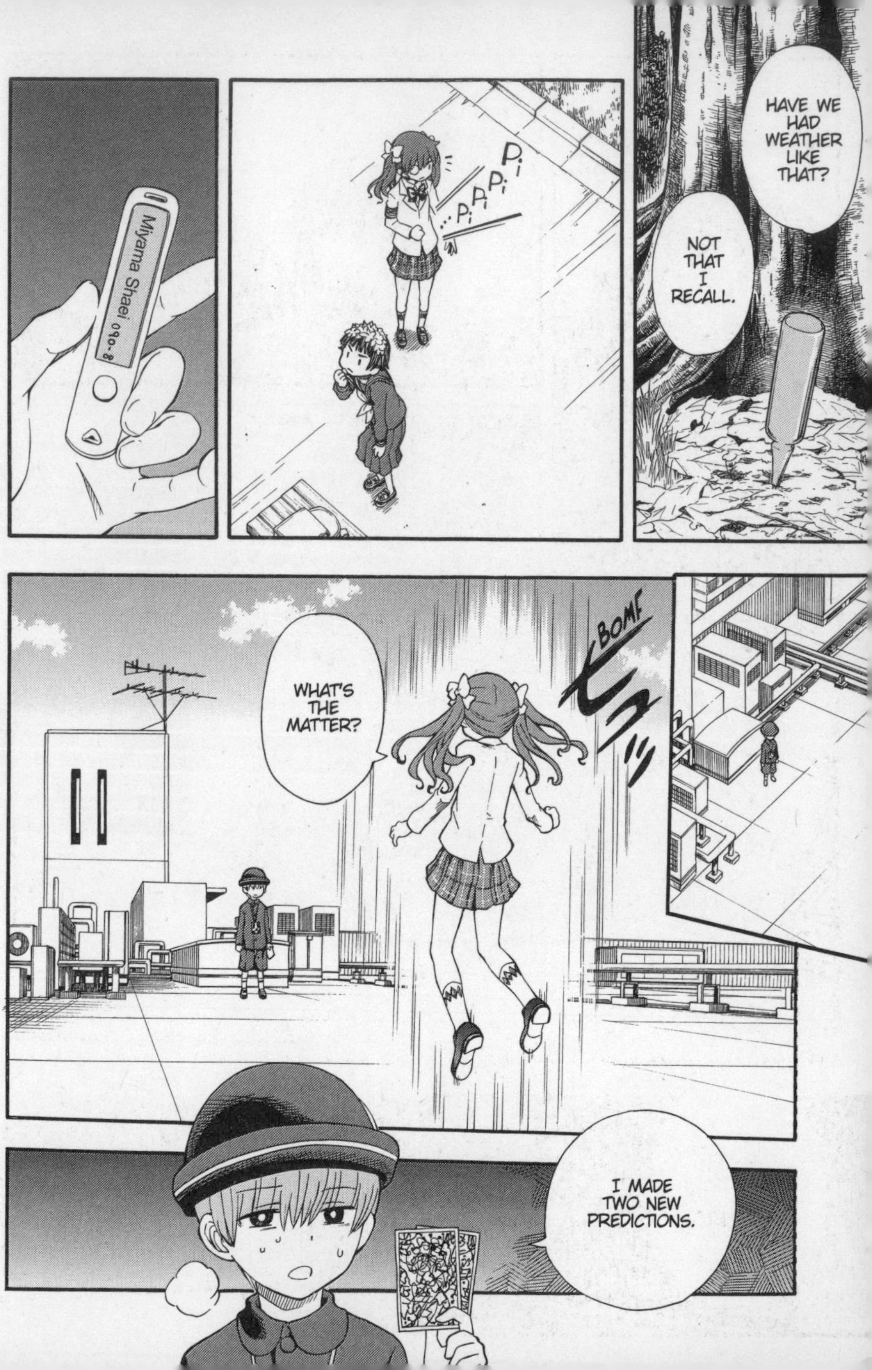
HAVE WE HAD WEATHER LIKE THAT?
NOT THAT I RECALL.
Pi Pi Pi Pi
Miyama Shaei 090-8
BOMF
WHAT'S THE MATTER?
I MADE TWO NEW PREDICTIONS.

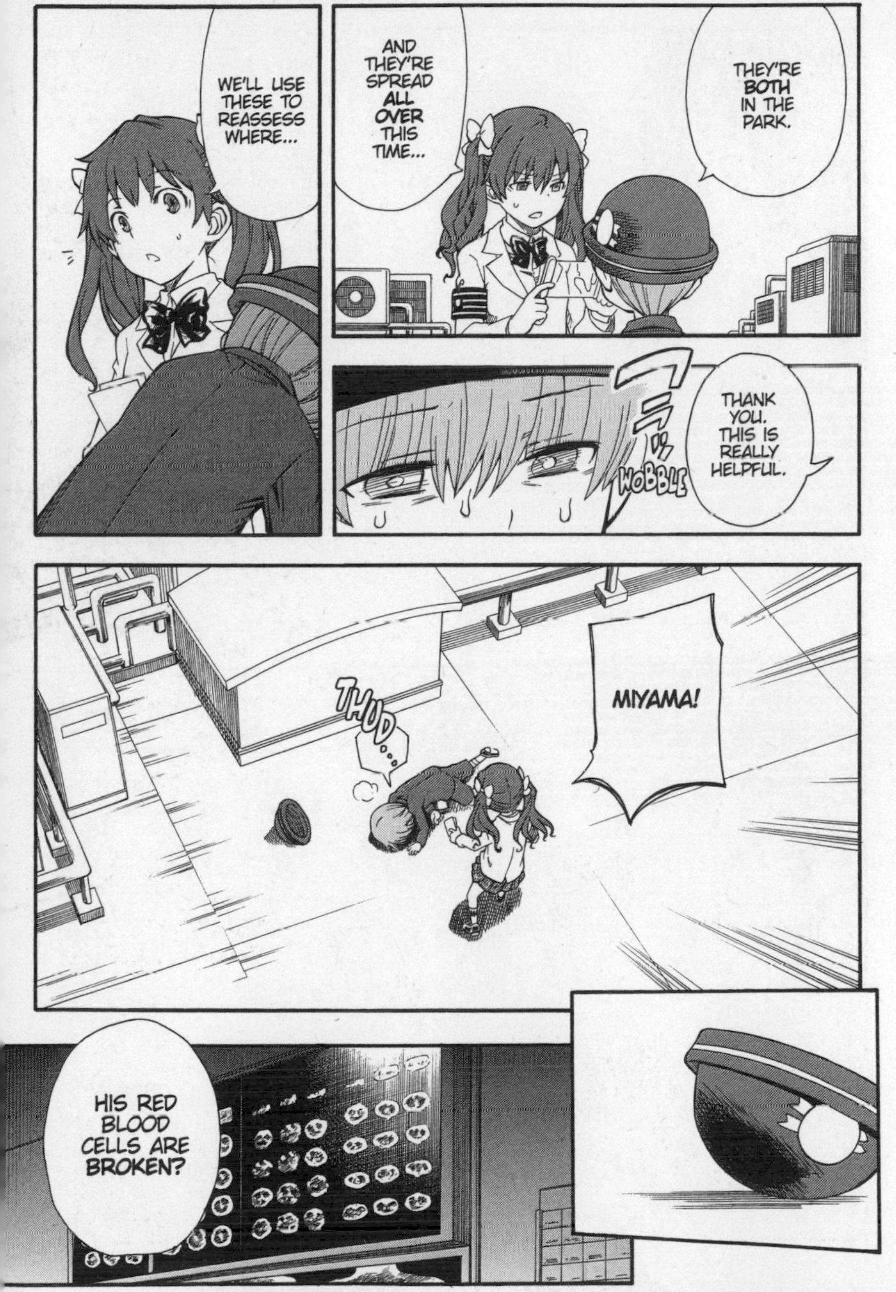
THEY'RE BOTH IN THE PARK.
AND THEY'RE SPREAD ALL OVER THIS TIME...
THANK YOU. THIS IS REALLY HELPFUL.
WOBBLE
WE'LL USE THESE TO REASSESS WHERE...
MIYAMA!
THUD...
HIS RED BLOOD CELLS ARE BROKEN?

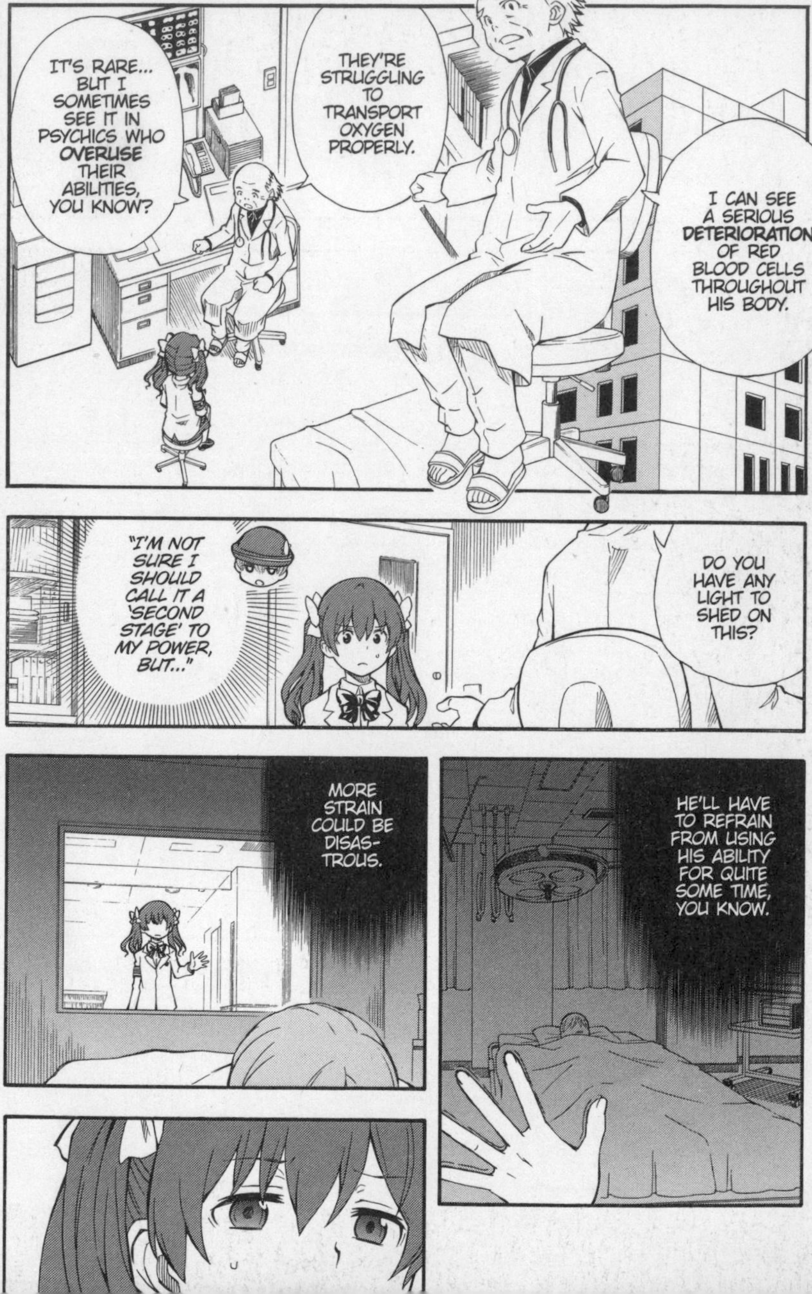
I CAN SEE A SERIOUS DETERIORATION OF RED BLOOD CELLS THROUGHOUT HIS BODY.
THEY'RE STRUGGLING TO TRANSPORT OXYGEN PROPERLY.
IT'S RARE... BUT I SOMETIMES SEE IT IN PSYCHICS WHO OVERUSE THEIR ABILITIES, YOU KNOW?
DO YOU HAVE ANY LIGHT TO SHED ON THIS?
"I'M NOT SURE I SHOULD CALL IT A 'SECOND STAGE' TO MY POWER, BUT..."
HE'LL HAVE TO REFRAIN FROM USING HIS ABILITY FOR QUITE SOME TIME, YOU KNOW.
MORE STRAIN COULD BE DISAS-TROUS.

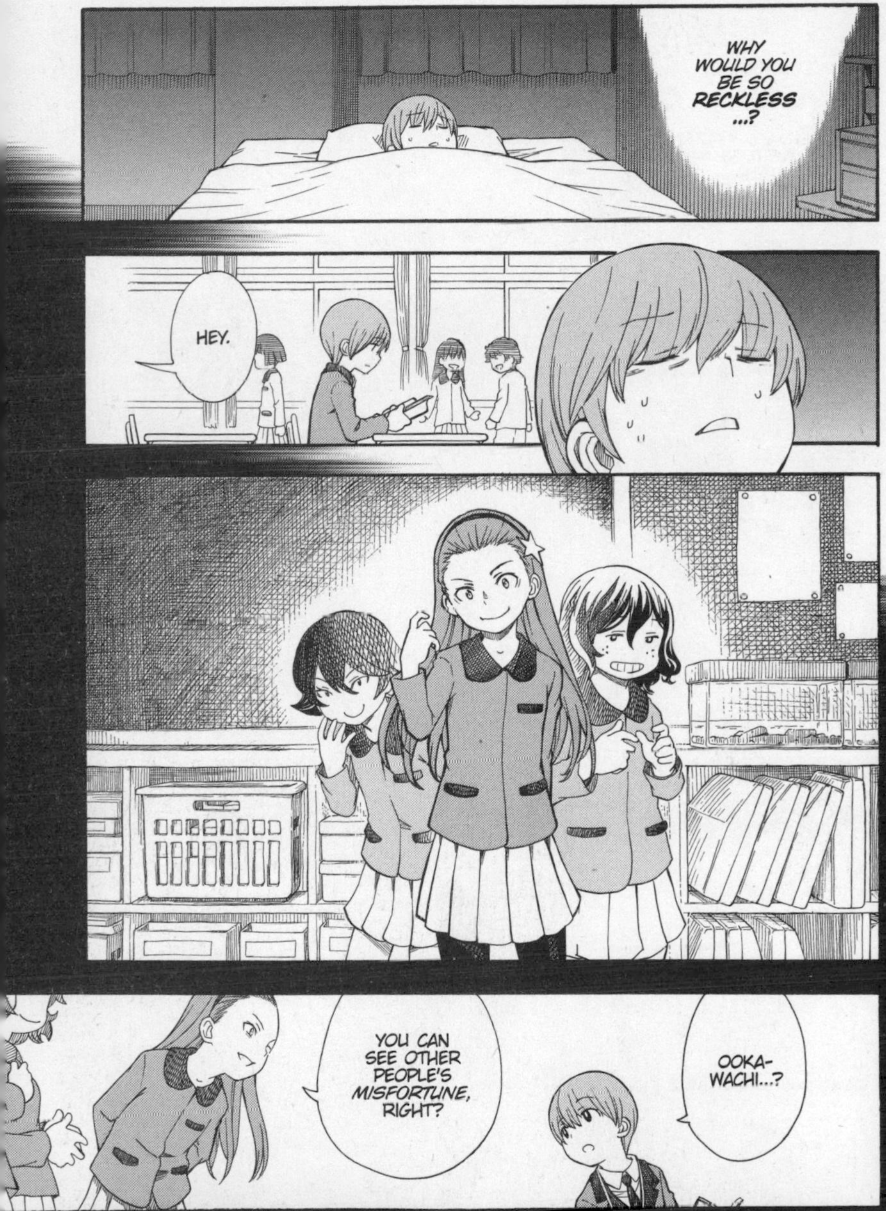
WHY WOULD YOU BE SO RECKLESS ...?
HEY.
OOKA-WACHI...?
YOU CAN SEE OTHER PEOPLE'S MISFORTUNE, RIGHT?

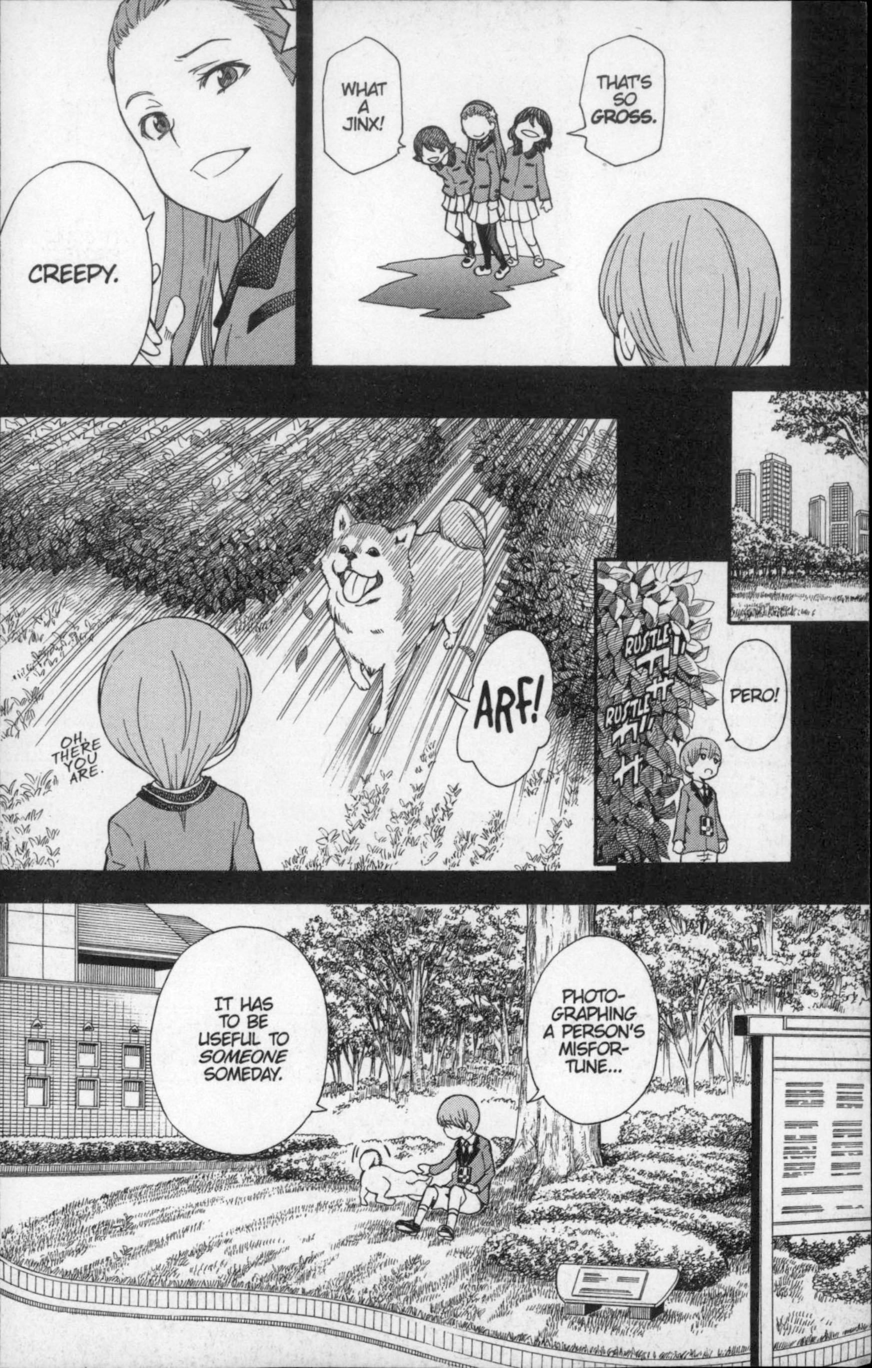
THAT'S SO GROSS.
WHAT A JINX!
CREEPY.
RUSTLE
RUSTLE
PERO!
ARF!
OH, THERE YOU ARE.
PHOTO-GRAPHING A PERSON'S MISFOR-TUNE...
IT HAS TO BE USEFUL TO *SOMEONE* SOMEDAY.

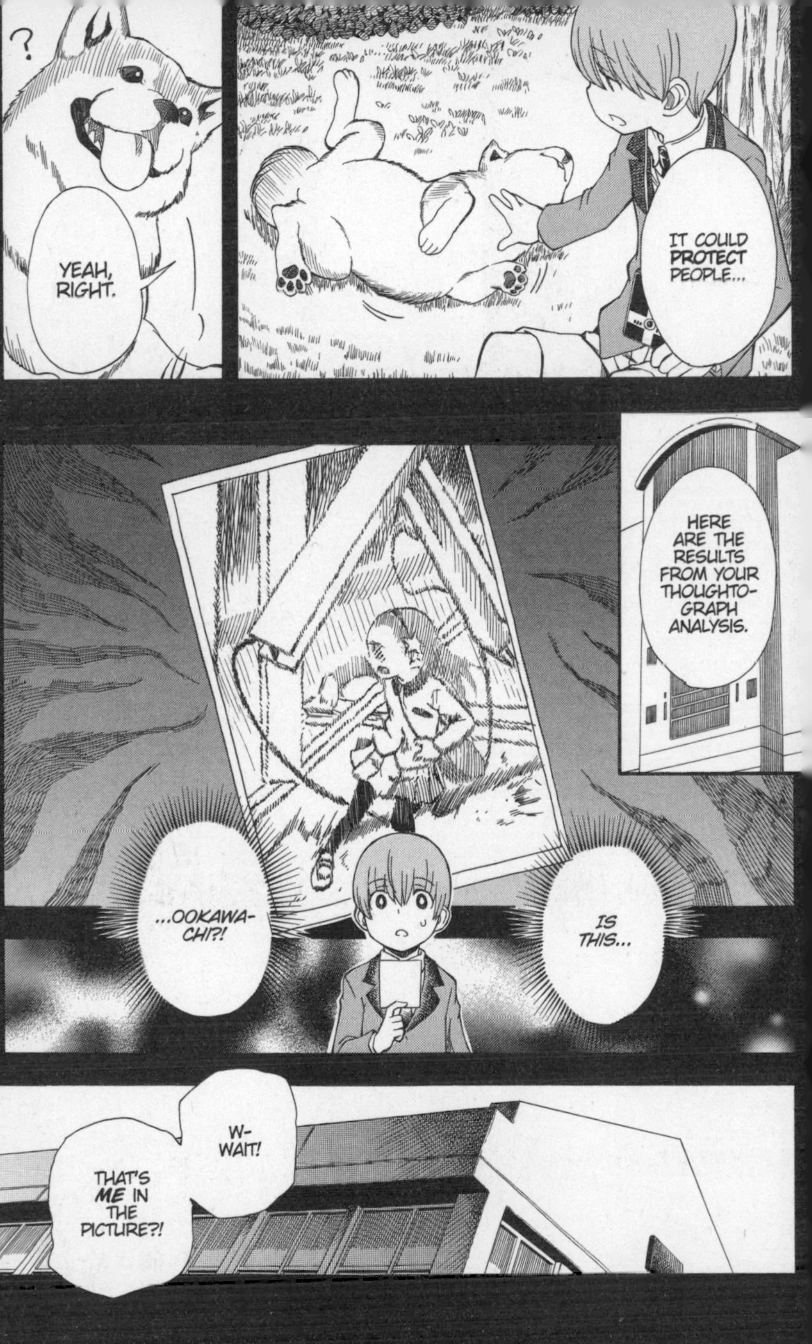
IT COULD PROTECT PEOPLE...
?
YEAH, RIGHT.
HERE ARE THE RESULTS FROM YOUR THOUGHTOGRAPH ANALYSIS.
IS THIS...
...OOKAWACHI?!
W-WAIT!
THAT'S ME IN THE PICTURE?!

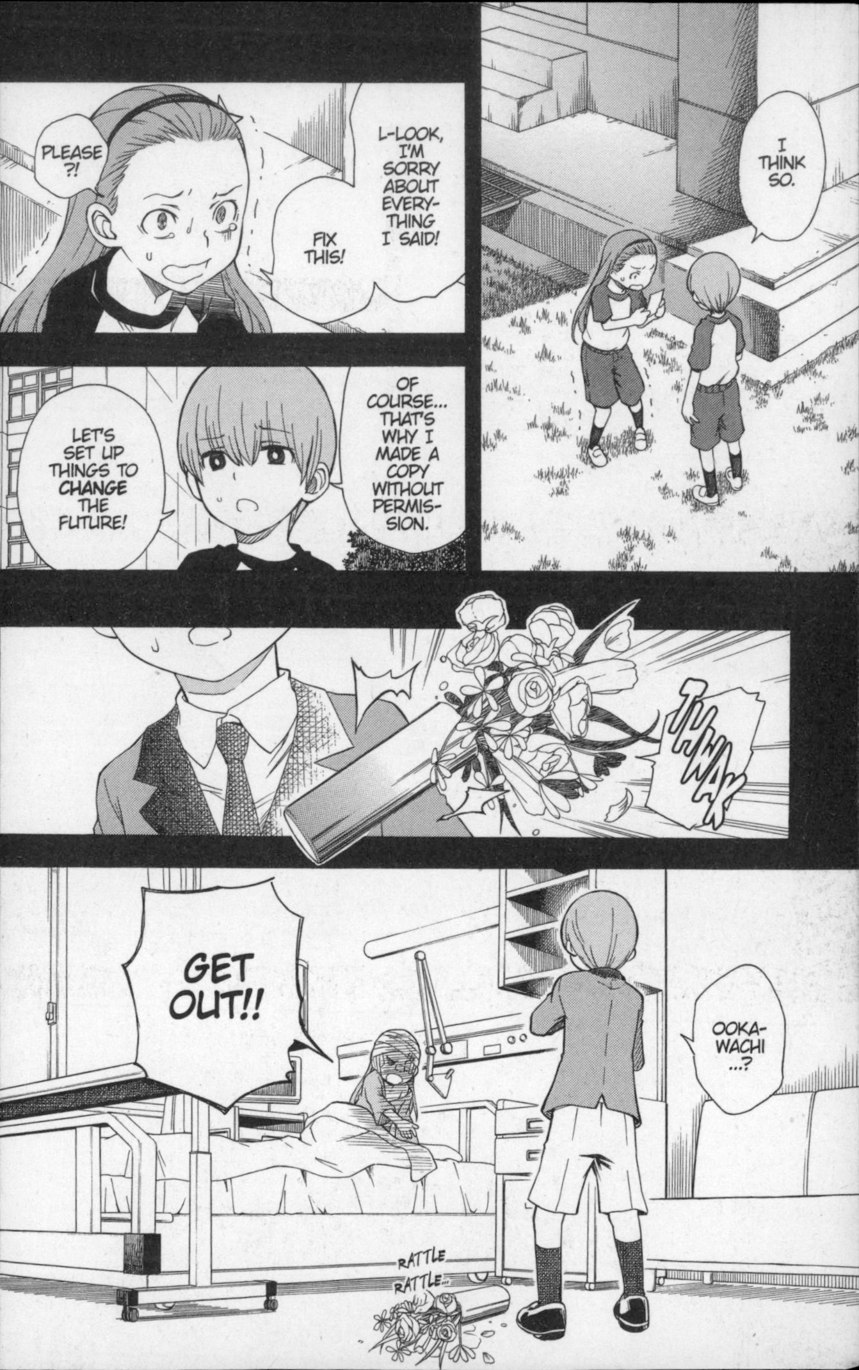
I THINK SO.
L-LOOK, I'M SORRY ABOUT EVERY-THING I SAID!
FIX THIS!
PLEASE?!
OF COURSE... THAT'S WHY I MADE A COPY WITHOUT PERMIS-SION.
LET'S SET UP THINGS TO CHANGE THE FUTURE!
THWAK
OOKA-WACHI...?
GET OUT!!
RATTLE RATTLE...

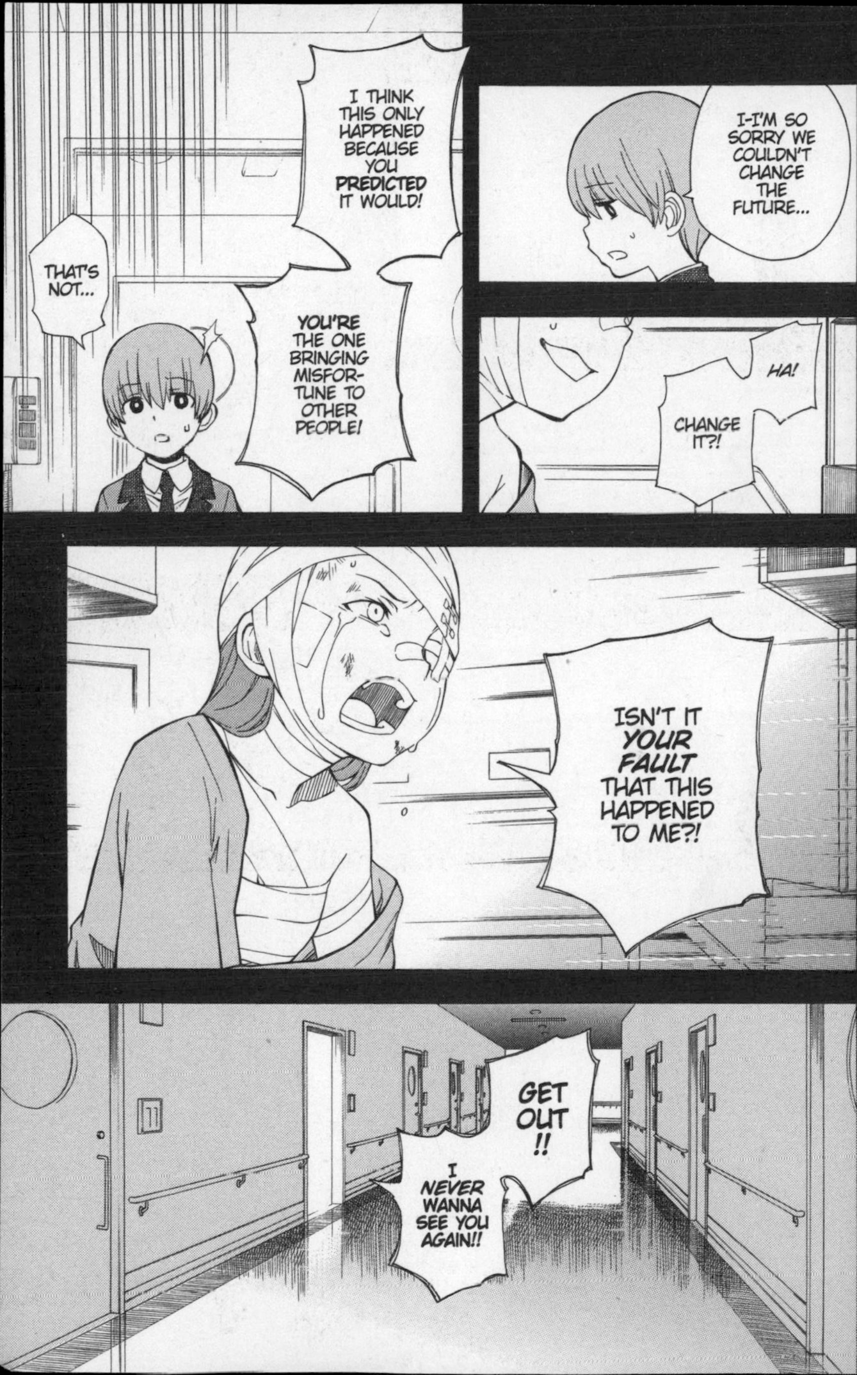
I-I'M SO SORRY WE COULDN'T CHANGE THE FUTURE...
HA!
CHANGE IT?!
I THINK THIS ONLY HAPPENED BECAUSE YOU PREDICTED IT WOULD!
YOU'RE THE ONE BRINGING MISFORTUNE TO OTHER PEOPLE!
THAT'S NOT...
ISN'T IT YOUR FAULT THAT THIS HAPPENED TO ME?!
GET OUT!!
I NEVER WANNA SEE YOU AGAIN!!

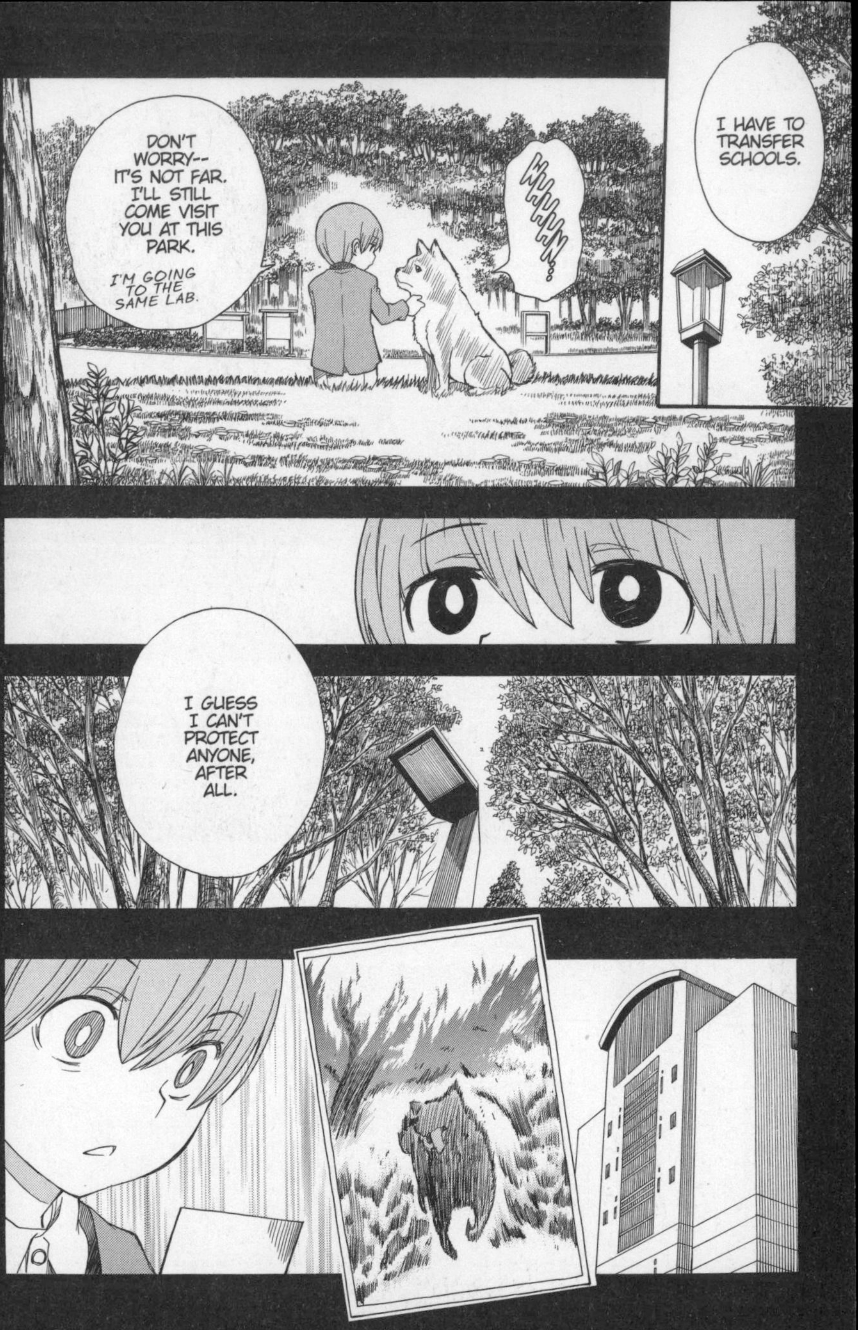
I HAVE TO TRANSFER SCHOOLS.
WHHHN...
DON'T WORRY-- IT'S NOT FAR. I'LL STILL COME VISIT YOU AT THIS PARK.
I'M GOING TO THE SAME LAB.
I GUESS I CAN'T PROTECT ANYONE, AFTER ALL.

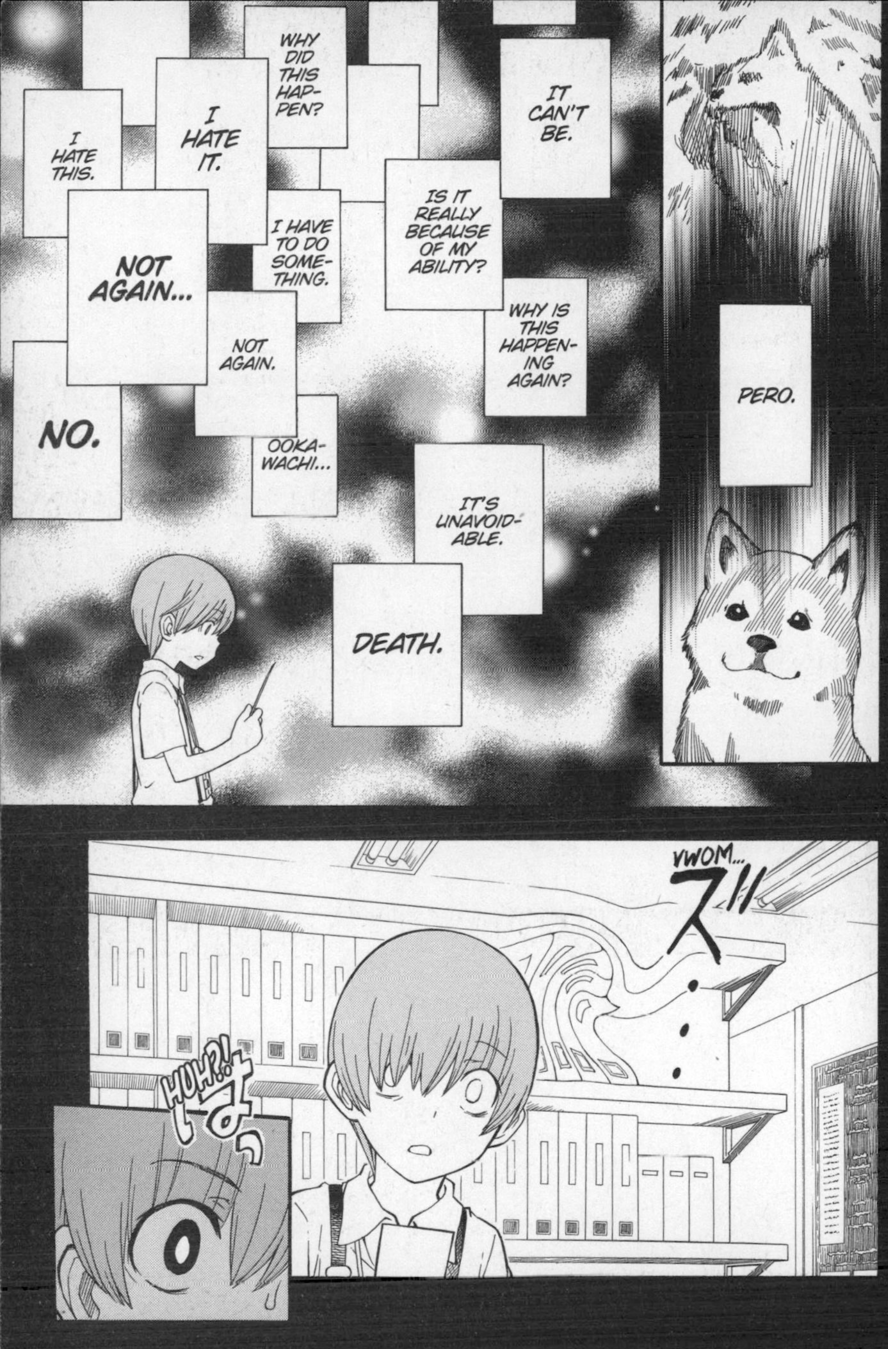
PERO.
IT CAN'T BE.
WHY DID THIS HAP-PEN?
I HATE IT.
I HATE THIS.
IS IT REALLY BECAUSE OF MY ABILITY?
I HAVE TO DO SOME-THING.
NOT AGAIN...
WHY IS THIS HAPPEN-ING AGAIN?
NOT AGAIN.
NO.
OOKA-WACHI...
IT'S UNAVOID-ABLE.
DEATH.
VWOM...
HUH?!

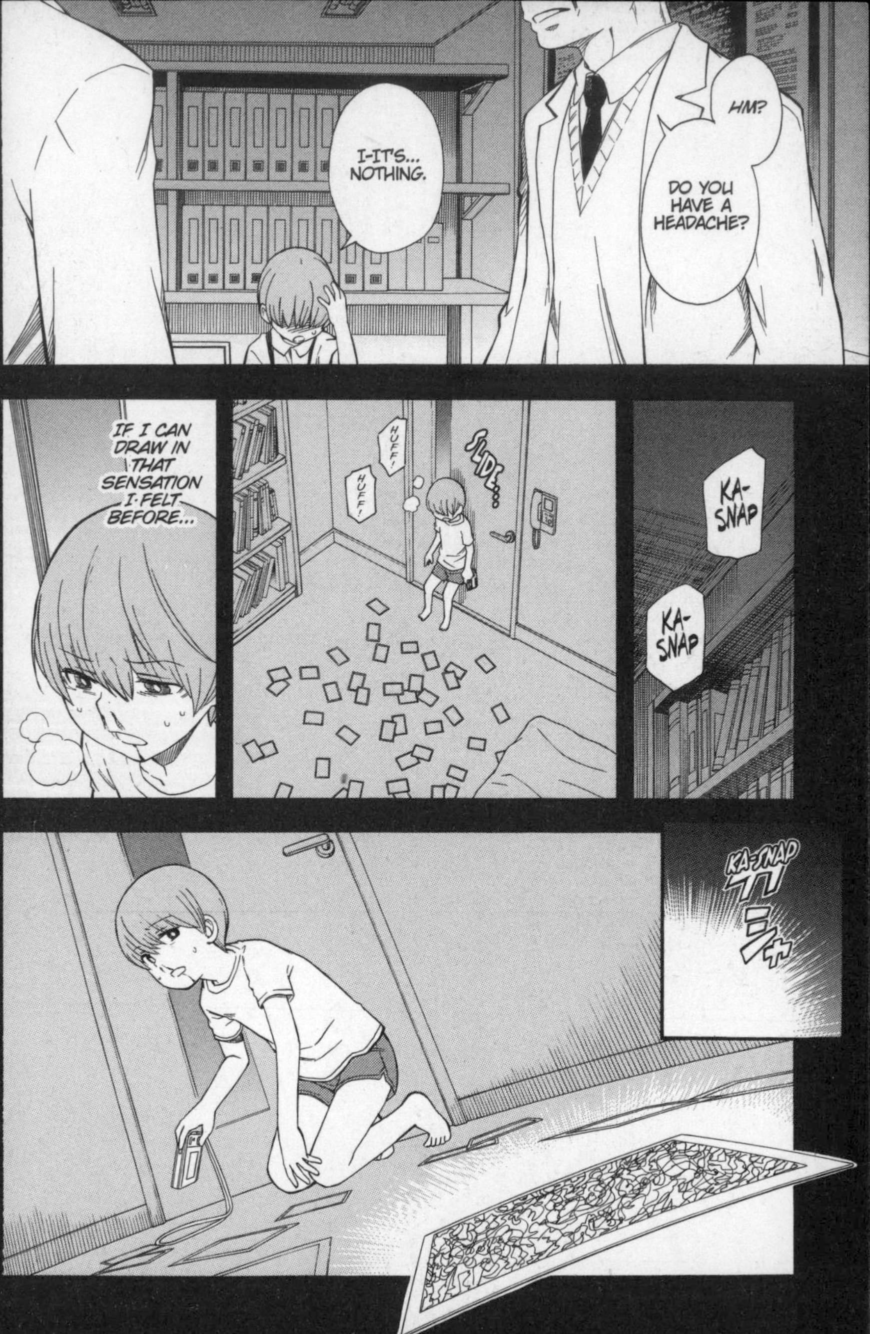
HM?
DO YOU HAVE A HEADACHE?
I-IT'S... NOTHING.
KA-SNAP
KA-SNAP
SLIDE...
HUFF!
HUFF!
IF I CAN DRAW IN THAT SENSATION I FELT BEFORE...
KA-SNAP

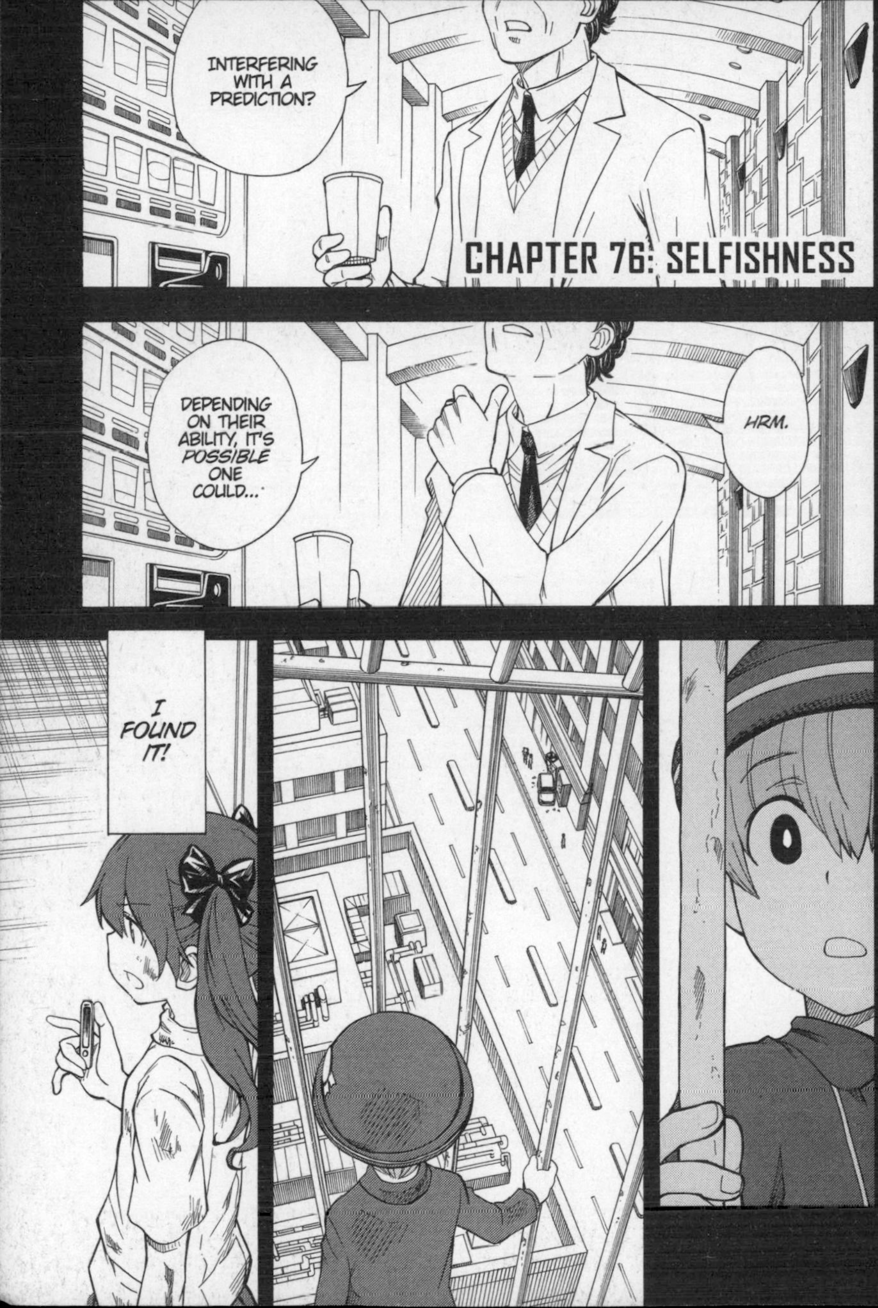
INTERFERING WITH A PREDICTION?
CHAPTER 76: SELFISHNESS
HRM.
DEPENDING ON THEIR ABILITY, IT'S POSSIBLE ONE COULD...
I FOUND IT!

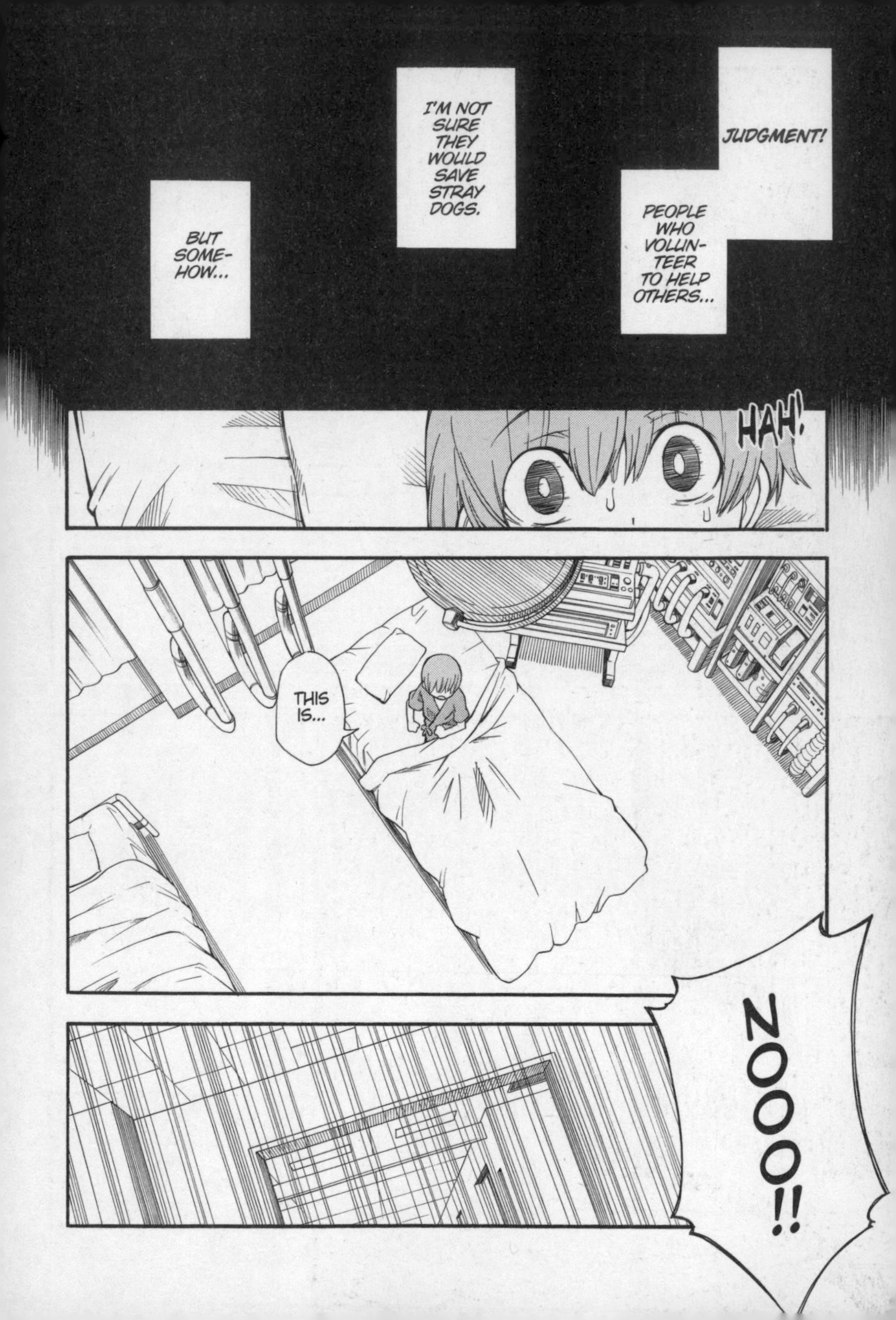
JUDGMENT!
PEOPLE WHO VOLUN-TEER TO HELP OTHERS...
I'M NOT SURE THEY WOULD SAVE STRAY DOGS.
BUT SOME-HOW...
HAH!
THIS IS...
NOOO!!

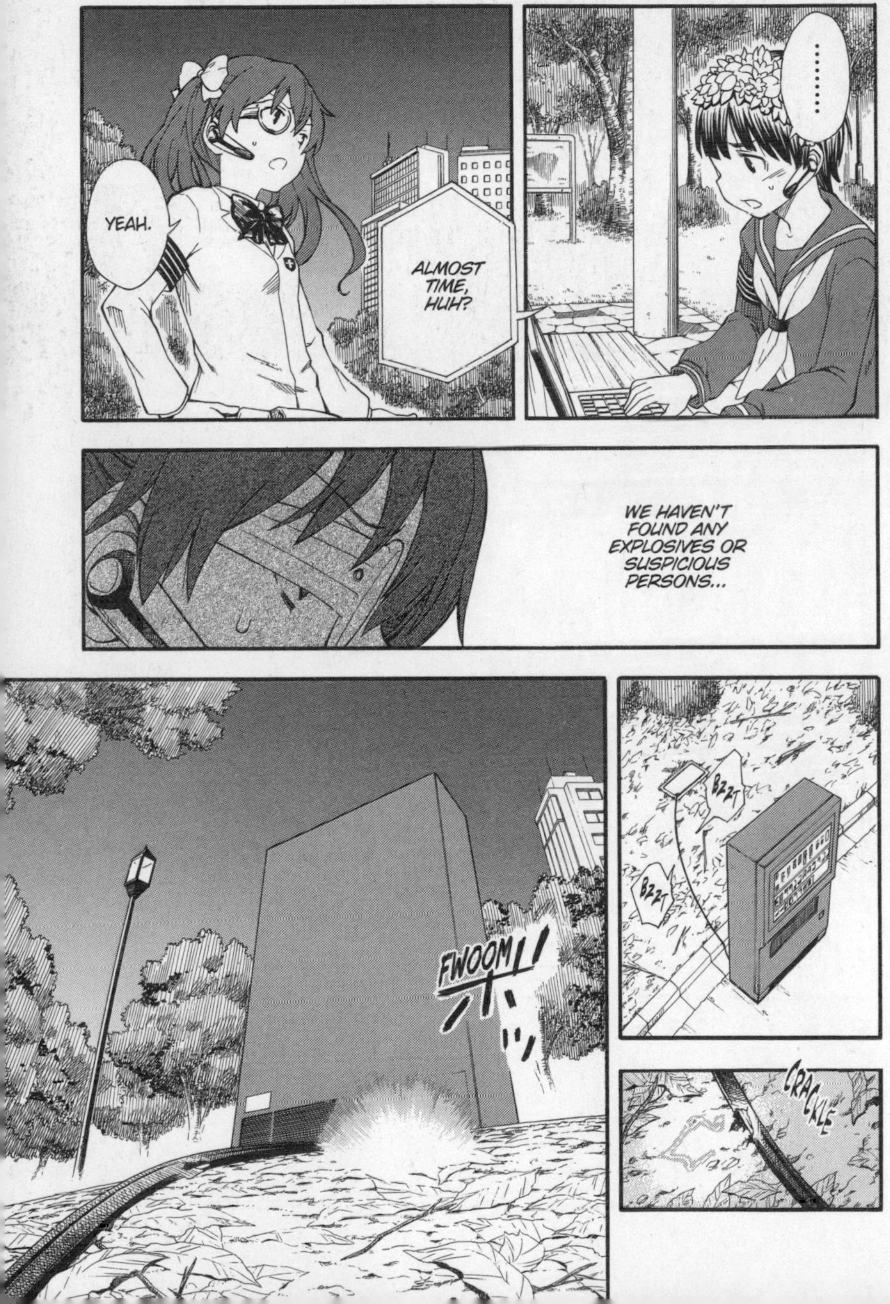
......
ALMOST TIME, HUH?
YEAH.
WE HAVEN'T FOUND ANY EXPLOSIVES OR SUSPICIOUS PERSONS...
BZZT
BZZT
CRACKLE
FWOOM!!

IT'S NOT LIKE THERE'S A GAS LINE OR UNDER- GROUND SHOPPING CENTER BENEATH HERE.

AND IT WOULD BE A STRETCH FOR THINGS TO ORIGINATE OUTSIDE THE PARK.

SO WHAT COULD POSSIBLY...

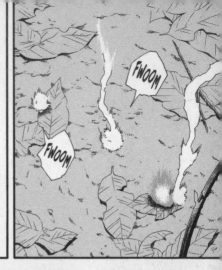

FWOOM

FWOOM

ニュ

FSSSSSH

FWOOM...!!

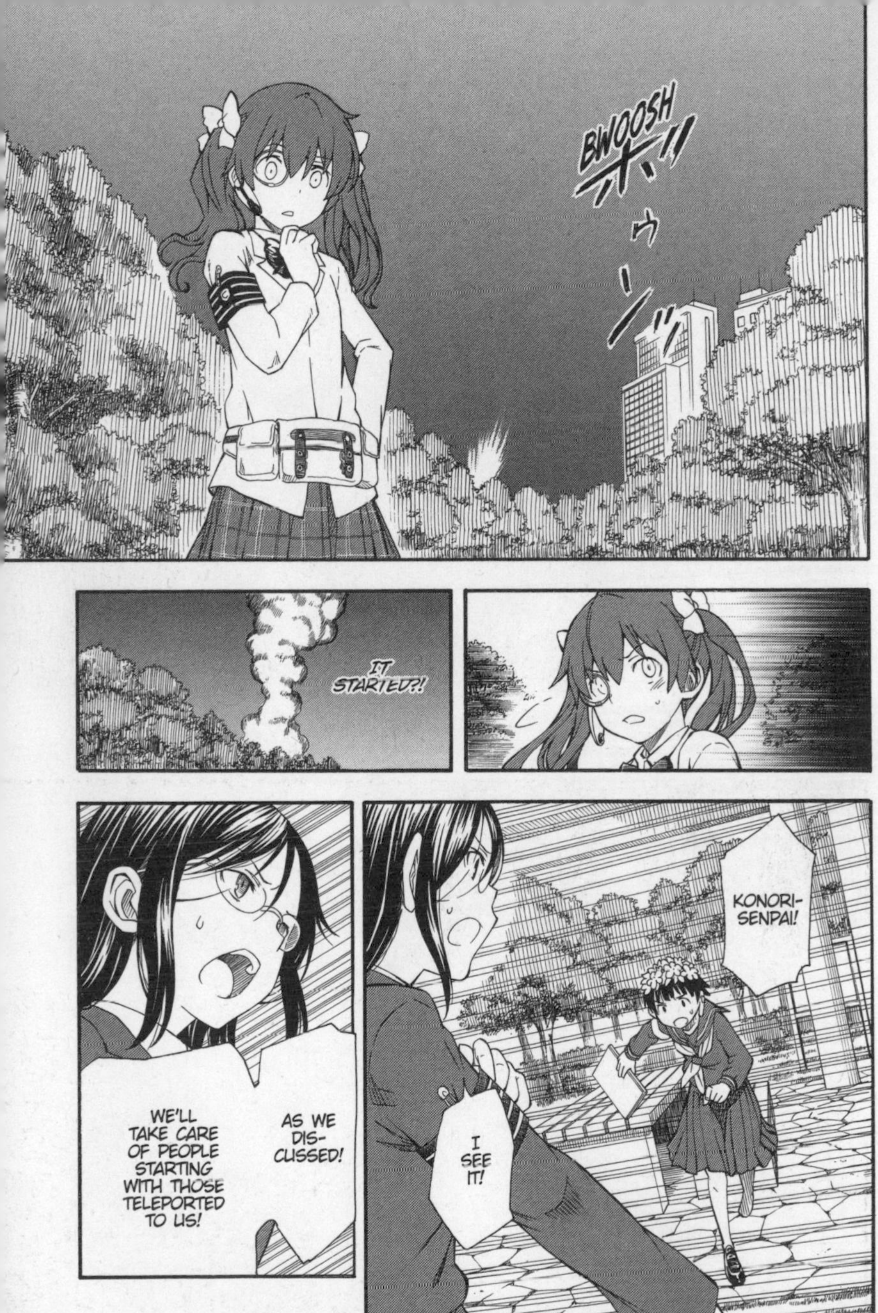
BWOOSH
IT STARTED?!
KONORI-SENPAI!
I SEE IT!
AS WE DIS-CUSSED!
WE'LL TAKE CARE OF PEOPLE STARTING WITH THOSE TELEPORTED TO US!

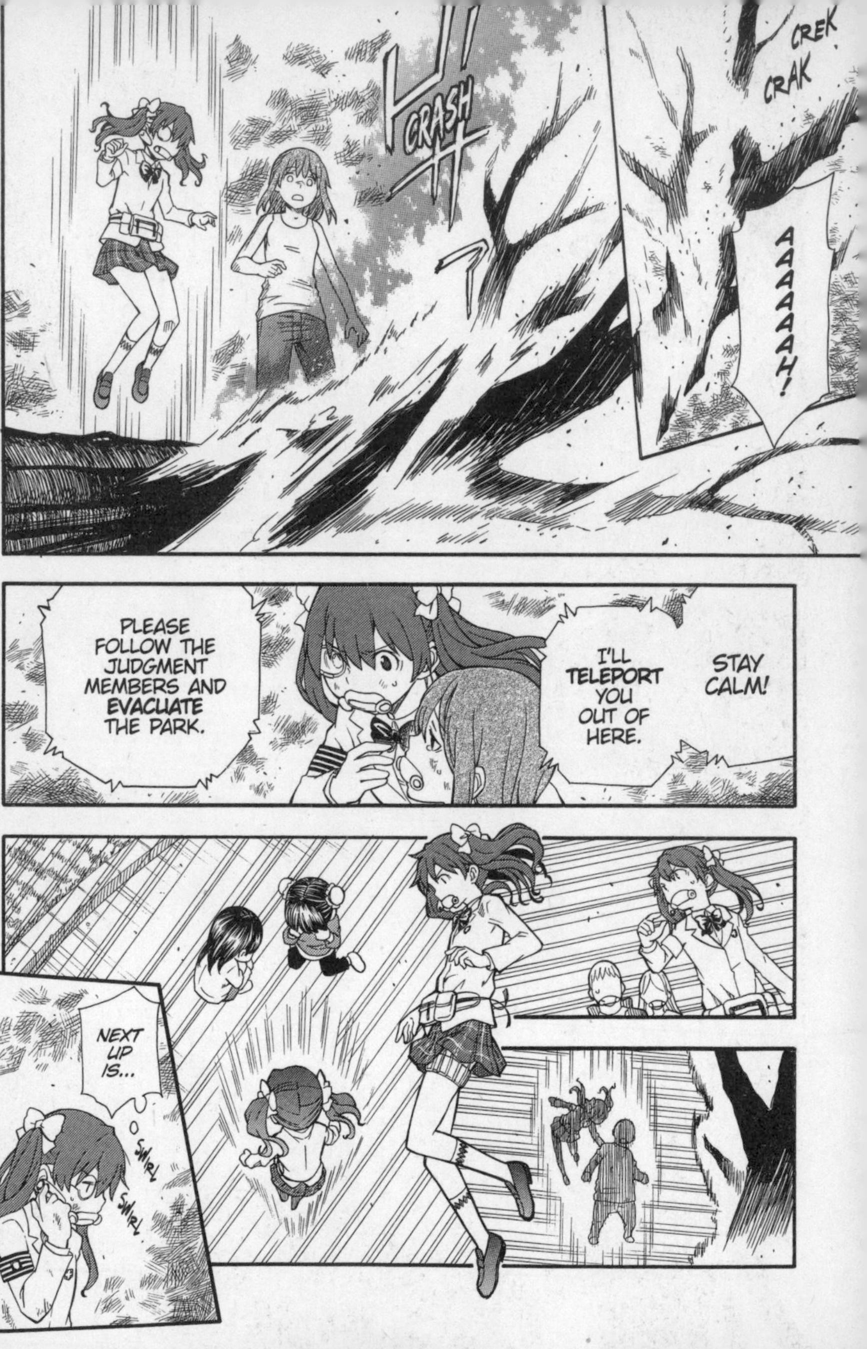
CREK
CRAK
AAAAAAAH!
CRASH
STAY CALM!
I'LL TELEPORT YOU OUT OF HERE.
PLEASE FOLLOW THE JUDGMENT MEMBERS AND EVACUATE THE PARK.
NEXT UP IS...
SWIRL
SWIRL

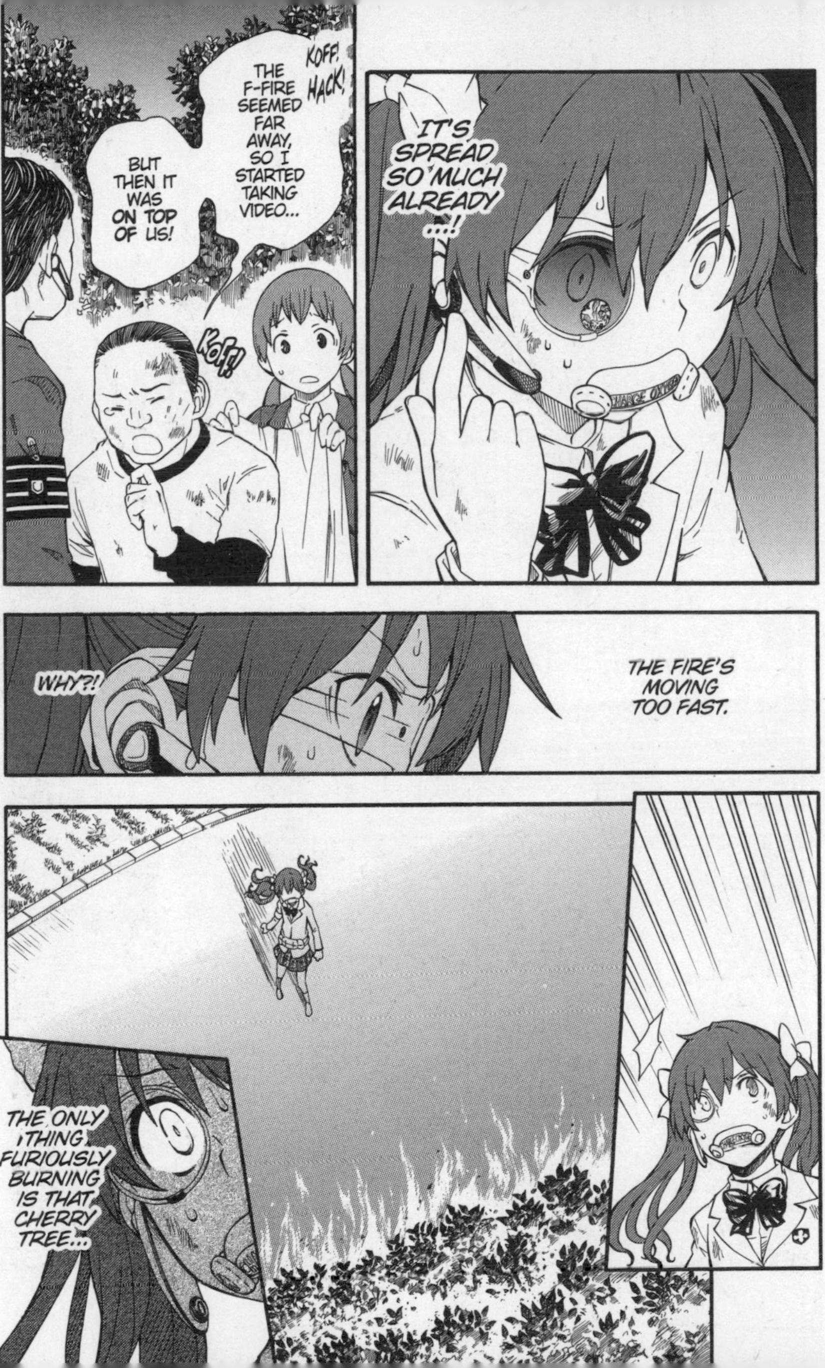
IT'S SPREAD SO MUCH ALREADY ...!
KOFF! HACK!
THE F-FIRE SEEMED FAR AWAY, SO I STARTED TAKING VIDEO...
BUT THEN IT WAS ON TOP OF US!
KOFF!
THE FIRE'S MOVING TOO FAST.
WHY?!
THE ONLY THING FURIOUSLY BURNING IS THAT CHERRY TREE...

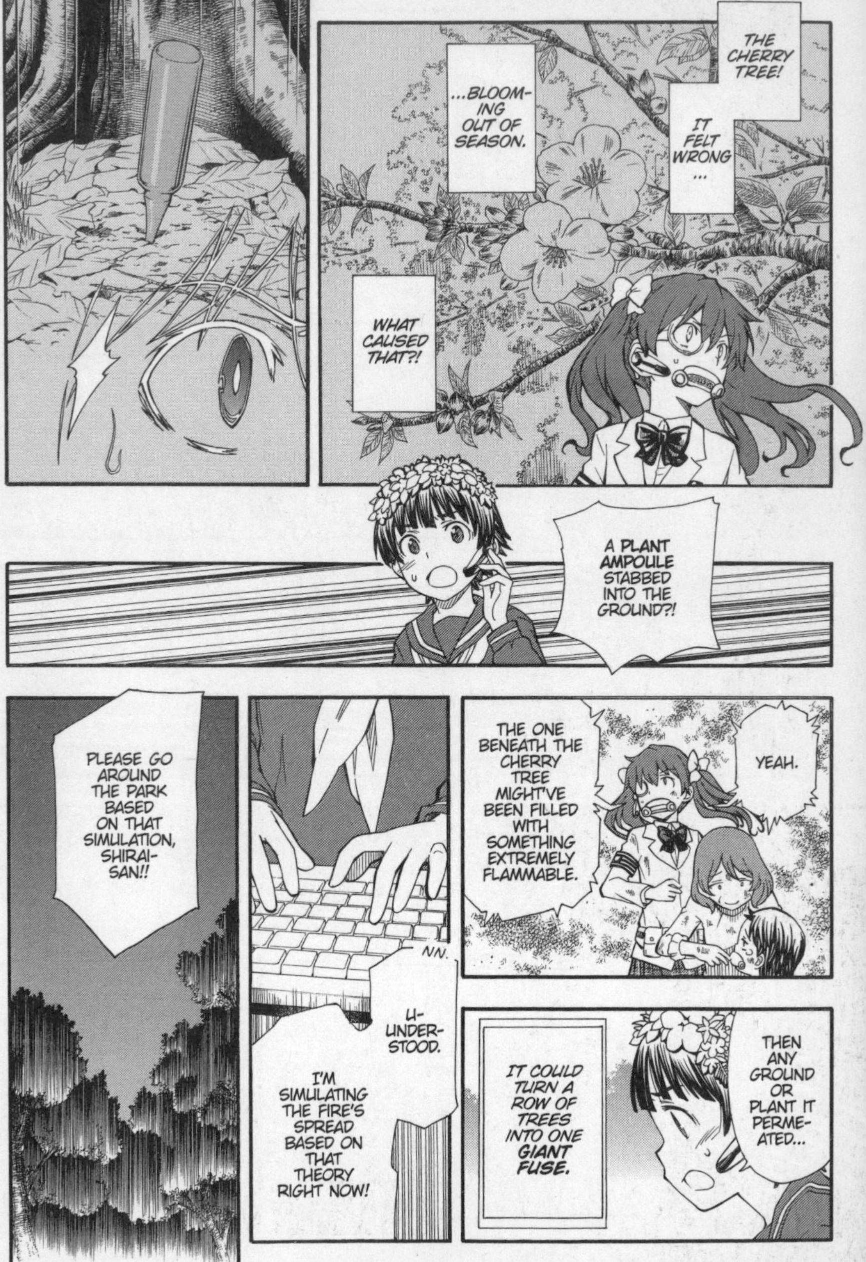
THE CHERRY TREE!
IT FELT WRONG...
...BLOOMING OUT OF SEASON.
WHAT CAUSED THAT?!
A PLANT AMPOULE STABBED INTO THE GROUND?!
YEAH.
THE ONE BENEATH THE CHERRY TREE MIGHT'VE BEEN FILLED WITH SOMETHING EXTREMELY FLAMMABLE.
THEN ANY GROUND OR PLANT IT PERMEATED...
IT COULD TURN A ROW OF TREES INTO ONE GIANT FUSE.
NN.
U-UNDERSTOOD.
I'M SIMULATING THE FIRE'S SPREAD BASED ON THAT THEORY RIGHT NOW!
PLEASE GO AROUND THE PARK BASED ON THAT SIMULATION, SHIRAI-SAN!!

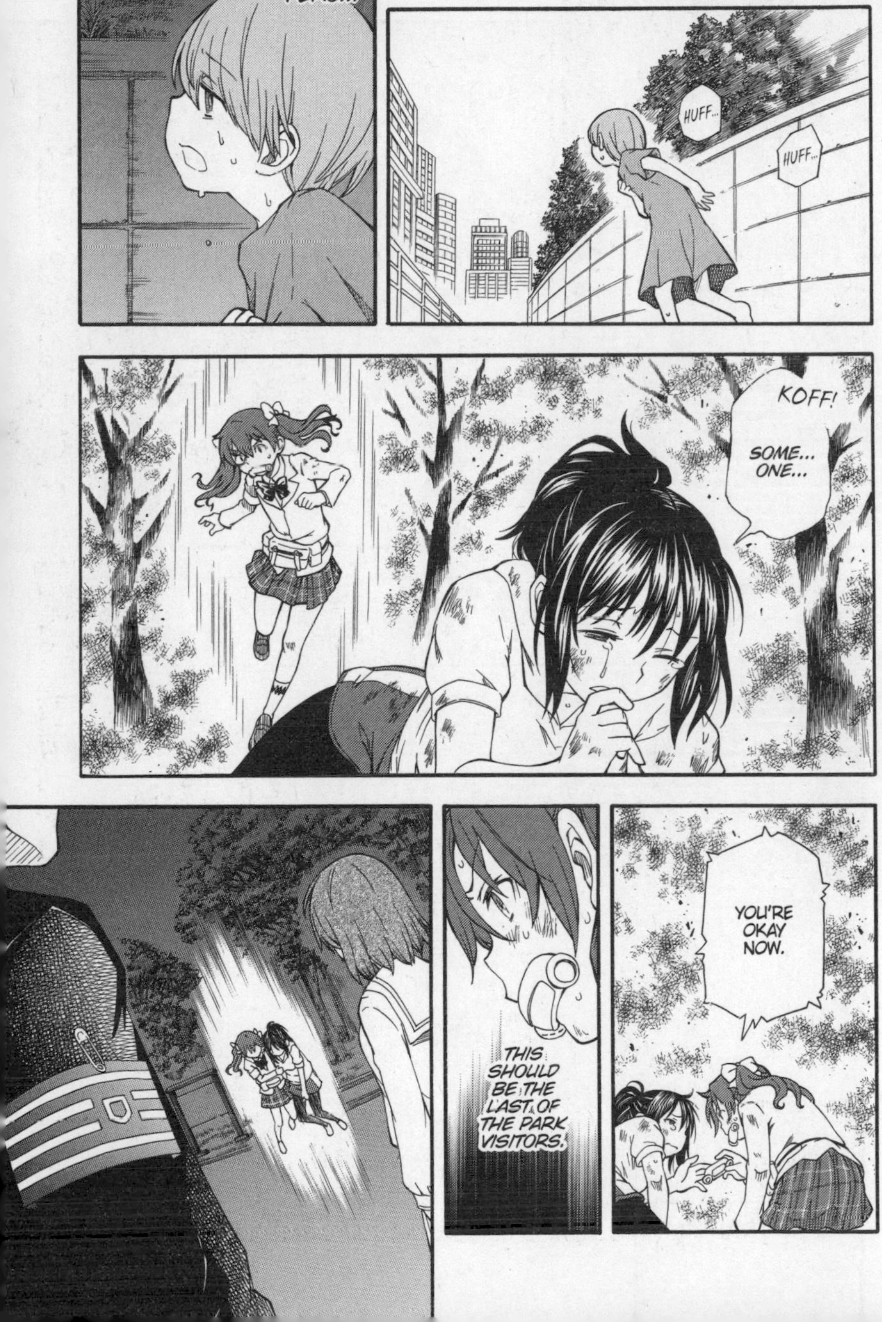
HUFF...
HUFF...
PERO...
KOFF!
SOME... ONE...
YOU'RE OKAY NOW.
THIS SHOULD BE THE LAST OF THE PARK VISITORS.

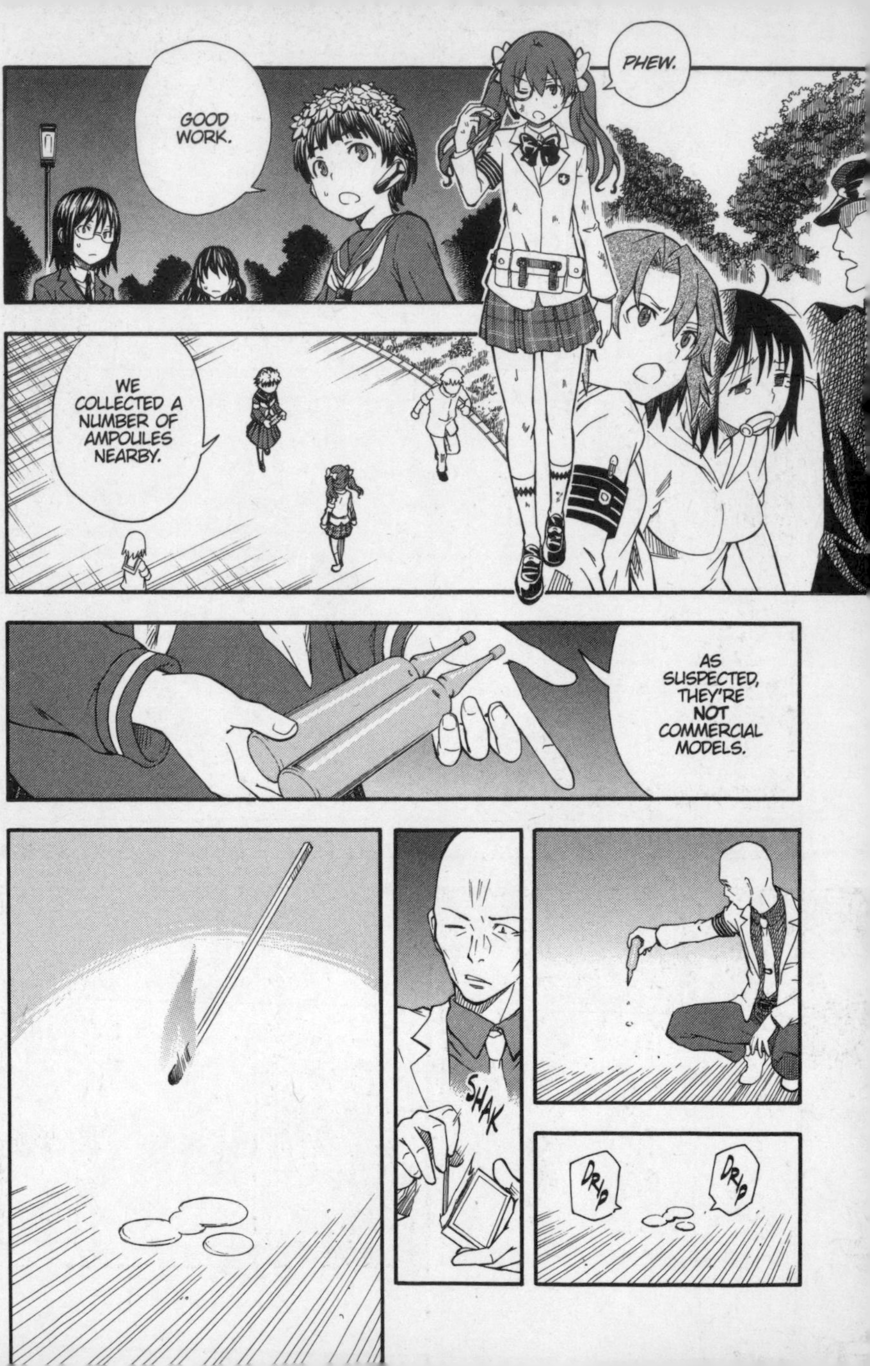
PHEW.
GOOD WORK.
WE COLLECTED A NUMBER OF AMPOULES NEARBY.
AS SUSPECTED, THEY'RE NOT COMMERCIAL MODELS.
DRIP
DRIP
SHAK

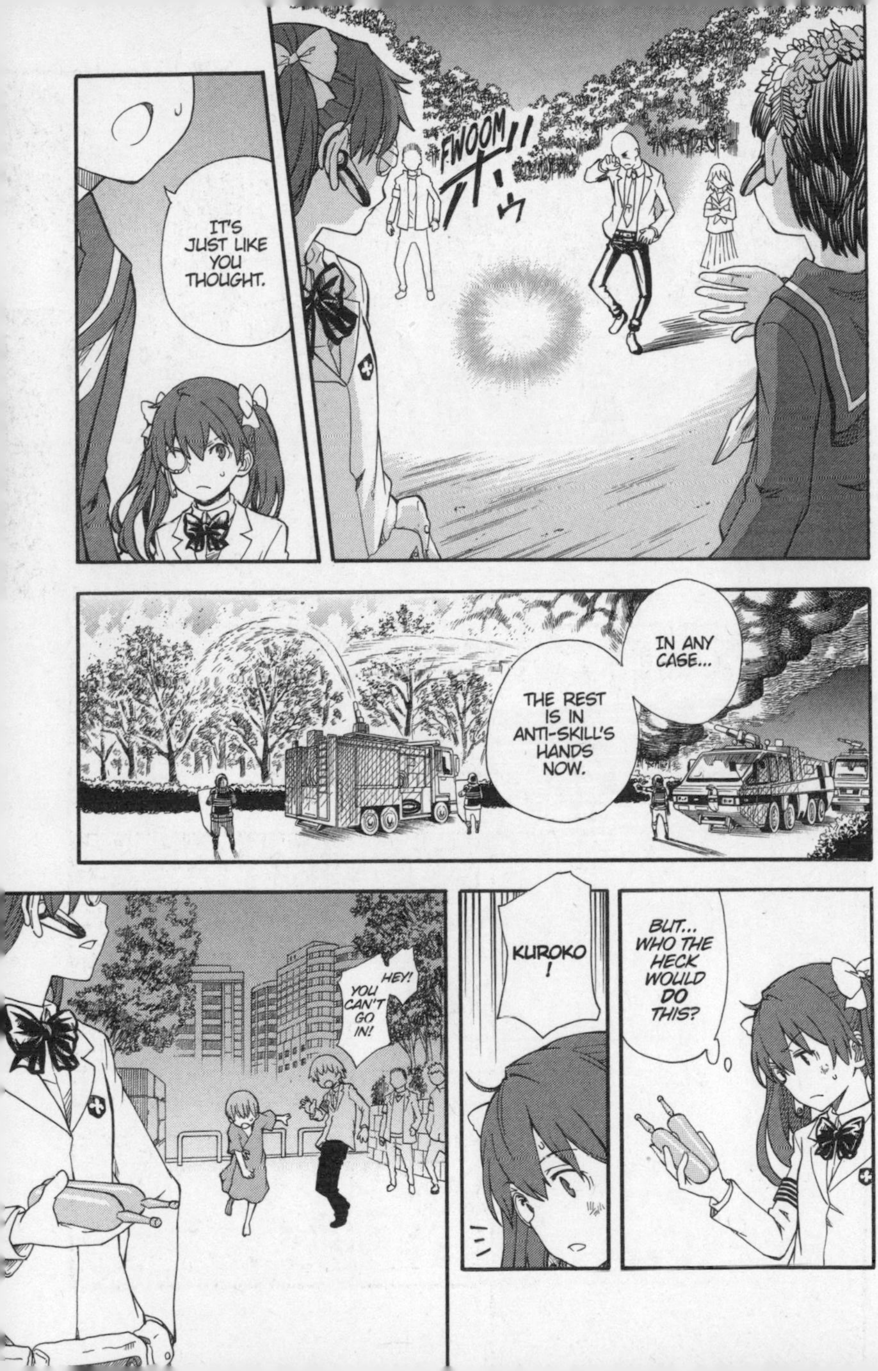
FWOOM
IT'S JUST LIKE YOU THOUGHT.
IN ANY CASE...
THE REST IS IN ANTI-SKILL'S HANDS NOW.
BUT... WHO THE HECK WOULD DO THIS?
KUROKO!
HEY! YOU CAN'T GO IN!

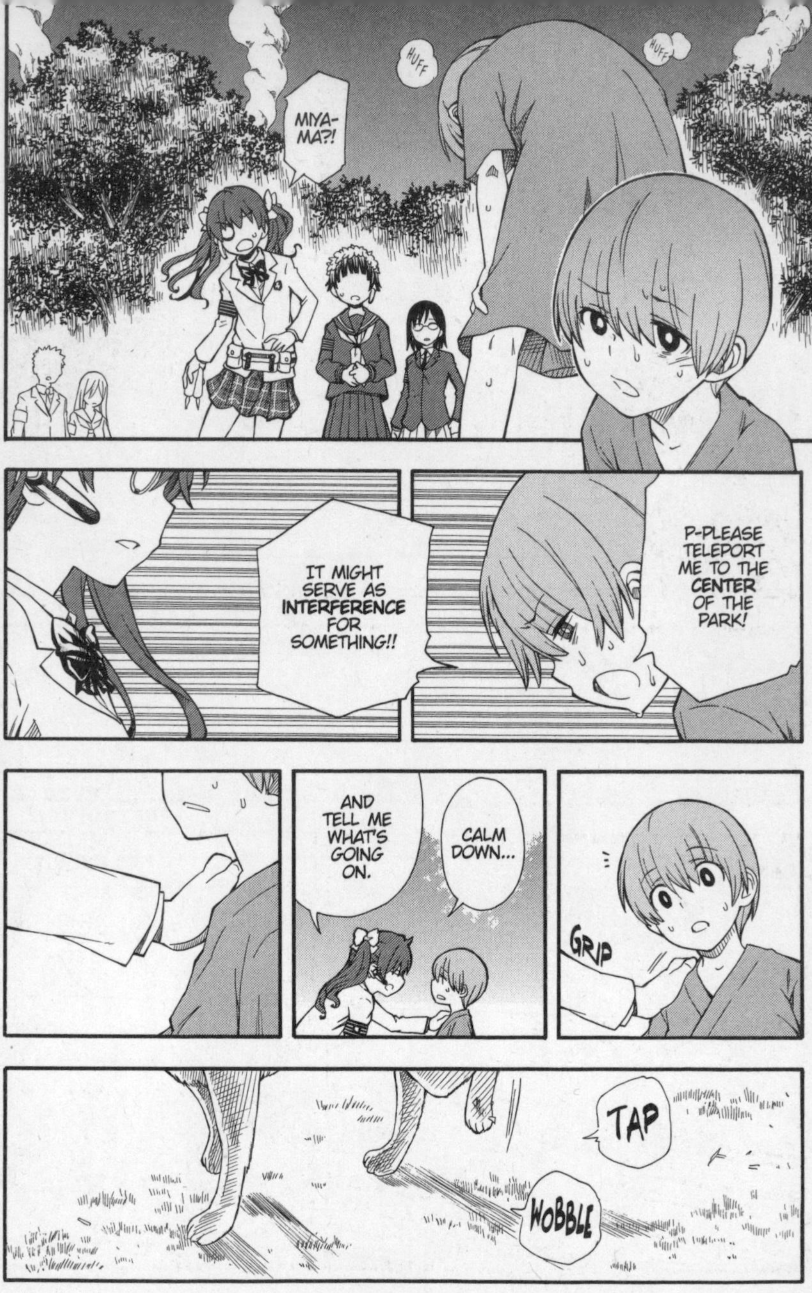
HUFF
HUFF
MIYA-MA?!
P-PLEASE TELEPORT ME TO THE CENTER OF THE PARK!
IT MIGHT SERVE AS INTERFERENCE FOR SOMETHING!!
GRIP
CALM DOWN...
AND TELL ME WHAT'S GOING ON.
TAP
WOBBLE

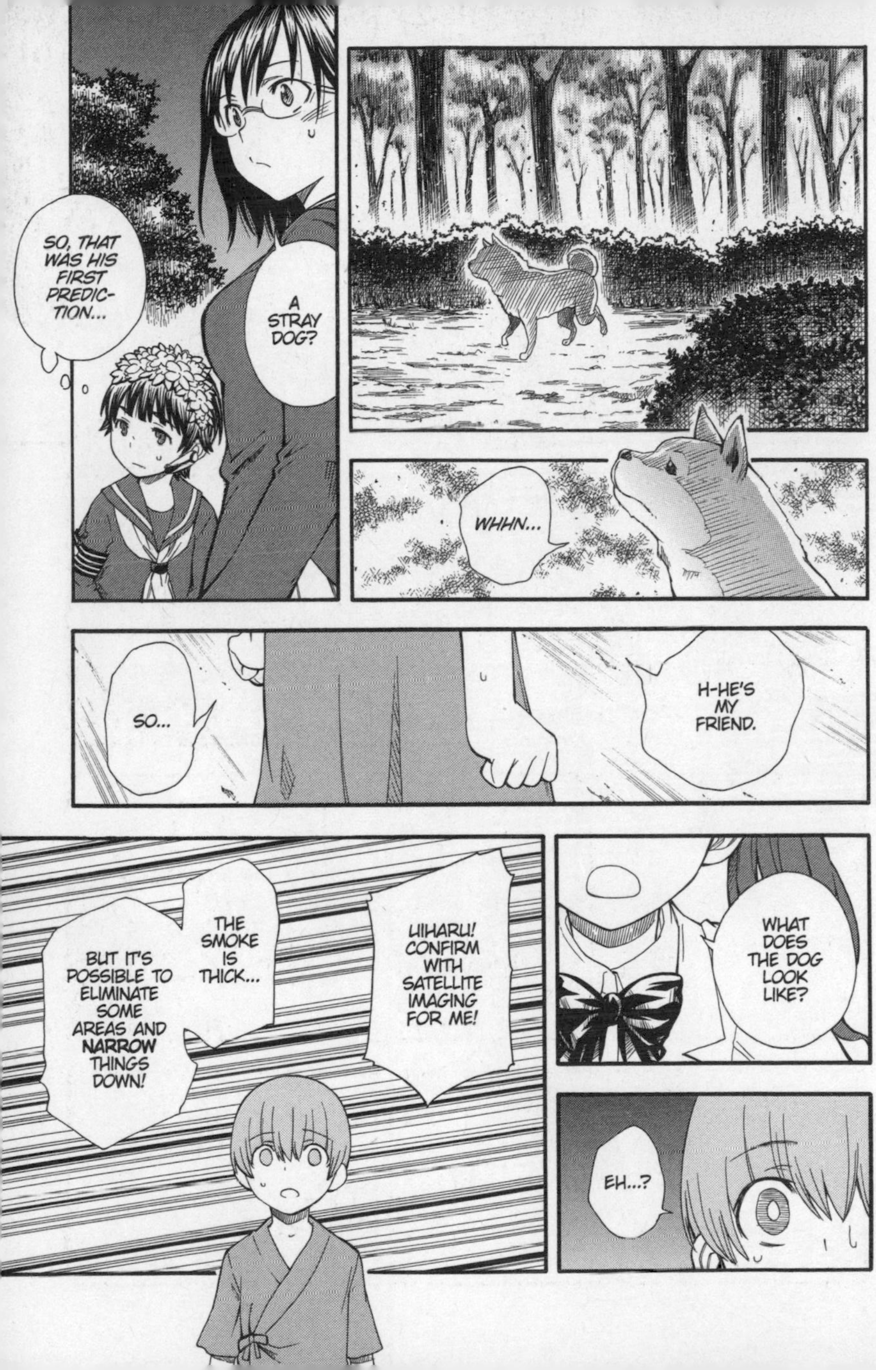
WHHN...
A STRAY DOG?
SO, THAT WAS HIS FIRST PREDICTION...
H-HE'S MY FRIEND.
SO...
WHAT DOES THE DOG LOOK LIKE?
EH...?
UIHARU! CONFIRM WITH SATELLITE IMAGING FOR ME!
THE SMOKE IS THICK...
BUT IT'S POSSIBLE TO ELIMINATE SOME AREAS AND NARROW THINGS DOWN!

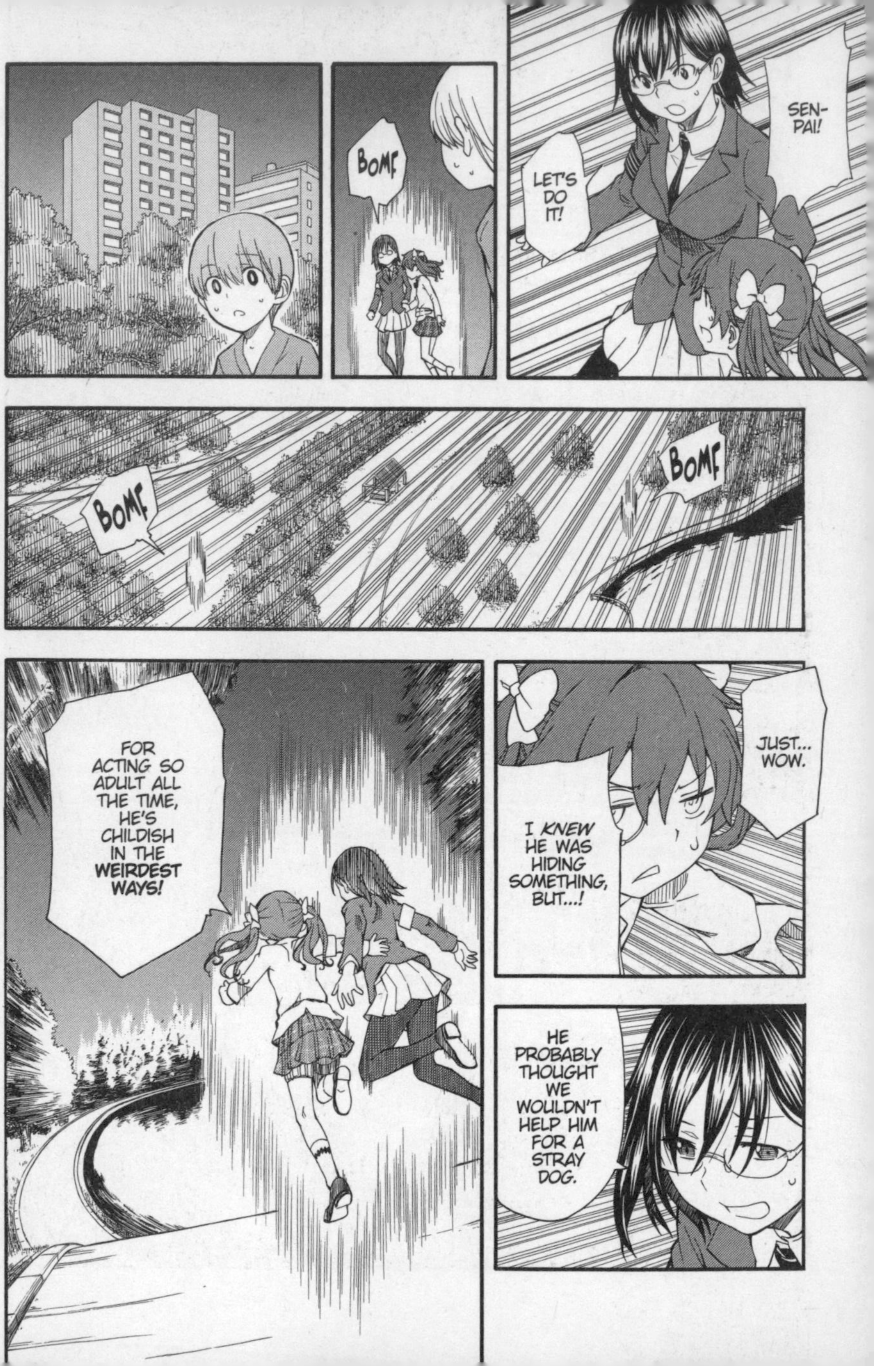
SEN-PAI!
LET'S DO IT!
BOMF
BOMF
BOMF
JUST... WOW.
I *KNEW* HE WAS HIDING SOMETHING, BUT...!
HE PROBABLY THOUGHT WE WOULDN'T HELP HIM FOR A STRAY DOG.
FOR ACTING SO ADULT ALL THE TIME, HE'S CHILDISH IN THE **WEIRDEST WAYS!**

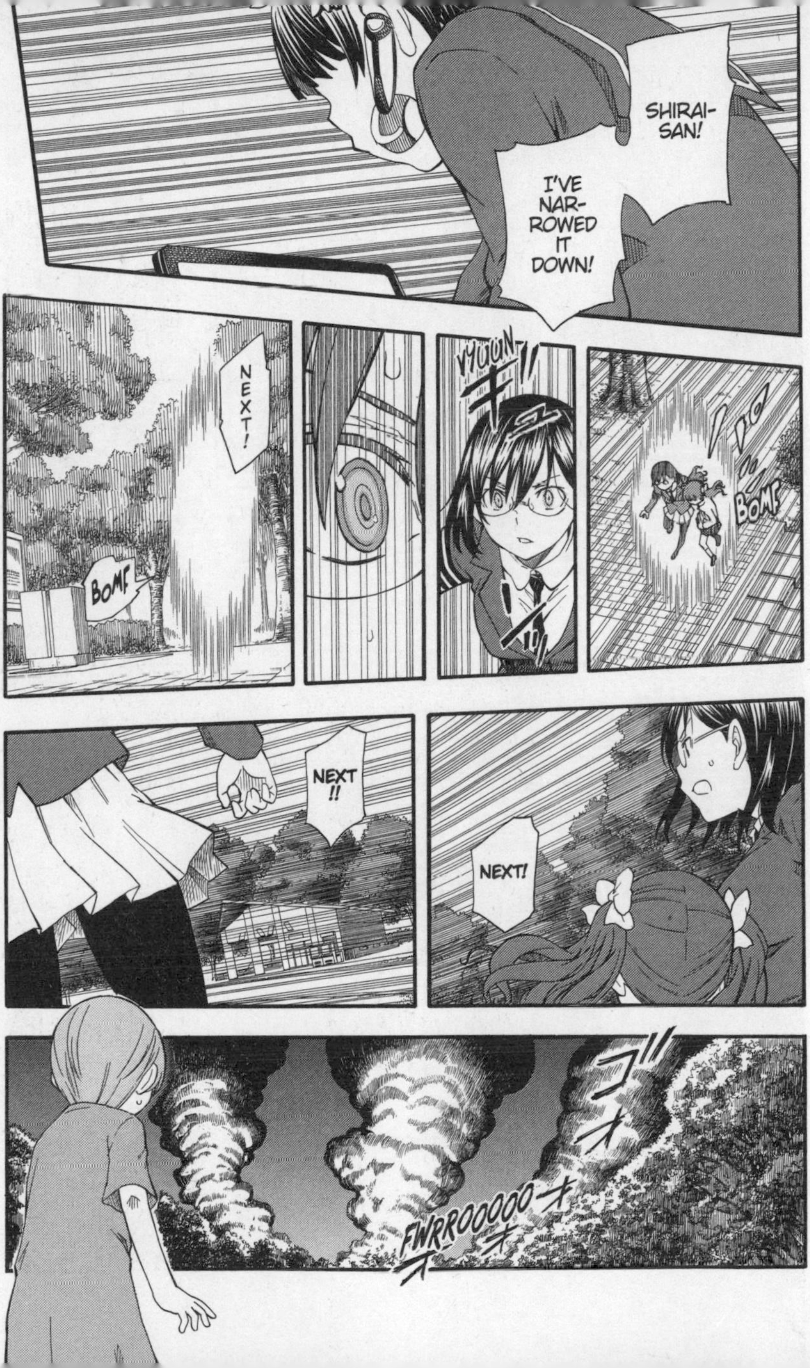
SHIRAI-SAN!
I'VE NAR-ROWED IT DOWN!
BOMF
VYUUN
NEXT!
BOMF
NEXT!
NEXT !!
FWRROOOOO

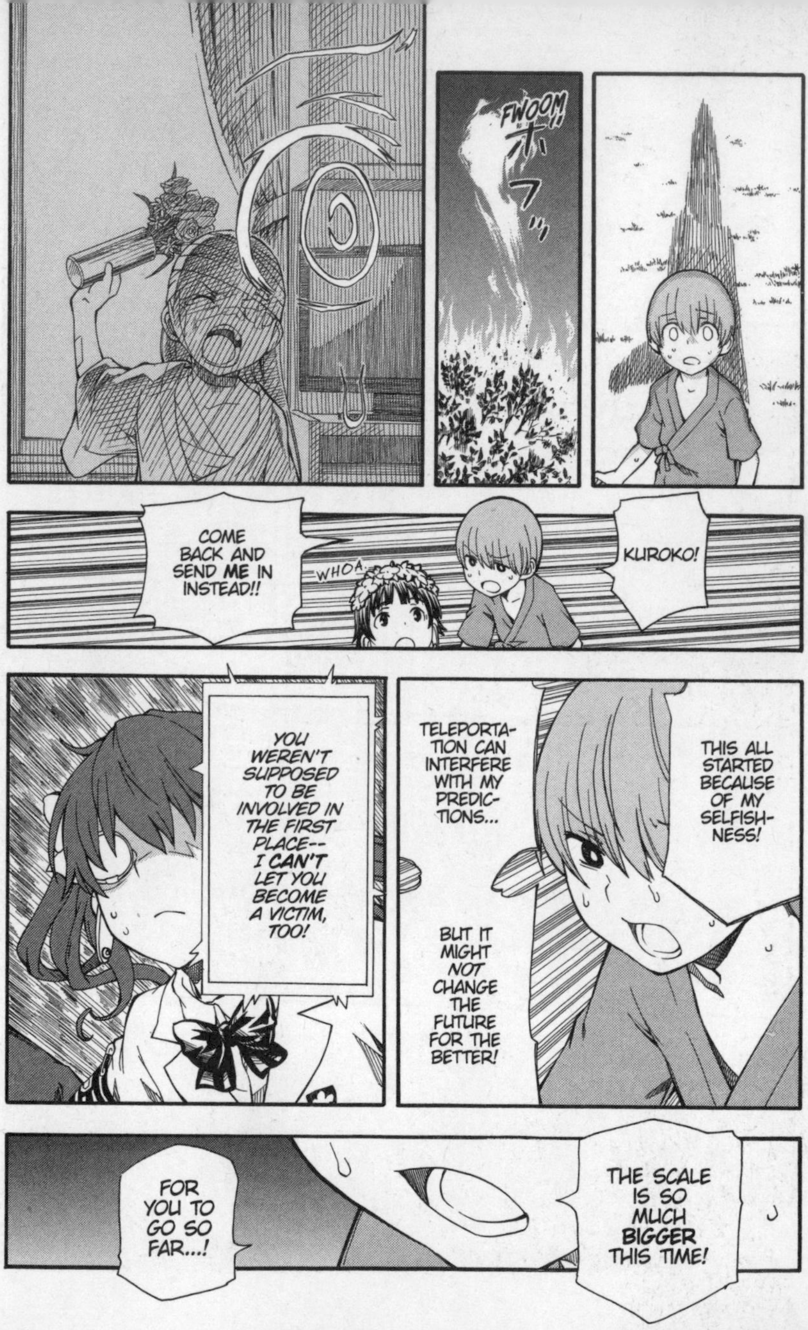
FWOOM!!
ホフッ
KUROKO!
WHOA
COME BACK AND SEND ME IN INSTEAD!!
THIS ALL STARTED BECAUSE OF MY SELFISHNESS!
TELEPORTATION CAN INTERFERE WITH MY PREDICTIONS...
BUT IT MIGHT NOT CHANGE THE FUTURE FOR THE BETTER!
YOU WEREN'T SUPPOSED TO BE INVOLVED IN THE FIRST PLACE-- I CAN'T LET YOU BECOME A VICTIM, TOO!
THE SCALE IS SO MUCH BIGGER THIS TIME!
FOR YOU TO GO SO FAR...!

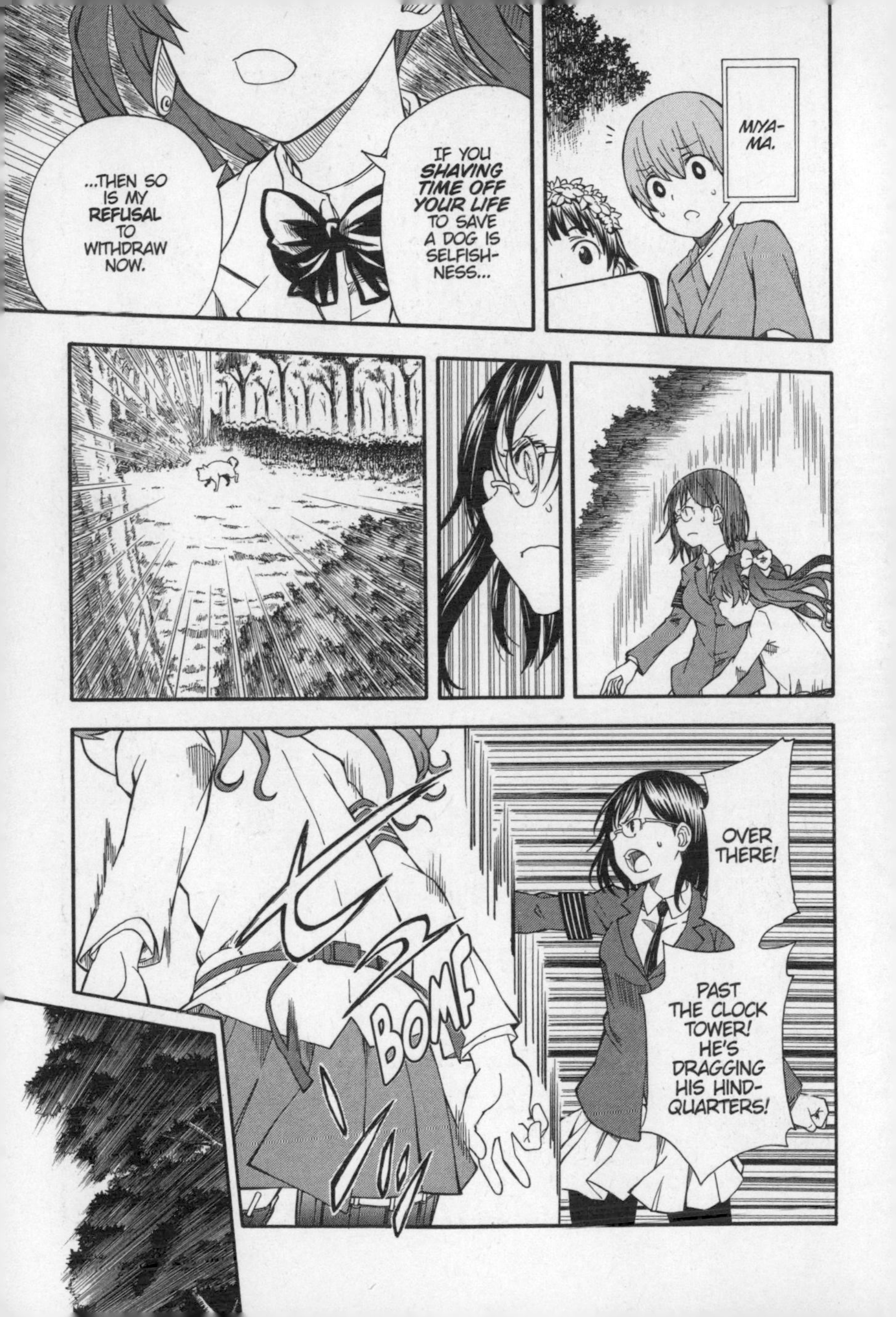
MIYA-MA.
IF YOU SHAVING TIME OFF YOUR LIFE TO SAVE A DOG IS SELFISH-NESS...
...THEN SO IS MY REFUSAL TO WITHDRAW NOW.
OVER THERE!
PAST THE CLOCK TOWER! HE'S DRAGGING HIS HIND-QUARTERS!
BOMF

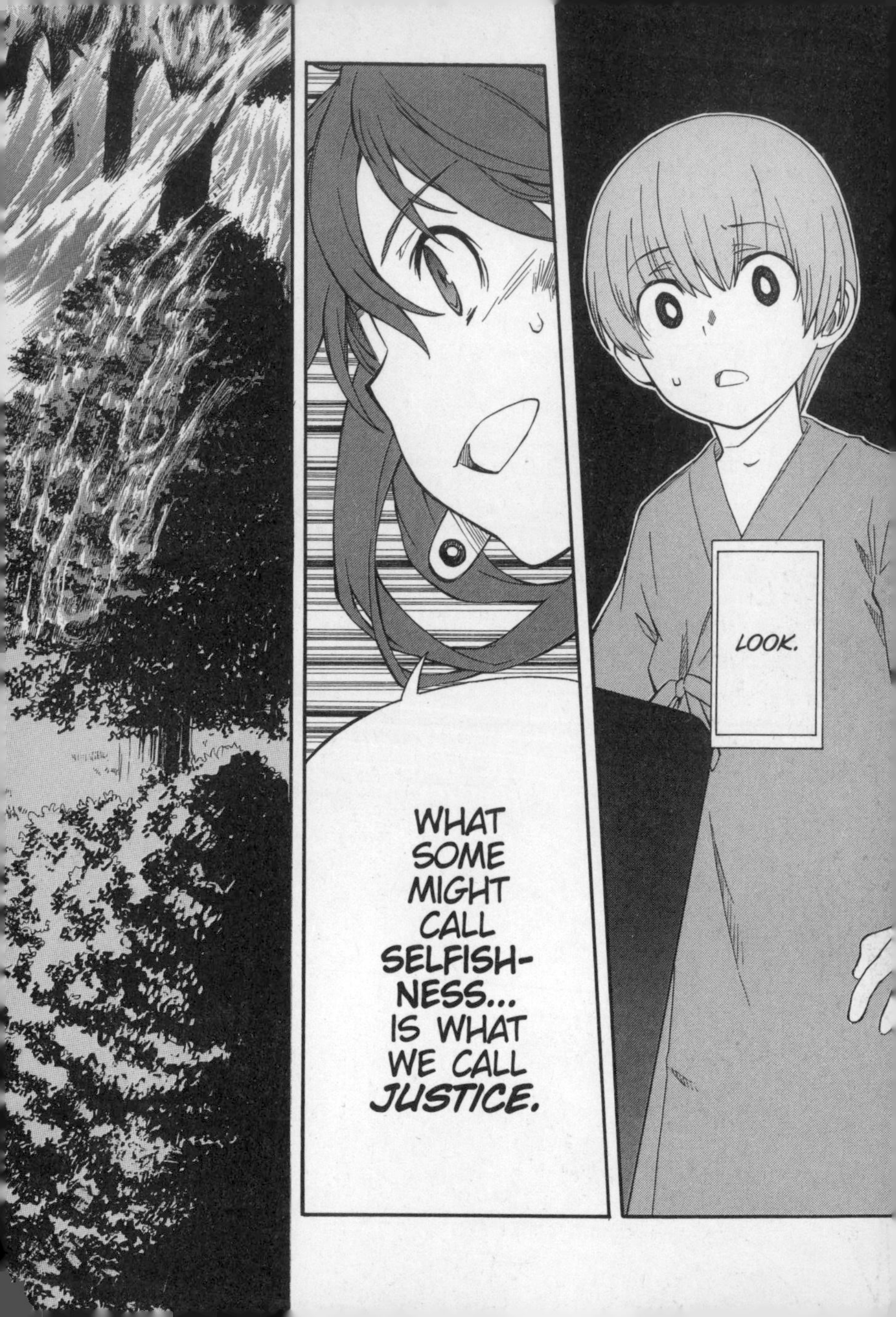
LOOK.
WHAT SOME MIGHT CALL SELFISHNESS... IS WHAT WE CALL JUSTICE.

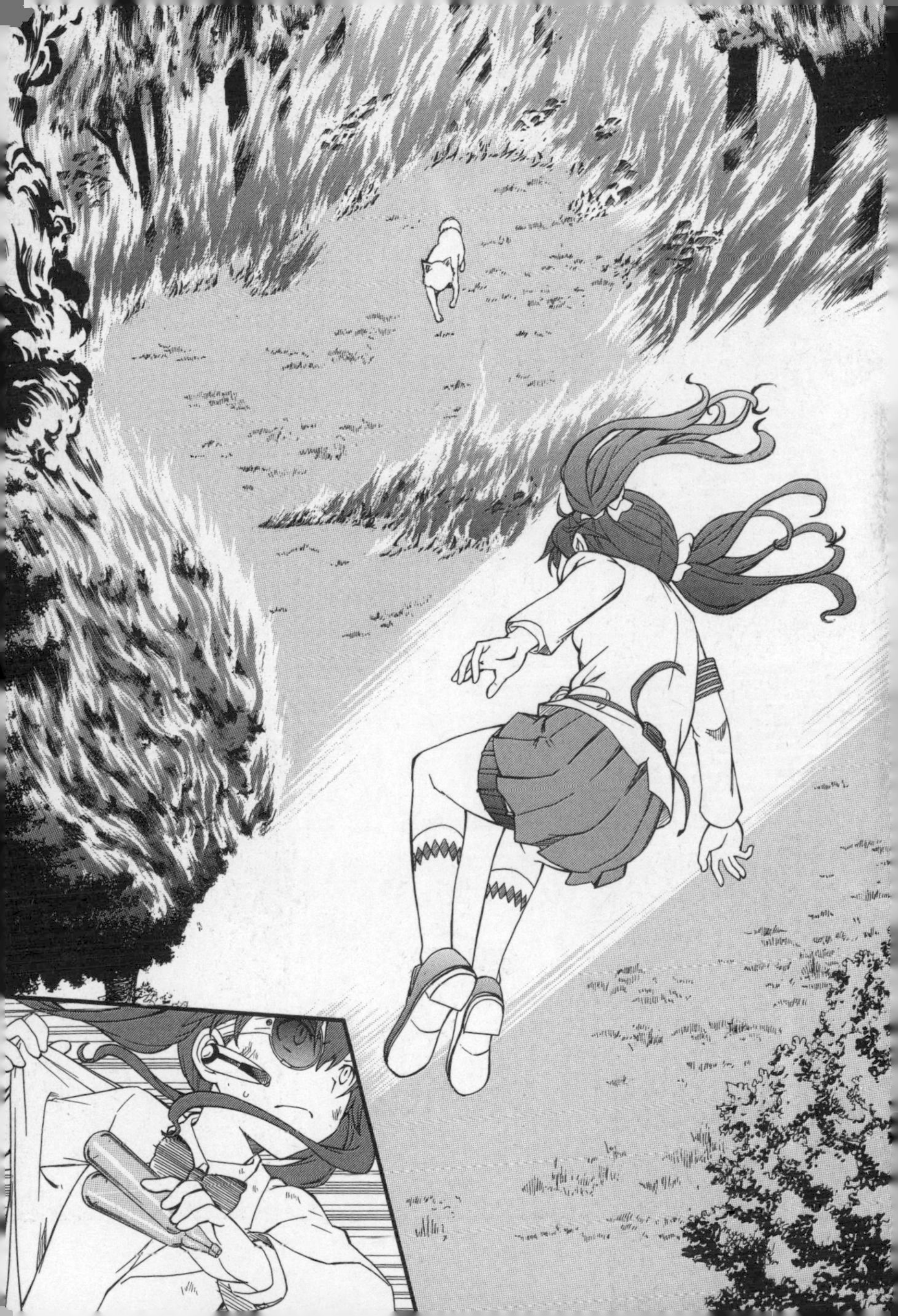

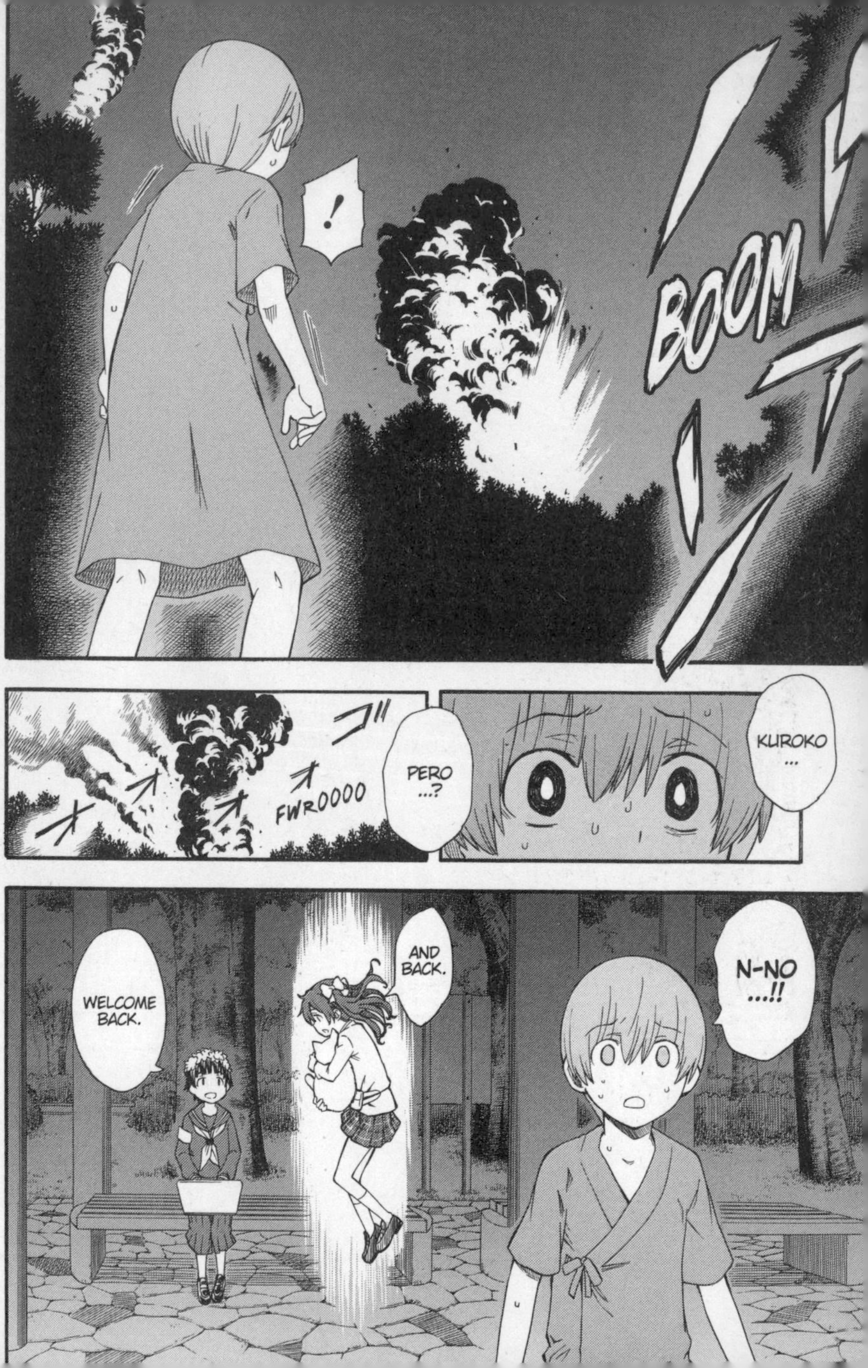
BOOM
!
KUROKO ...
PERO ...?
FWROOOO
N-NO ...!!
AND BACK.
WELCOME BACK.

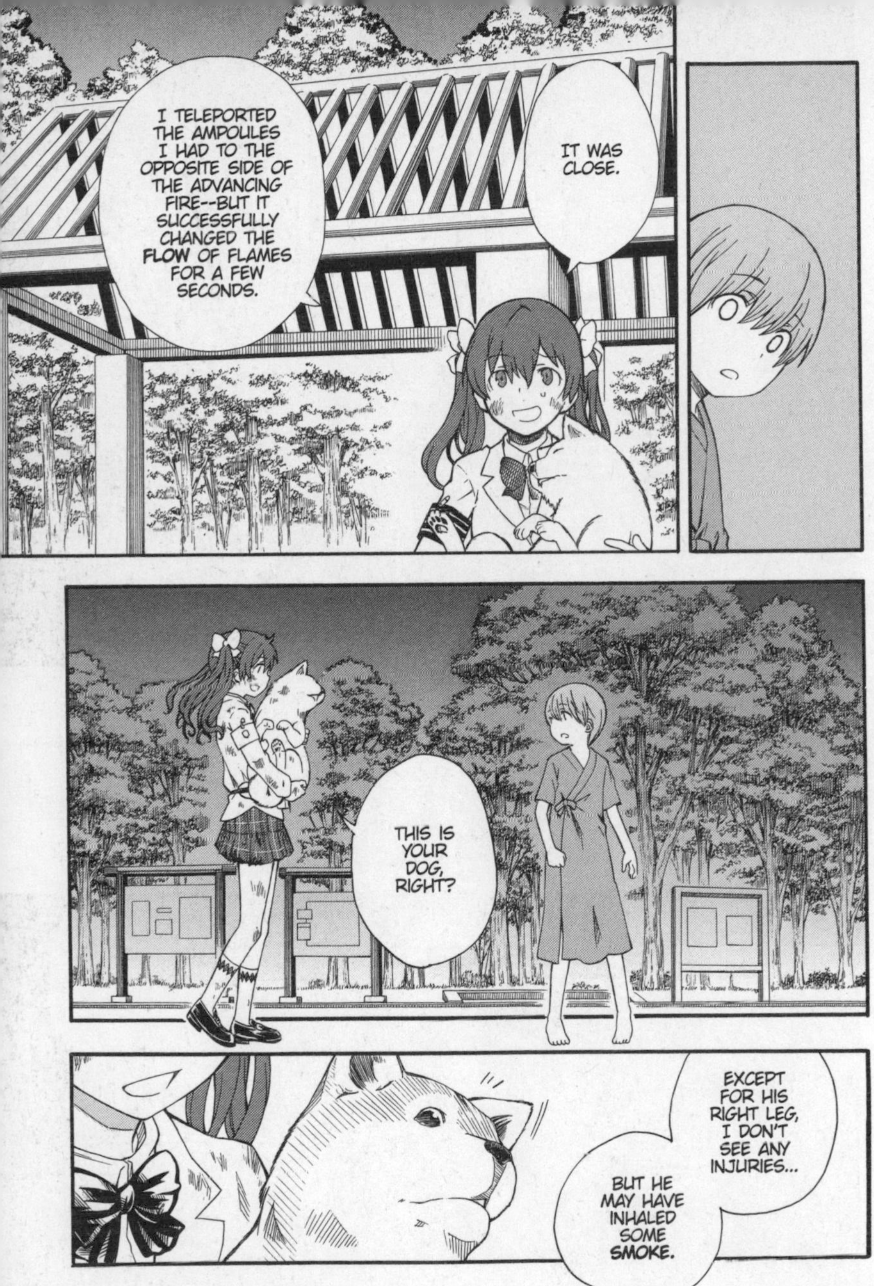
IT WAS CLOSE.
I TELEPORTED THE AMPOULES I HAD TO THE OPPOSITE SIDE OF THE ADVANCING FIRE--BUT IT SUCCESSFULLY CHANGED THE FLOW OF FLAMES FOR A FEW SECONDS.
THIS IS YOUR DOG, RIGHT?
EXCEPT FOR HIS RIGHT LEG, I DON'T SEE ANY INJURIES...
BUT HE MAY HAVE INHALED SOME SMOKE.

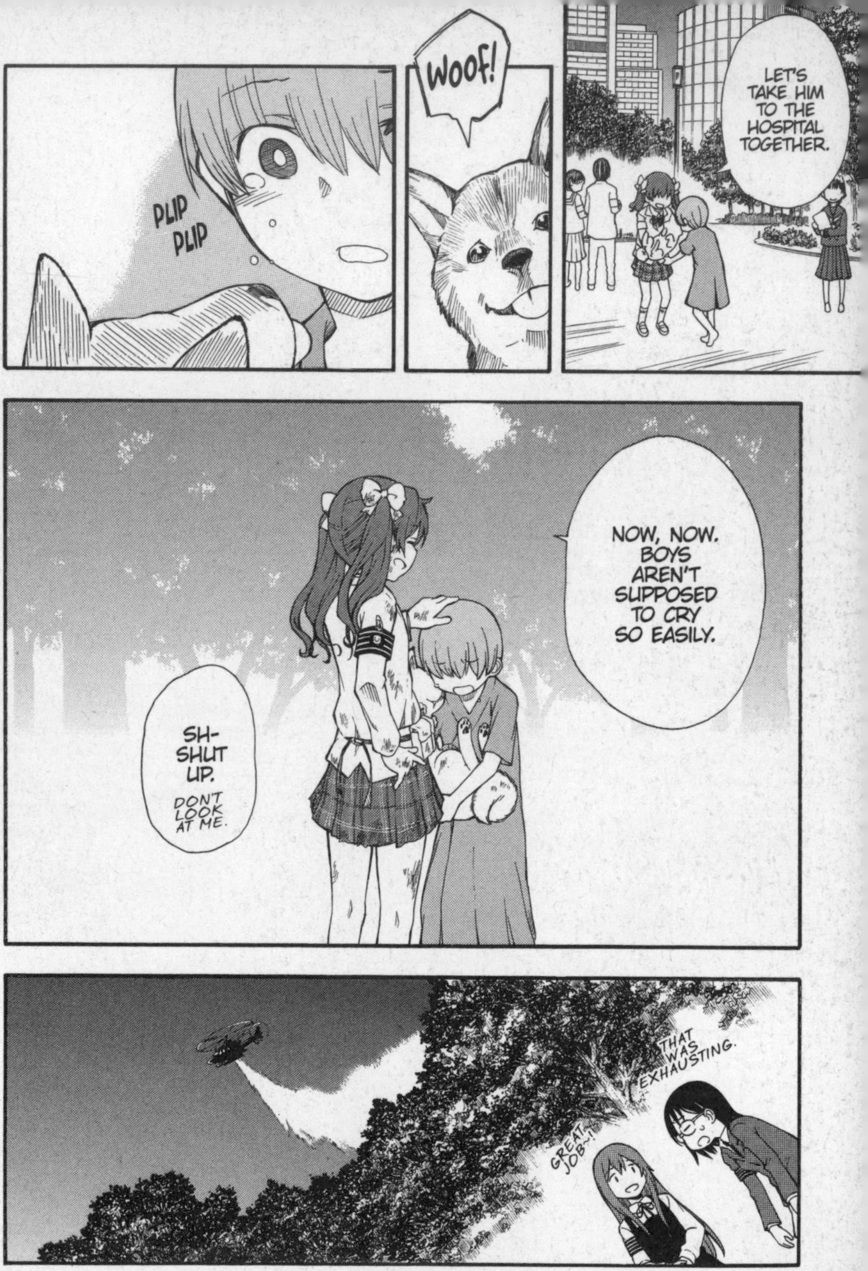
LET'S TAKE HIM TO THE HOSPITAL TOGETHER.
WOOF!
PLIP PLIP
NOW, NOW. BOYS AREN'T SUPPOSED TO CRY SO EASILY.
SH-SHUT UP.
DON'T LOOK AT ME.
THAT WAS EXHAUSTING.
GREAT JOB~!

A Certain SCIENTIFIC Railgun

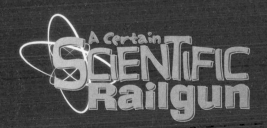

A Certain SCIENTIFIC Railgun

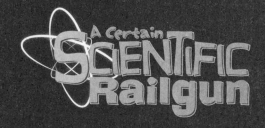

CHAPTER 77: DREAMS

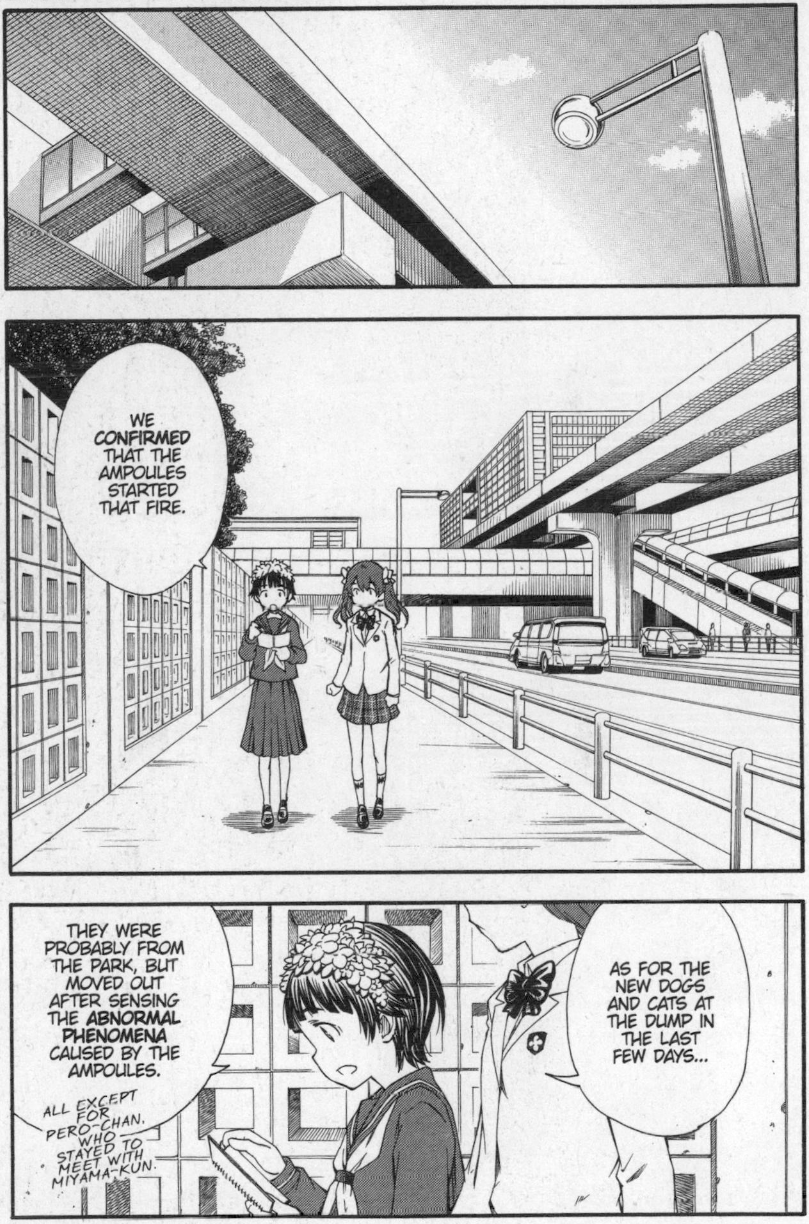
WE CONFIRMED THAT THE AMPOULES STARTED THAT FIRE.
AS FOR THE NEW DOGS AND CATS AT THE DUMP IN THE LAST FEW DAYS...
THEY WERE PROBABLY FROM THE PARK, BUT MOVED OUT AFTER SENSING THE ABNORMAL PHENOMENA CAUSED BY THE AMPOULES.
ALL EXCEPT FOR PERO-CHAN, WHO STAYED TO MEET WITH MIYAMA-KUN.

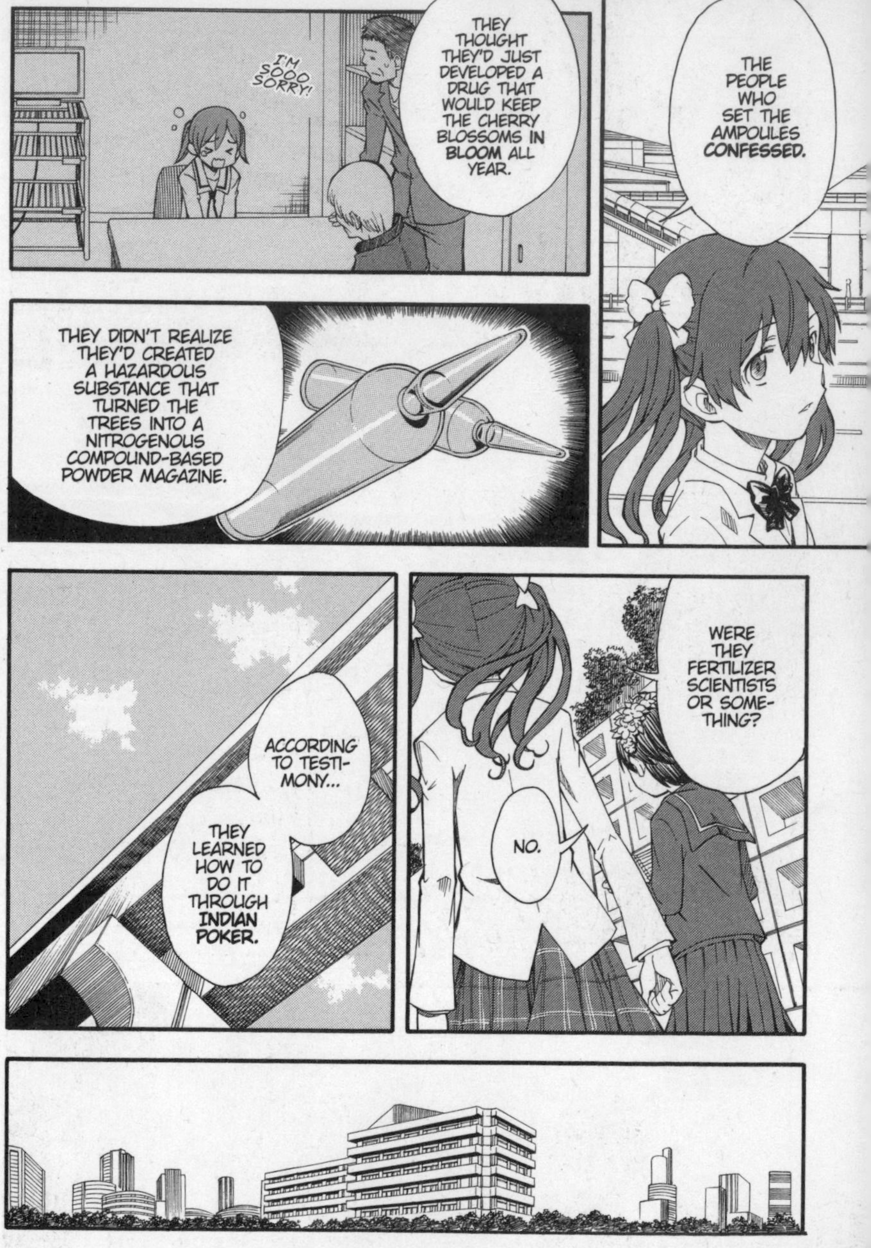
THE PEOPLE WHO SET THE AMPOULES CONFESSED.
THEY THOUGHT THEY'D JUST DEVELOPED A DRUG THAT WOULD KEEP THE CHERRY BLOSSOMS IN BLOOM ALL YEAR.
I'M SOOO SORRY!
THEY DIDN'T REALIZE THEY'D CREATED A HAZARDOUS SUBSTANCE THAT TURNED THE TREES INTO A NITROGENOUS COMPOUND-BASED POWDER MAGAZINE.
WERE THEY FERTILIZER SCIENTISTS OR SOME-THING?
NO.
ACCORDING TO TESTI-MONY...
THEY LEARNED HOW TO DO IT THROUGH INDIAN POKER.

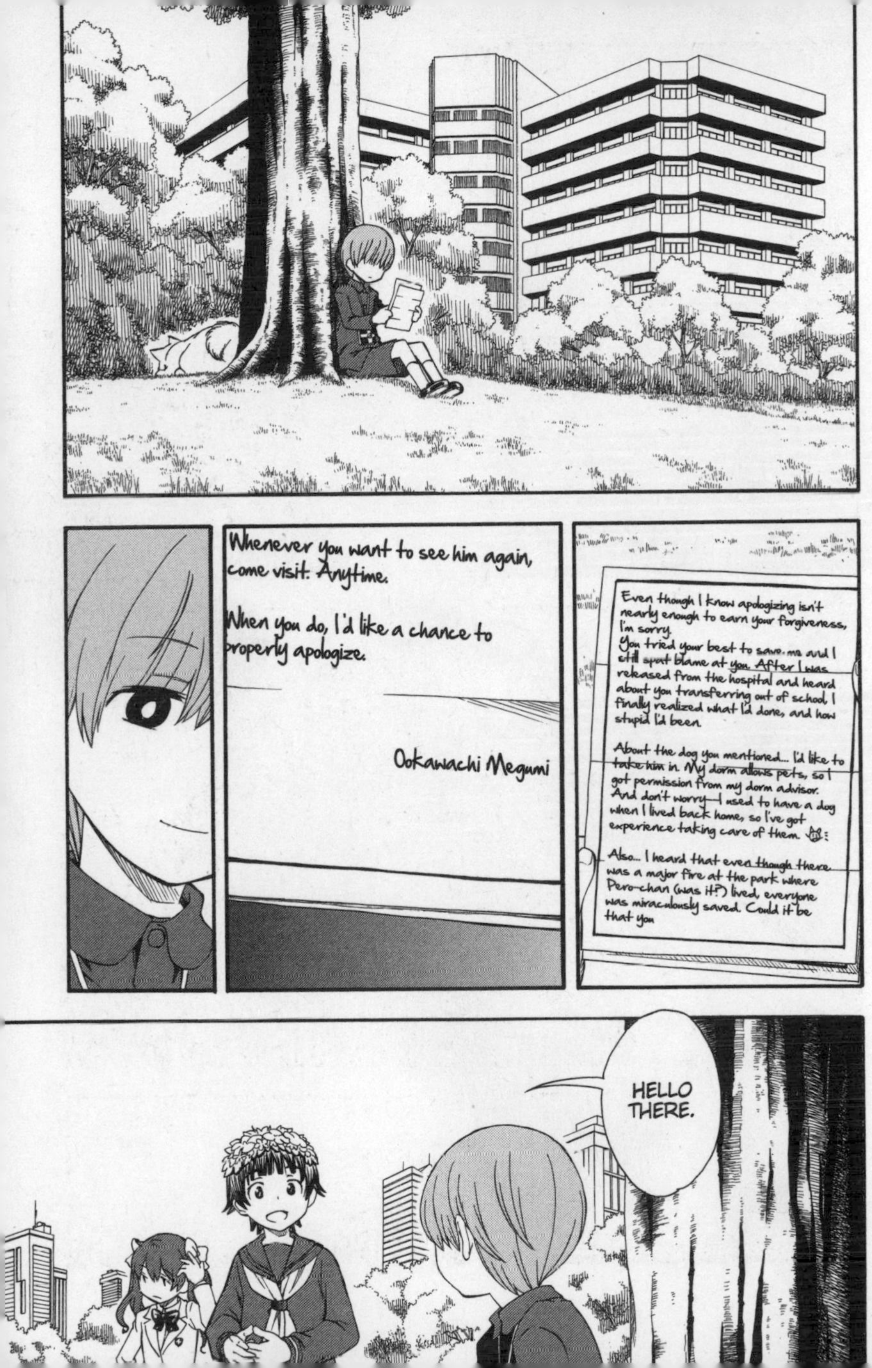
Even though I know apologizing isn't nearly enough to earn your forgiveness, I'm sorry.
You tried your best to save me and I still spat blame at you. After I was released from the hospital and heard about you transferring out of school, I finally realized what I'd done, and how stupid I'd been.
About the dog you mentioned... I'd like to take him in. My dorm allows pets, so I got permission from my dorm advisor. And don't worry—I used to have a dog when I lived back home, so I've got experience taking care of them.
Also... I heard that even though there was a major fire at the park where Pero-chan (was it?) lived, everyone was miraculously saved. Could it be that you
Whenever you want to see him again, come visit. Anytime.
When you do, I'd like a chance to properly apologize.
Ookawachi Megumi
HELLO THERE.

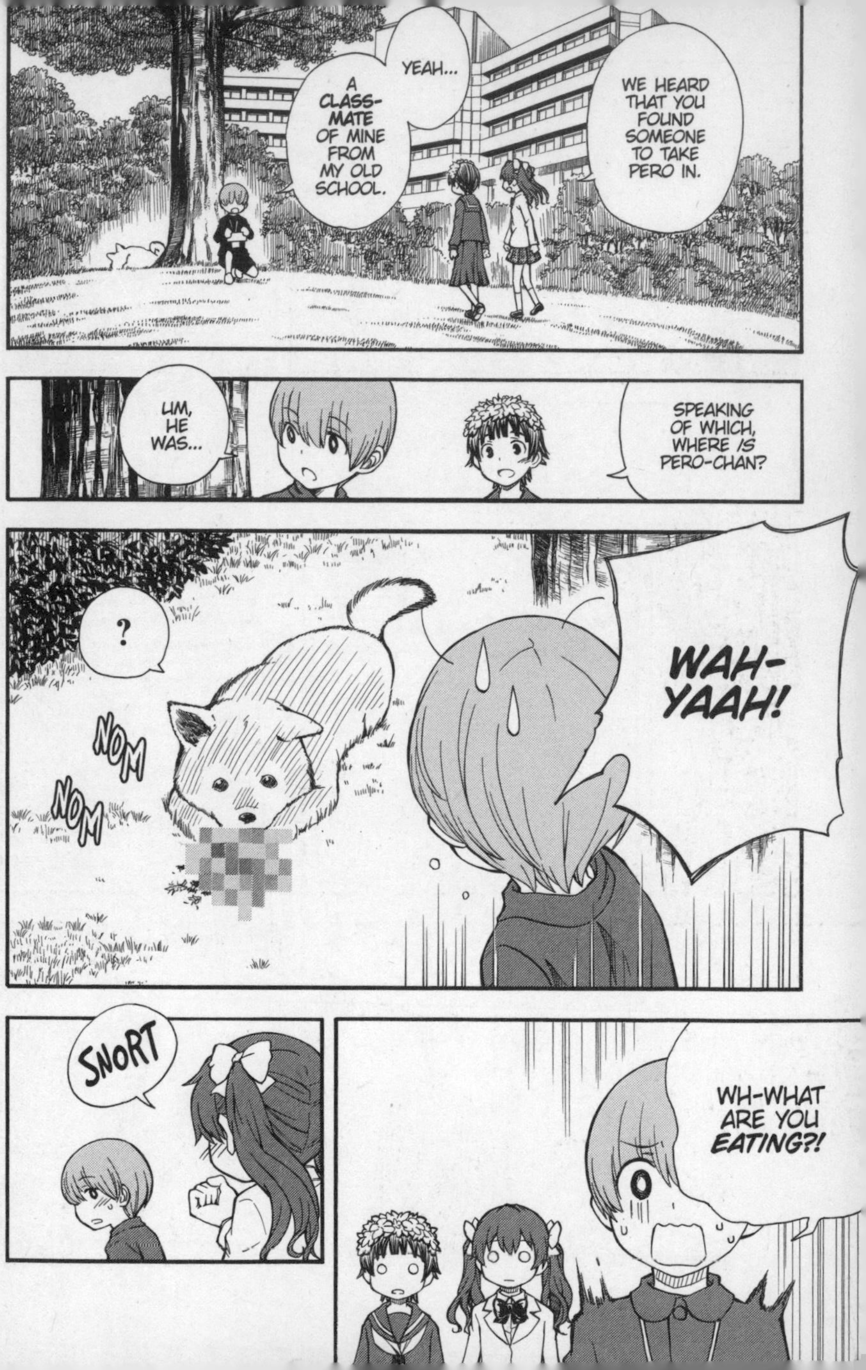
WE HEARD THAT YOU FOUND SOMEONE TO TAKE PERO IN.
YEAH...
A CLASSMATE OF MINE FROM MY OLD SCHOOL.
SPEAKING OF WHICH, WHERE IS PERO-CHAN?
UM, HE WAS...
WAH-YAAH!
?
NOM
NOM
WH-WHAT ARE YOU EATING?!
SNORT

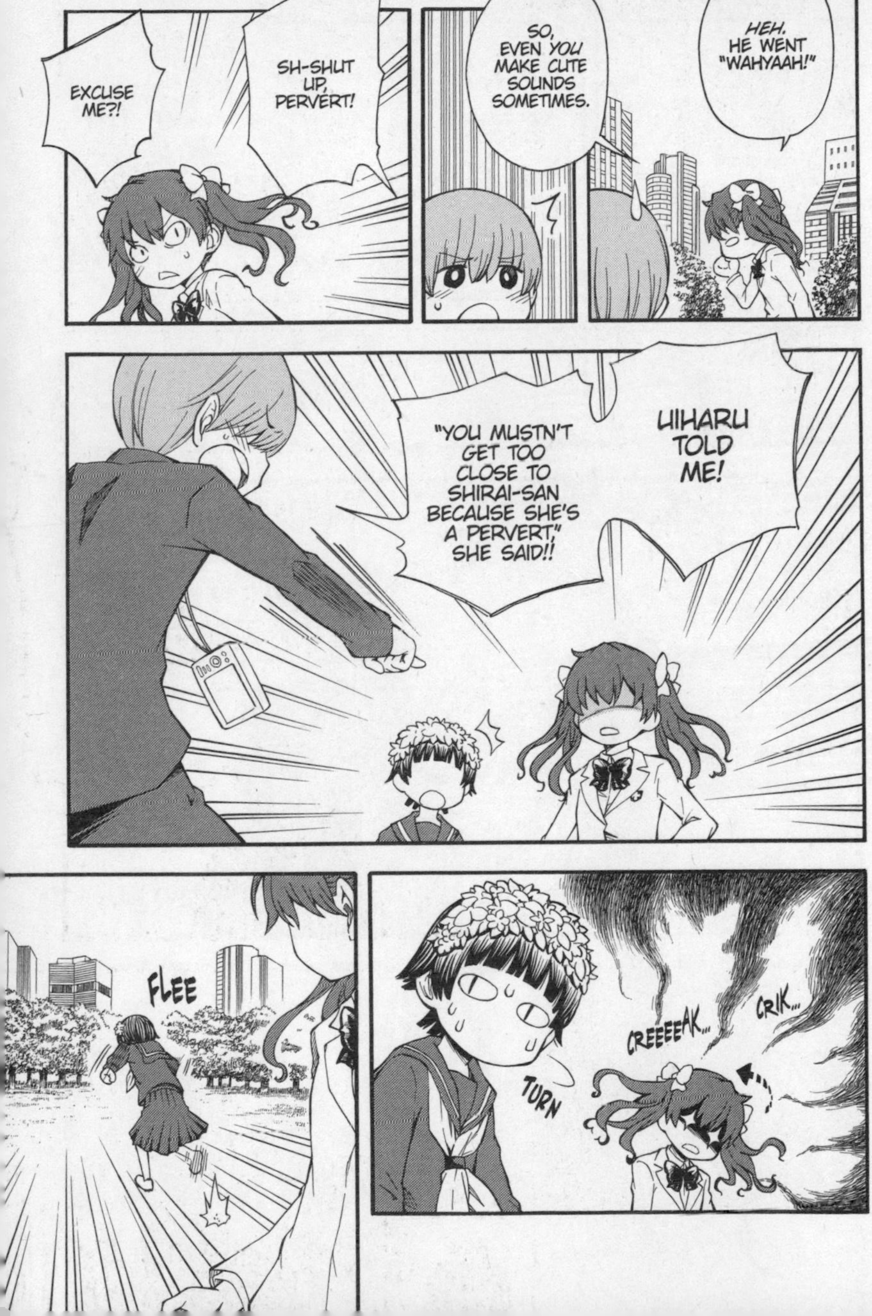
HEH. HE WENT "WAHYAAH!"
SO, EVEN YOU MAKE CUTE SOUNDS SOMETIMES.
SH-SHUT UP, PERVERT!
EXCUSE ME?!
UIHARU TOLD ME!
"YOU MUSTN'T GET TOO CLOSE TO SHIRAI-SAN BECAUSE SHE'S A PERVERT," SHE SAID!!
CRIK...
CREEEEAK...
TURN
FLEE

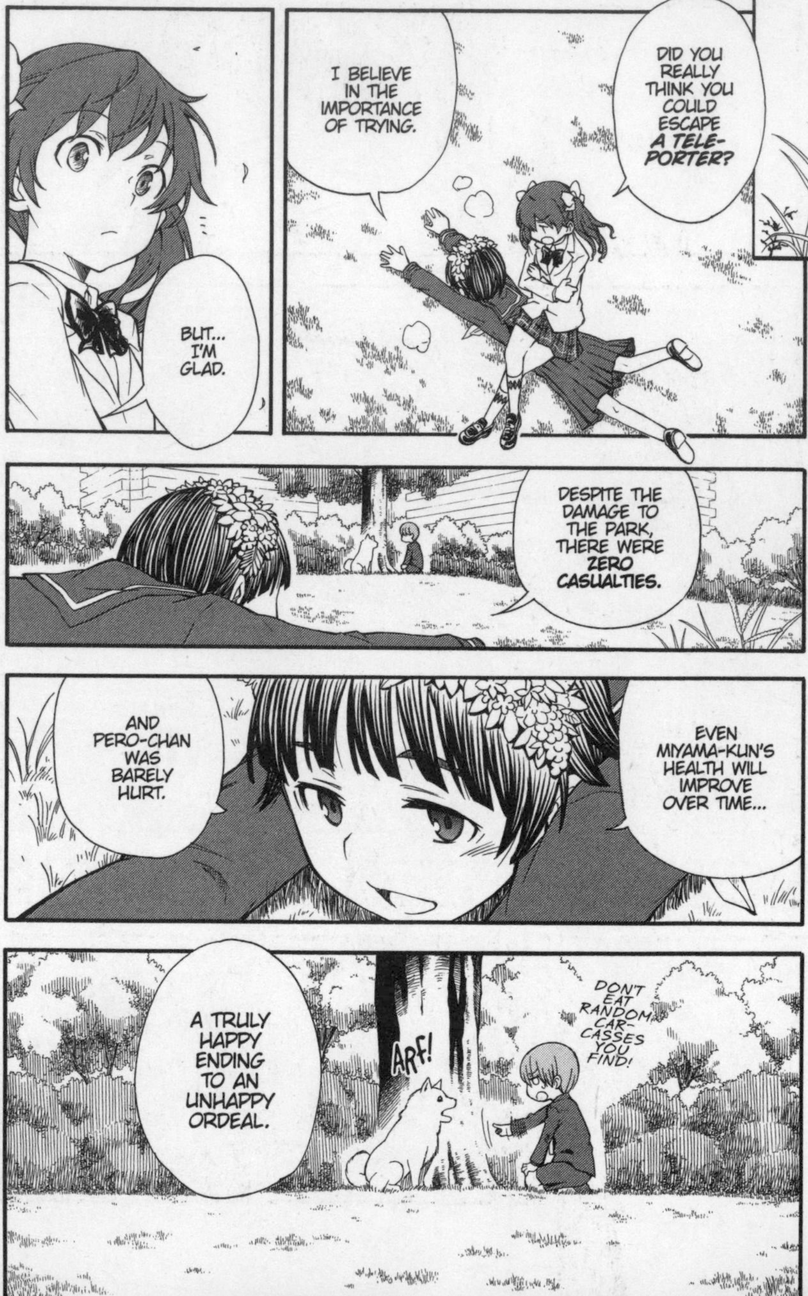
DID YOU REALLY THINK YOU COULD ESCAPE **A TELE-PORTER?**
I BELIEVE IN THE IMPORTANCE OF TRYING.
BUT... I'M GLAD.
DESPITE THE DAMAGE TO THE PARK, THERE WERE ZERO CASUALTIES.
EVEN MIYAMA-KUN'S HEALTH WILL IMPROVE OVER TIME...
AND PERO-CHAN WAS BARELY HURT.
DON'T EAT RANDOM CAR-CASSES YOU FIND!
ARF!
A TRULY HAPPY ENDING TO AN UNHAPPY ORDEAL.

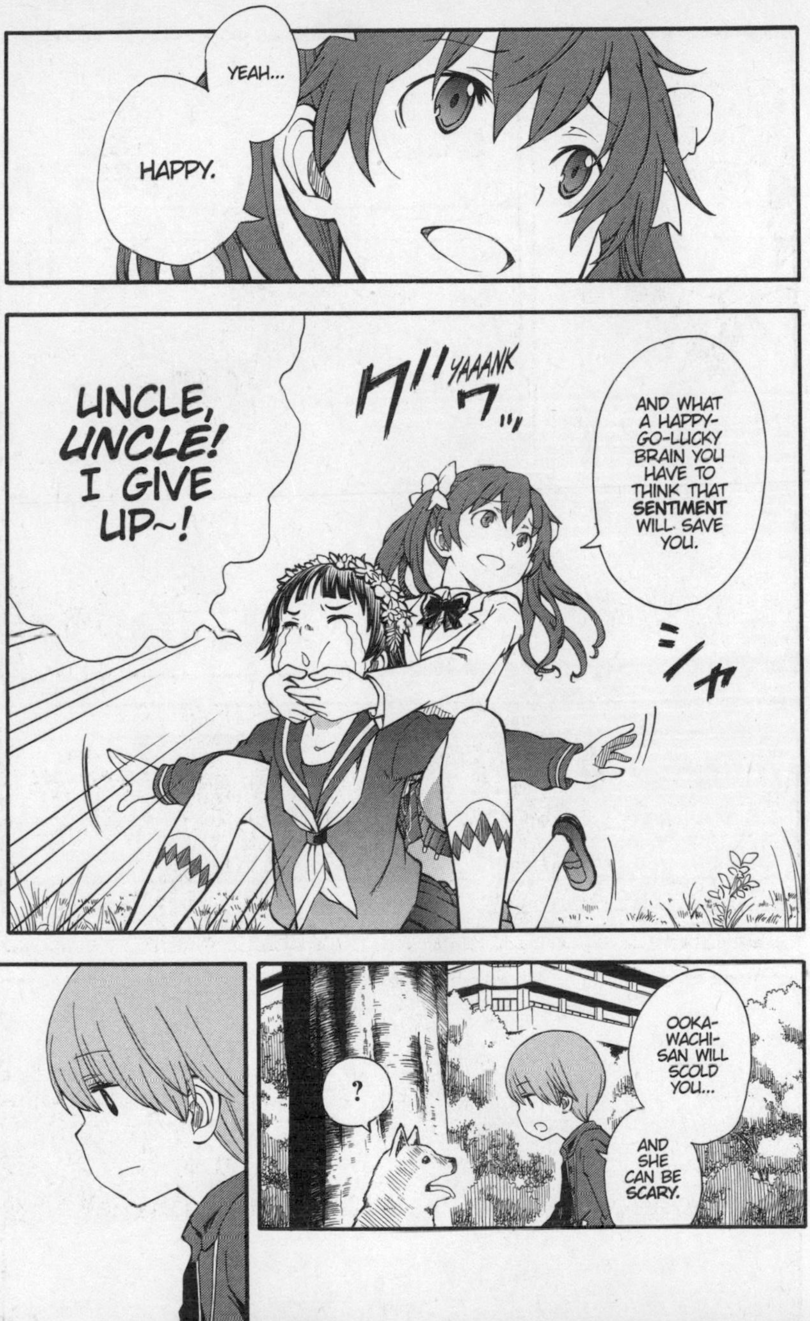
YEAH...
HAPPY.
AND WHAT A HAPPY-GO-LUCKY BRAIN YOU HAVE TO THINK THAT SENTIMENT WILL SAVE YOU.
YAAANK
UNCLE, UNCLE! I GIVE UP~!
OOKA-WACHI-SAN WILL SCOLD YOU...
AND SHE CAN BE SCARY.
?

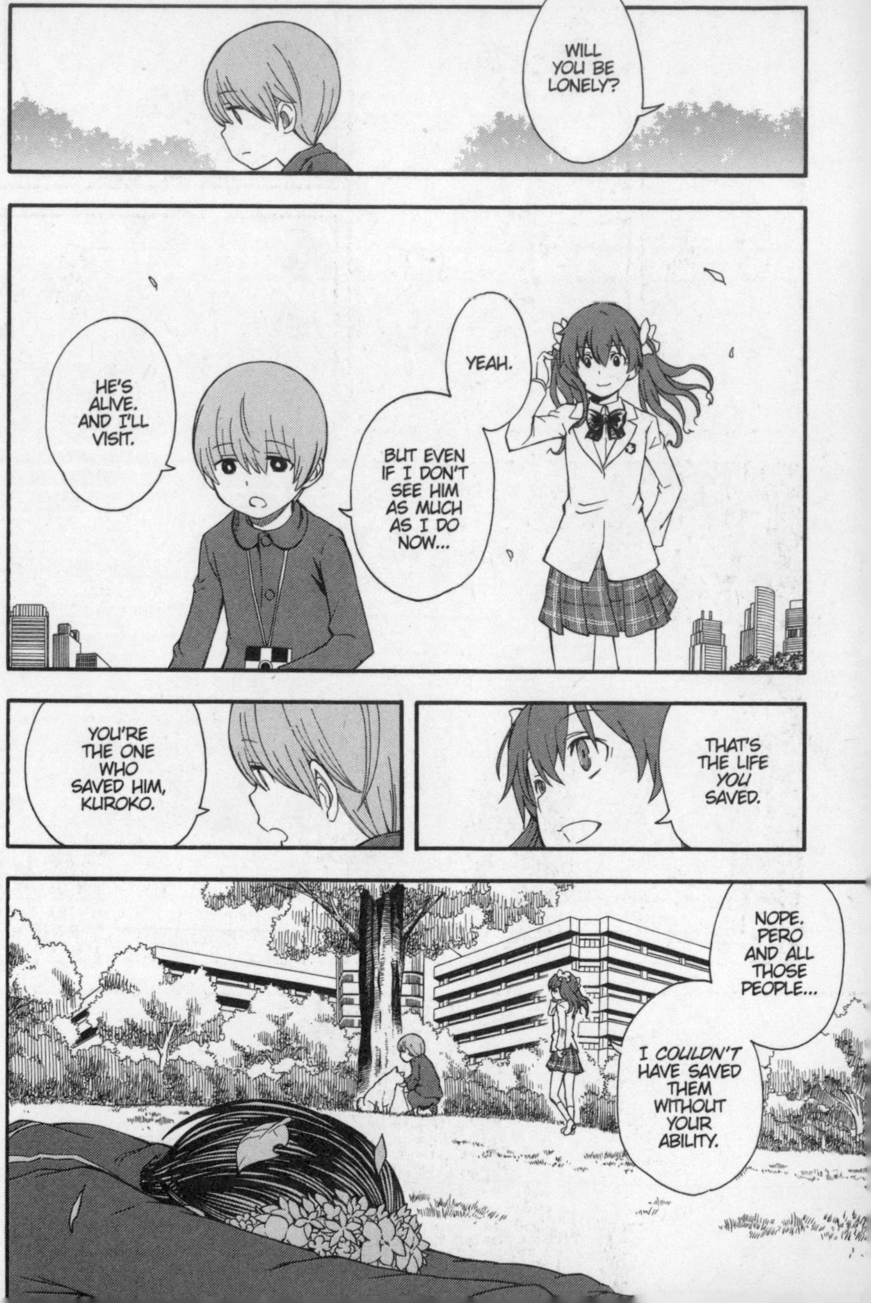
WILL YOU BE LONELY?
YEAH.
BUT EVEN IF I DON'T SEE HIM AS MUCH AS I DO NOW...
HE'S ALIVE. AND I'LL VISIT.
THAT'S THE LIFE *YOU* SAVED.
YOU'RE THE ONE WHO SAVED HIM, KUROKO.
NOPE. PERO AND ALL THOSE PEOPLE...
I COULDN'T HAVE SAVED THEM WITHOUT YOUR ABILITY.

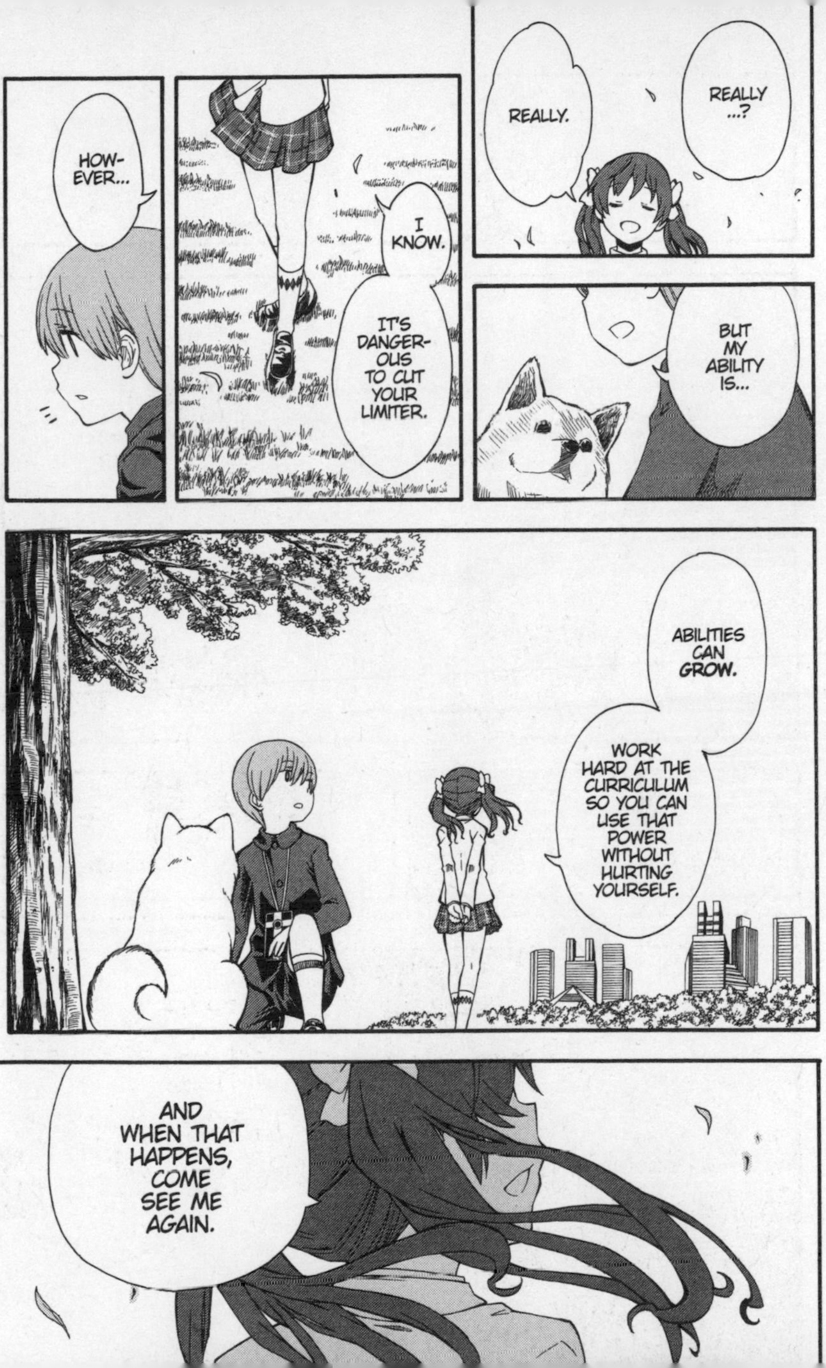
REALLY ...?
REALLY.
BUT MY ABILITY IS...
I KNOW.
IT'S DANGER-OUS TO CUT YOUR LIMITER.
HOW-EVER...
ABILITIES CAN GROW.
WORK HARD AT THE CURRICULUM SO YOU CAN USE THAT POWER WITHOUT HURTING YOURSELF.
AND WHEN THAT HAPPENS, COME SEE ME AGAIN.

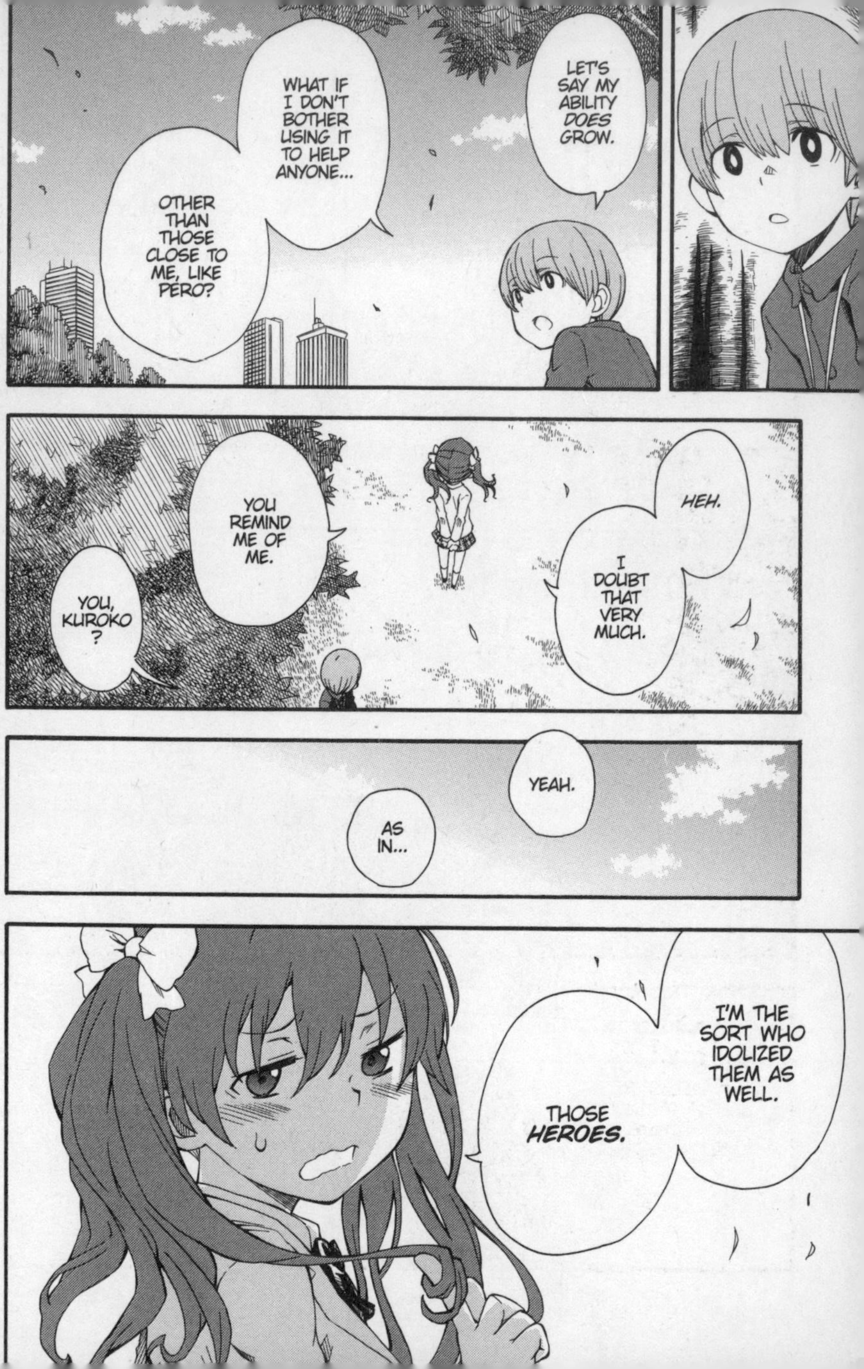
LET'S SAY MY ABILITY DOES GROW.
WHAT IF I DON'T BOTHER USING IT TO HELP ANYONE...
OTHER THAN THOSE CLOSE TO ME, LIKE PERO?
HEH.
I DOUBT THAT VERY MUCH.
YOU REMIND ME OF ME.
YOU, KUROKO?
YEAH.
AS IN...
I'M THE SORT WHO IDOLIZED THEM AS WELL.
THOSE HEROES.

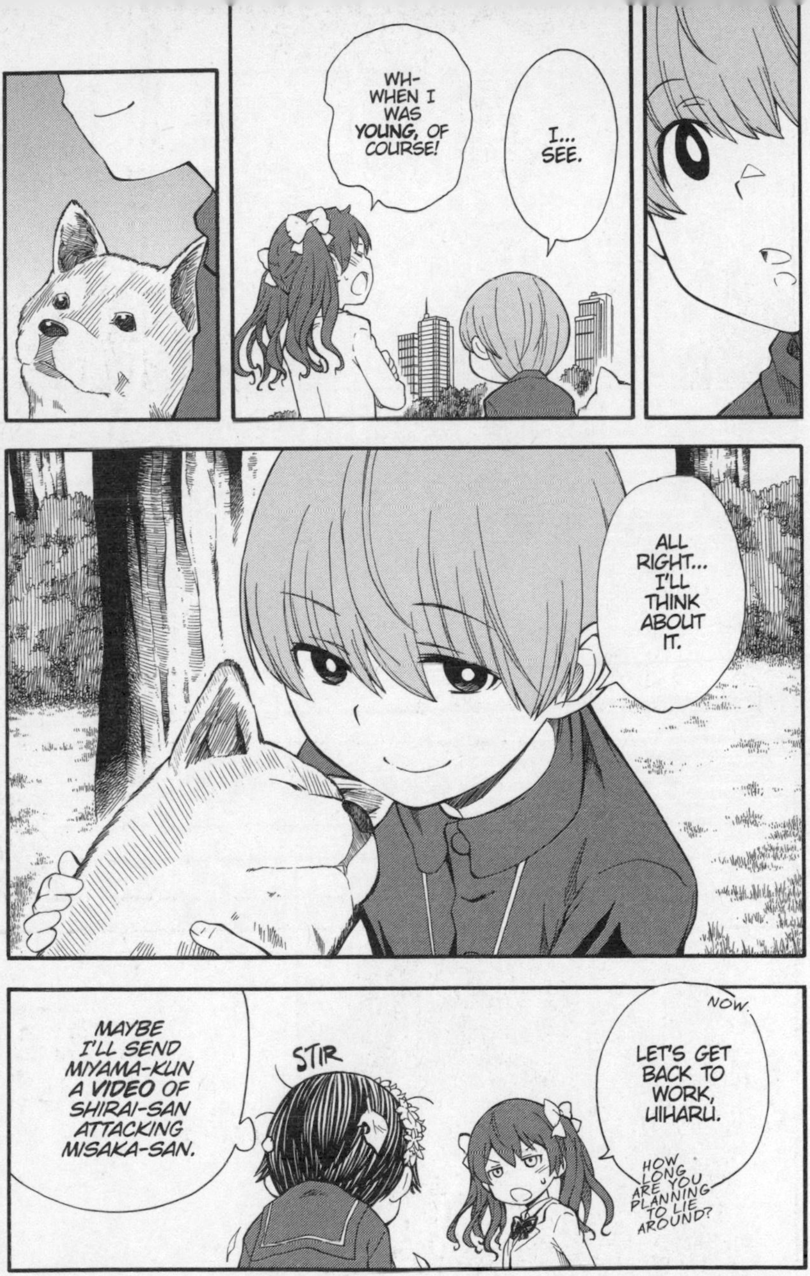
WH- WHEN I WAS YOUNG, OF COURSE!
I... SEE.
ALL RIGHT... I'LL THINK ABOUT IT.
NOW.
LET'S GET BACK TO WORK, UIHARU.
HOW LONG ARE YOU PLANNING TO LIE AROUND?
STIR
MAYBE I'LL SEND MIYAMA-KUN A VIDEO OF SHIRAI-SAN ATTACKING MISAKA-SAN.

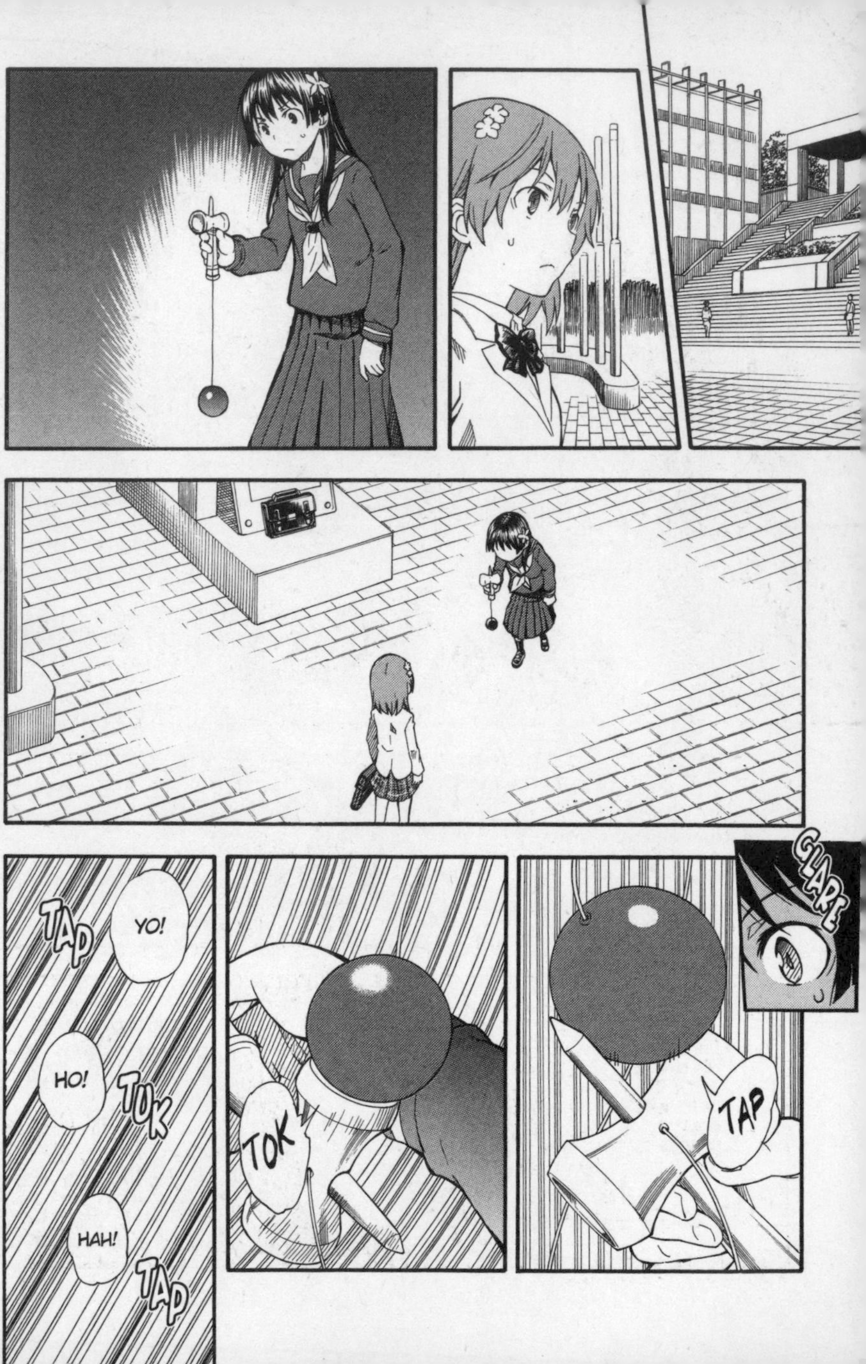
GLARE
TAP
TOK
YO!
TAP
HO!
TUK
HAH!
TAP

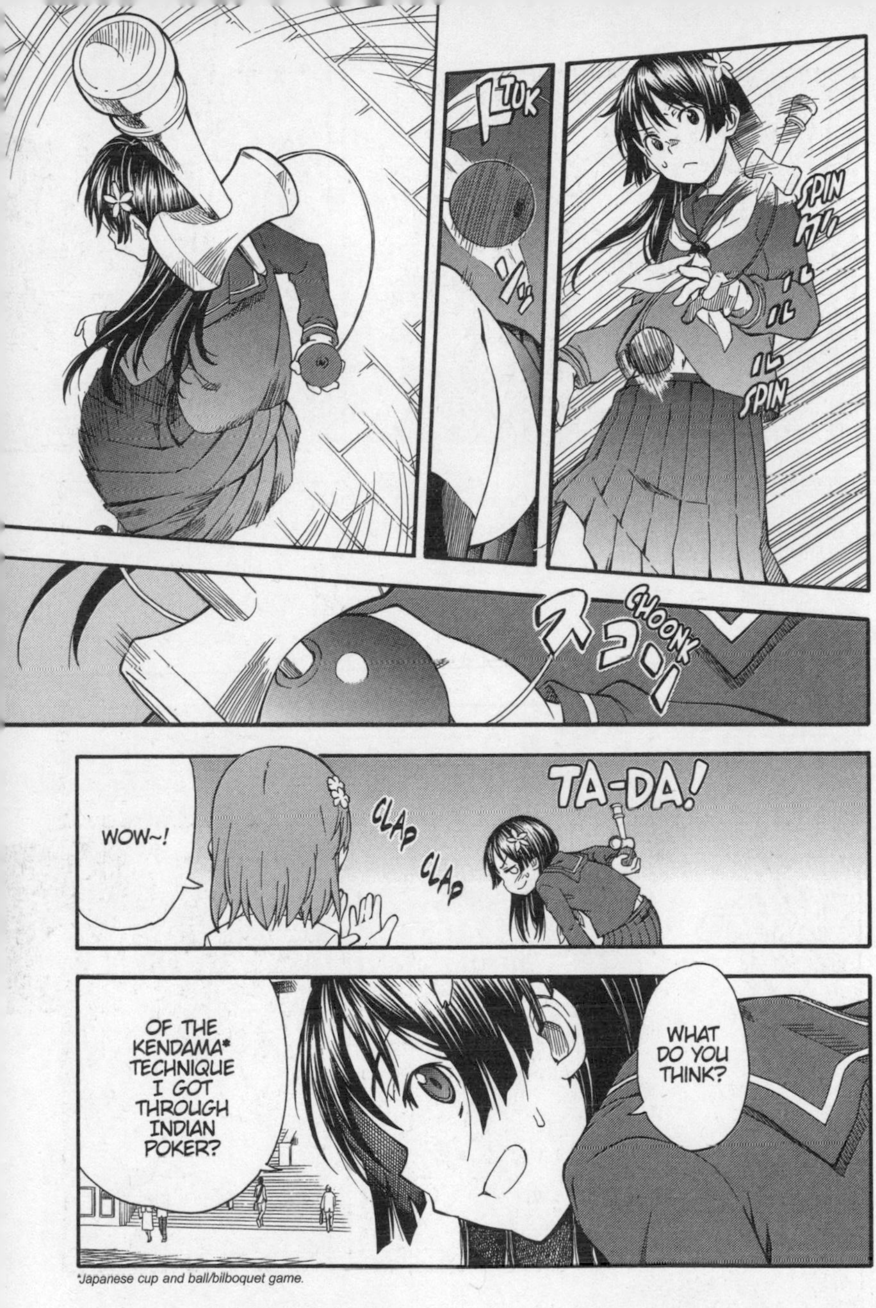
SPIN
SPIN
TUK
CHOONK
TA-DA!
CLAP
CLAP
WOW~!
WHAT DO YOU THINK?
OF THE KENDAMA* TECHNIQUE I GOT THROUGH INDIAN POKER?

*Japanese cup and ball/bilboquet game.

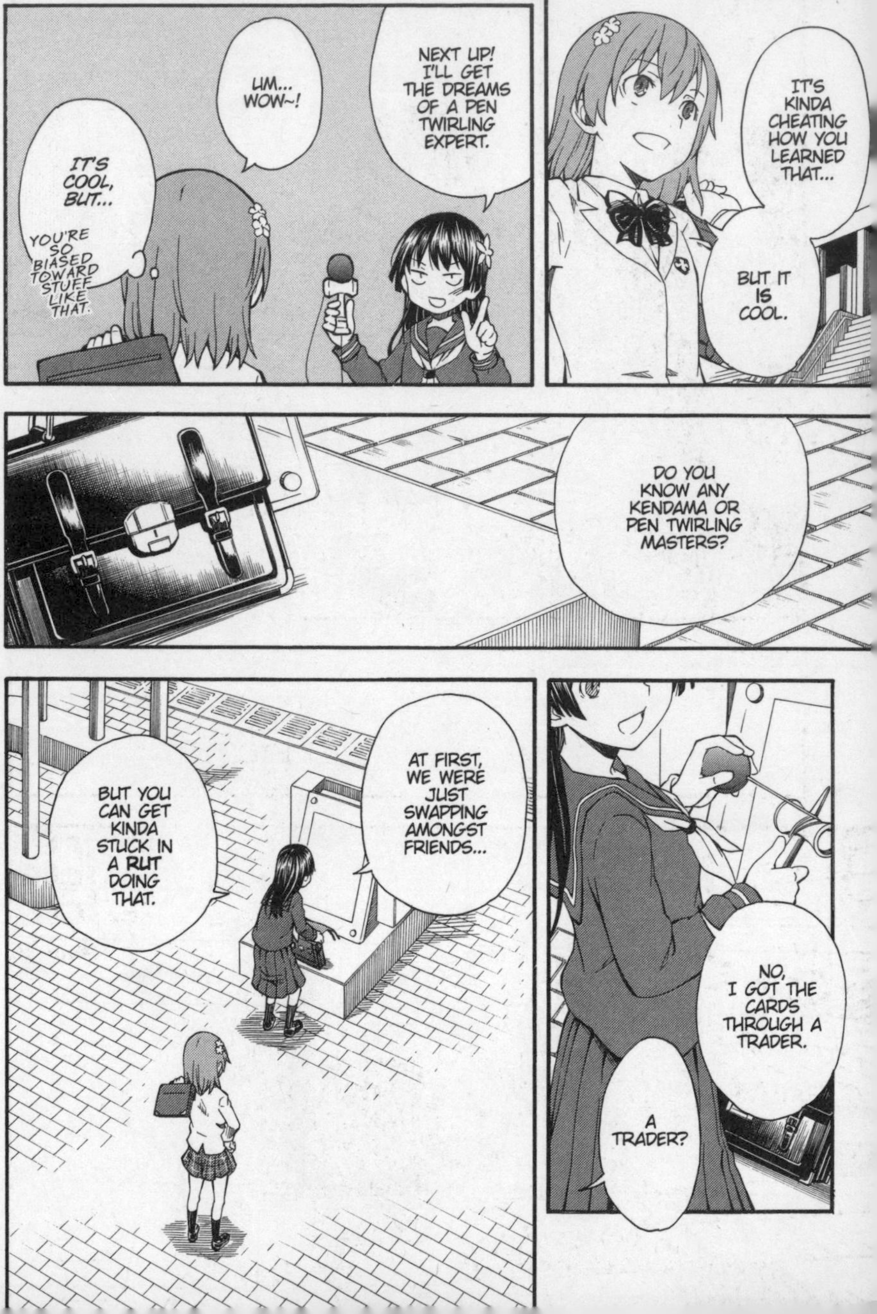
IT'S KINDA CHEATING HOW YOU LEARNED THAT...
BUT IT IS COOL.
NEXT UP! I'LL GET THE DREAMS OF A PEN TWIRLING EXPERT.
UM... WOW~!
IT'S COOL, BUT...
YOU'RE SO BIASED TOWARD STUFF LIKE THAT.
DO YOU KNOW ANY KENDAMA OR PEN TWIRLING MASTERS?
NO, I GOT THE CARDS THROUGH A TRADER.
A TRADER?
AT FIRST, WE WERE JUST SWAPPING AMONGST FRIENDS...
BUT YOU CAN GET KINDA STUCK IN A RUT DOING THAT.

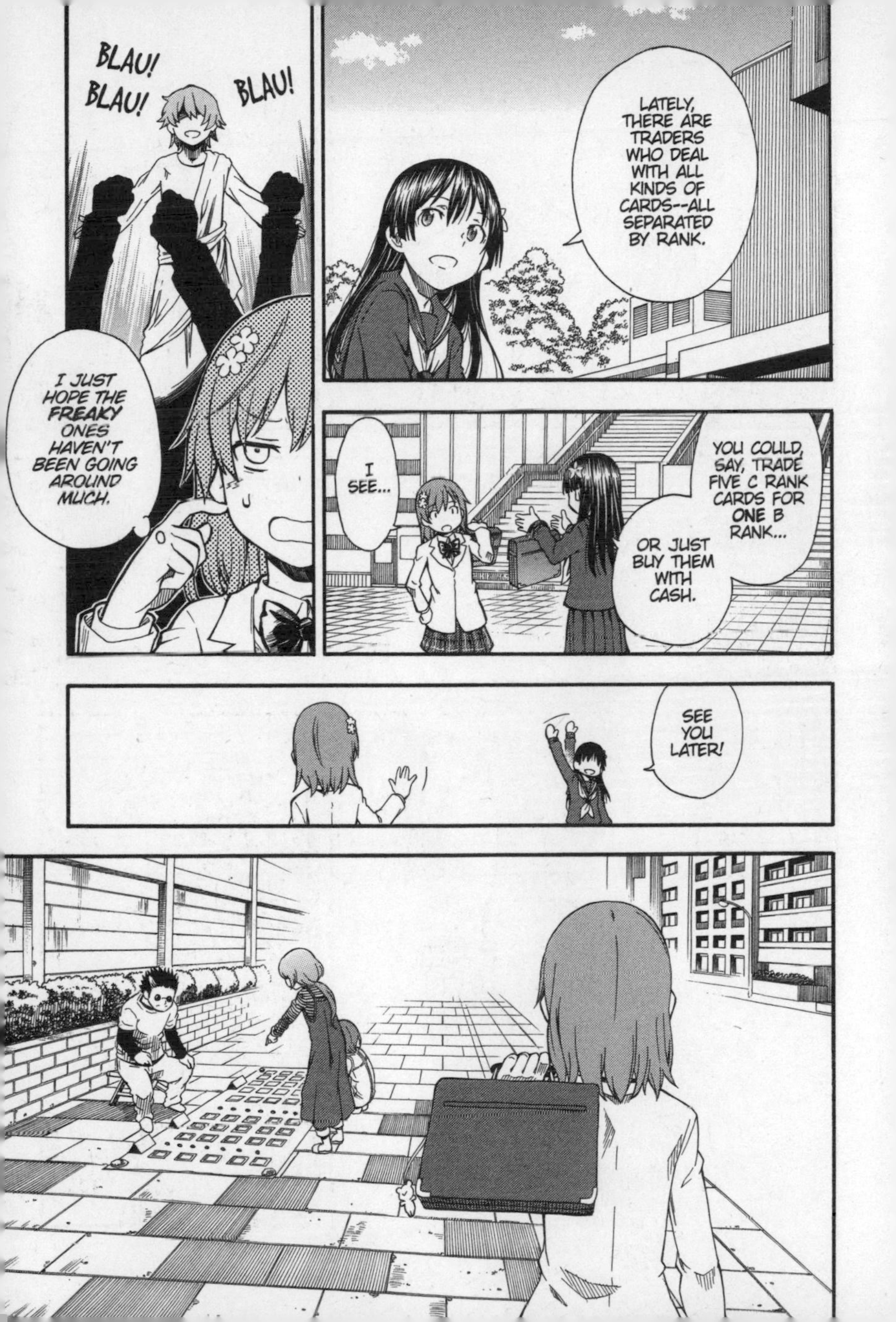
LATELY, THERE ARE TRADERS WHO DEAL WITH ALL KINDS OF CARDS--ALL SEPARATED BY RANK.
YOU COULD, SAY, TRADE FIVE C RANK CARDS FOR ONE B RANK...
OR JUST BUY THEM WITH CASH.
I SEE...
BLAU!
BLAU!
BLAU!
I JUST HOPE THE FREAKY ONES HAVEN'T BEEN GOING AROUND MUCH.
SEE YOU LATER!

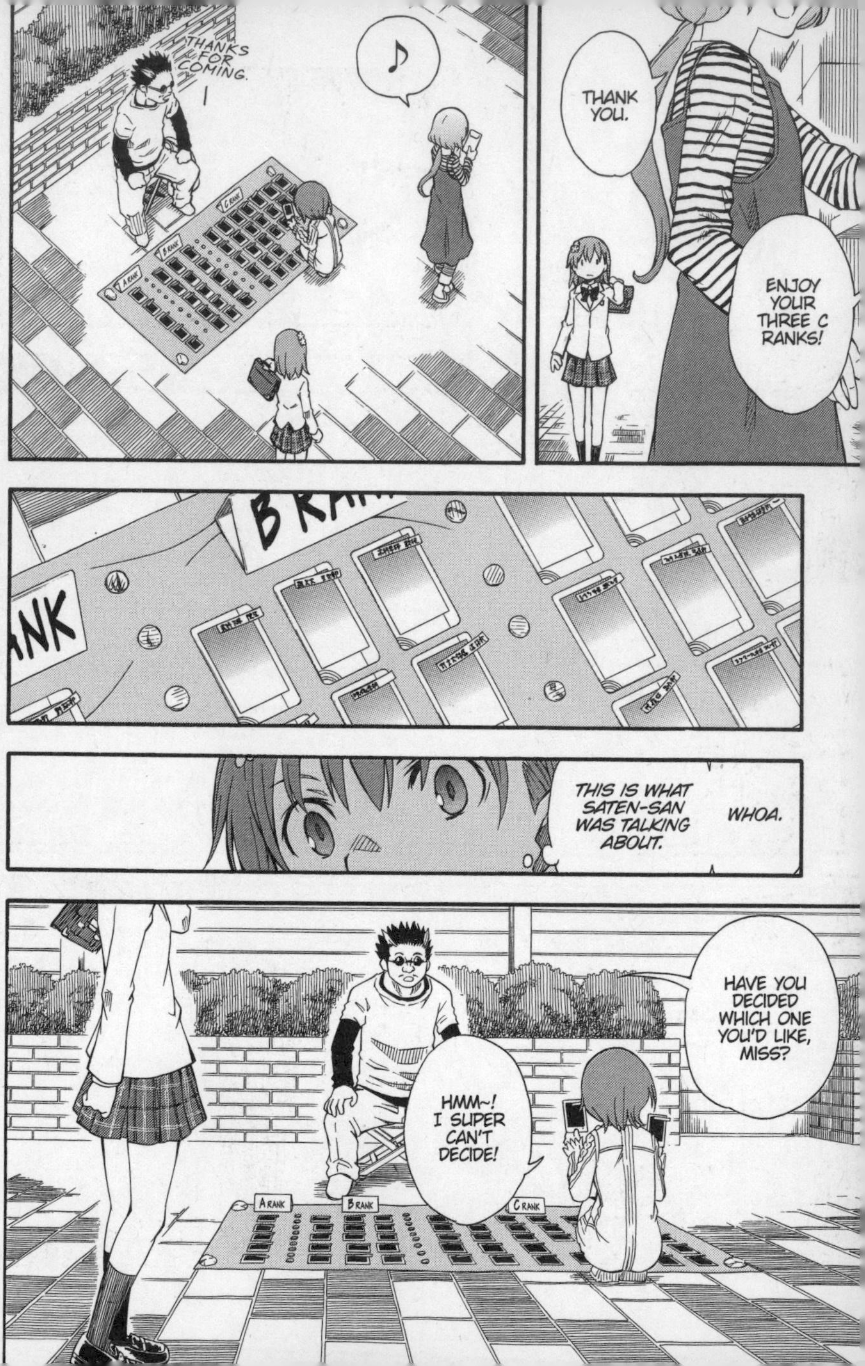
THANK YOU.
ENJOY YOUR THREE C RANKS!
♪
THANKS FOR COMING.
WHOA.
THIS IS WHAT SATEN-SAN WAS TALKING ABOUT.
HAVE YOU DECIDED WHICH ONE YOU'D LIKE, MISS?
HMM~! I SUPER CAN'T DECIDE!
A RANK
B RANK
C RANK

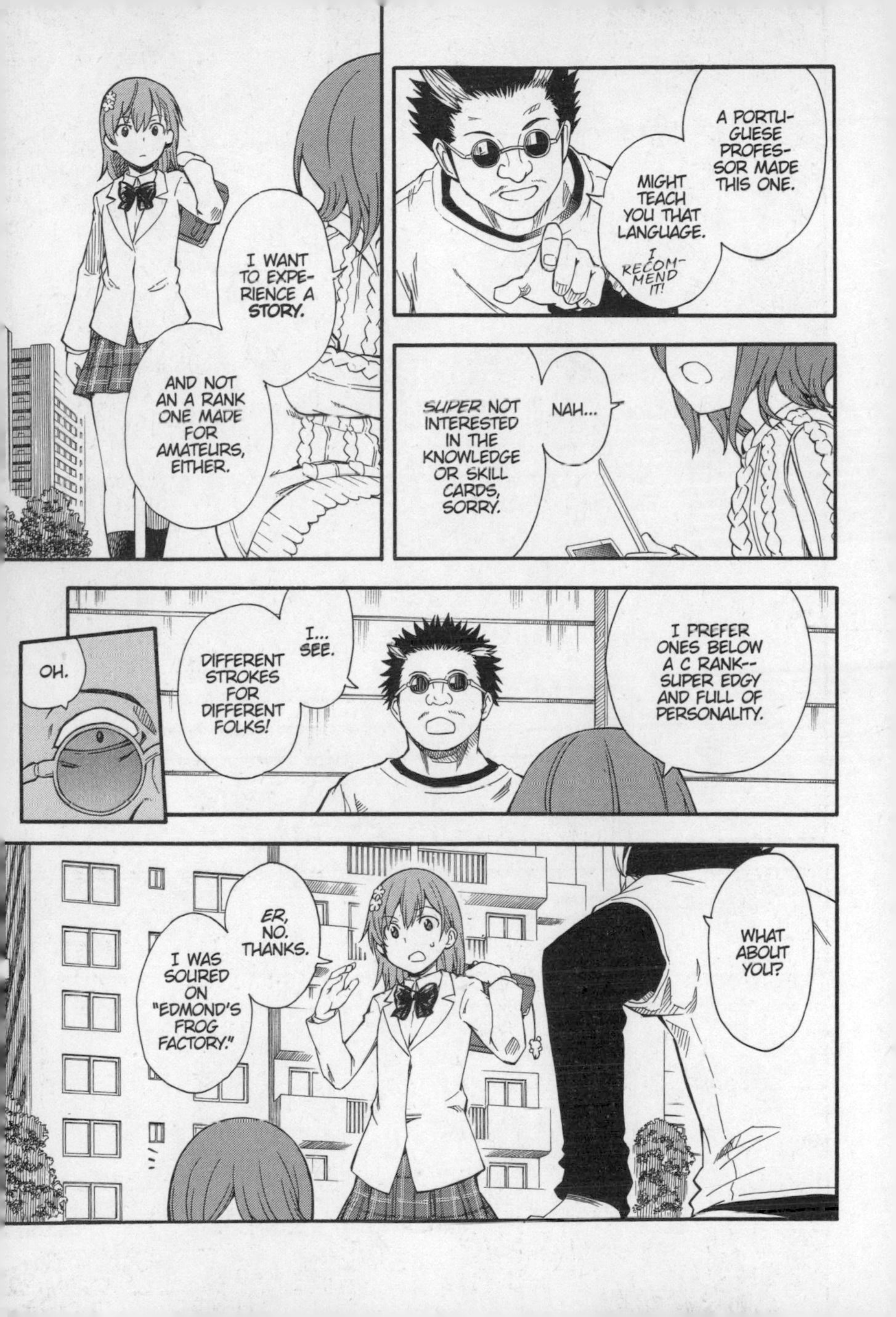
A PORTUGUESE PROFESSOR MADE THIS ONE.
MIGHT TEACH YOU THAT LANGUAGE.
I RECOMMEND IT!
NAH...
SUPER NOT INTERESTED IN THE KNOWLEDGE OR SKILL CARDS, SORRY.
I WANT TO EXPERIENCE A STORY.
AND NOT AN A RANK ONE MADE FOR AMATEURS, EITHER.
I PREFER ONES BELOW A C RANK-- SUPER EDGY AND FULL OF PERSONALITY.
I... SEE.
DIFFERENT STROKES FOR DIFFERENT FOLKS!
OH.
WHAT ABOUT YOU?
ER, NO. THANKS.
I WAS SOURED ON "EDMOND'S FROG FACTORY."

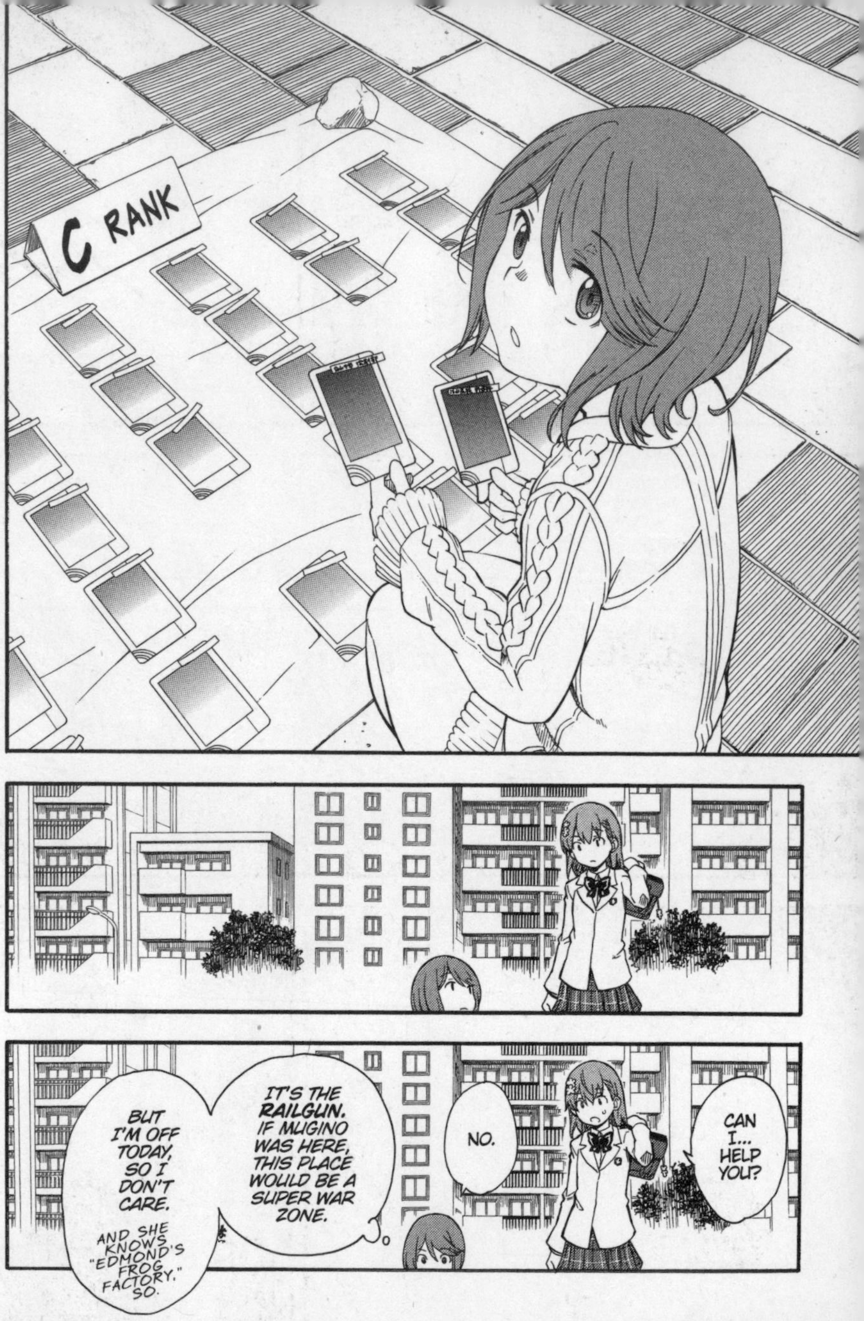
C RANK
CAN I... HELP YOU?
NO.
IT'S THE RAILGUN. IF MUGINO WAS HERE, THIS PLACE WOULD BE A SUPER WAR ZONE.
BUT I'M OFF TODAY, SO I DON'T CARE.
AND SHE KNOWS "EDMOND'S FROG FACTORY." SO.

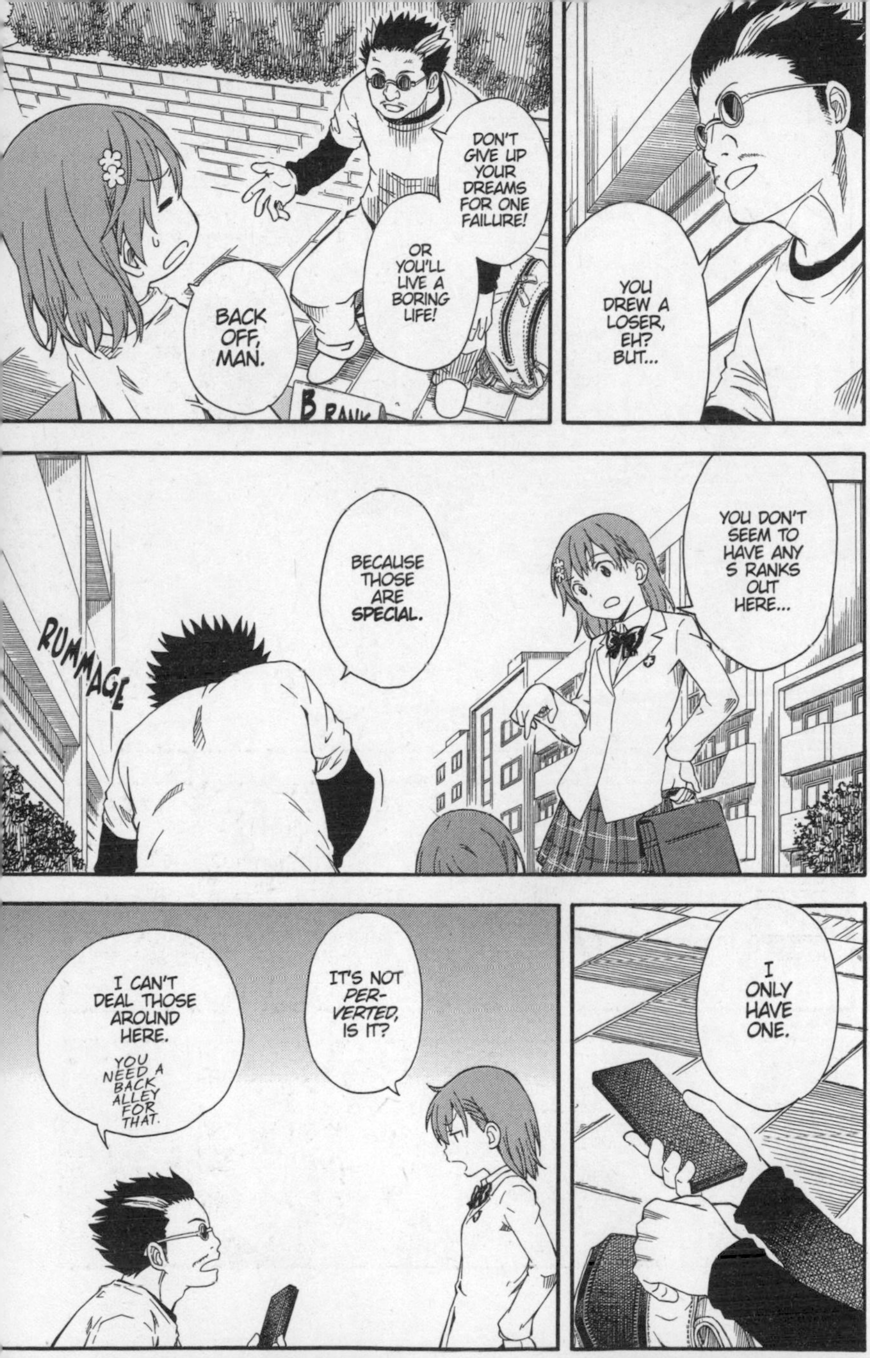
YOU DREW A LOSER, EH? BUT...
DON'T GIVE UP YOUR DREAMS FOR ONE FAILURE!
OR YOU'LL LIVE A BORING LIFE!
BACK OFF, MAN.
YOU DON'T SEEM TO HAVE ANY S RANKS OUT HERE...
BECAUSE THOSE ARE SPECIAL.
RUMMAGE
I ONLY HAVE ONE.
IT'S NOT PER-VERTED, IS IT?
I CAN'T DEAL THOSE AROUND HERE.
YOU NEED A BACK ALLEY FOR THAT.

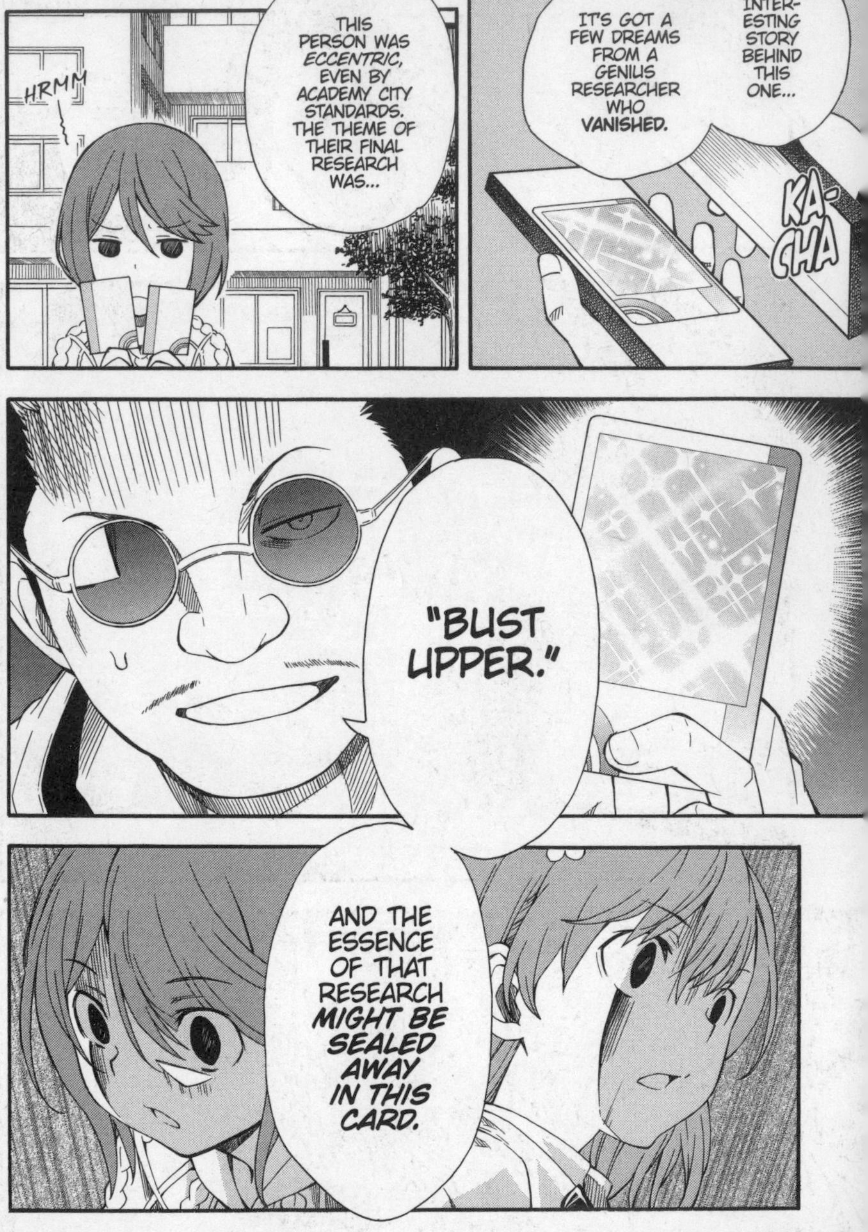
INTERESTING STORY BEHIND THIS ONE...
IT'S GOT A FEW DREAMS FROM A GENIUS RESEARCHER WHO VANISHED.
KA-CHA
HRMM
THIS PERSON WAS ECCENTRIC, EVEN BY ACADEMY CITY STANDARDS. THE THEME OF THEIR FINAL RESEARCH WAS...
"BUST UPPER."
AND THE ESSENCE OF THAT RESEARCH MIGHT BE SEALED AWAY IN THIS CARD.

CHAPTER 78: BREASTS

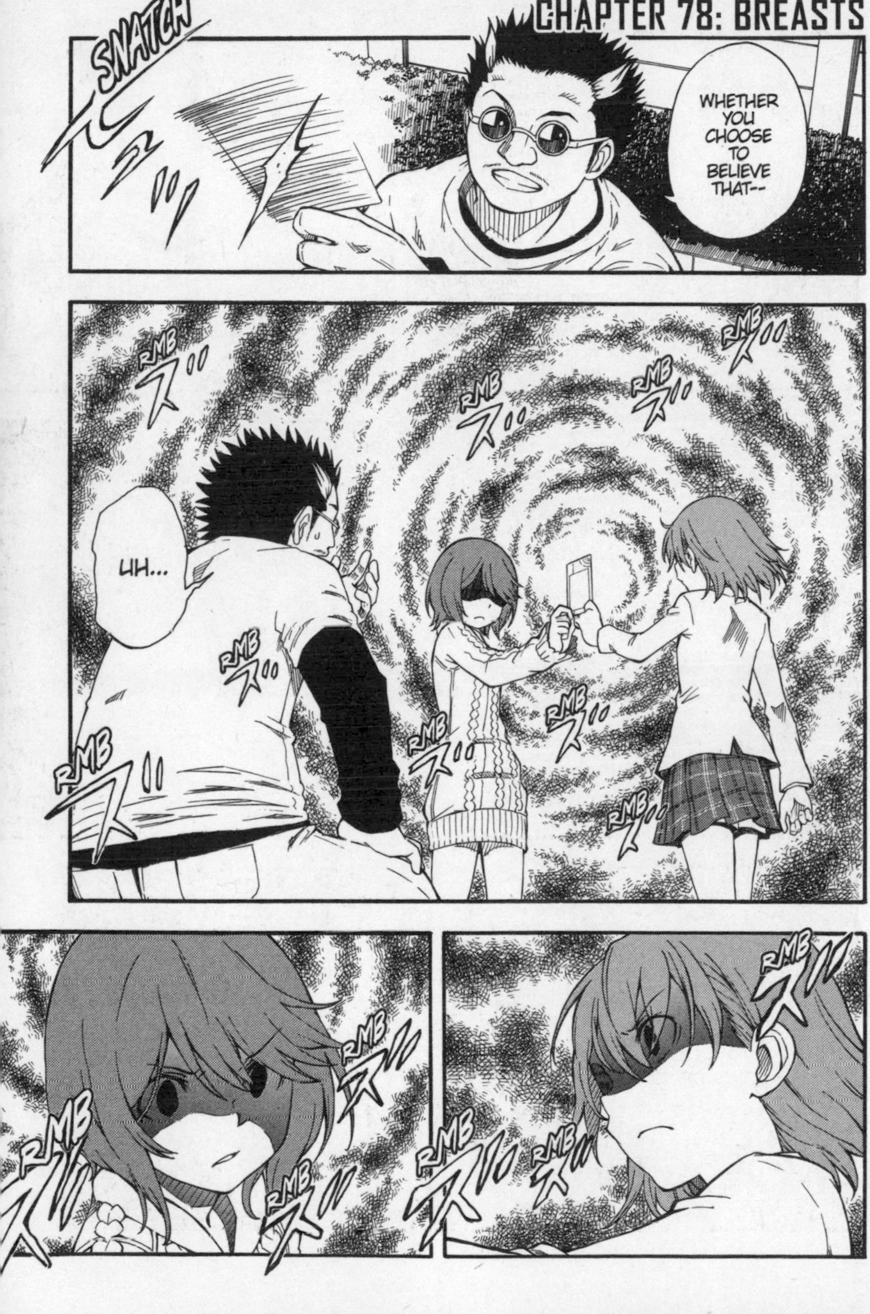
SNATCH
WHETHER YOU CHOOSE TO BELIEVE THAT--
RMB
RMB
RMB
UH...
RMB
RMB
RMB
RMB
RMB
RMB
RMB
RMB
RMB
RMB
RMB

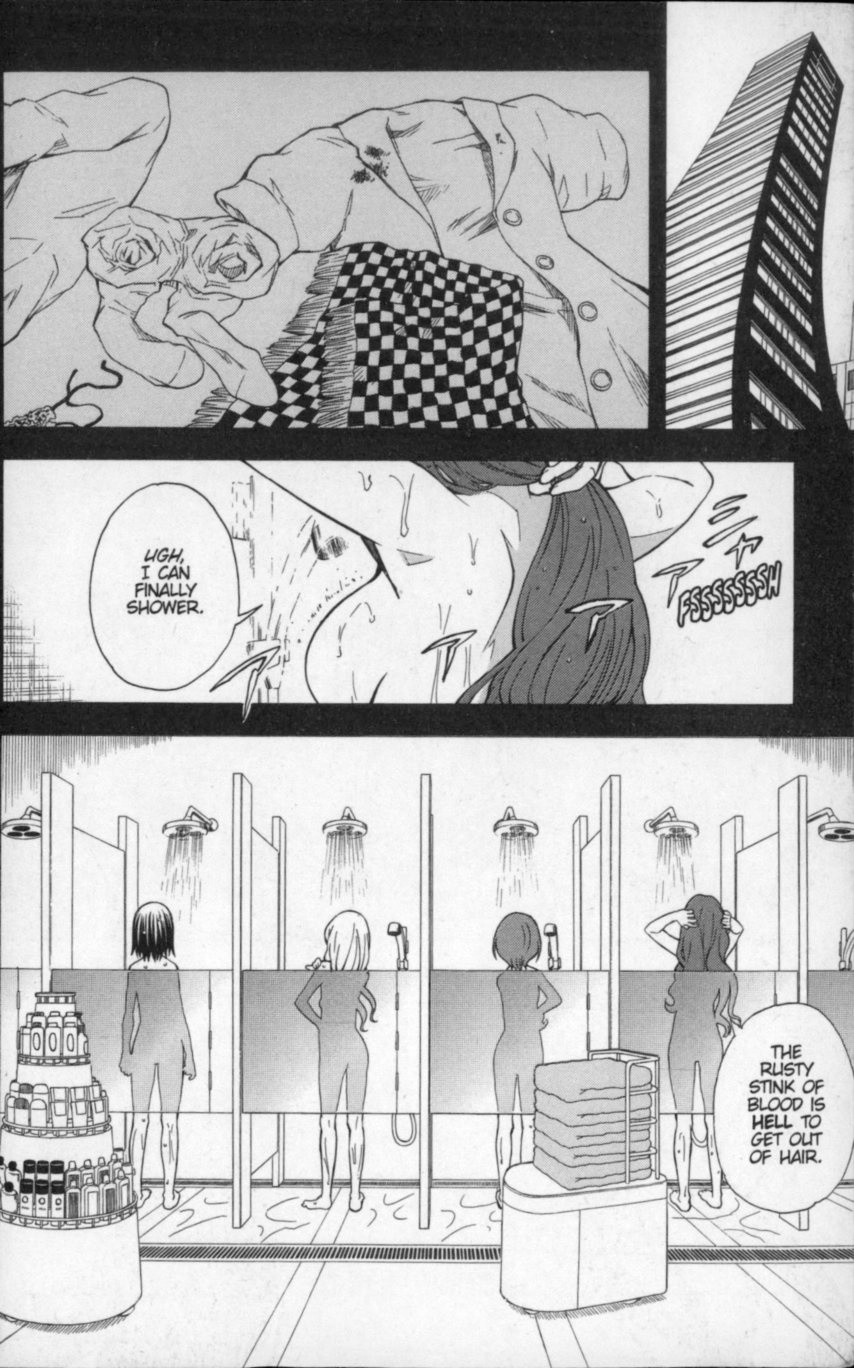
FSSSSSSSH
UGH, I CAN FINALLY SHOWER.
THE RUSTY STINK OF BLOOD IS HELL TO GET OUT OF HAIR.

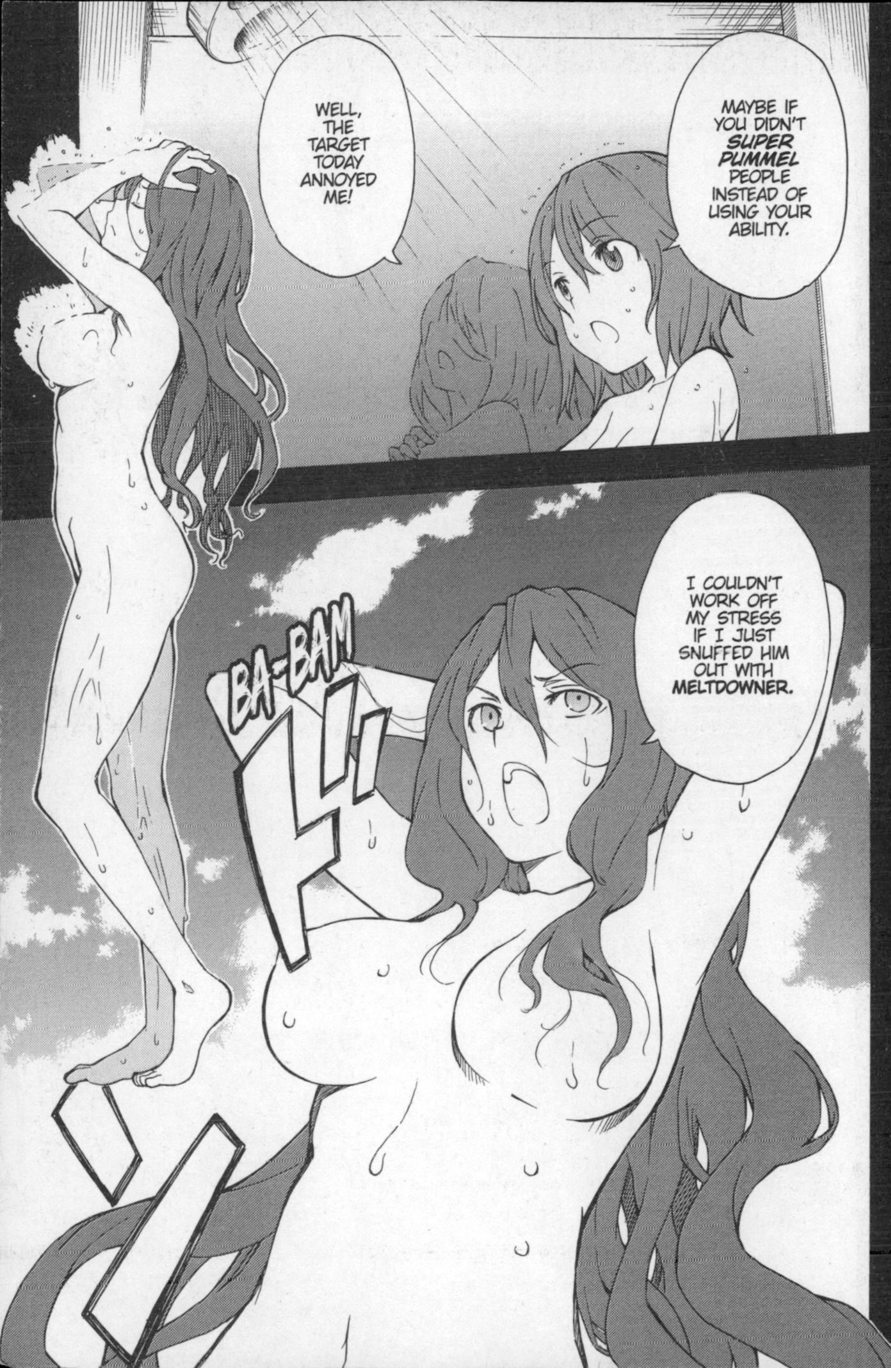
MAYBE IF YOU DIDN'T SUPER PUMMEL PEOPLE INSTEAD OF USING YOUR ABILITY.
WELL, THE TARGET TODAY ANNOYED ME!
I COULDN'T WORK OFF MY STRESS IF I JUST SNUFFED HIM OUT WITH MELTDOWNER.
BA-BAM

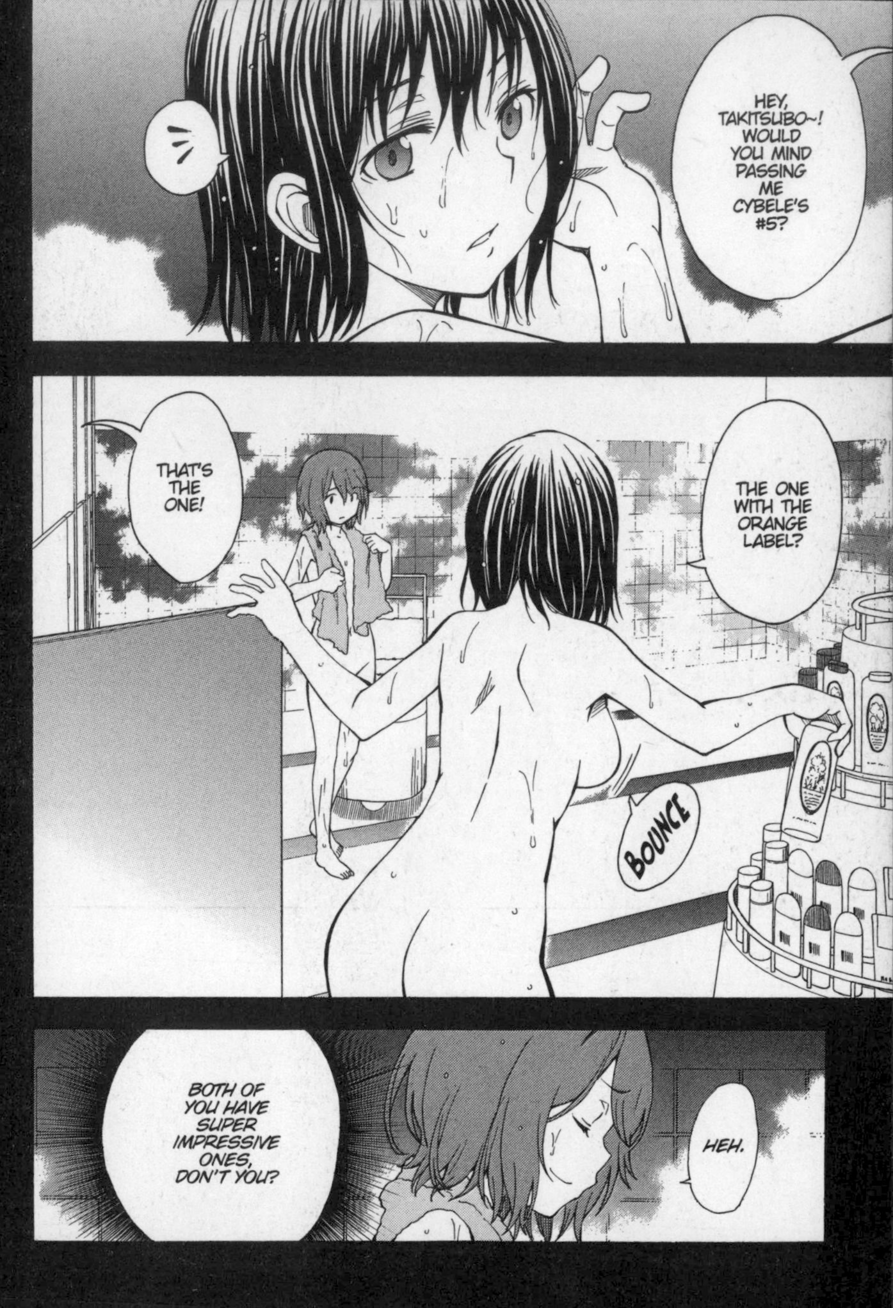
HEY, TAKITSUBO~! WOULD YOU MIND PASSING ME CYBELE'S #5?
THE ONE WITH THE ORANGE LABEL?
THAT'S THE ONE!
BOUNCE
HEH.
BOTH OF YOU HAVE SUPER IMPRESSIVE ONES, DON'T YOU?

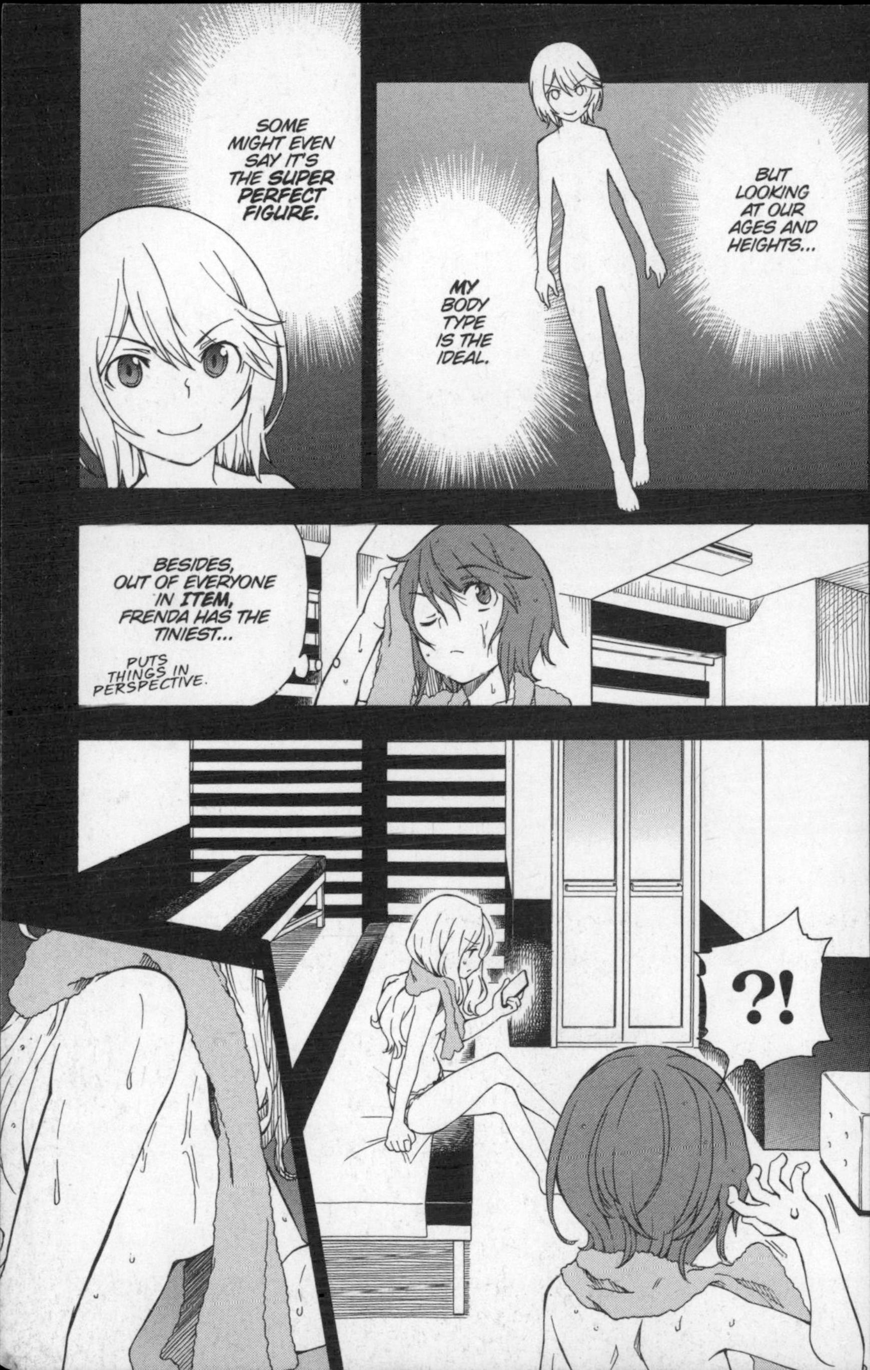
BUT LOOKING AT OUR AGES AND HEIGHTS...
MY BODY TYPE IS THE IDEAL.
SOME MIGHT EVEN SAY IT'S THE SUPER PERFECT FIGURE.
BESIDES, OUT OF EVERYONE IN ITEM, FRENDA HAS THE TINIEST...
PUTS THINGS IN PERSPECTIVE.
?!

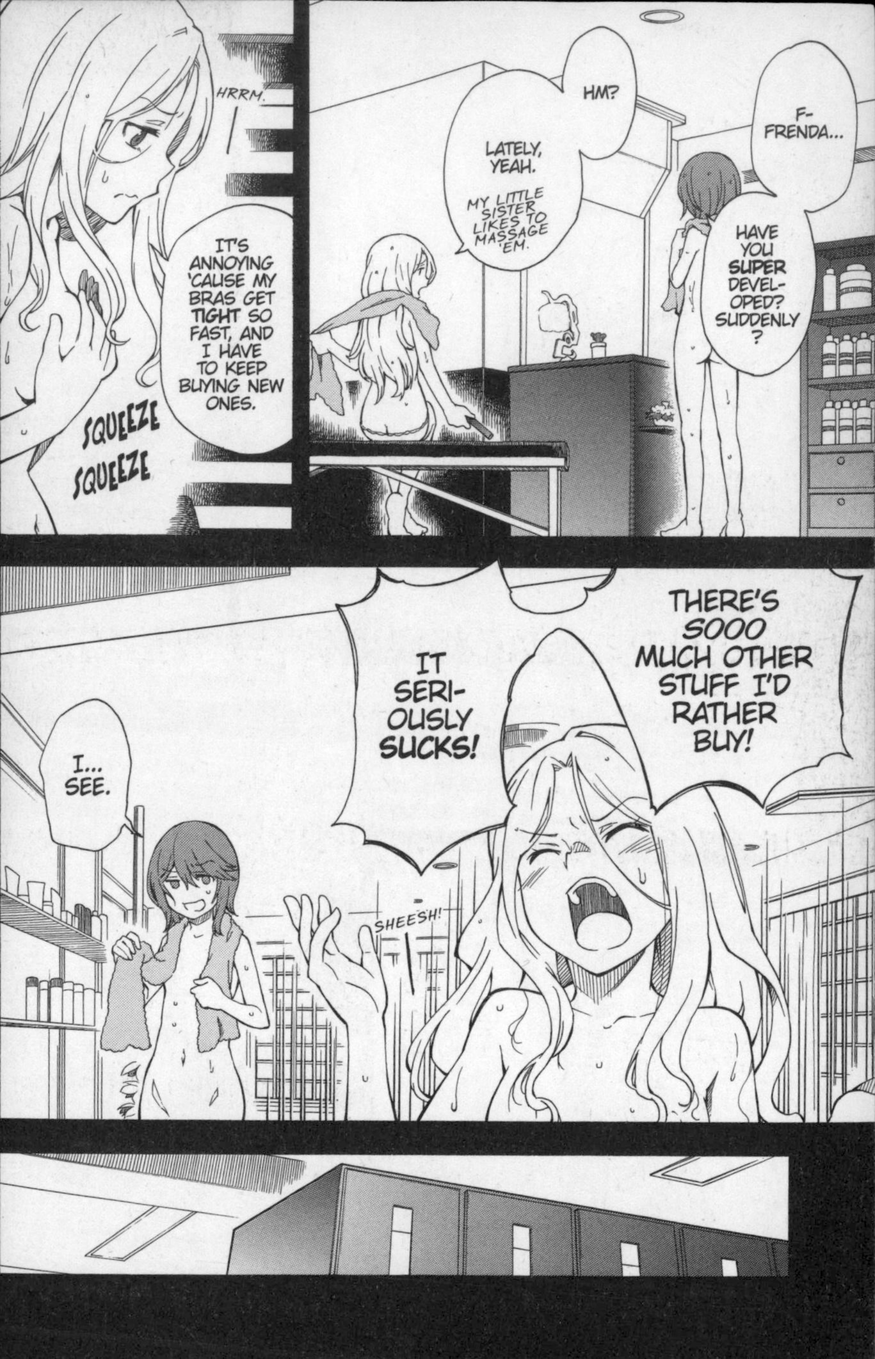
F-FRENDA...
HAVE YOU SUPER DEVELOPED? SUDDENLY?
HM?
LATELY, YEAH.
MY LITTLE SISTER LIKES TO MASSAGE 'EM.
HRRM.
IT'S ANNOYING 'CAUSE MY BRAS GET TIGHT SO FAST, AND I HAVE TO KEEP BUYING NEW ONES.
SQUEEZE
SQUEEZE
THERE'S SOOO MUCH OTHER STUFF I'D RATHER BUY!
IT SERIOUSLY SUCKS!
SHEESH!
I... SEE.

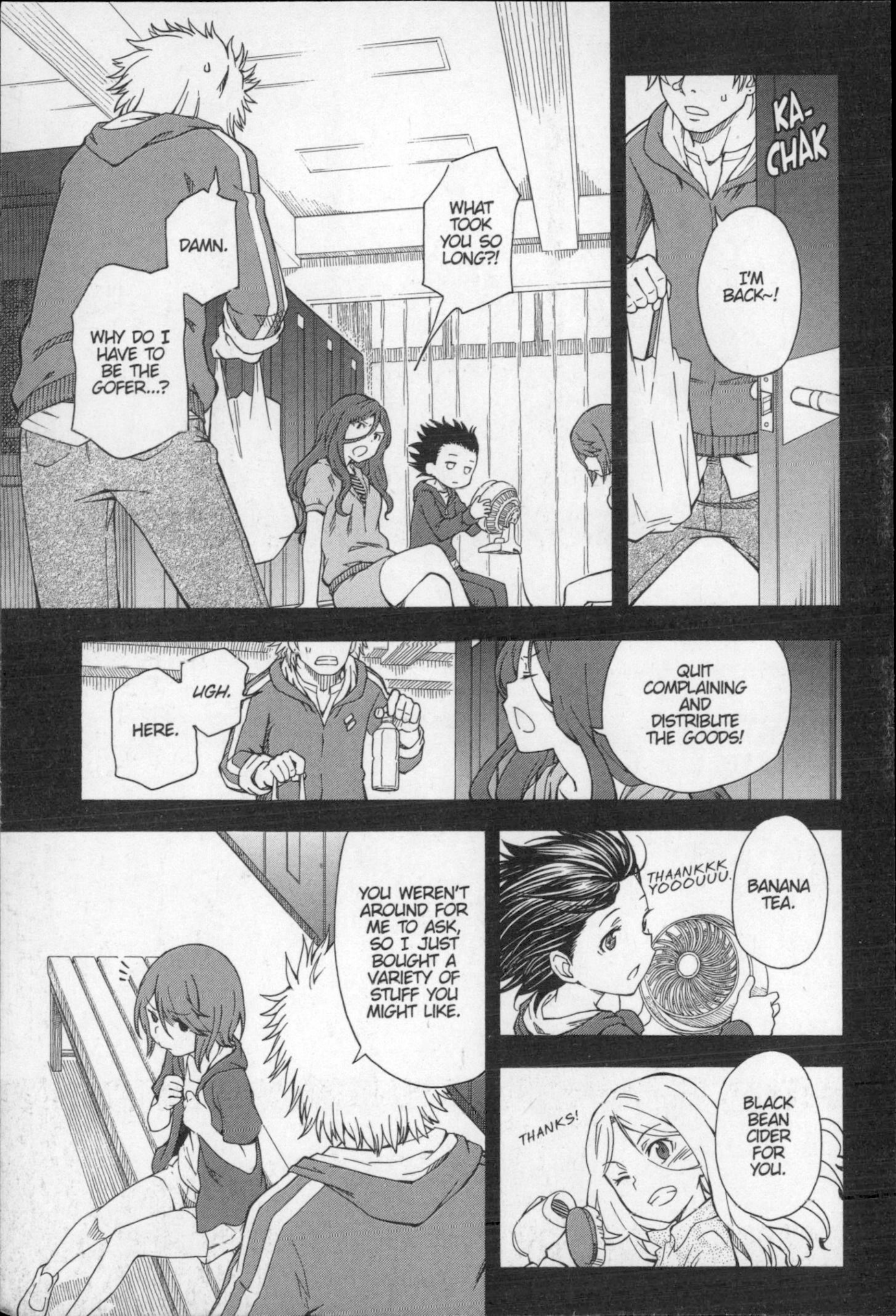
KA-CHAK
I'M BACK~!
WHAT TOOK YOU SO LONG?!
DAMN.
WHY DO I HAVE TO BE THE GOFER...?
QUIT COMPLAINING AND DISTRIBUTE THE GOODS!
UGH.
HERE.
BANANA TEA.
THAANKKK YOOOUUU.
BLACK BEAN CIDER FOR YOU.
THANKS!
YOU WEREN'T AROUND FOR ME TO ASK, SO I JUST BOUGHT A VARIETY OF STUFF YOU MIGHT LIKE.

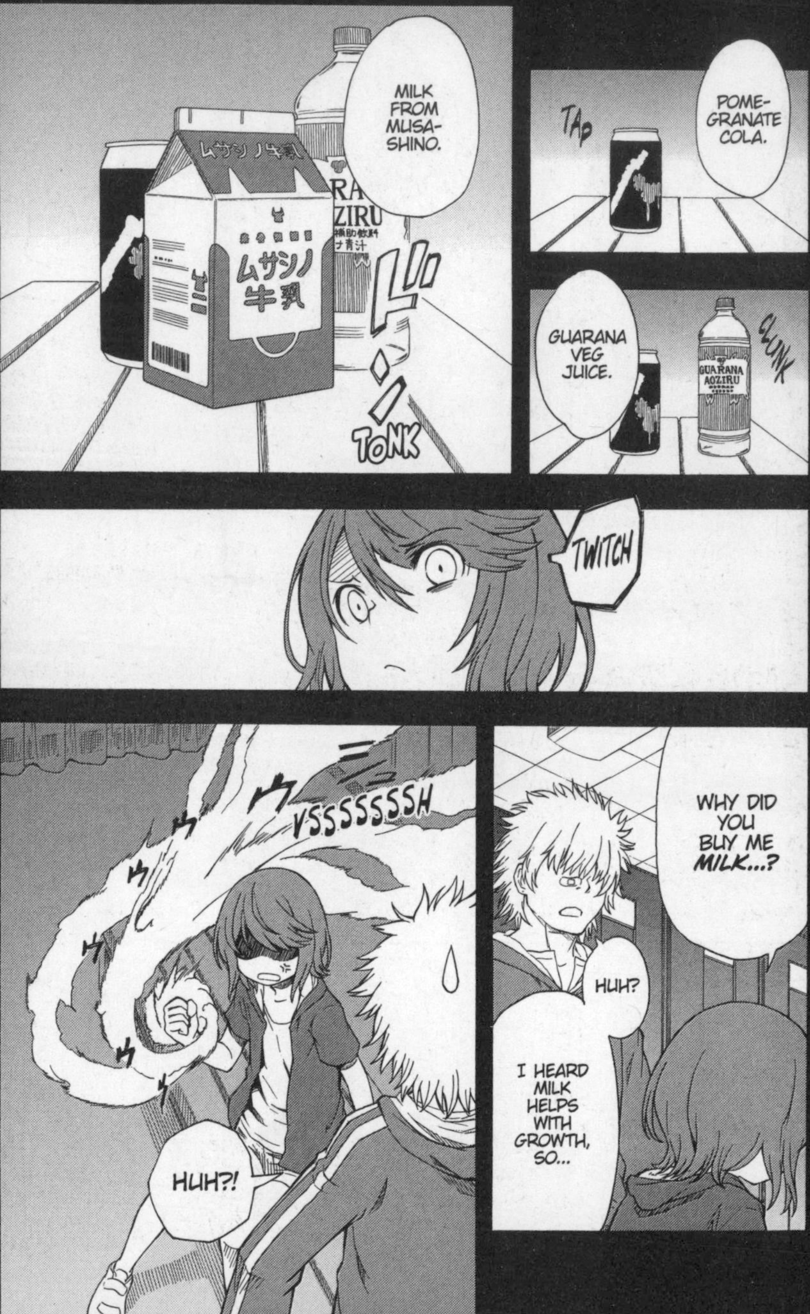
TAP
POME-GRANATE COLA.
GUARANA VEG JUICE.
GUARANA AOZIRU
CLUNK
MILK FROM MUSA-SHINO.
ムサシノ牛乳
ムサシノ牛乳
TONK
TWITCH
WHY DID YOU BUY ME *MILK*...?
HUH?
I HEARD MILK HELPS WITH GROWTH, SO...
VSSSSSSSH
HUH?!

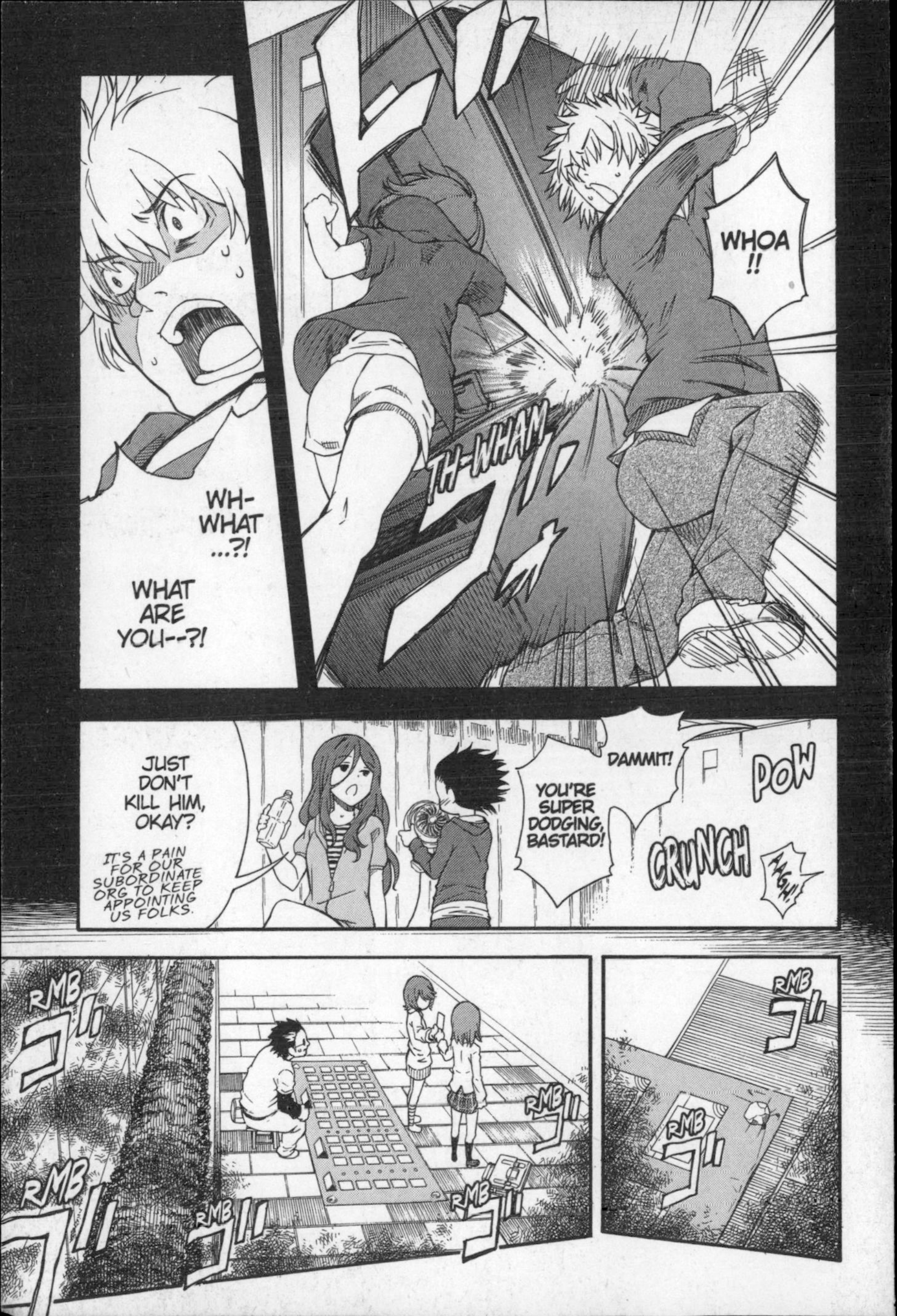
WHOA !!
TH-WHAM
WH- WHAT ...?!
WHAT ARE YOU--?!
POW
DAMMIT!
YOU'RE SUPER DODGING, BASTARD!
CRUNCH
AAGH!!
JUST DON'T KILL HIM, OKAY?
IT'S A PAIN FOR OUR SUBORDINATE ORG TO KEEP APPOINTING US FOLKS.
RMB
RMB
RMB
RMB
RMB
RMB
RMB
RMB

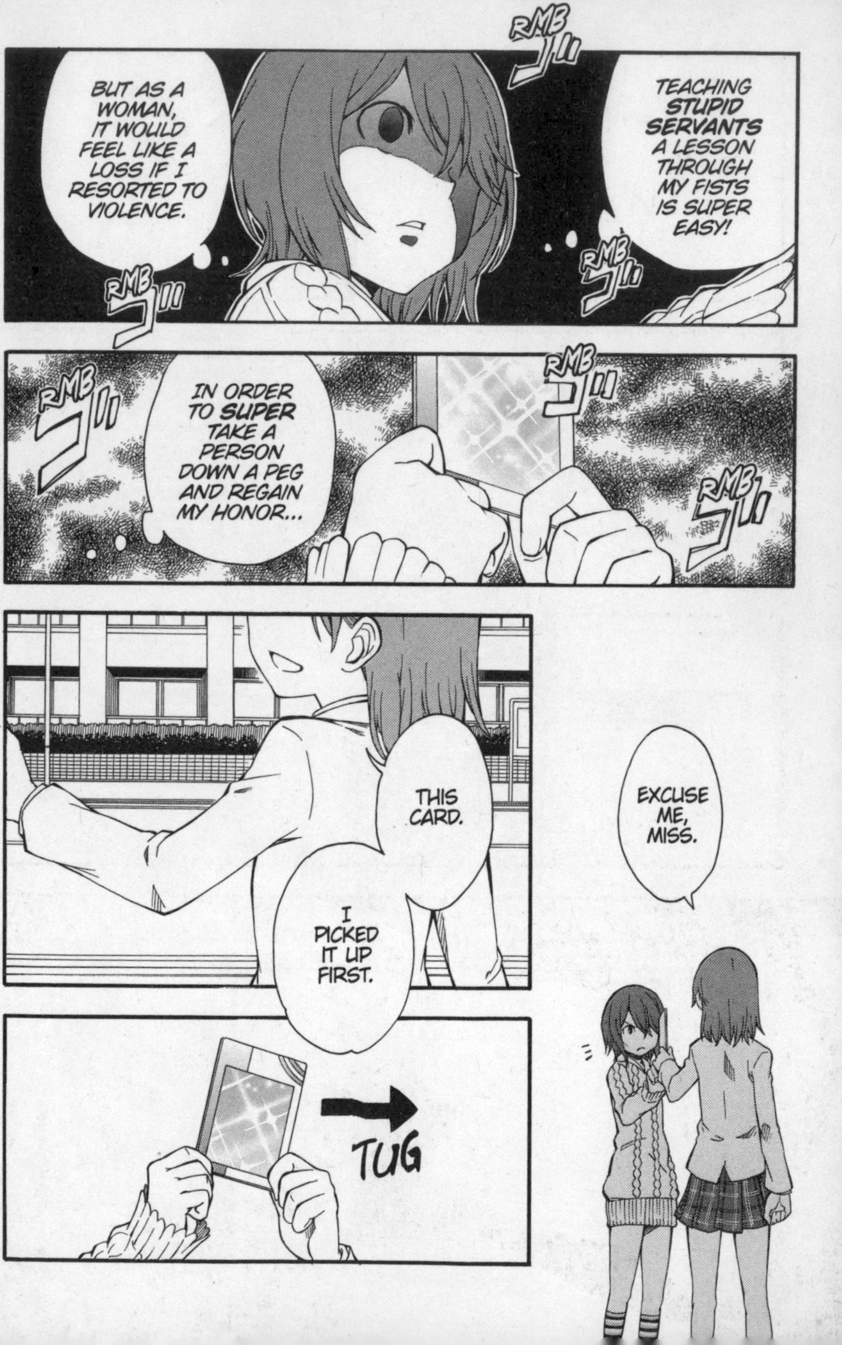
RMB
TEACHING STUPID SERVANTS A LESSON THROUGH MY FISTS IS SUPER EASY!
RMB
BUT AS A WOMAN, IT WOULD FEEL LIKE A LOSS IF I RESORTED TO VIOLENCE.
RMB
RMB
RMB
IN ORDER TO SUPER TAKE A PERSON DOWN A PEG AND REGAIN MY HONOR...
RMB
EXCUSE ME, MISS.
THIS CARD.
I PICKED IT UP FIRST.
TUG

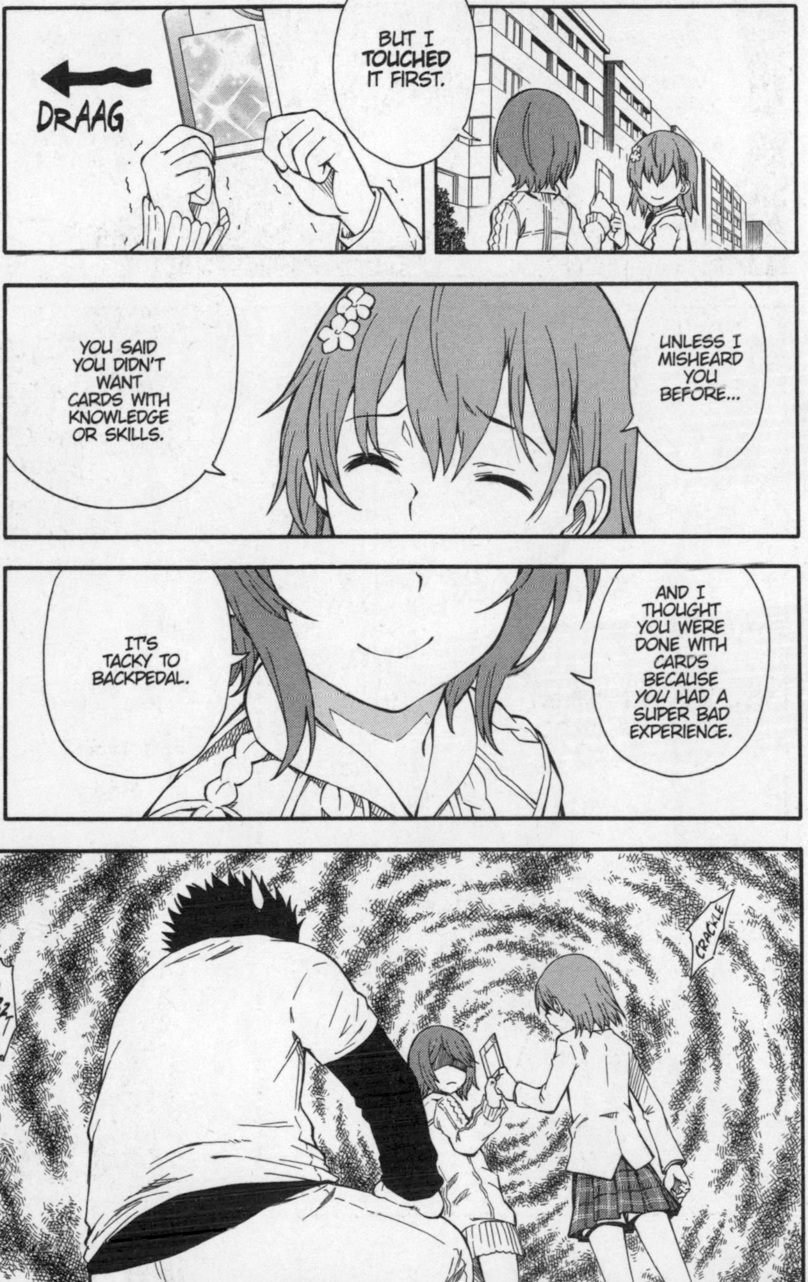

BUT I TOUCHED IT FIRST.
DRAAG
UNLESS I MISHEARD YOU BEFORE...
YOU SAID YOU DIDN'T WANT CARDS WITH KNOWLEDGE OR SKILLS.
AND I THOUGHT YOU WERE DONE WITH CARDS BECAUSE *YOU* HAD A SUPER BAD EXPERIENCE.
IT'S TACKY TO BACKPEDAL.
CRACKLE
BZZ

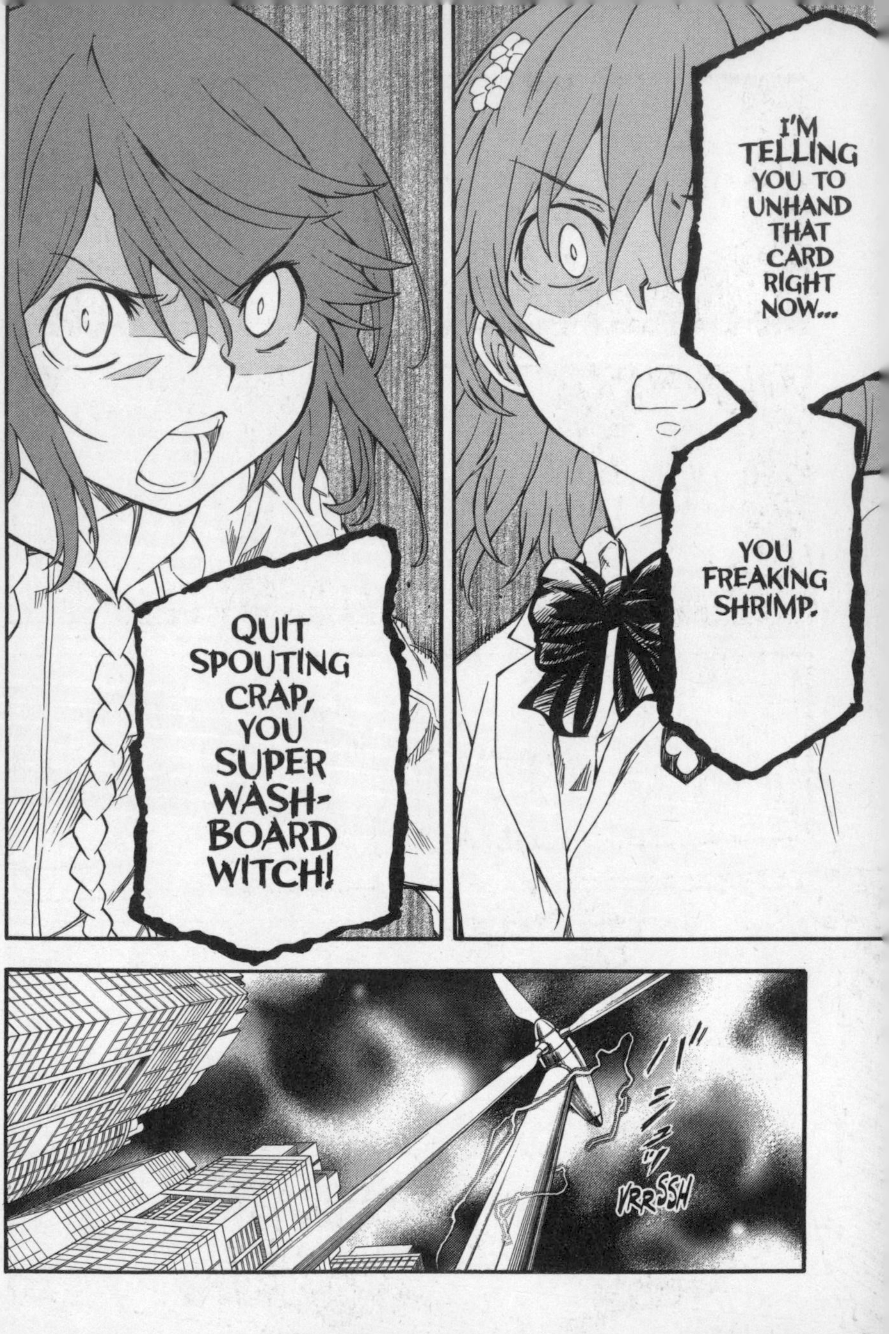
I'M TELLING YOU TO UNHAND THAT CARD RIGHT NOW...
YOU FREAKING SHRIMP.
QUIT SPOUTING CRAP, YOU SUPER WASH-BOARD WITCH!
VRRSSH

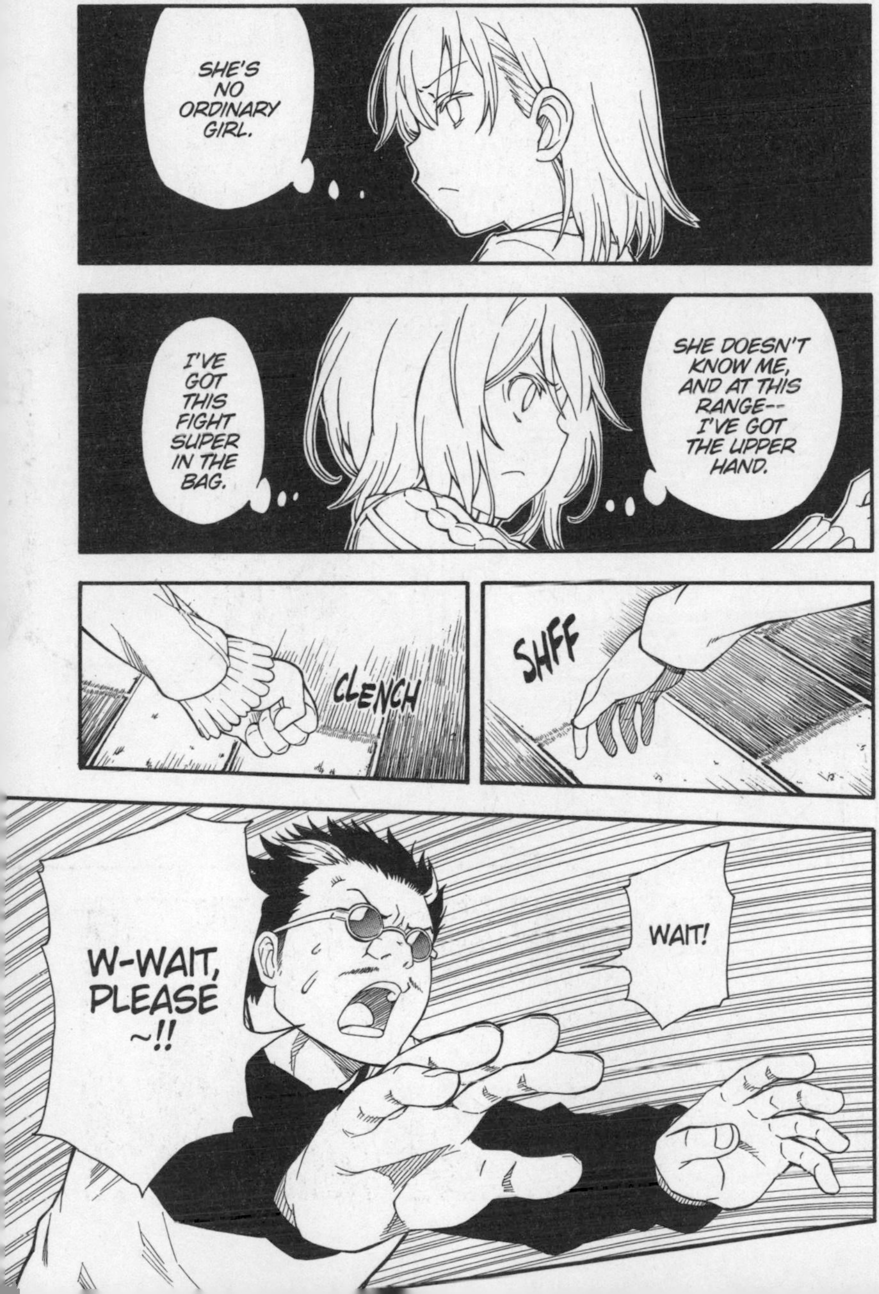
SHE'S NO ORDINARY GIRL.
SHE DOESN'T KNOW ME, AND AT THIS RANGE-- I'VE GOT THE UPPER HAND.
I'VE GOT THIS FIGHT SUPER IN THE BAG.
SHFF
CLENCH
WAIT!
W-WAIT, PLEASE ~!!

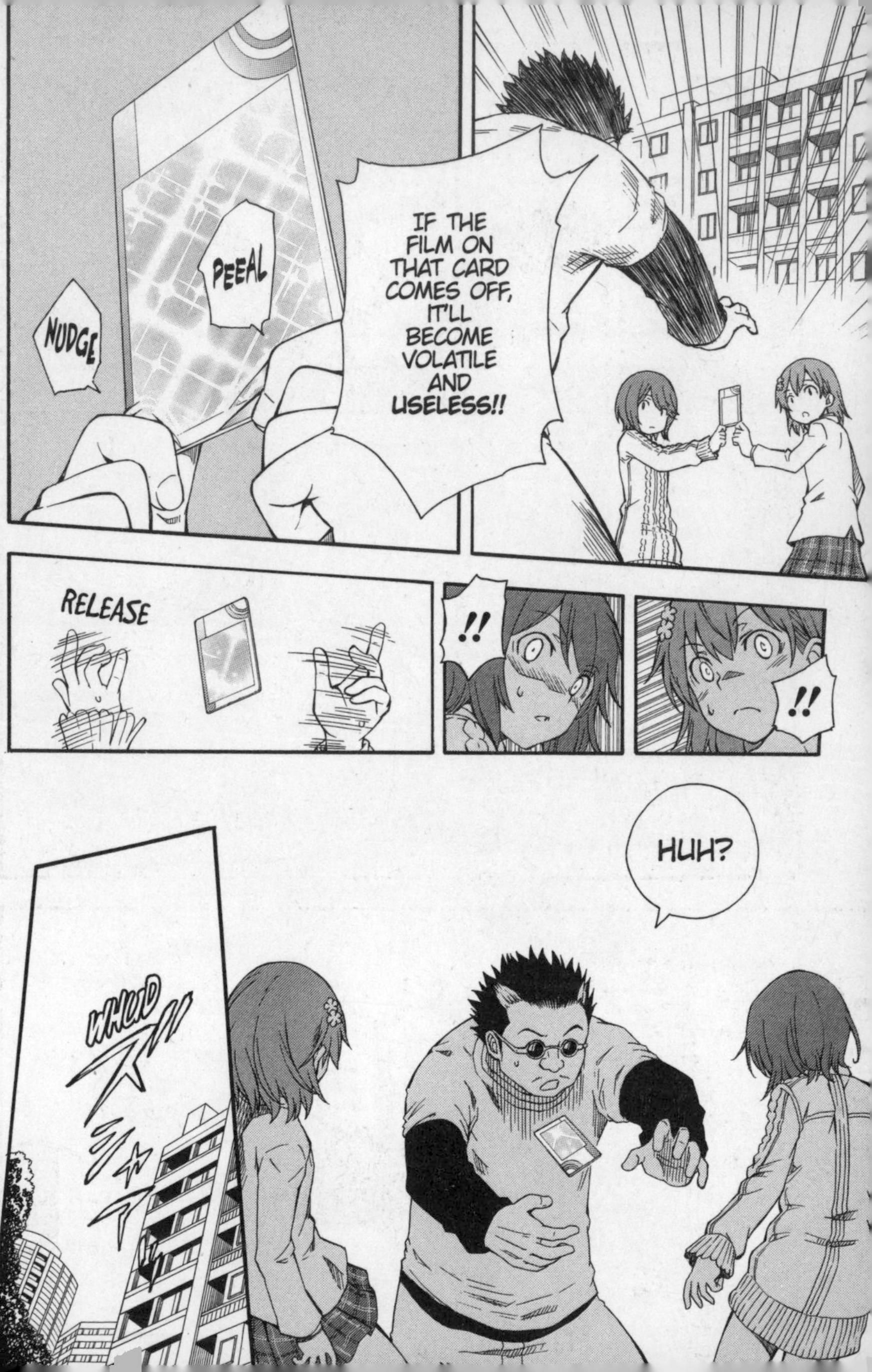
IF THE FILM ON THAT CARD COMES OFF, IT'LL BECOME VOLATILE AND USELESS!!
PEEAL
NUDGE
!!
!!
RELEASE
HUH?
WHUD

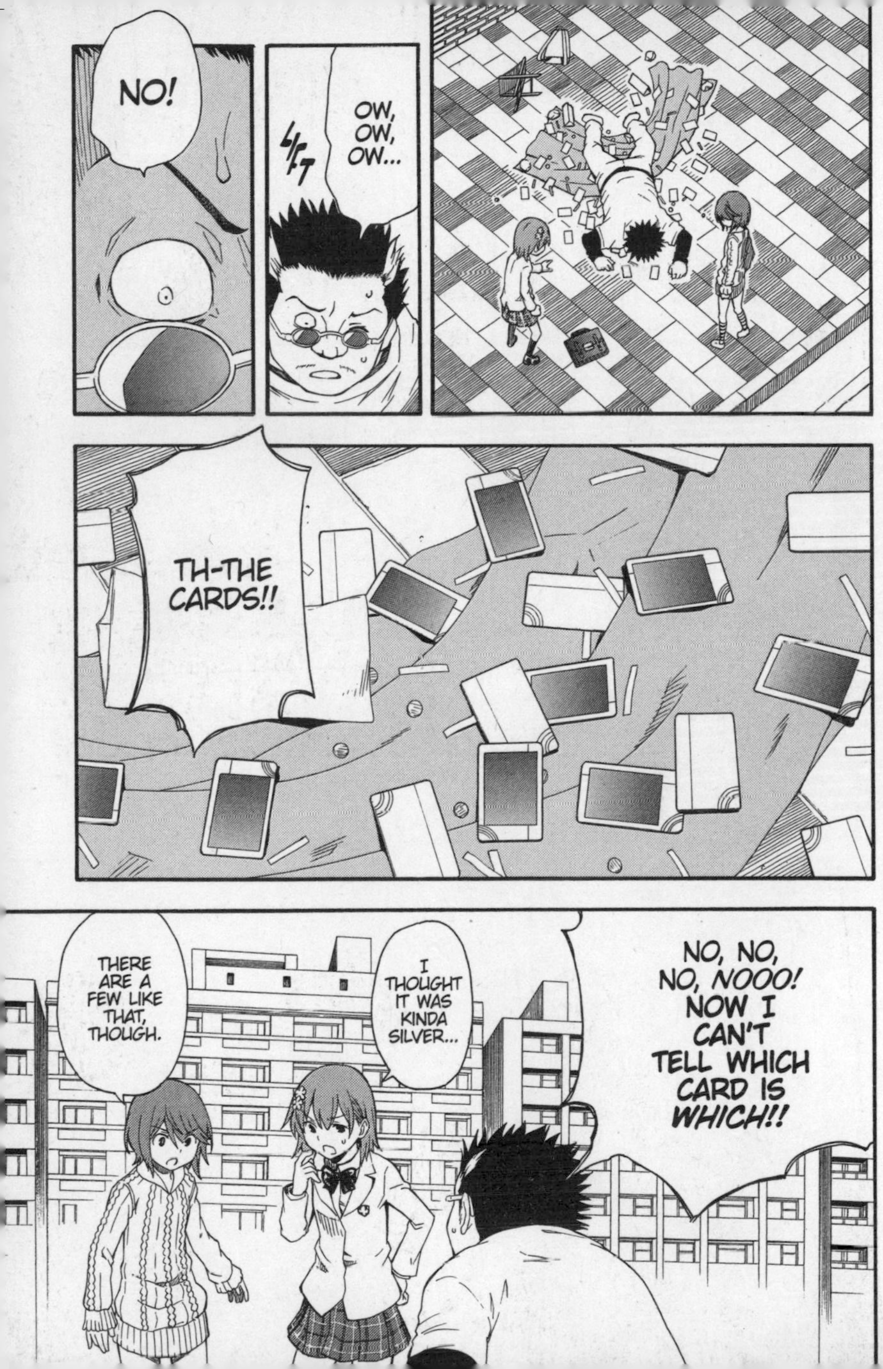
OW, OW, OW...
NO!
TH-THE CARDS!!
NO, NO, NO, NOOO! NOW I CAN'T TELL WHICH CARD IS WHICH!!
I THOUGHT IT WAS KINDA SILVER...
THERE ARE A FEW LIKE THAT, THOUGH.

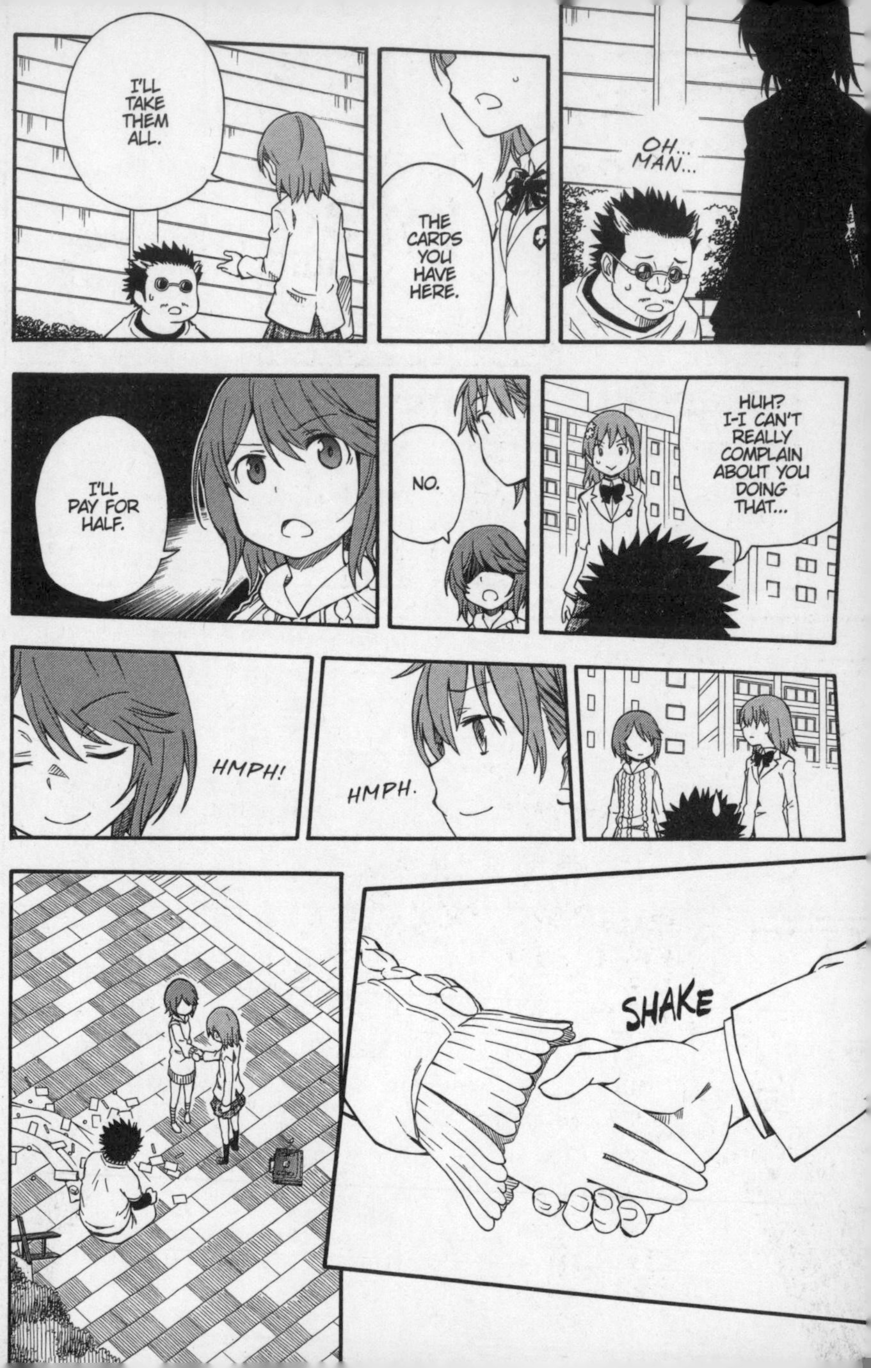
OH... MAN...
THE CARDS YOU HAVE HERE.
I'LL TAKE THEM ALL.
HUH? I-I CAN'T REALLY COMPLAIN ABOUT YOU DOING THAT...
NO.
I'LL PAY FOR HALF.
HMPH.
HMPH!
SHAKE

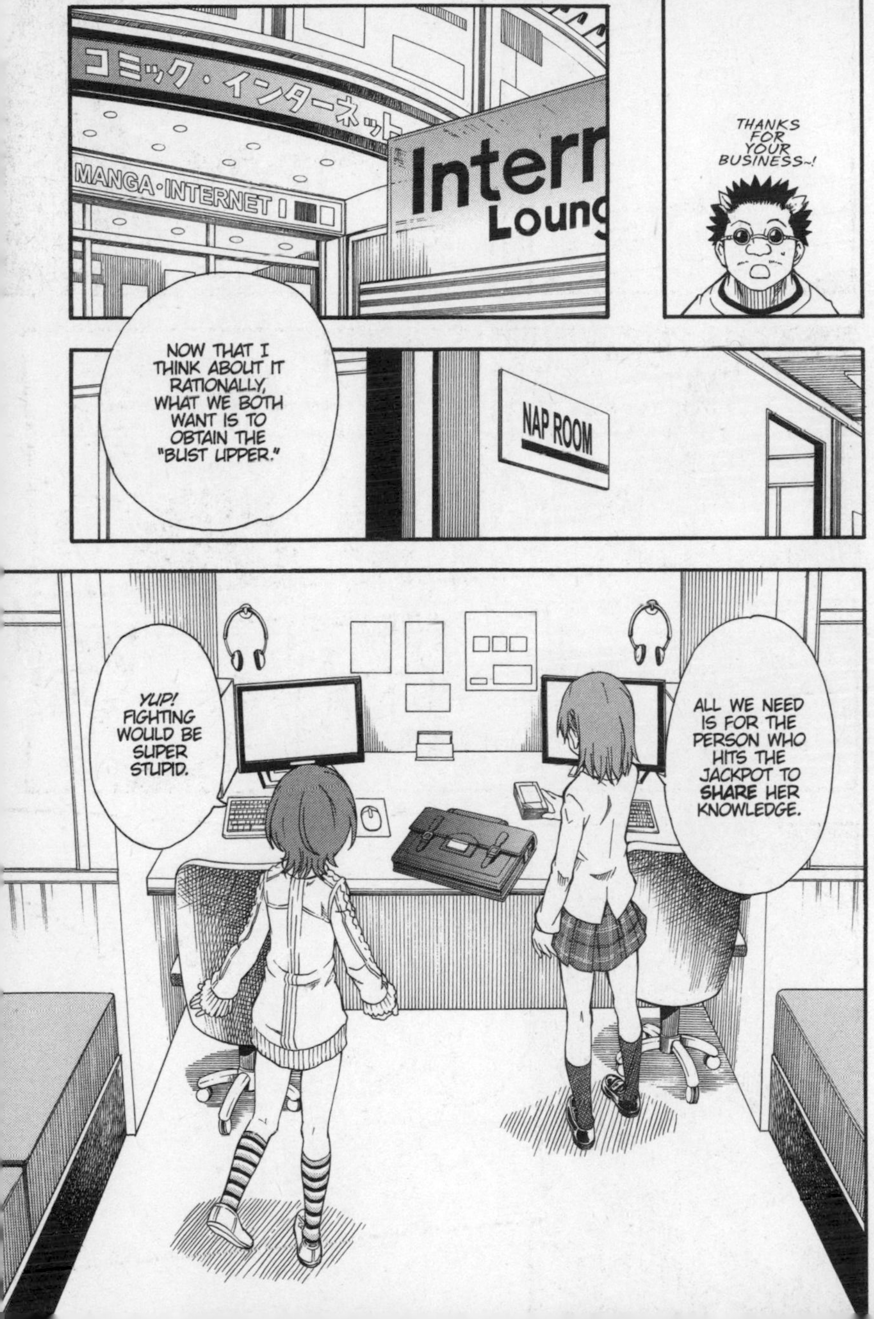
THANKS FOR YOUR BUSINESS~!
コミック・インターネット
MANGA·INTERNET
NOW THAT I THINK ABOUT IT RATIONALLY, WHAT WE BOTH WANT IS TO OBTAIN THE "BUST UPPER."
NAP ROOM
ALL WE NEED IS FOR THE PERSON WHO HITS THE JACKPOT TO SHARE HER KNOWLEDGE.
YUP! FIGHTING WOULD BE SUPER STUPID.

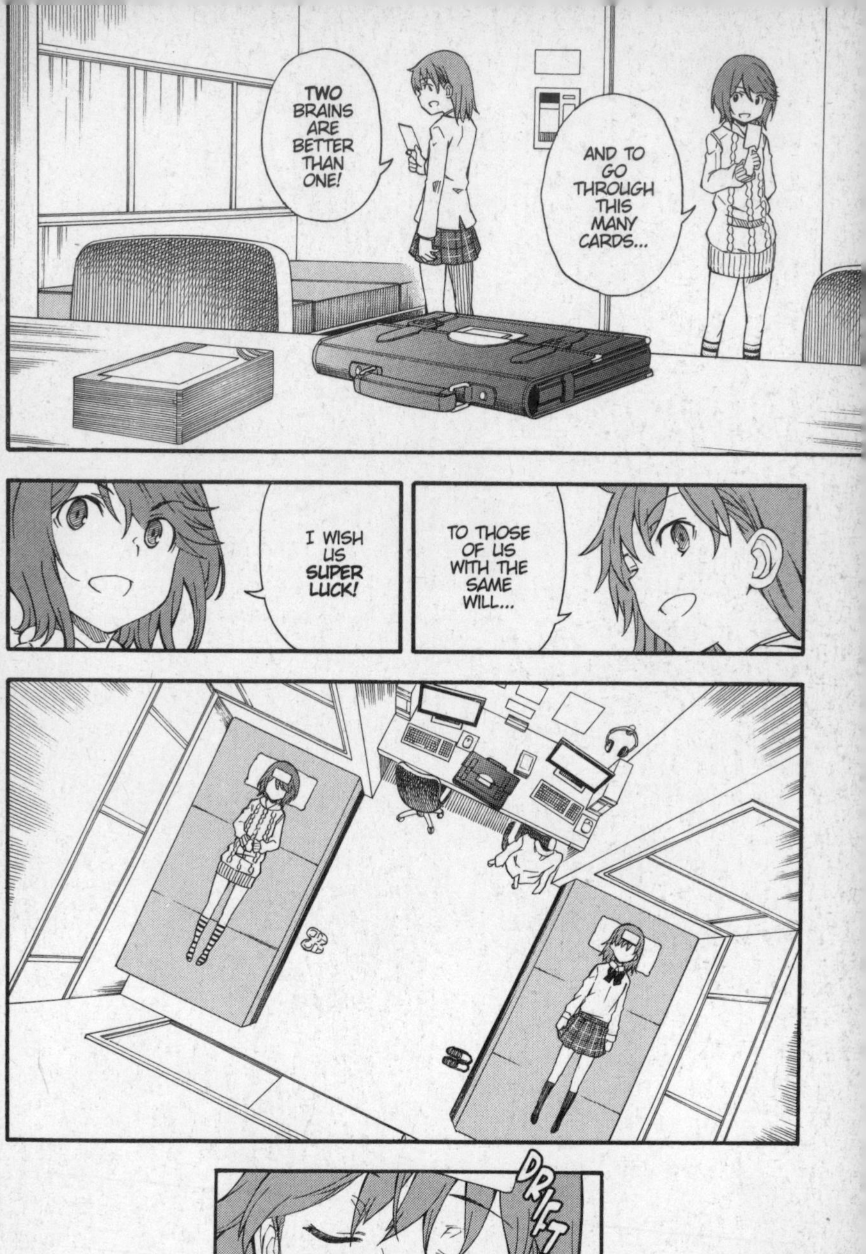
AND TO GO THROUGH THIS MANY CARDS...
TWO BRAINS ARE BETTER THAN ONE!
TO THOSE OF US WITH THE SAME WILL...
I WISH US SUPER LUCK!
DRIFT...

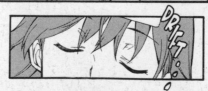

A Certain SCIENTIFIC Railgun

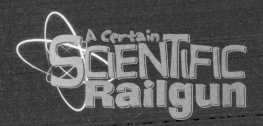

A Certain SCIENTIFIC Railgun

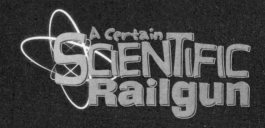

CHAPTER 79: REVELATION

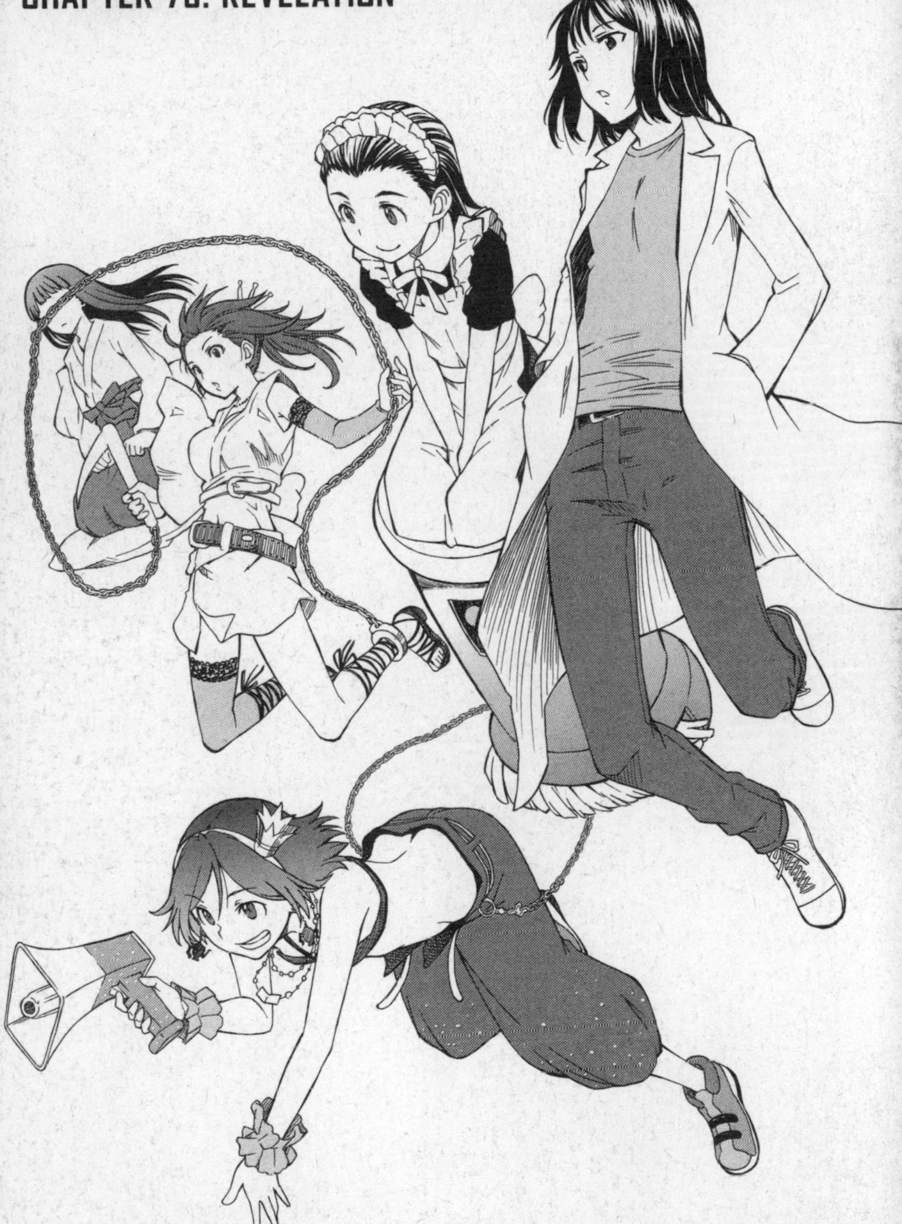

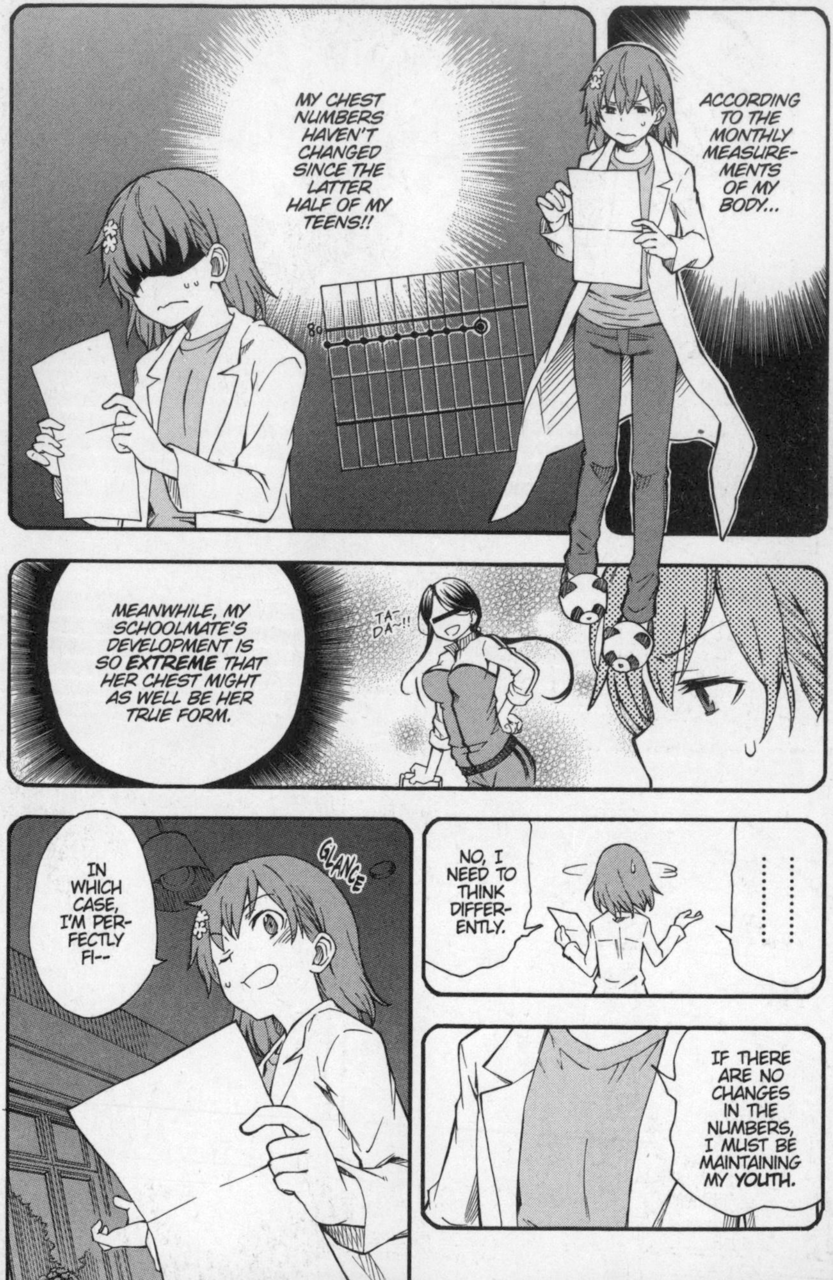
ACCORDING TO THE MONTHLY MEASUREMENTS OF MY BODY...
MY CHEST NUMBERS HAVEN'T CHANGED SINCE THE LATTER HALF OF MY TEENS!!
80
TA-DA~!!
MEANWHILE, MY SCHOOLMATE'S DEVELOPMENT IS SO **EXTREME** THAT HER CHEST MIGHT AS WELL BE HER TRUE FORM.
......
NO, I NEED TO THINK DIFFERENTLY.
IF THERE ARE NO CHANGES IN THE NUMBERS, I MUST BE MAINTAINING MY **YOUTH**.
GLANCE
IN WHICH CASE, I'M PERFECTLY FI--

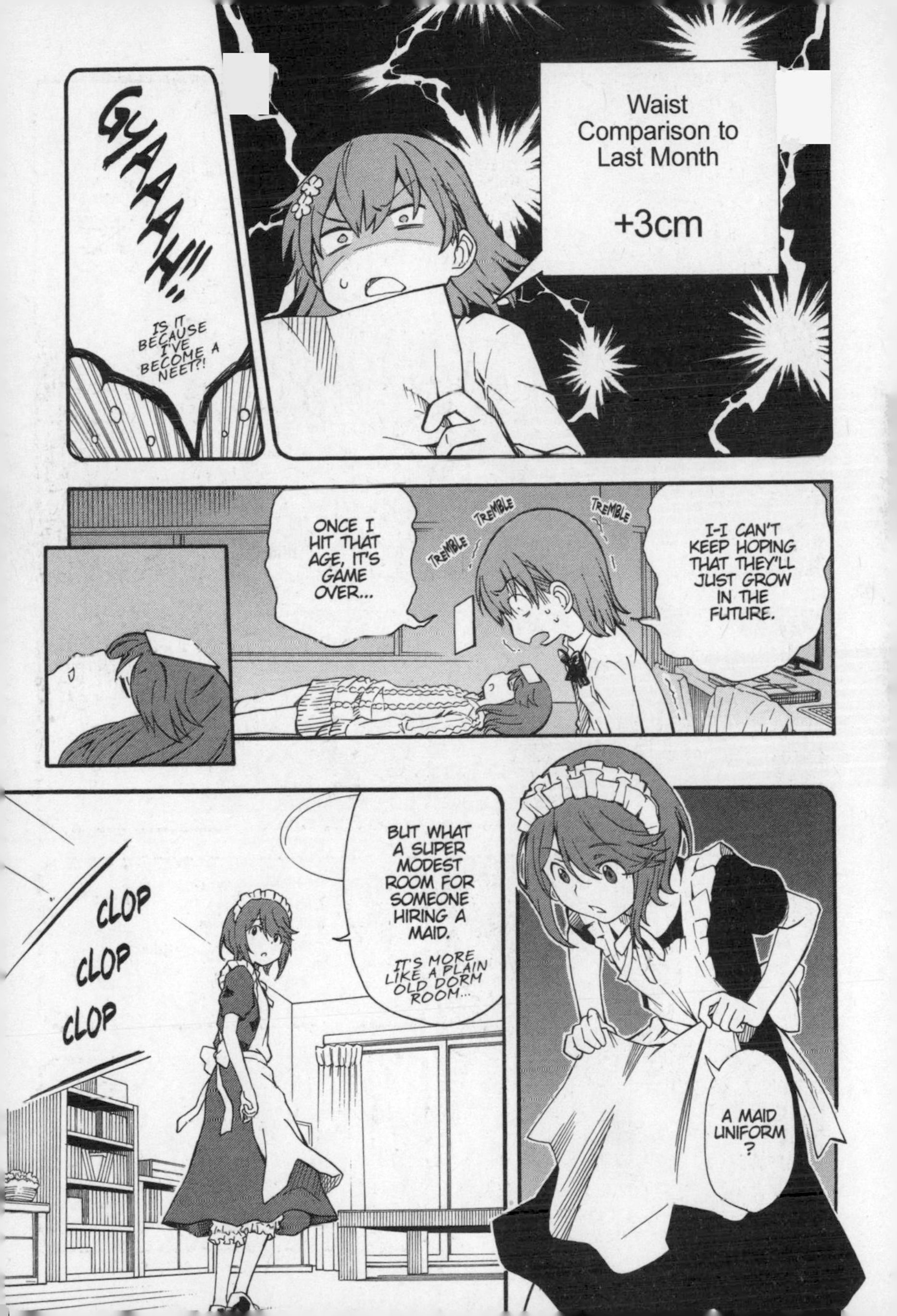
Waist Comparison to Last Month
+3cm
GYAAAH!!
IS IT BECAUSE I'VE BECOME A NEET?!
TREMBLE
I-I CAN'T KEEP HOPING THAT THEY'LL JUST GROW IN THE FUTURE.
TREMBLE
ONCE I HIT THAT AGE, IT'S GAME OVER...
TREMBLE
A MAID UNIFORM?
BUT WHAT A SUPER MODEST ROOM FOR SOMEONE HIRING A MAID.
IT'S MORE LIKE A PLAIN OLD DORM ROOM...
CLOP
CLOP
CLOP

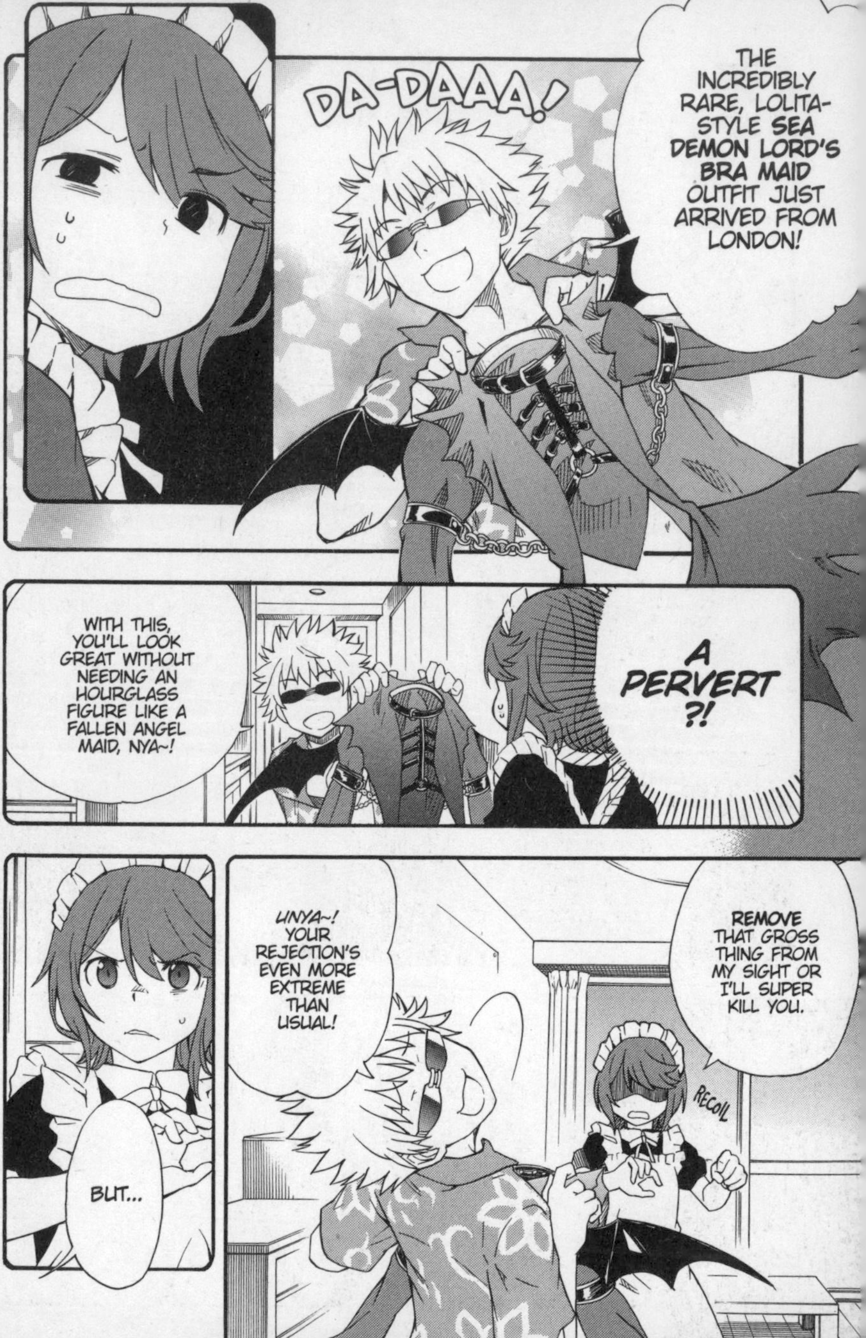
THE INCREDIBLY RARE, LOLITA-STYLE SEA DEMON LORD'S BRA MAID OUTFIT JUST ARRIVED FROM LONDON!
DA-DAAA!
A PERVERT?!
WITH THIS, YOU'LL LOOK GREAT WITHOUT NEEDING AN HOURGLASS FIGURE LIKE A FALLEN ANGEL MAID, NYA~!
REMOVE THAT GROSS THING FROM MY SIGHT OR I'LL SUPER KILL YOU.
RECOIL
UNYA~! YOUR REJECTION'S EVEN MORE EXTREME THAN USUAL!
BUT...

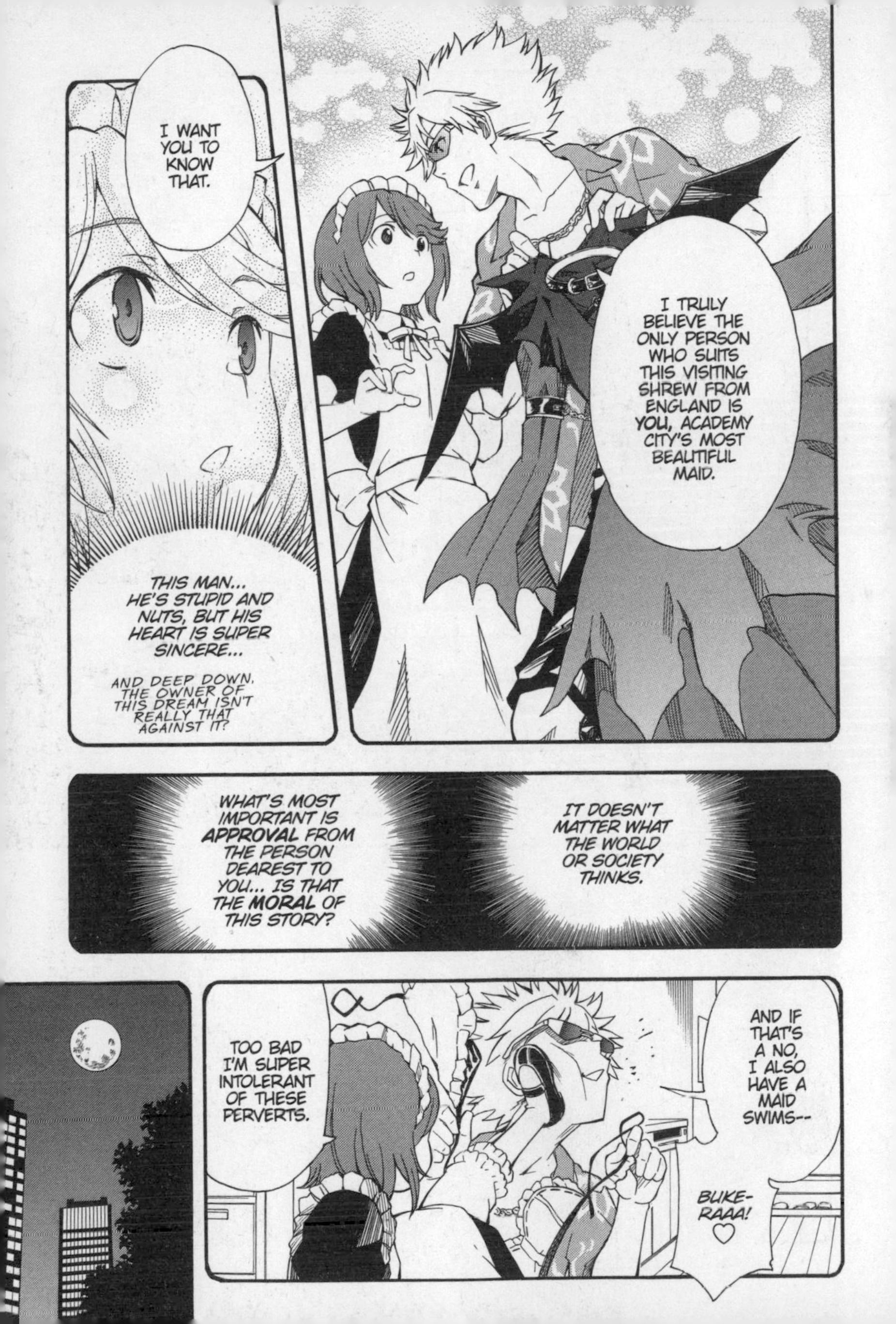
I TRULY BELIEVE THE ONLY PERSON WHO SUITS THIS VISITING SHREW FROM ENGLAND IS YOU, ACADEMY CITY'S MOST BEAUTIFUL MAID.
I WANT YOU TO KNOW THAT.
THIS MAN... HE'S STUPID AND NUTS, BUT HIS HEART IS SUPER SINCERE...
AND DEEP DOWN, THE OWNER OF THIS DREAM ISN'T REALLY THAT AGAINST IT?
IT DOESN'T MATTER WHAT THE WORLD OR SOCIETY THINKS.
WHAT'S MOST IMPORTANT IS APPROVAL FROM THE PERSON DEAREST TO YOU... IS THAT THE MORAL OF THIS STORY?
AND IF THAT'S A NO, I ALSO HAVE A MAID SWIMS--
BUKE-RAAA! ♡
TOO BAD I'M SUPER INTOLERANT OF THESE PERVERTS.

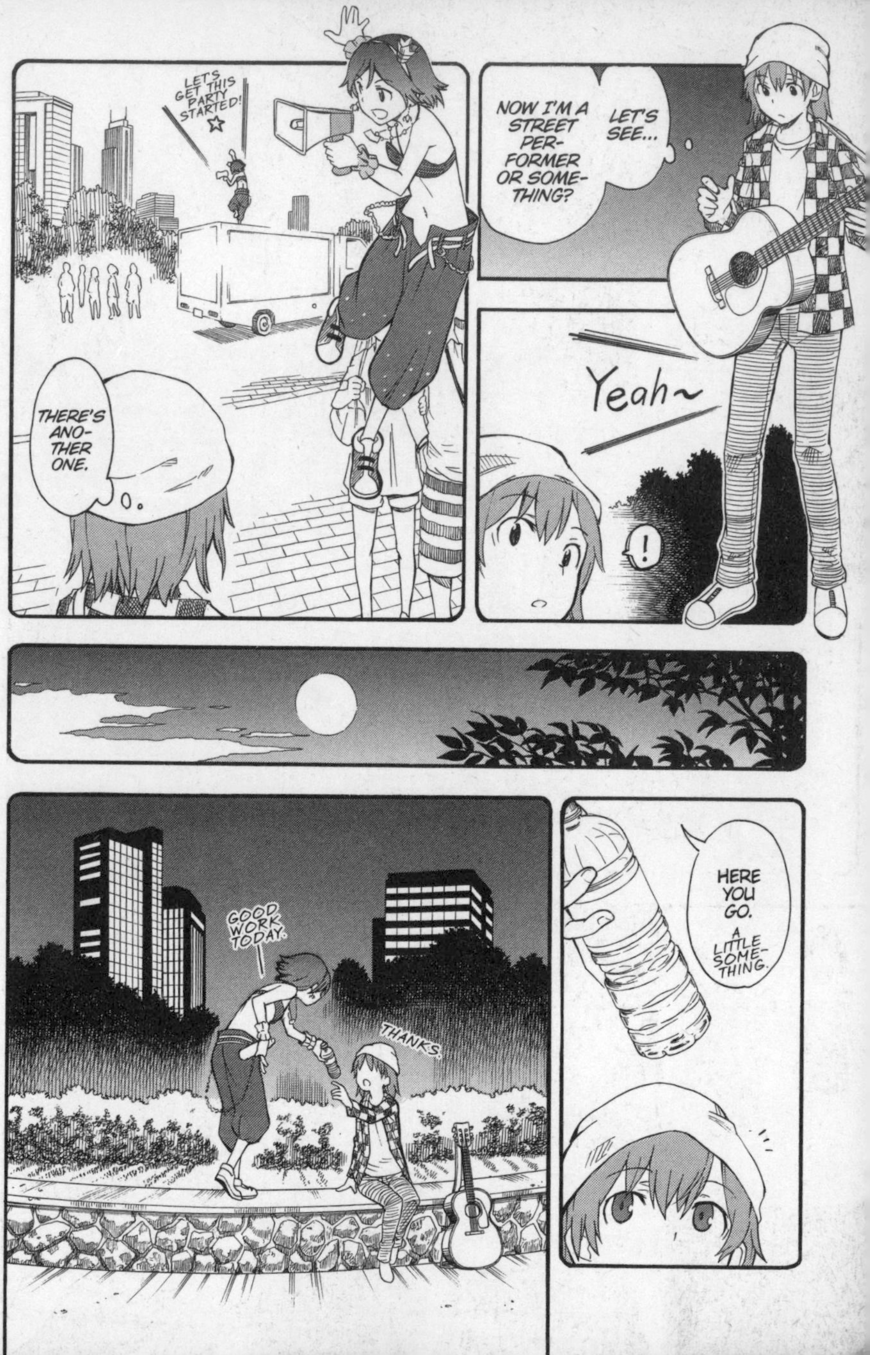
LET'S SEE...
NOW I'M A STREET PERFORMER OR SOMETHING?
Yeah~
!
LET'S GET THIS PARTY STARTED! ☆
THERE'S ANOTHER ONE.
HERE YOU GO.
A LITTLE SOMETHING.
GOOD WORK TODAY.
THANKS.

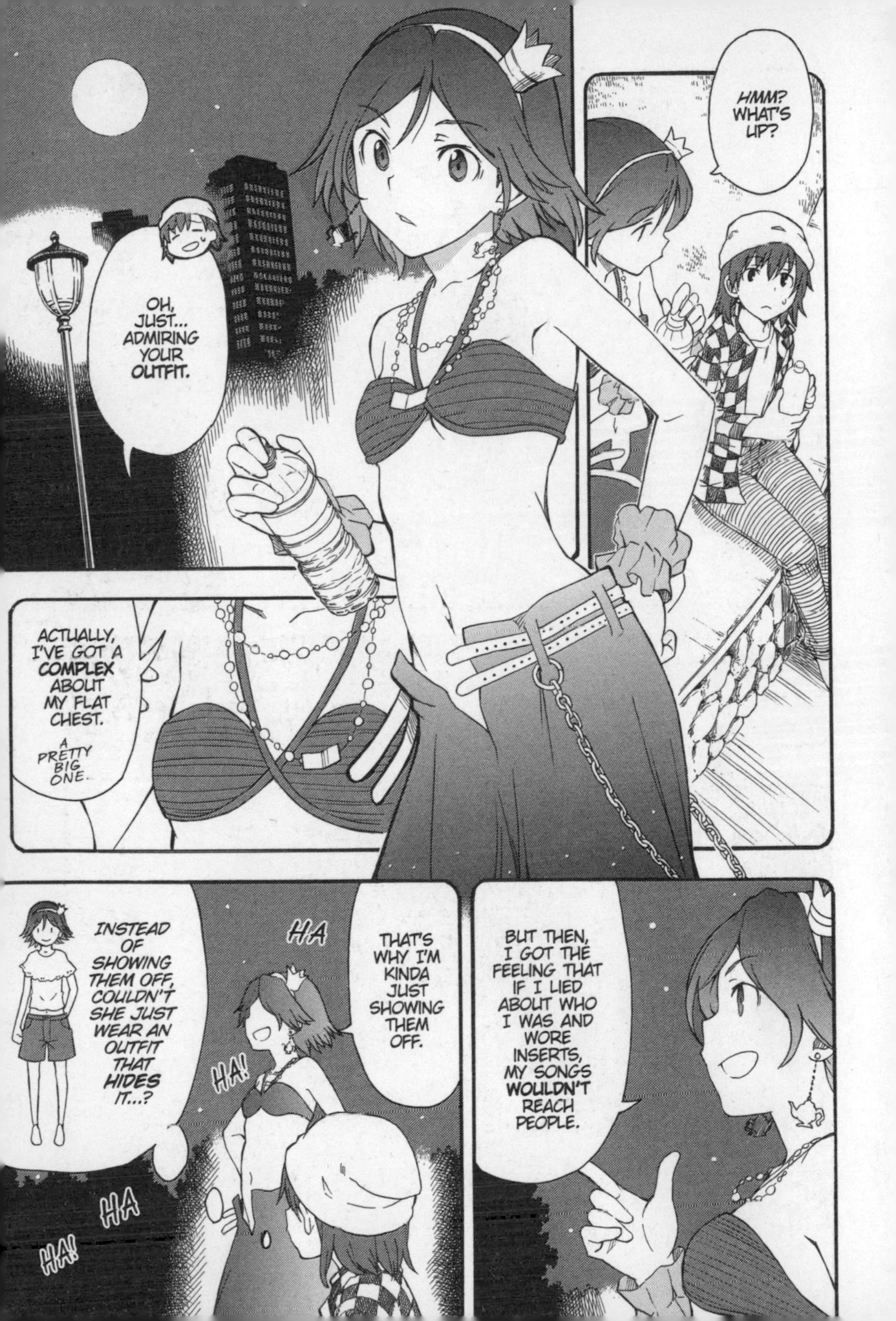
HMM? WHAT'S UP?
OH, JUST... ADMIRING YOUR OUTFIT.
ACTUALLY, I'VE GOT A COMPLEX ABOUT MY FLAT CHEST.
A PRETTY BIG ONE.
BUT THEN, I GOT THE FEELING THAT IF I LIED ABOUT WHO I WAS AND WORE INSERTS, MY SONGS WOULDN'T REACH PEOPLE.
THAT'S WHY I'M KINDA JUST SHOWING THEM OFF.
HA
HA!
HA
HA!
INSTEAD OF SHOWING THEM OFF, COULDN'T SHE JUST WEAR AN OUTFIT THAT HIDES IT...?

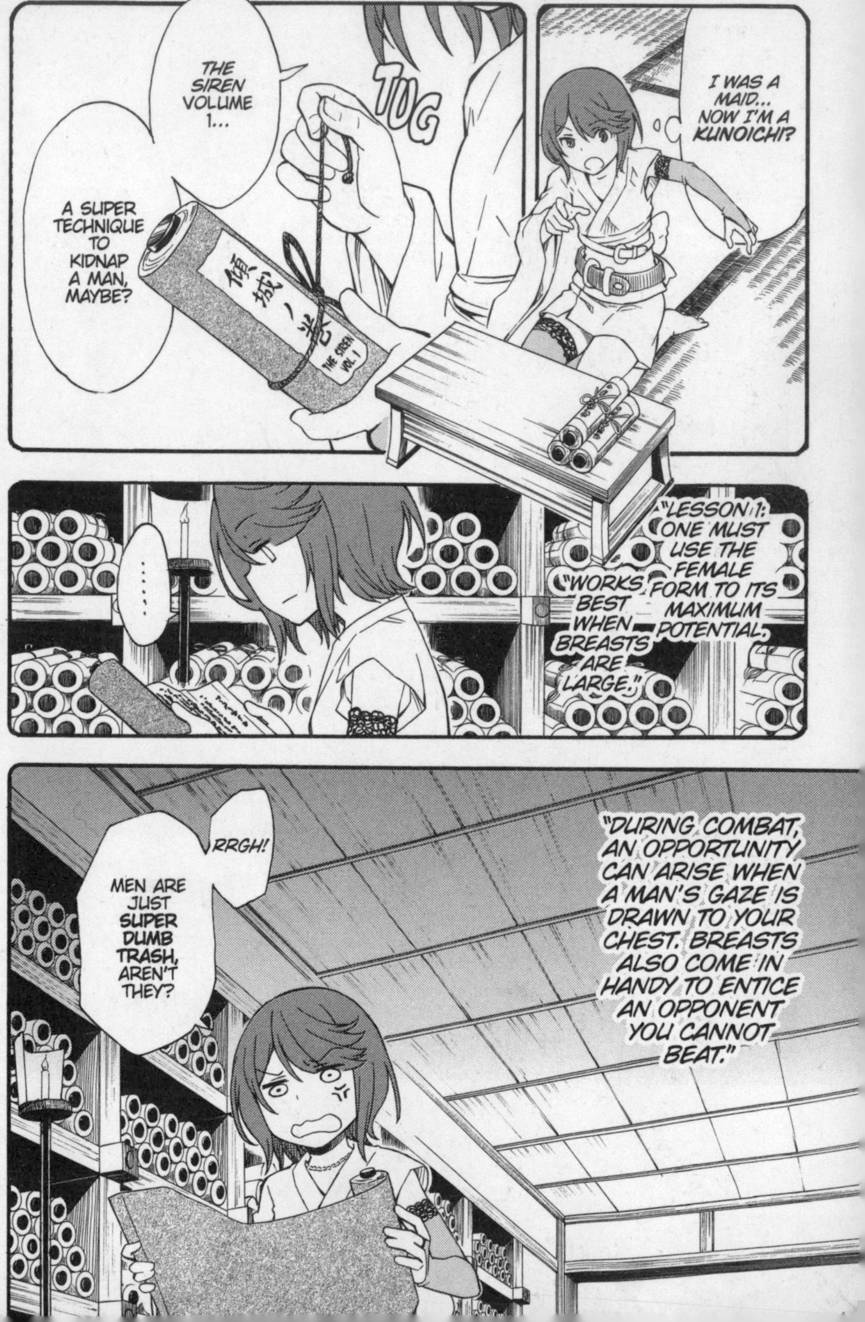
I WAS A MAID... NOW I'M A KUNOICHI?
TUG
THE SIREN VOLUME 1...
A SUPER TECHNIQUE TO KIDNAP A MAN, MAYBE?
傾城一巻
THE SIREN VOL. 1
"LESSON 1: ONE MUST USE THE FEMALE FORM TO ITS MAXIMUM POTENTIAL.
"WORKS BEST WHEN BREASTS ARE LARGE."
......
"DURING COMBAT, AN OPPORTUNITY CAN ARISE WHEN A MAN'S GAZE IS DRAWN TO YOUR CHEST. BREASTS ALSO COME IN HANDY TO ENTICE AN OPPONENT YOU CANNOT BEAT."
RRGH!
MEN ARE JUST SUPER DUMB TRASH, AREN'T THEY?

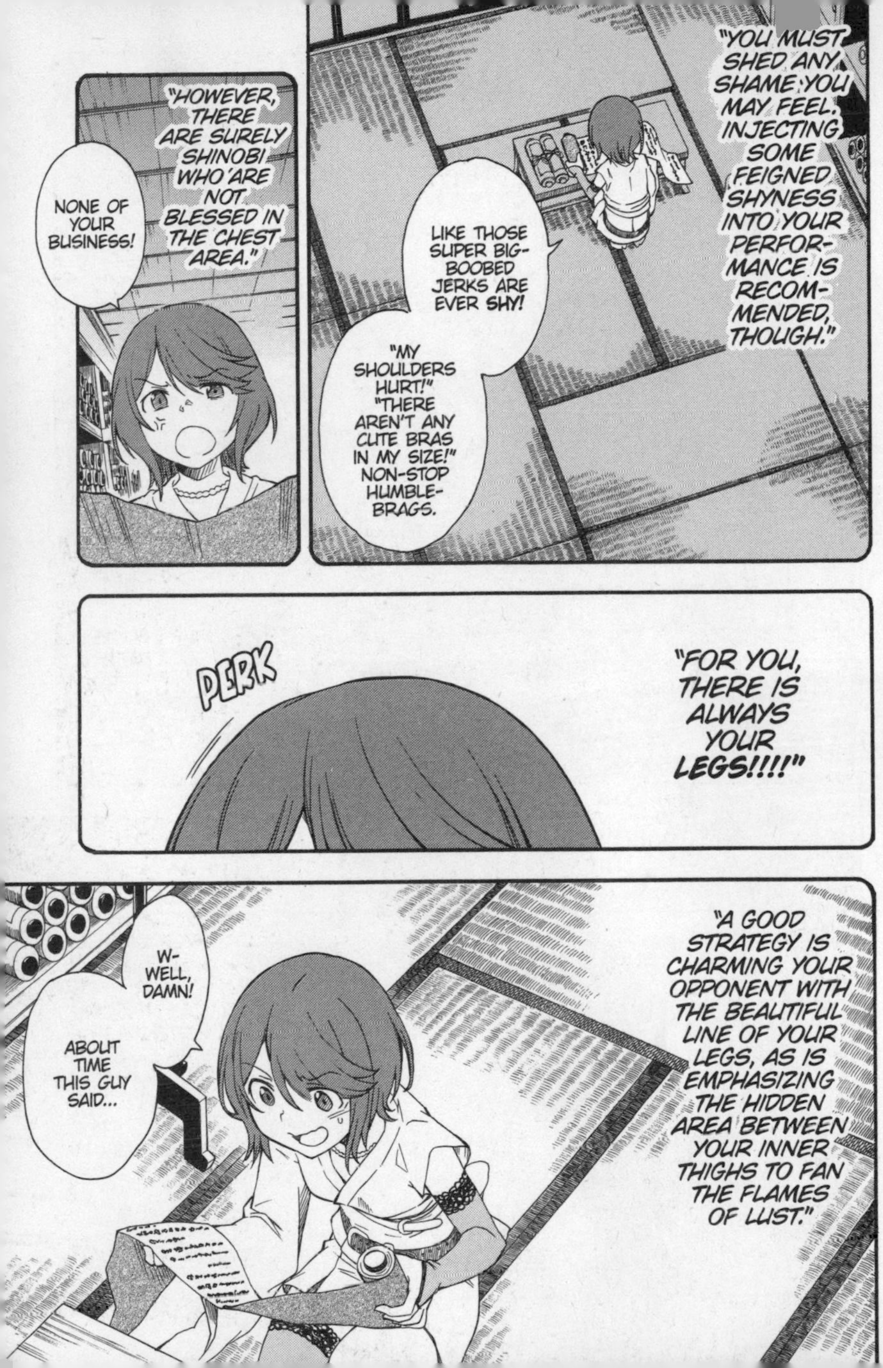
"YOU MUST SHED ANY SHAME YOU MAY FEEL. INJECTING SOME FEIGNED SHYNESS INTO YOUR PERFORMANCE IS RECOMMENDED, THOUGH."
LIKE THOSE SUPER BIG-BOOBED JERKS ARE EVER SHY!
"MY SHOULDERS HURT!" "THERE AREN'T ANY CUTE BRAS IN MY SIZE!" NON-STOP HUMBLE-BRAGS.
"HOWEVER, THERE ARE SURELY SHINOBI WHO ARE NOT BLESSED IN THE CHEST AREA."
NONE OF YOUR BUSINESS!
"FOR YOU, THERE IS ALWAYS YOUR LEGS!!!!"
PERK
"A GOOD STRATEGY IS CHARMING YOUR OPPONENT WITH THE BEAUTIFUL LINE OF YOUR LEGS, AS IS EMPHASIZING THE HIDDEN AREA BETWEEN YOUR INNER THIGHS TO FAN THE FLAMES OF LUST."
W-WELL, DAMN!
ABOUT TIME THIS GUY SAID...

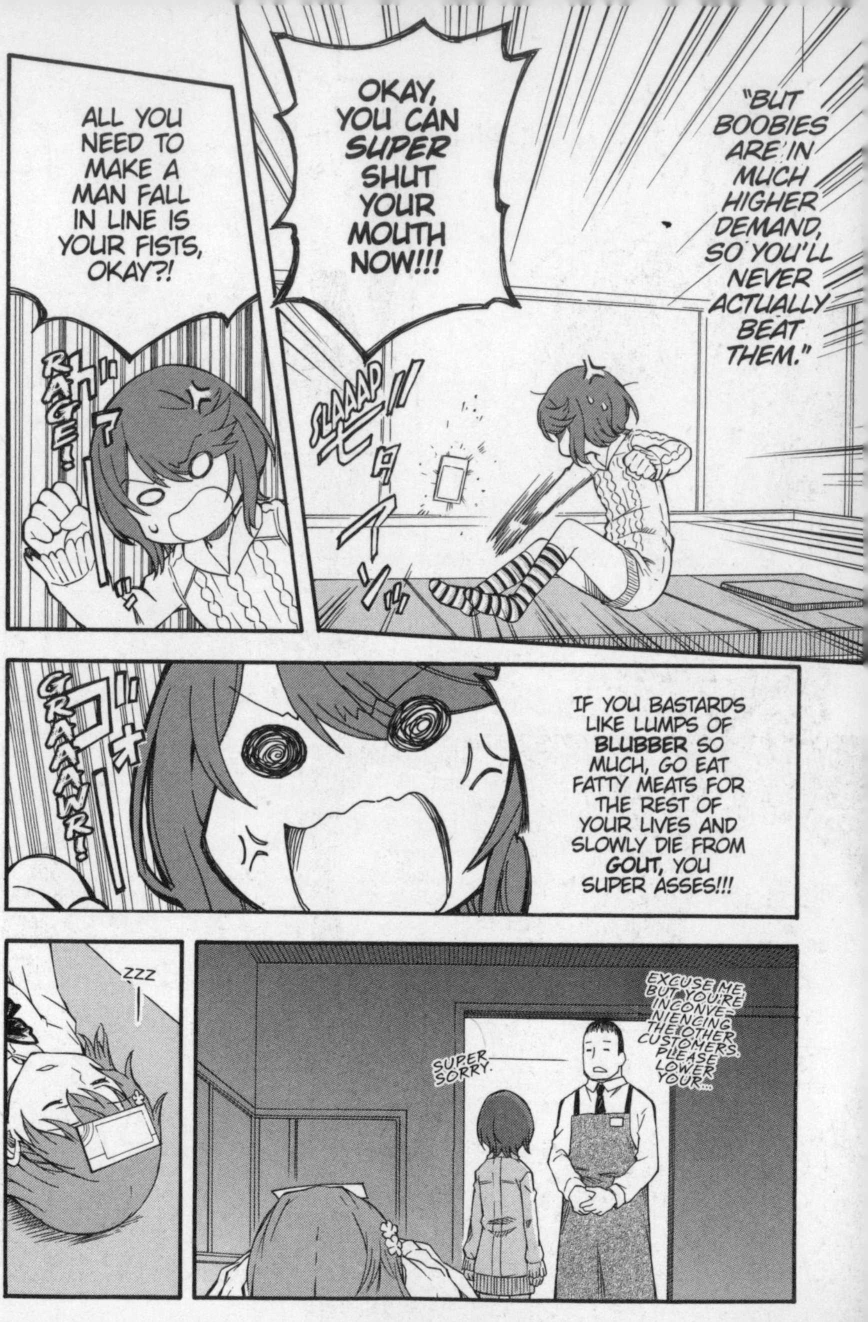
"BUT BOOBIES ARE IN MUCH HIGHER DEMAND, SO YOU'LL NEVER ACTUALLY BEAT THEM."
OKAY, YOU CAN SUPER SHUT YOUR MOUTH NOW!!!
SLAAAP!
ALL YOU NEED TO MAKE A MAN FALL IN LINE IS YOUR FISTS, OKAY?!
RAGE!
IF YOU BASTARDS LIKE LUMPS OF BLUBBER SO MUCH, GO EAT FATTY MEATS FOR THE REST OF YOUR LIVES AND SLOWLY DIE FROM GOUT, YOU SUPER ASSES!!!
GRAAAAWR!
EXCUSE ME, BUT YOU'RE INCONVENIENCING THE OTHER CUSTOMERS. PLEASE LOWER YOUR...
SUPER SORRY.
ZZZ

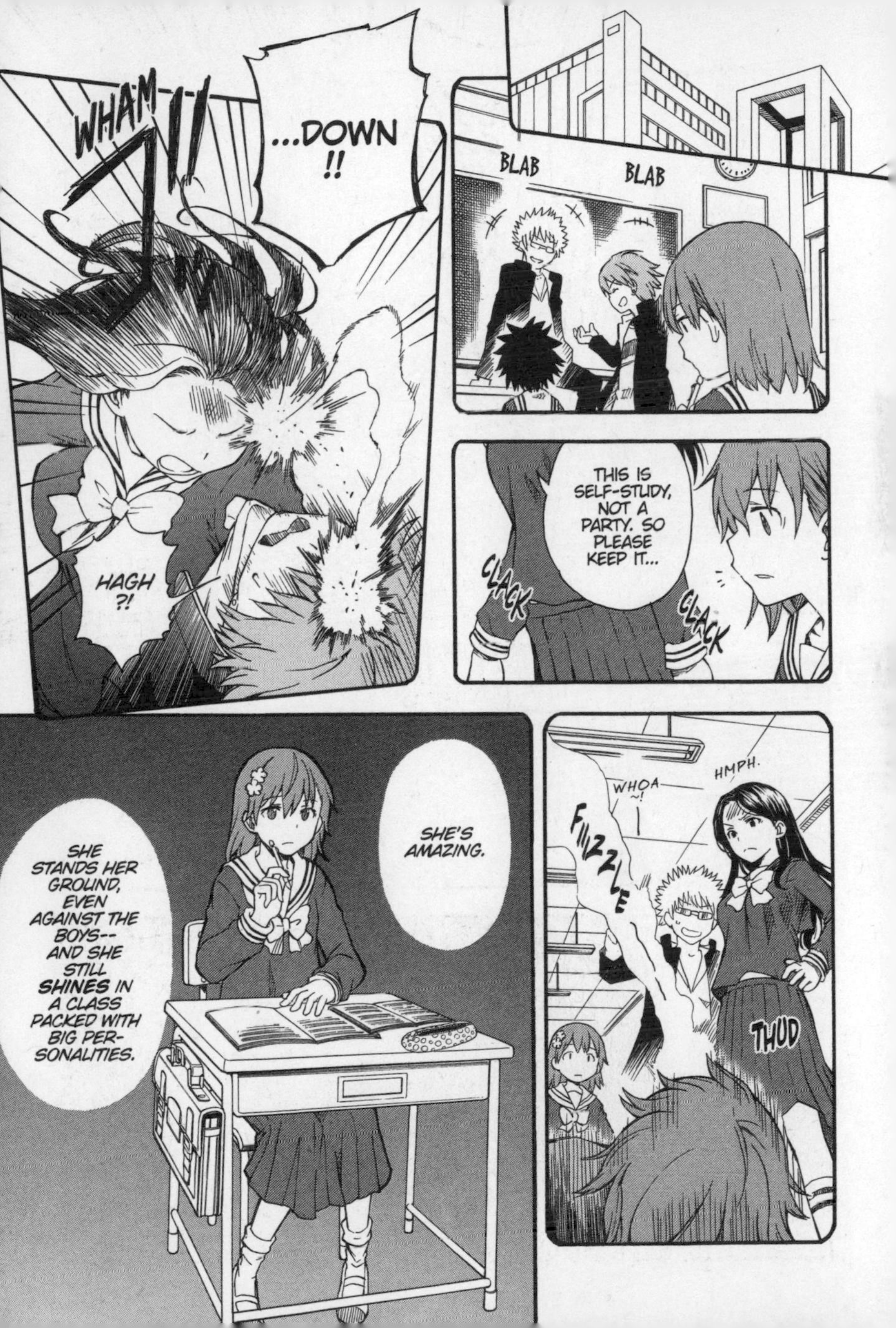
BLAB
BLAB
THIS IS SELF-STUDY, NOT A PARTY. SO PLEASE KEEP IT...
CLACK
CLACK
...DOWN !!
WHAM!!
HAGH ?!
HMPH.
WHOA ~!
FIZZLE
THUD
SHE'S AMAZING.
SHE STANDS HER GROUND, EVEN AGAINST THE BOYS-- AND SHE STILL SHINES IN A CLASS PACKED WITH BIG PER-SONALITIES.

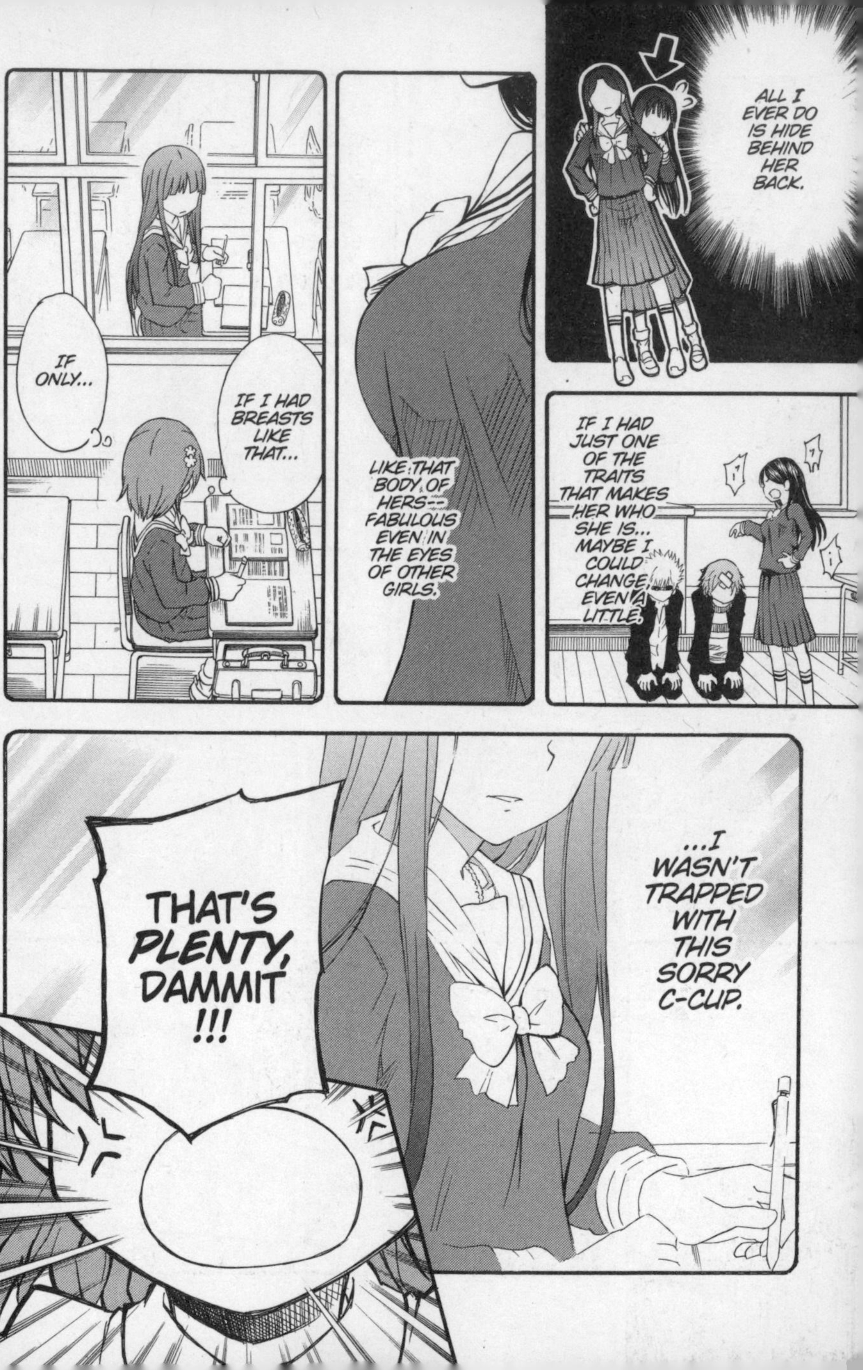
ALL I EVER DO IS HIDE BEHIND HER BACK.
IF I HAD JUST ONE OF THE TRAITS THAT MAKES HER WHO SHE IS... MAYBE I COULD CHANGE, EVEN A LITTLE.
LIKE THAT BODY OF HERS-- FABULOUS EVEN IN THE EYES OF OTHER GIRLS.
IF ONLY...
IF I HAD BREASTS LIKE THAT...
...I WASN'T TRAPPED WITH THIS SORRY C-CUP.
THAT'S PLENTY, DAMMIT!!!

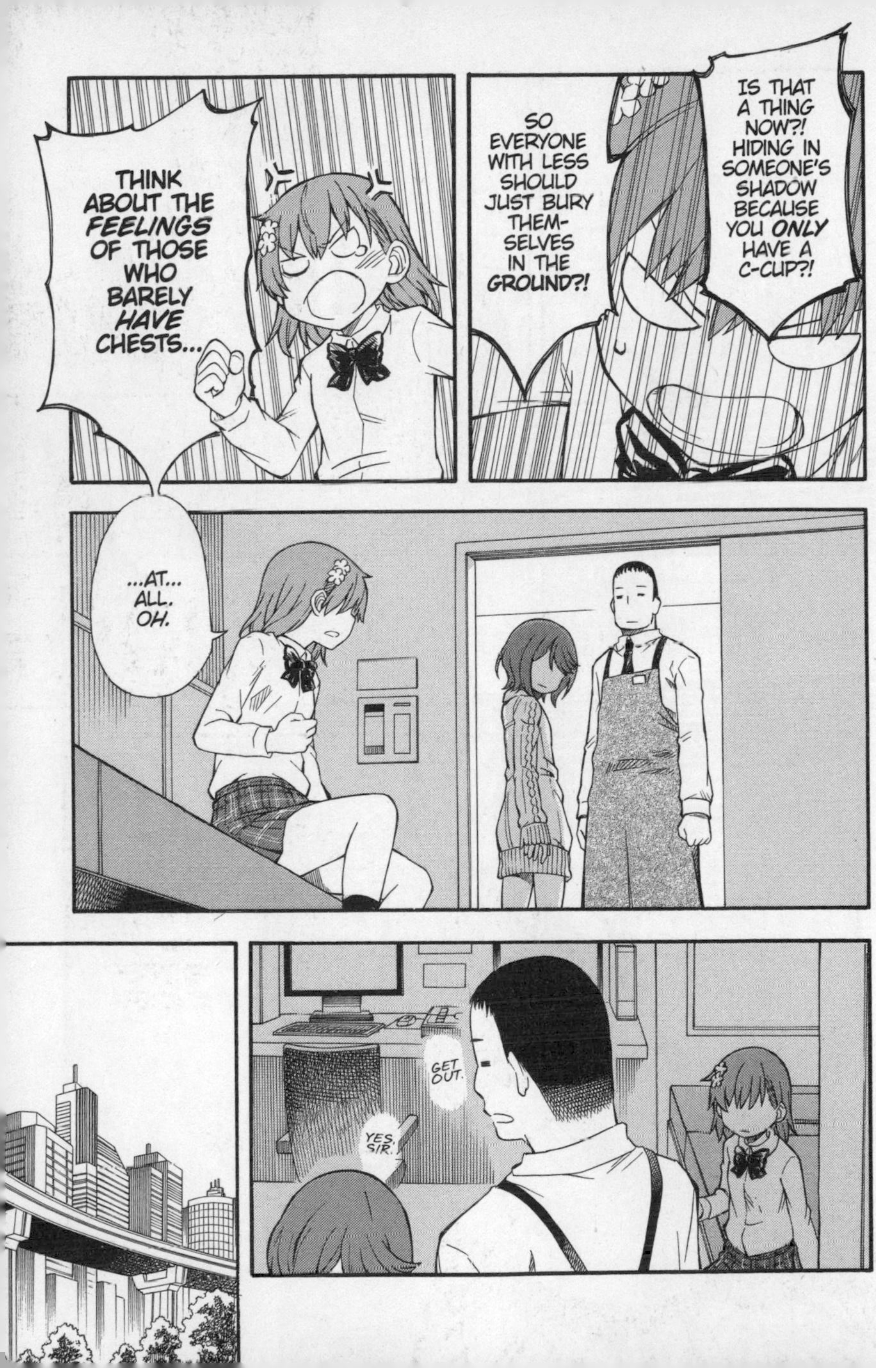
IS THAT A THING NOW?! HIDING IN SOMEONE'S SHADOW BECAUSE YOU ONLY HAVE A C-CUP?!
SO EVERYONE WITH LESS SHOULD JUST BURY THEMSELVES IN THE GROUND?!
THINK ABOUT THE FEELINGS OF THOSE WHO BARELY HAVE CHESTS...
...AT... ALL. OH.
GET OUT.
YES, SIR.

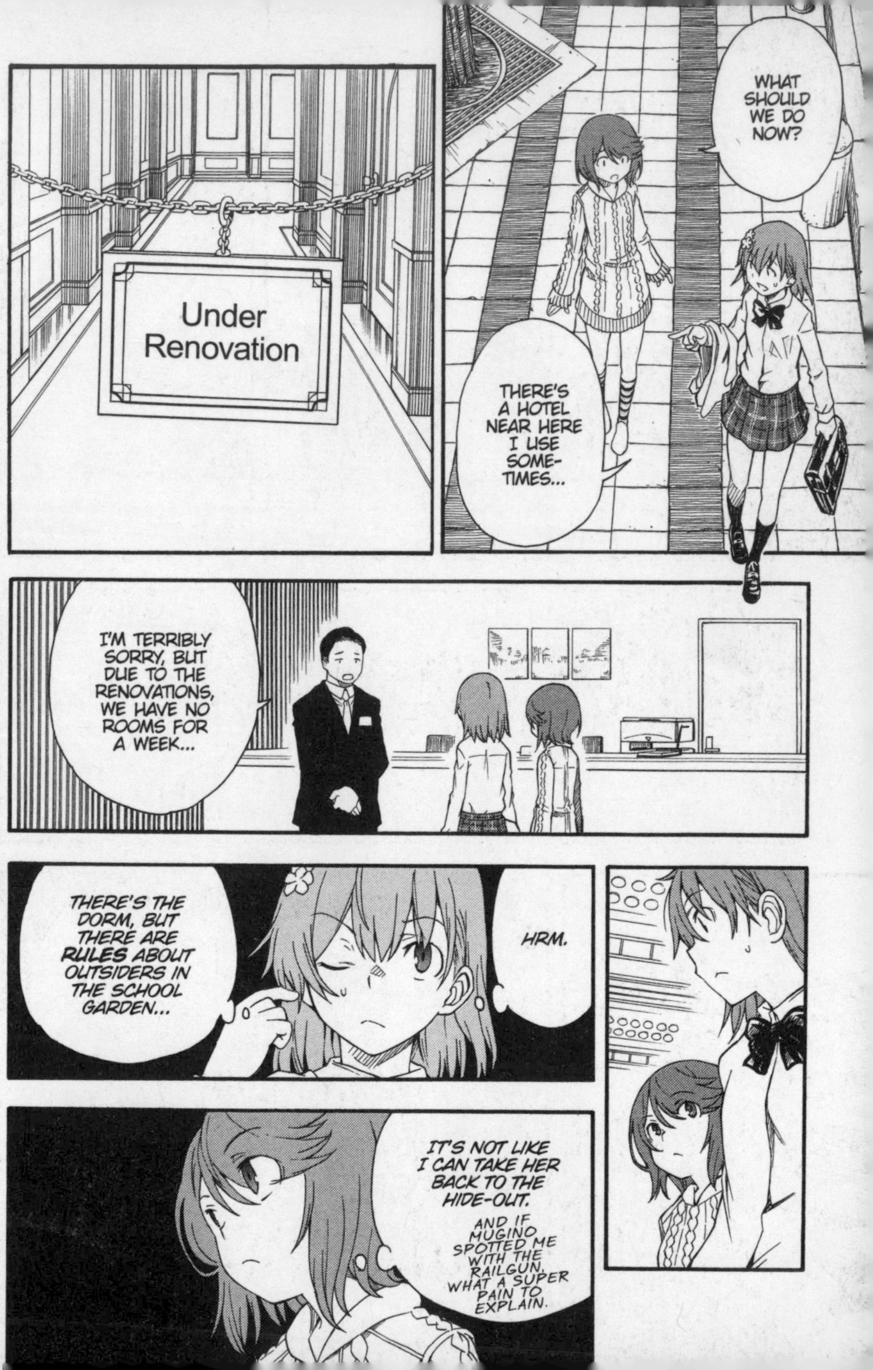
WHAT SHOULD WE DO NOW?
THERE'S A HOTEL NEAR HERE I USE SOME-TIMES...
Under Renovation
I'M TERRIBLY SORRY, BUT DUE TO THE RENOVATIONS, WE HAVE NO ROOMS FOR A WEEK...
HRM.
THERE'S THE DORM, BUT THERE ARE RULES ABOUT OUTSIDERS IN THE SCHOOL GARDEN...
IT'S NOT LIKE I CAN TAKE HER BACK TO THE HIDE-OUT.
AND IF MUGINO SPOTTED ME WITH THE RAILGUN, WHAT A SUPER PAIN TO EXPLAIN.

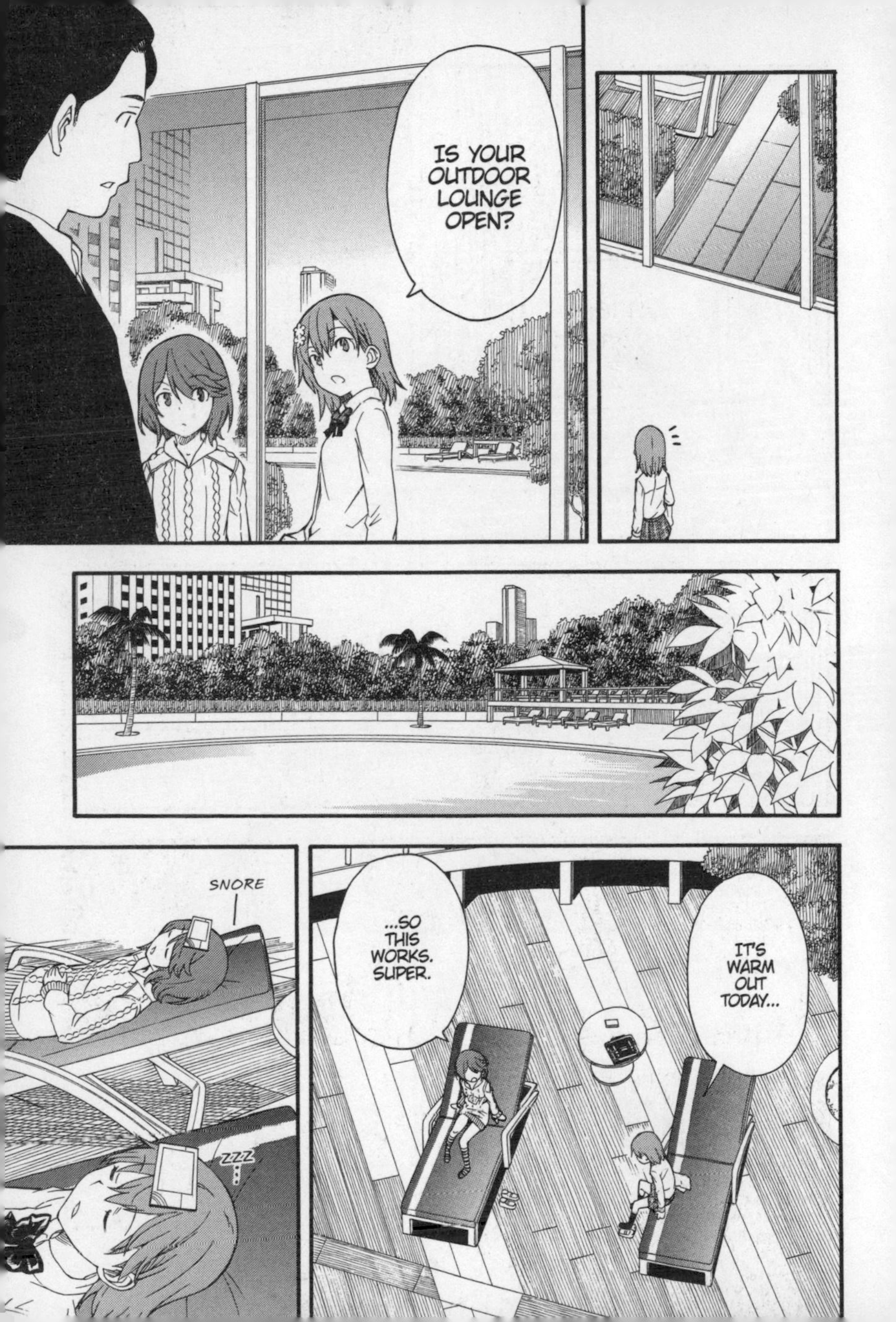
IS YOUR OUTDOOR LOUNGE OPEN?
IT'S WARM OUT TODAY...
...SO THIS WORKS. SUPER.
SNORE
ZZZ...

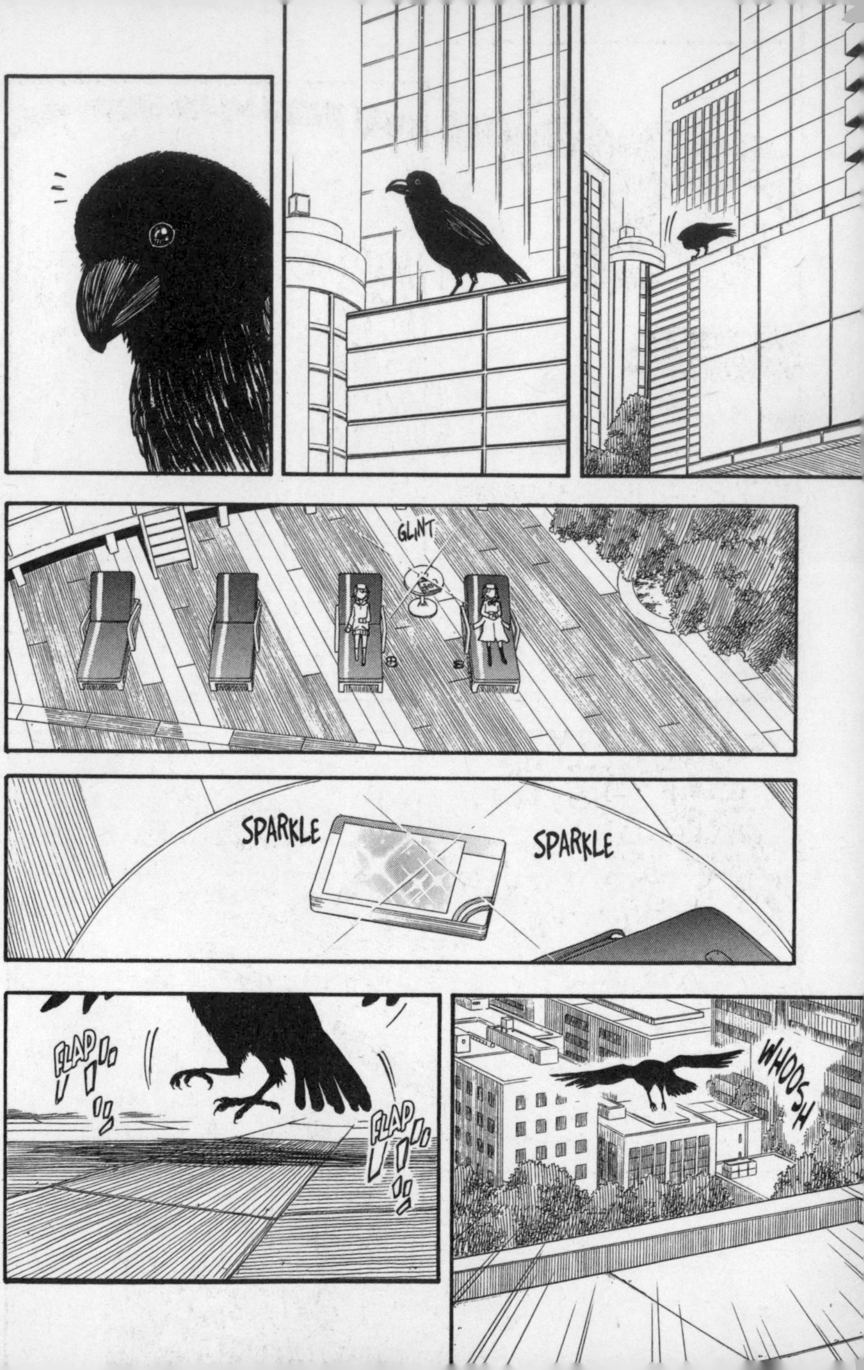
GLINT
SPARKLE
SPARKLE
WHOOSH
FLAP
FLAP

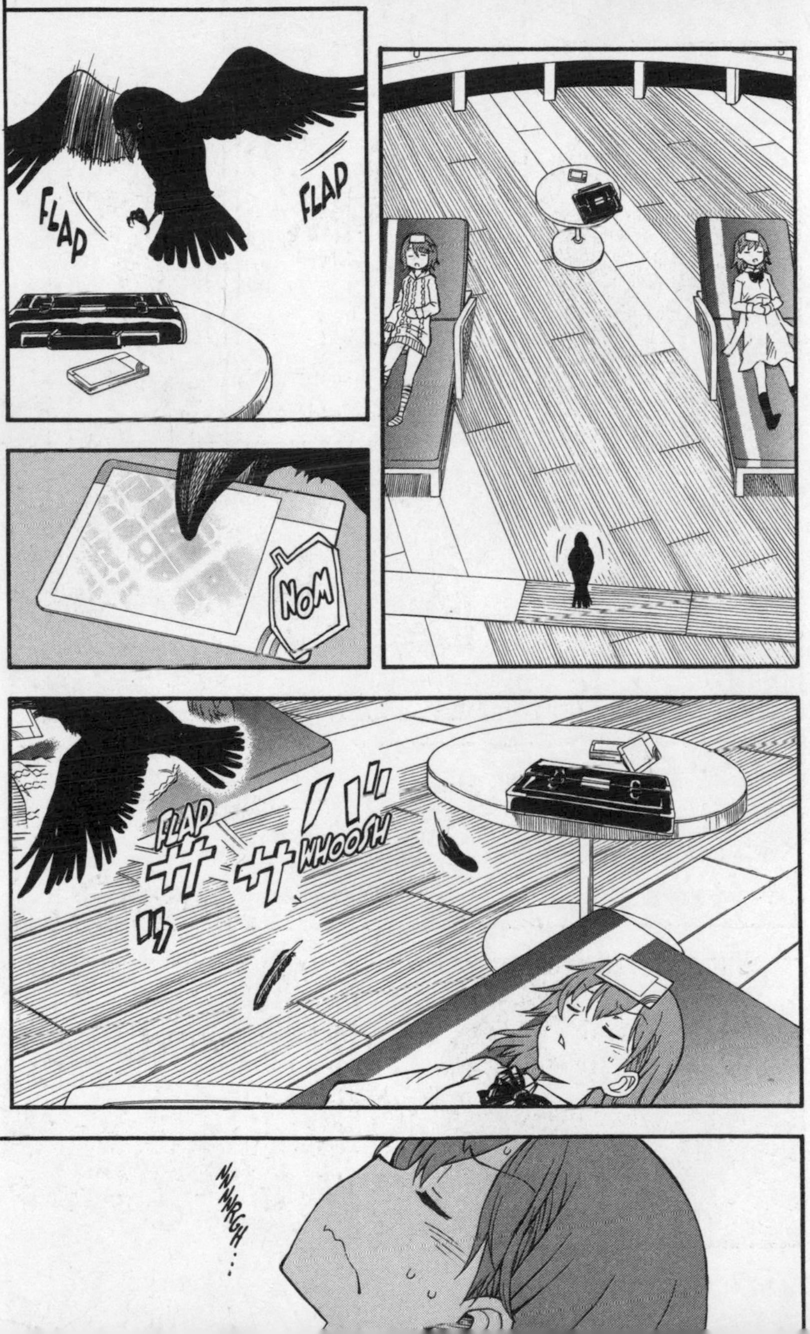
FLAP
FLAP
NOM
FLAP
WHOOSH
NNNRGH...

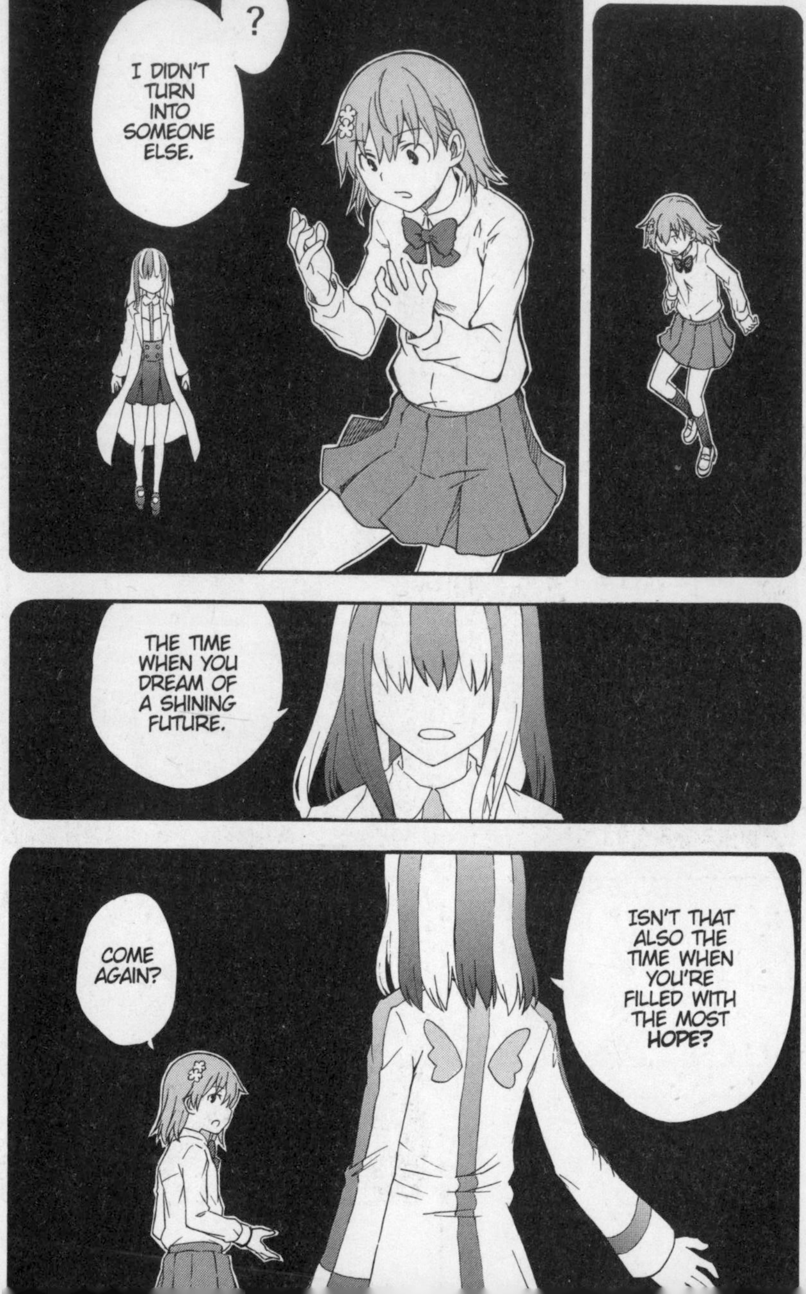
?
I DIDN'T TURN INTO SOMEONE ELSE.
THE TIME WHEN YOU DREAM OF A SHINING FUTURE.
ISN'T THAT ALSO THE TIME WHEN YOU'RE FILLED WITH THE MOST HOPE?
COME AGAIN?

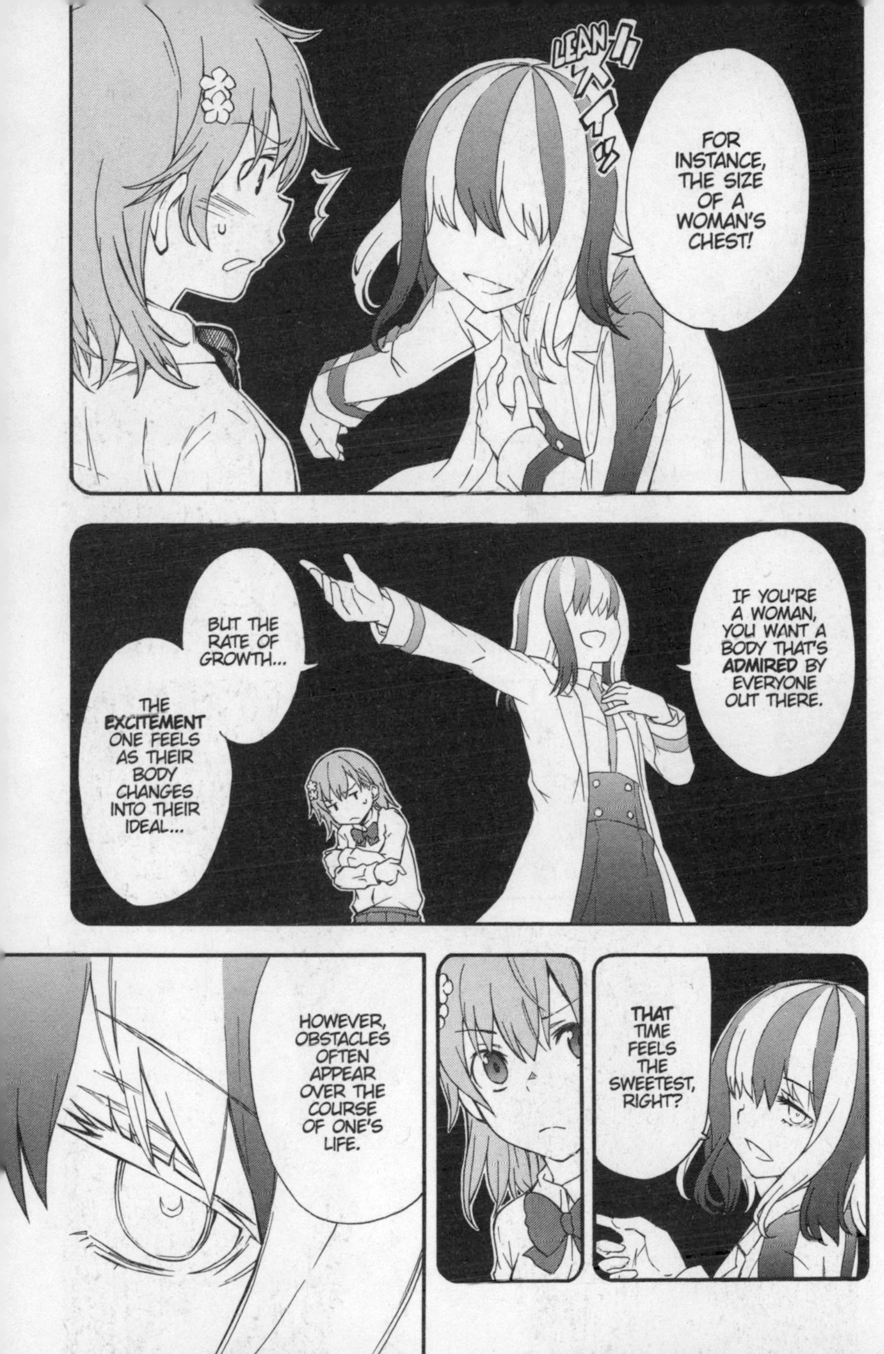
LEAN-
FOR INSTANCE, THE SIZE OF A WOMAN'S CHEST!
IF YOU'RE A WOMAN, YOU WANT A BODY THAT'S **ADMIRED** BY EVERYONE OUT THERE.
BUT THE RATE OF GROWTH...
THE **EXCITEMENT** ONE FEELS AS THEIR BODY CHANGES INTO THEIR IDEAL...
THAT TIME FEELS THE SWEETEST, RIGHT?
HOWEVER, OBSTACLES OFTEN APPEAR OVER THE COURSE OF ONE'S LIFE.

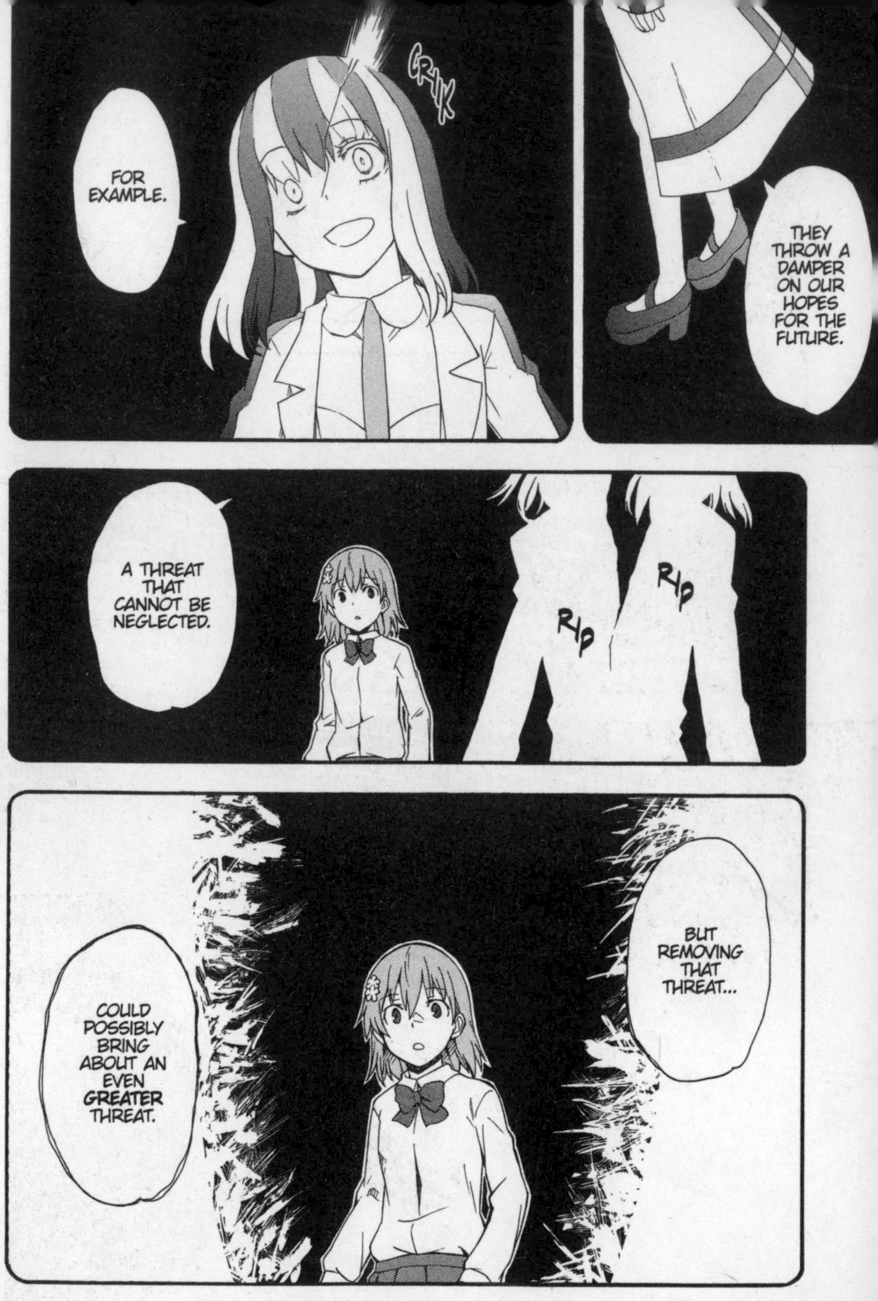
THEY THROW A DAMPER ON OUR HOPES FOR THE FUTURE.
CRIIK
FOR EXAMPLE.
A THREAT THAT CANNOT BE NEGLECTED.
RIP
RIP
BUT REMOVING THAT THREAT...
COULD POSSIBLY BRING ABOUT AN EVEN GREATER THREAT.

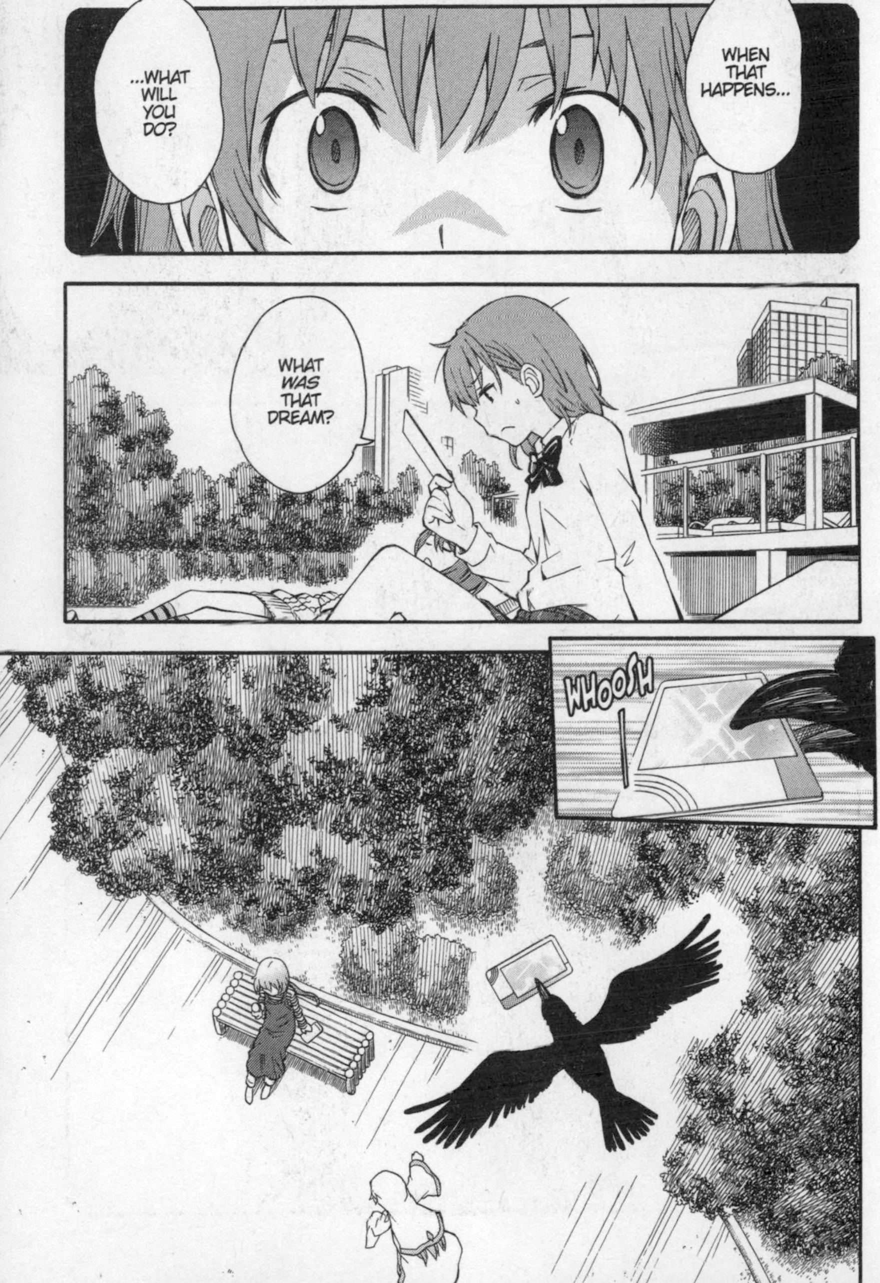
WHEN THAT HAPPENS...
...WHAT WILL YOU DO?
WHAT *WAS* THAT DREAM?
WHOOSH

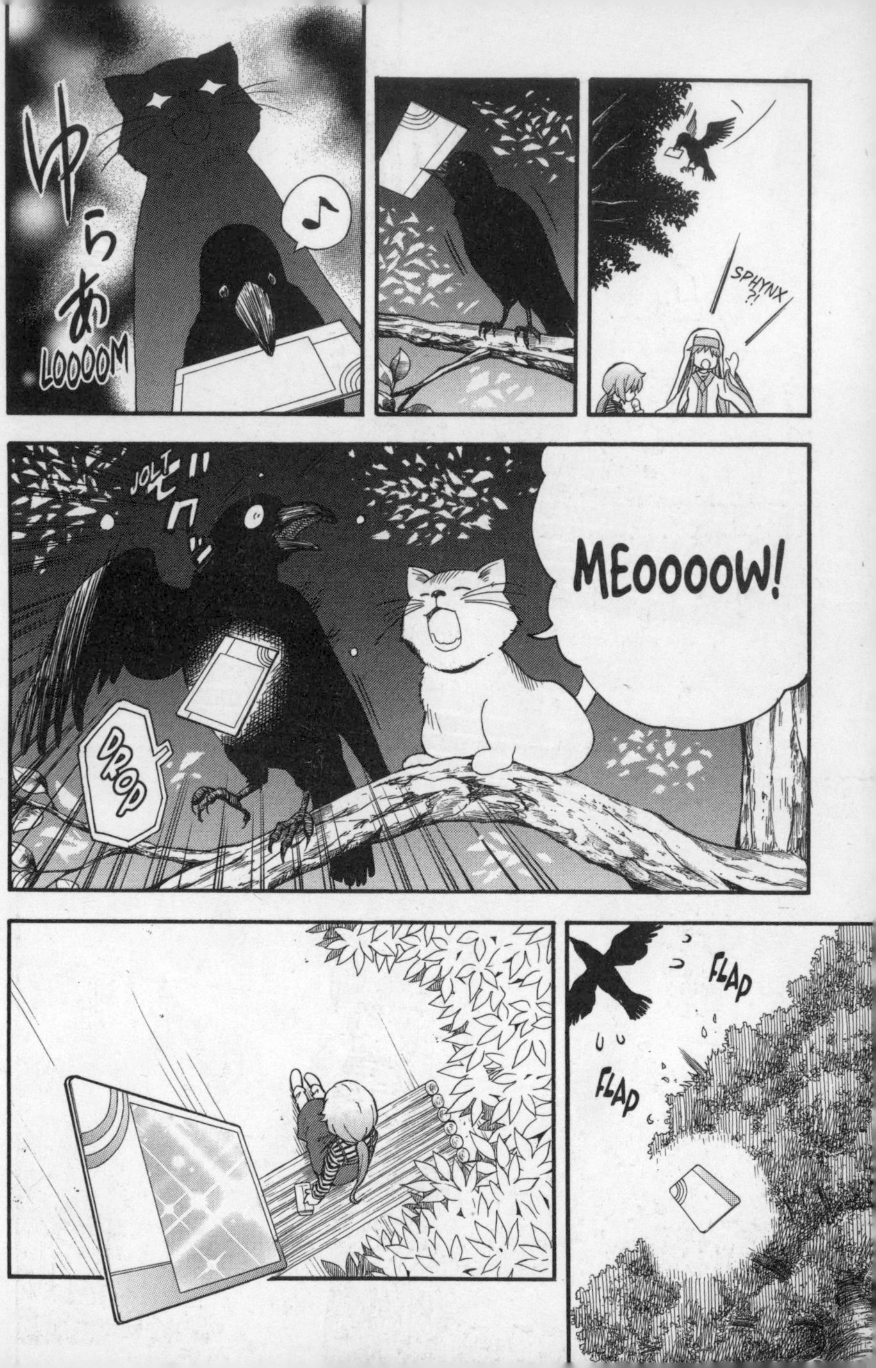
SPHYNX ?!
ゆらあ
LOOOOM
♪
MEOOOOW!
JOLT
DROP
FLAP
FLAP

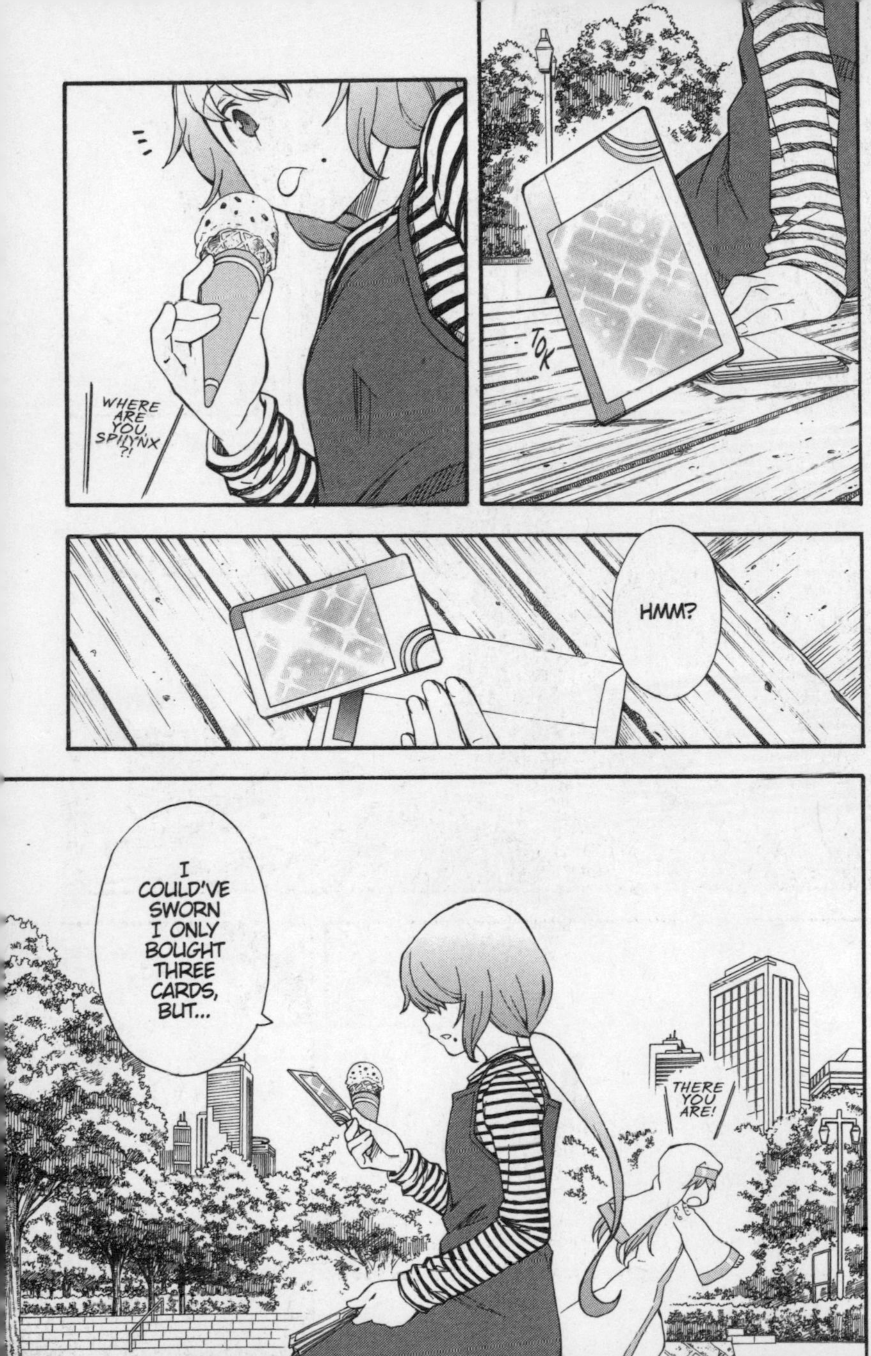
TOK
WHERE ARE YOU, SPILYNX?!
HMM?
I COULD'VE SWORN I ONLY BOUGHT THREE CARDS, BUT...
THERE YOU ARE!

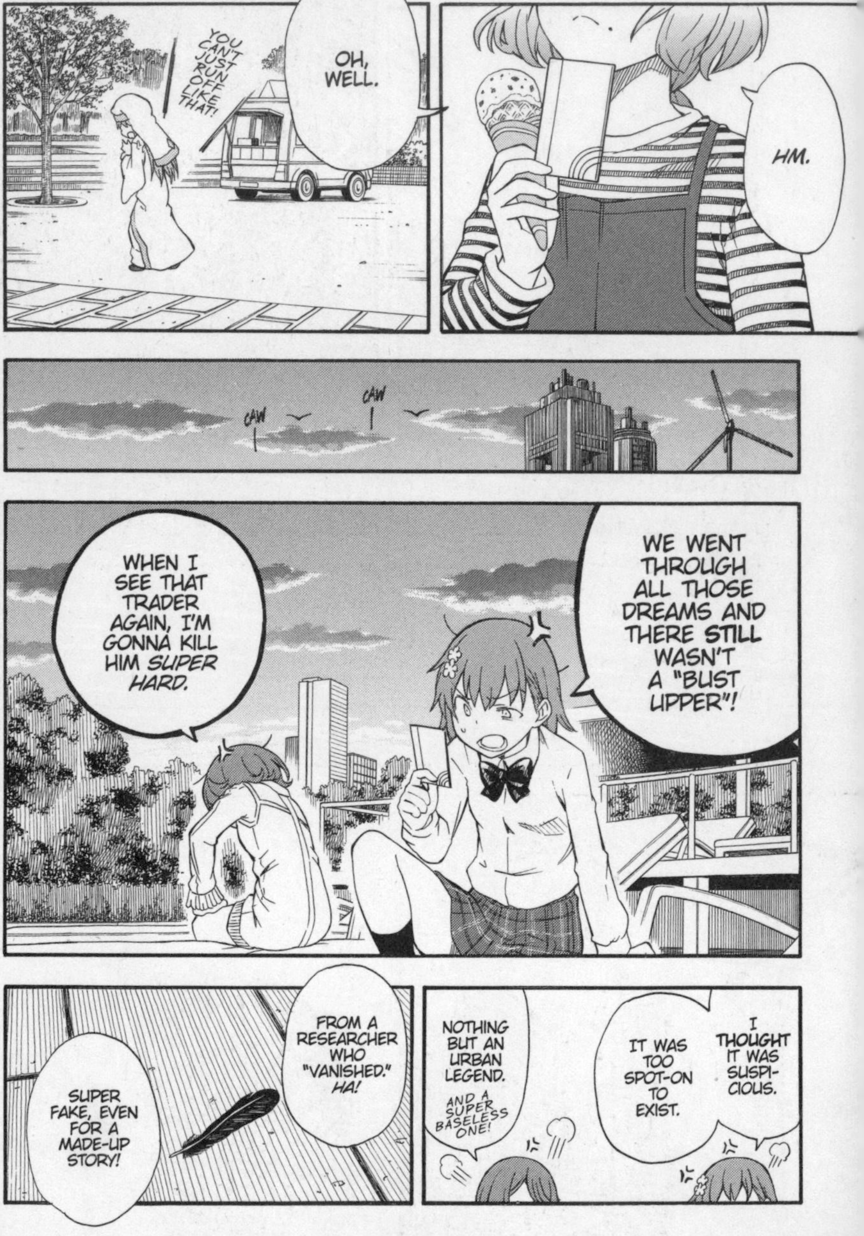
HM.
OH, WELL.
YOU CAN'T JUST RUN OFF LIKE THAT!
CAW
CAW
WE WENT THROUGH ALL THOSE DREAMS AND THERE STILL WASN'T A "BUST UPPER"!
WHEN I SEE THAT TRADER AGAIN, I'M GONNA KILL HIM SUPER HARD.
I THOUGHT IT WAS SUSPICIOUS.
IT WAS TOO SPOT-ON TO EXIST.
NOTHING BUT AN URBAN LEGEND.
AND A SUPER BASELESS ONE!
FROM A RESEARCHER WHO "VANISHED." HA!
SUPER FAKE, EVEN FOR A MADE-UP STORY!

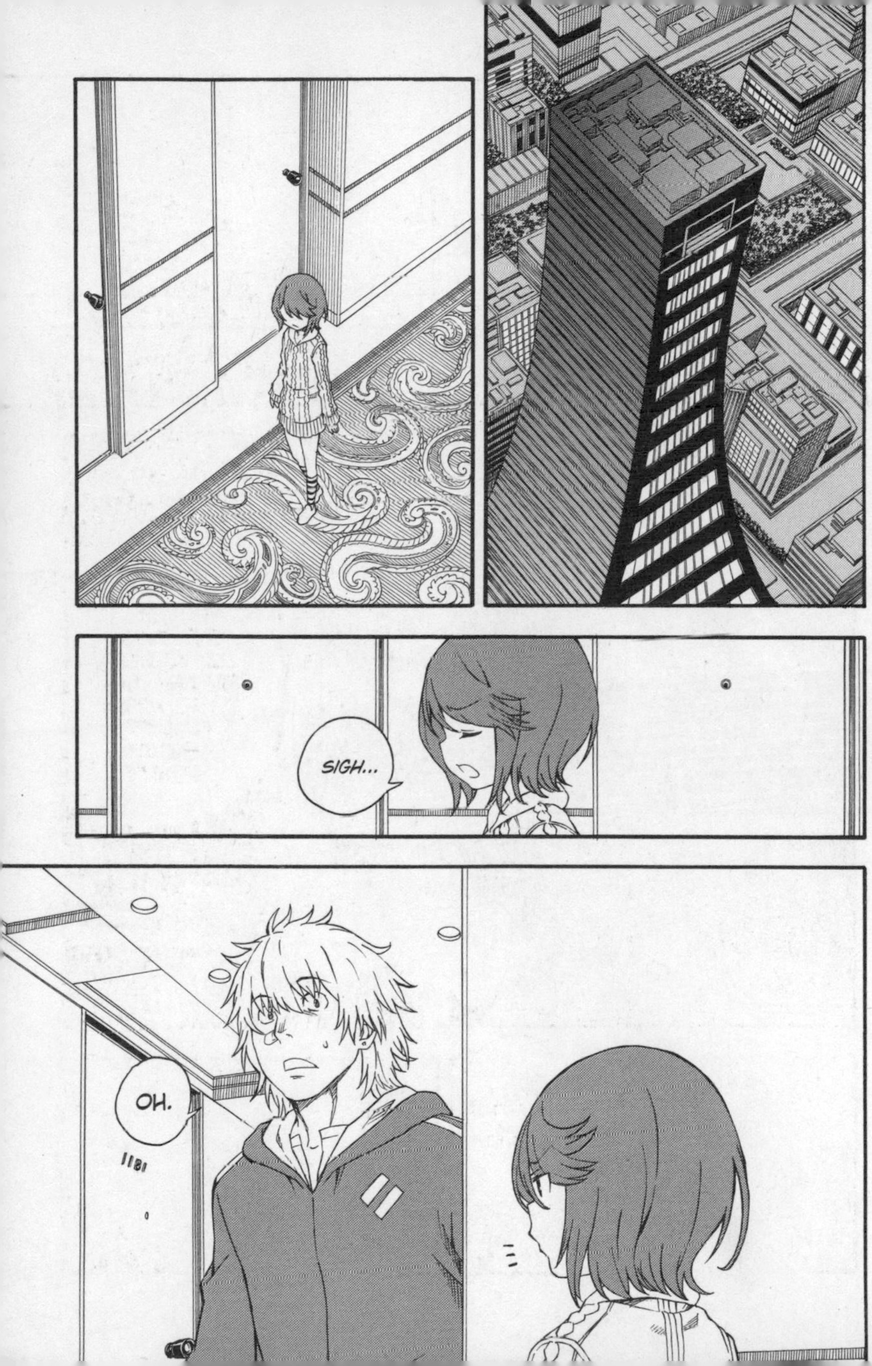
SIGH...
OH.

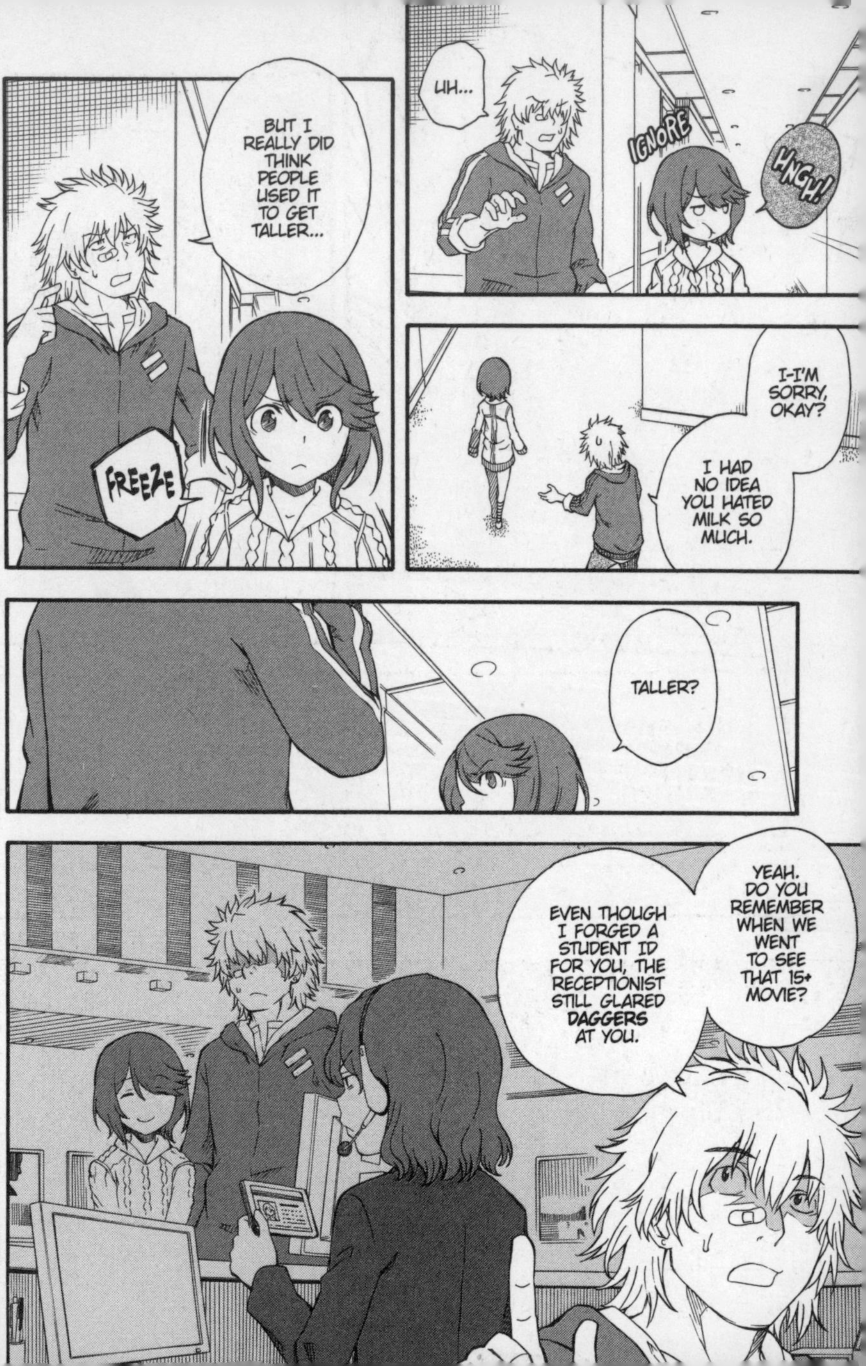
UH...
IGNORE
HNGH!
I-I'M SORRY, OKAY?
I HAD NO IDEA YOU HATED MILK SO MUCH.
BUT I REALLY DID THINK PEOPLE USED IT TO GET TALLER...
FREEZE
TALLER?
YEAH. DO YOU REMEMBER WHEN WE WENT TO SEE THAT 15+ MOVIE?
EVEN THOUGH I FORGED A STUDENT ID FOR YOU, THE RECEPTIONIST STILL GLARED DAGGERS AT YOU.

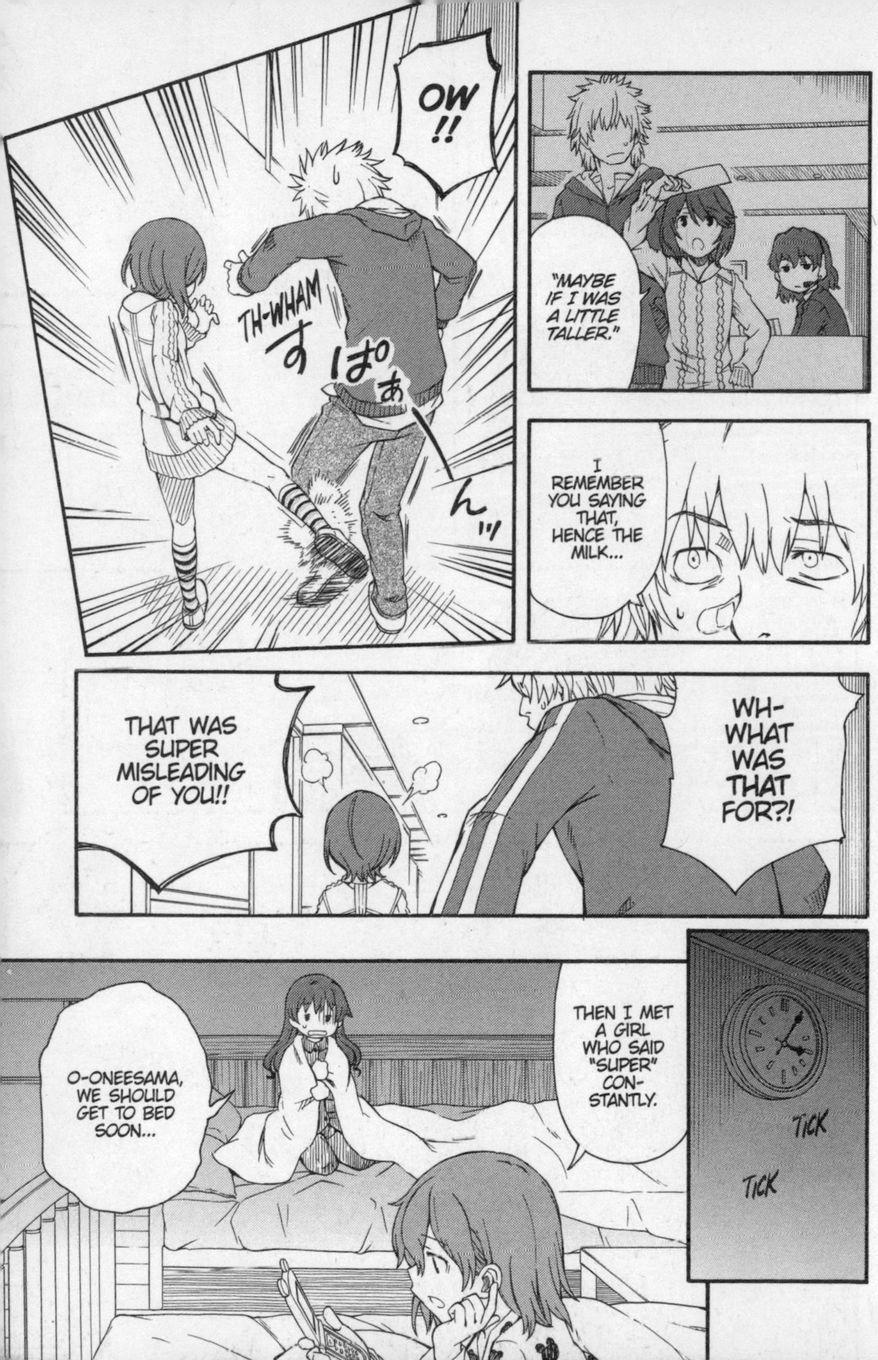
"MAYBE IF I WAS A LITTLE TALLER."
I REMEMBER YOU SAYING THAT, HENCE THE MILK...
OW !!
TH-WHAM
すぽぁんッ
WH-WHAT WAS THAT FOR?!
THAT WAS SUPER MISLEADING OF YOU!!
TICK
TICK
THEN I MET A GIRL WHO SAID "SUPER" CON-STANTLY.
O-ONEESAMA, WE SHOULD GET TO BED SOON...

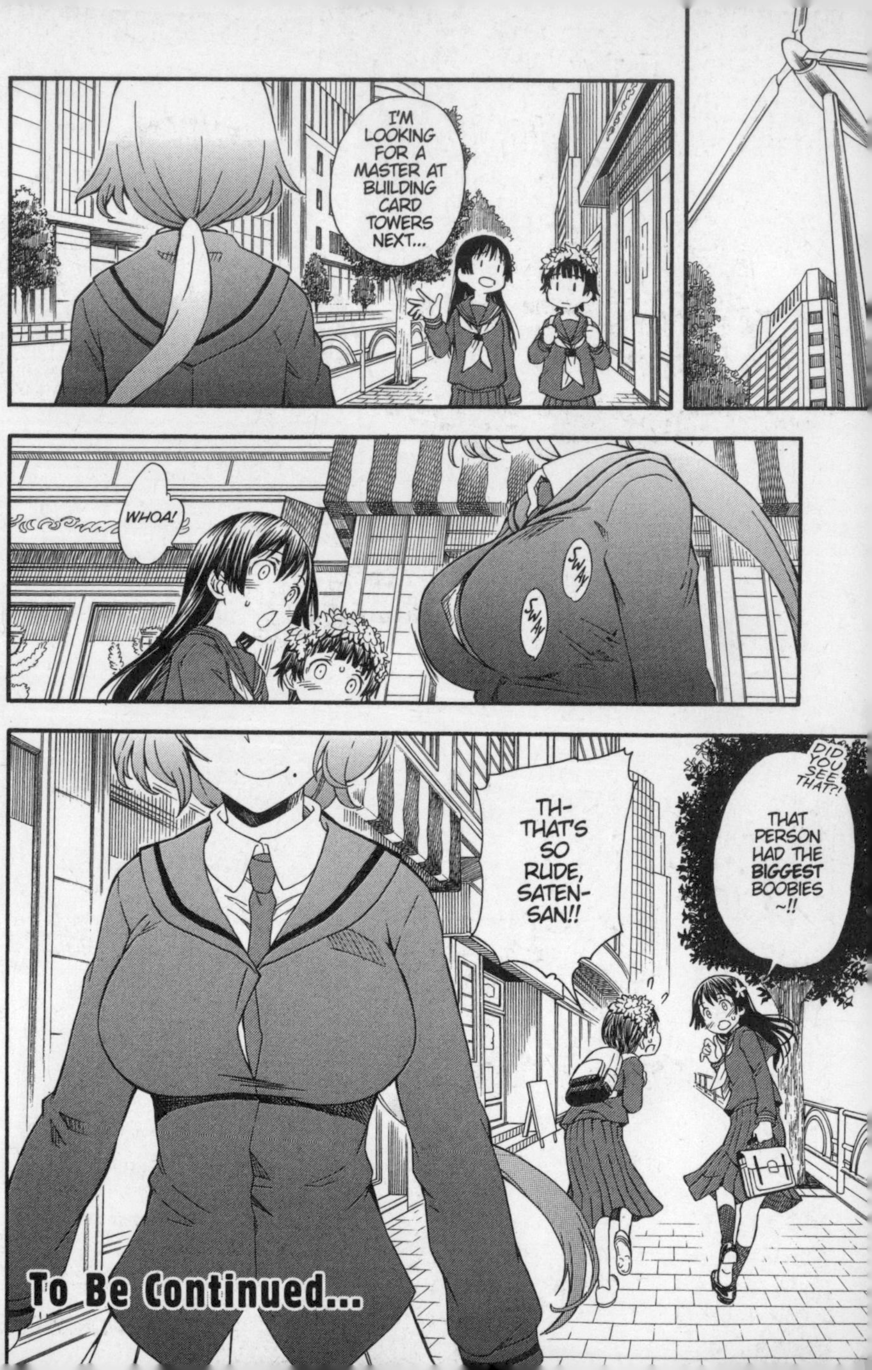
I'M LOOKING FOR A MASTER AT BUILDING CARD TOWERS NEXT...
WHOA!
SWAY
SWAY
DID YOU SEE THAT?!
THAT PERSON HAD THE BIGGEST BOOBIES ~!!
TH-THAT'S SO RUDE, SATEN-SAN!!
To Be Continued...

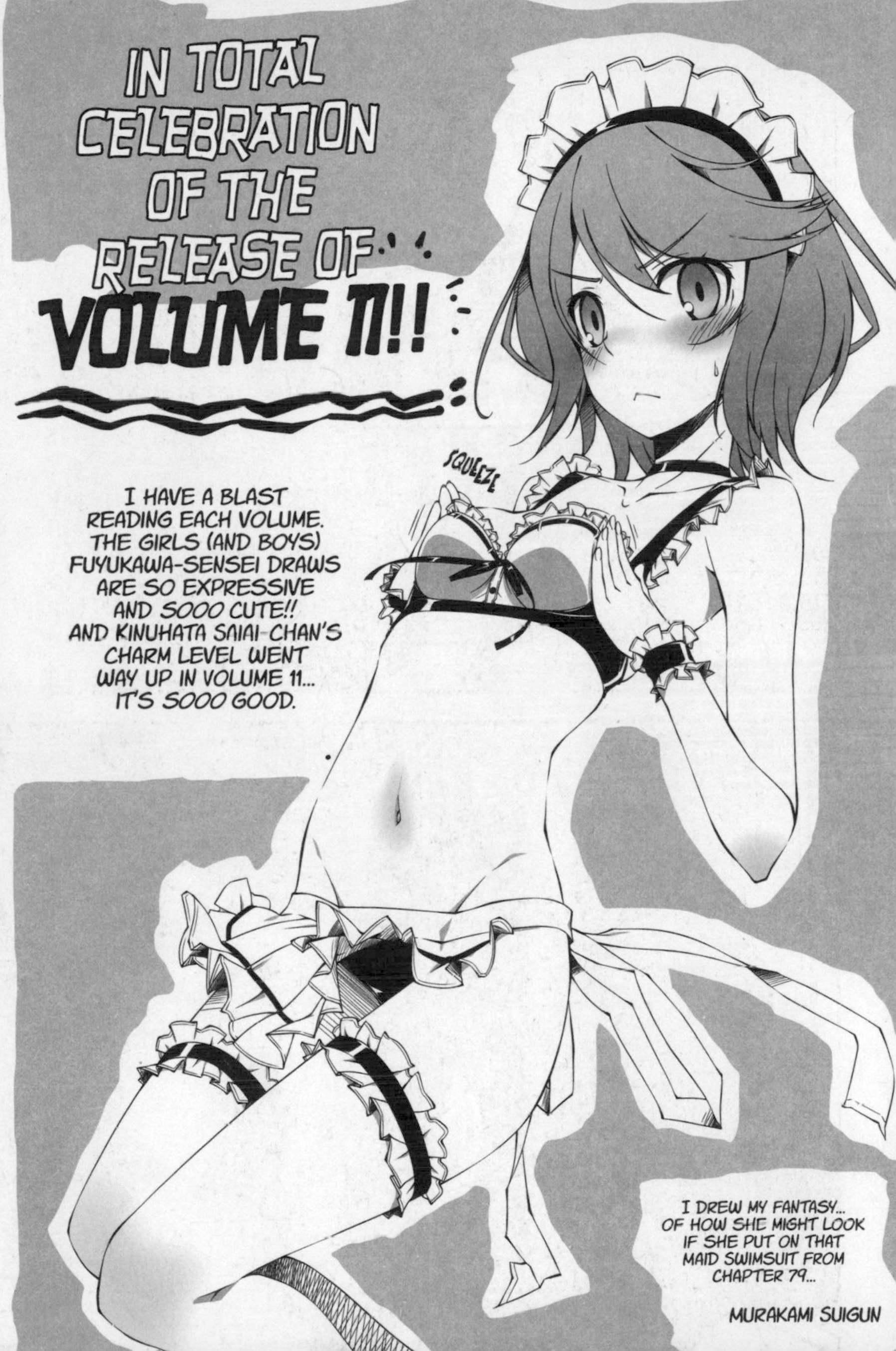
IN TOTAL CELEBRATION OF THE RELEASE OF VOLUME 11!!
SQUEEZE
I HAVE A BLAST READING EACH VOLUME. THE GIRLS (AND BOYS) FUYUKAWA-SENSEI DRAWS ARE SO EXPRESSIVE AND SOOO CUTE!! AND KINUHATA SAIAI-CHAN'S CHARM LEVEL WENT WAY UP IN VOLUME 11... IT'S SOOO GOOD.
I DREW MY FANTASY... OF HOW SHE MIGHT LOOK IF SHE PUT ON THAT MAID SWIMSUIT FROM CHAPTER 79...
MURAKAMI SUIGUN

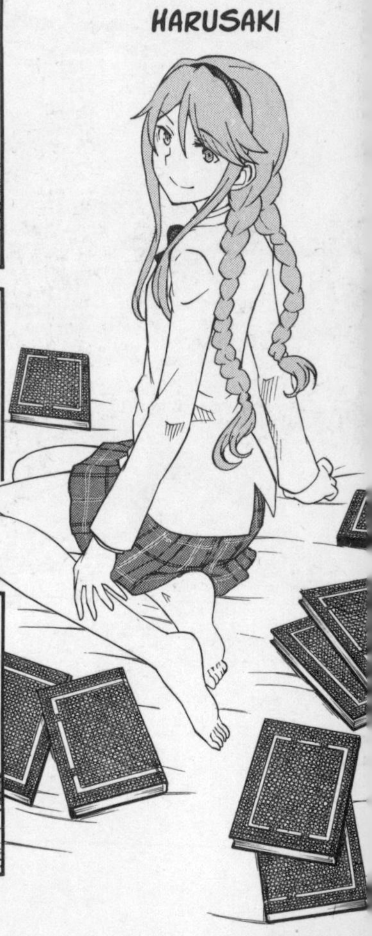
HARUSAKI

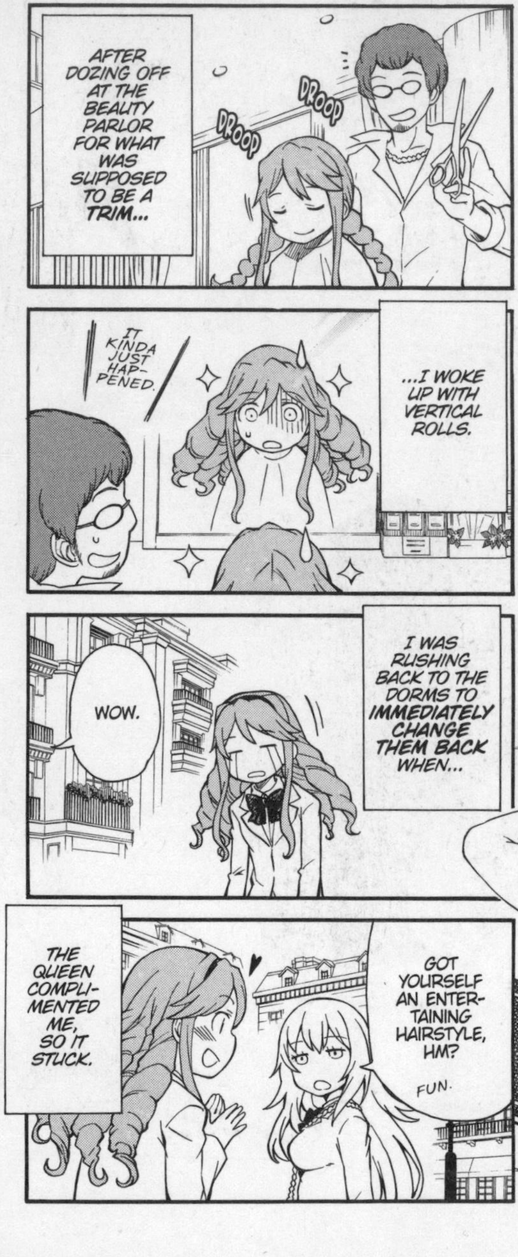
DROOP
DROOP
AFTER DOZING OFF AT THE BEAUTY PARLOR FOR WHAT WAS SUPPOSED TO BE A **TRIM**...
...I WOKE UP WITH VERTICAL ROLLS.
IT KINDA JUST HAPPENED.
I WAS RUSHING BACK TO THE DORMS TO ***IMMEDIATELY CHANGE THEM BACK*** WHEN...
WOW.
GOT YOURSELF AN ENTERTAINING HAIRSTYLE, HM?
FUN.
THE QUEEN COMPLIMENTED ME, SO IT STUCK.

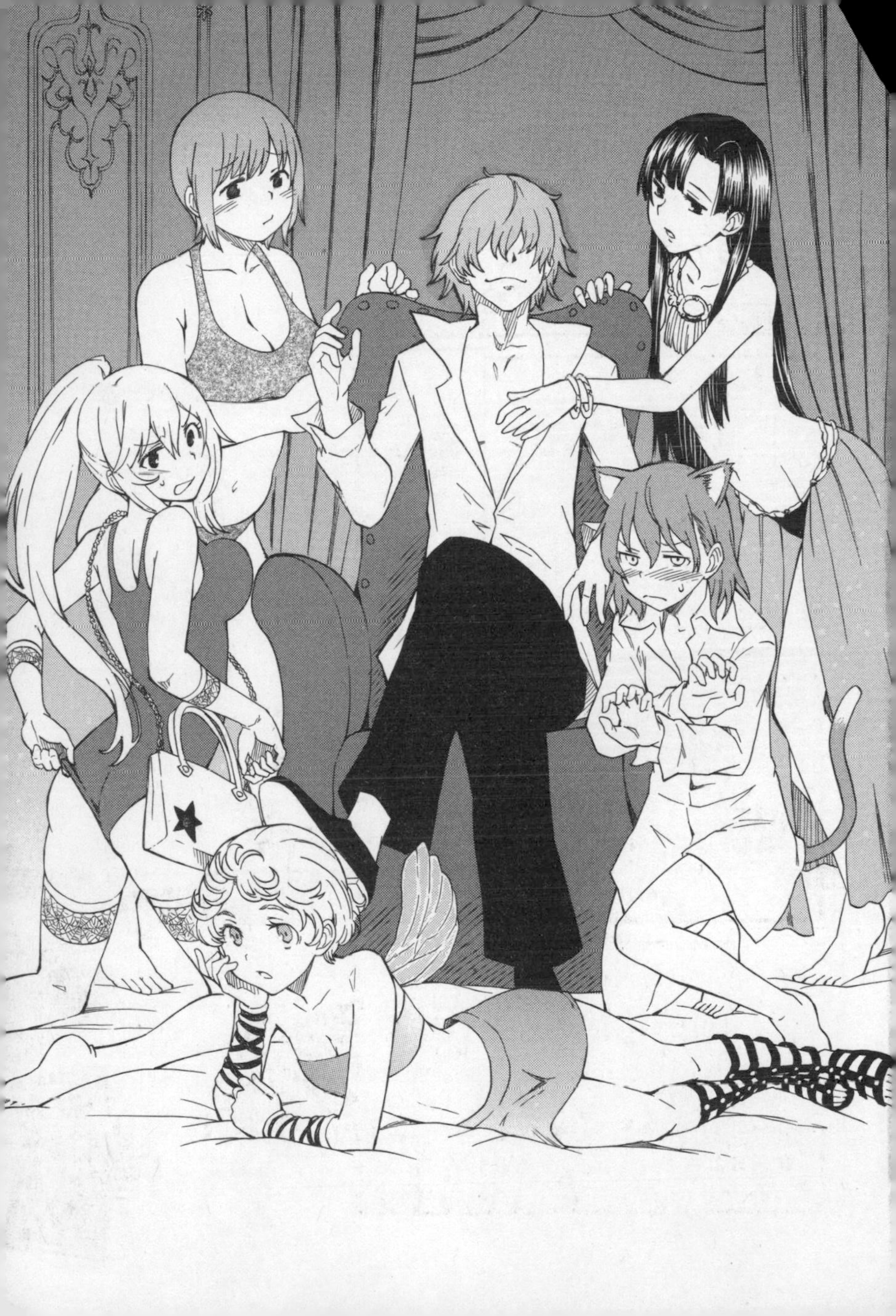

SEVEN SEAS ENTERTAINMENT PRESENTS

A Certain SCIENTIFIC Railgun

story by **KAZUMA KAMACHI** / art by **MOTOI FUYUKAWA** VOLUME 11

TRANSLATION
Nan Rymer

ADAPTATION
Maggie Danger

LETTERING
Roland Amago

LAYOUT
Bambi Eloriaga-Amago

COVER DESIGN
Nicky Lim

PROOFREADER
Shanti Whitesides
Janet Houck

PRODUCTION MANAGER
Lissa Pattillo

EDITOR-IN-CHIEF
Adam Arnold

PUBLISHER
Jason DeAngelis

Edited by ASCII MEDIA WORKS.
First published in Japan in 2015 by KADOKAWA CORPORATION, Tokyo.

ISBN: 978-1-626922-16-7

Printed in Canada

First Printing: June 2016

10 9 8 7 6 5 4 3 2 1

FOLLOW US ONLINE: ***www.gomanga.com***

READING DIRECTIONS

This book reads from ***right to left***, Japanese style. If this is your first time reading manga, you start reading from the top right panel on each page and take it from there. If you get lost, just follow the numbered diagram here. It may seem backwards at first, but you'll get the hang of it! Have fun!!

1
2
3
4
5
6
7
8
9

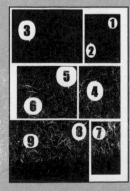